The Life of Madie Hall Xuma

WOMEN, GENDER, AND SEXUALITY
IN AMERICAN HISTORY

Editorial Advisors:
Susan K. Cahn
Wanda A. Hendricks
Deborah Gray White

Anne Firor Scott, Founding Editor Emerita

*A list of books in the series appears
at the end of this book.*

The Life of Madie Hall Xuma

Black Women's Global Activism
during Jim Crow and Apartheid

WANDA A. HENDRICKS

UNIVERSITY OF
ILLINOIS PRESS
Urbana, Chicago, and Springfield

Publication was supported by a grant from the
Howard D. and Marjorie L. Brooks Fund for
Progressive Thought.

Library of Congress Cataloging-in-Publication Data
Names: Hendricks, Wanda A., author.
Title: The life of Madie Hall Xuma : black women's
   global activism during Jim Crow and apartheid /
   Wanda A. Hendricks.
Description: Urbana : University of Illinois Press,
   2022. | Series: Women, gender, and sexuality
   in American history | Includes bibliographical
   references and index.
Identifiers: LCCN 2022004937 (print) | LCCN
   2022004938 (ebook) | ISBN 9780252044564
   (cloth) | ISBN 9780252086649 (paperback) | ISBN
   9780252053573 (ebook)
Subjects: LCSH: Xuma, Madie Hall, 1894–1982. | African
   Americans—South Africa—Biography. | African
   American women political activists—Biography. |
   African American women social activists—Biography.
   | Xuma, Alfred B. (Alfred Bitini), 1893–1962—Family.
   | African National Congress—Biography. | South
   Africa—Politics and government—20th century.
   | African American women educators—North
   Carolina—Winston Salem—Biography. | Winston
   Salem (N.C.)—Biography. | BISAC: SOCIAL
   SCIENCE / Black Studies (Global) | BIOGRAPHY &
   AUTOBIOGRAPHY / Cultural, Ethnic & Regional /
   African American & Black
Classification: LCC DT1927.X865 H46 2022 (print)
   | LCC DT1927.X865 (ebook) | DDC 968.05092
   [B]—dc23/eng/20220217
LC record available at https://lccn.loc.gov/2022004937
LC ebook record available at https://lccn.loc.gov/2022004938

Contents

Preface

I met "Miss Madie" shortly before she died, but at the time, I had no idea who she was. I had been visiting her hometown of Winston-Salem, North Carolina, since I was a teenager and more than likely would never have come in contact with her if my great-aunt and -uncle Alma Hendricks Cardwell and John Cardwell as well as great-aunt Nola Hendricks Lash and cousin Barbara Lash had not sold their property on Stadium Drive where they had lived for decades, purchased two lots on Cameron Avenue, and built homes next door to each other. "Miss Madie" was their neighbor.

The city had been home to both families for generations, but Madie Beatrice Hall's family arrived first and was part of an old guard of prominent Blacks who began the process of building up Black Winston in the late nineteenth century. My great-aunts, on the other hand, were part of the wave of Black migrants who flocked to Winston-Salem in the second decade of the twentieth century just as the city was on the cusp of becoming a global tobacco empire. Their mother, Lavinia Ann Forney Hendricks, moved them from Kings Mountain, North Carolina, to seek a fresh start.

Born in 1862 in Cleveland County, North Carolina, Lavinia had been the only child of Peter and Chloe Forney. Her formerly enslaved parents valued education and sent her to Scotia Seminary in Concord, North Carolina, one of the first institutions of higher education established for Black women in the postslavery period. After graduation she taught in the Rutherford, North Carolina, school system and then married James Hendricks in 1884 and moved to his hometown of Kings Mountain. Over the next sixteen years, she bore seven children and mourned the death of one of them. By 1900 she was listed in the Census as the head of a household with six children ranging between the ages of five months to fourteen. Thirteen years later, she had found a new home in the bustling town of Winston-Salem. She parlayed her education and professional experience into a career in the city's segregated public schools, settled her family into the African American housing community of Columbian Heights (also referred to as Columbia Heights), and enrolled her daughters in one of the premier normal schools in the state, Slater Industrial Academy (now Winston-Salem State University).[1]

Lavinia probably lost her professional teaching position because of World War I and the influenza pandemic that ravaged the world in 1918, but she rebounded by gaining employment in the booming tobacco labor sector as a cigarette maker. Her young daughters also contributed to the family coffers by working at the Zinzendorf Hotel Laundry while attending school.[2] Their perseverance paid dividends. In 1919 Lavinia, like Hall's parents, became an entrepreneur, entering the real-estate business. She purchased a lot for $600 located on East Bank Street (also known as Idabelle Avenue) and used it to create a steady stream of income. Buying, selling, and leveraging property proved to be so profitable that from 1920 to 1927, five additional deeds of trust appear in the records under her name.[3]

Lavinia's business acumen advanced opportunities for her daughters. Alma graduated from Slater Normal School and by 1921 was employed as a teacher in Wadesboro, North Carolina. When Kimberly Park School, one of the elementary schools where Madie Hall taught, opened in Winston-Salem, she returned home and became part of the faculty. So committed to the profession, she enhanced her skills and credentials by enrolling in the first term of the summer school at Winston-Salem Teachers College (formally Slater Normal) in 1927. Nola joined her sister in the education profession in 1923 as she began her career in the rural community of Tobaccoville.[4]

By the 1930s, the Hendricks family had been rooted in the city for nearly two decades and were prominent enough that the newspaper often reported on them. For example, the paper announced that Lavinia hosted a birthday party celebration for her grandson Clyde Hendricks Jr., highlighted Alma's attendance at a dinner honoring the visit of a former Winston-Salem resident from Ohio, and reported on Nola's visit to Winston-Salem after she had migrated to New York. And when Lavinia's mother, Chloe Ann Forney, died in July 1932, she was remembered for her "faithful member[ship]" at Peoples Choice A.M.E. Zion Church in Columbian Heights.[5]

That determination to succeed and devotion to community, solidified over more than seven decades, enveloped me as a young adult when I spent time with my relatives during the summers. Aunt Nola, cousin Barbara, and I spent a great of time in a daily ritual of what I now fondly remember as our "sessions" on the front porch. The sessions usually began about midmorning and offered us a time to "just be." We talked a lot and watched the people and cars go by. Occasionally, Aunt Alma joined us, but mostly she remained inside her own house or on her own porch. A number of the usually widowed older Black women neighbors, however, would stroll down the street, stop in front of the house to greet us, make some comments about the weather, and continue on their walk. A few came up the walkway, perched themselves in one of the chairs on the porch, and stayed a while, chatting with us about a multitude of things.

During much of the time that I spent with my aunts and cousin, their neighbor "Miss Madie" never had a last name and was simply the woman who appeared on her porch in the mornings just long enough to greet us with a wave as we began our sessions. For some reason that is a mystery to me now, "Miss Madie" joined us for one of those sessions. Because so many years have passed, I can't quite recall exactly how the conversation with her began, but somehow the topic of Africa emerged. She mentioned something about having lived in South Africa, seemed to know a great deal about the country, and appeared to have been in the thick of the apartheid fight. Since I had just completed a South African graduate history course at the University of North Carolina at Charlotte, read several books on the country, and written a final paper on Alfred Bitini Xuma who was elected president of the African National Congress in 1940, I was intrigued. After she left and my aunt, cousin, and I had retreated into the house to escape the summer heat, I asked my aunt Nola what was "Miss Madie's" last name. Aunt Nola fumbled terribly in her attempts to pronounce the name. Finally, in exasperation she told me that her husband had been an African and that she had been somebody important in Africa. The realization that "Miss Madie" might have been someone whose name I had come across during my research on South Africa was immediate, but it still took some time before I actually connected her personally to Xuma. When I discovered that she was his wife and the woman whose personal correspondence I had actually read, I was stunned. I never forgot her.

Acknowledgments

This project was much larger and far more complex than I ever could have imagined. As a historian of Black American women's history, African American history, and American history, I had limited knowledge of South African history and only a rudimentary understanding of the expansive and complex history of the African continent and the history of women in a global context. Moreover, I do not read or speak Xhosa, the native language of Alfred B. Xuma, which means that, like my aunt Nola, I am unable to correctly pronounce Madie Beatrice Hall Xuma's last name. So, as I have waded into the raced, classed, and gendered geographies of her transnational experience, I remain acutely aware of my own limitations and shortcomings.

Hall Xuma's life has largely been ignored because she has been overshadowed by her husband's success and international fame and because most scholars simply have had no idea what to make of her. And, like so many women of the Black diaspora, she does not have an "archived collection" of her own papers. She, however, understood the power of documenting history and left a body of primary resources embedded in her husband's archived collection and in the oral interviews that she did shortly before her death. As a member of one of the prominent Black families in Winston-Salem, her life was also documented in media outlets throughout the late nineteenth century and the twentieth century. Piecing all of this information together to produce a coherent book, however, was a formidable task and possible only because of the dedicated and committed community of librarians and archivists who helped me.

I am deeply indebted to the University of South Carolina Cooper Library staff, particularly Kytt Moore Pavlakovich in the Interlibrary Loan Department for her dedication to me and this project over many years. I also thank

Beverly Pott, Eva Pough, Kathy Snediker, William Sudduth, and Ross Taylor who helped me navigate the resources available in Cooper Library. I am appreciative of the assistance of Thomas Flynn at the Winston-Salem State University Archives at the C. G. O'Kelly Library; the staff at the Z. Smith Reynolds Library at Wake Forest University in Winston-Salem; Fambrough L. Brownlee at the Forsyth County Public Library in Winston-Salem; Laura Adair Johnson at the Livingstone College Carnegie Library in Salisbury, North Carolina; the staff at the Albert and Shirley Small Special Collections Library at the University of Virginia in Charlottesville; the staff at the Stuart A. Rose Manuscript, Archives & Rare Book Library, Emory University in Atlanta; Maida Goodwin at the Sophia Smith Collection at Smith College in Northampton, Massachusetts; Jocelyn Wilk at the Columbia University Rare Book & Manuscript Library in New York; the staff at the Schomburg Center for Research in Black Culture in New York; Donald L. Ross who leads the Alpha Phi Alpha Fraternity Historical Commission and the Alpha Phi Alpha Publications Committee; Kevin B. Leonard at Northwestern University Archives in Evanston, Illinois; and Mackenzie Snare at the Wilberforce University Rembert E. Stokes Library Archives in Wilberforce, Ohio.

I am also grateful for the support that I received from the Historical Papers Research Archive University of the Witwatersrand in Johannesburg, South Africa, and the World Young Women's Christian Association (World YWCA) in Geneva. Archivist Gabriele Mohale, in particular, provided a detailed road map to finding Hall Xuma in the voluminous A. B. Xuma Papers and alerted me to new unprocessed materials in other collections. Elaine Carlson, who spent her career as a staff member at the World YWCA and currently serves as the cochair of the YWCA World Service Council, found my research so compelling that she invited me to make a presentation at a World Service Council meeting in New York in 2018, helped me situate Hall Xuma's activism in a transnational context, and introduced me to Casey Harden, the general secretary of the World YWCA; Alejandra Castillo, the chief executive officer of YWCA USA; and an international audience made up of some of the kindest women I have ever met.

After I was granted permission to visit the World YWCA archive in Geneva, I arrived there in September 2019 and worked with a wonderful coalition of savvy former staff members that included Jane Bennett, Mandy Nogarede, Jacqueline Urfer, Elsbeth Herzog, and Murielle Joye-Patry. They generously provided information on the organization, guided me through the World YWCA archive, and helped me find my way in Geneva. Murielle's deep roots in the World YWCA, in particular, accentuate the historical continuum of involvement in the YWCA in families and across generations. Her aunt Irene Pictet served her second term on the executive committee with

Hall Xuma in 1955 and was the treasurer of the governing body. Murielle followed in her aunt's footsteps as a member of the executive committee from 1983 to 1995 and as treasurer. The wonderful staff, including Caterina Lemp Bitsacopoulos, Talisa Avanthay Garcia, and several interns from countries around the globe, impressed me with their intellect, hopeful view of the world, and ability to converse in multiple languages. They reminded me of the reason that Hall Xuma championed the leadership and exchange programs that the World YWCA so fiercely pursued and promoted for women and girls.

A community of scholars have enriched my intellectual life and provided me with assistance as I navigated the complexities of this book. J. Edwin Hendricks introduced me to the history of the Black community in Winston-Salem nearly forty years ago when I was a graduate student at Wake Forest University and taught me how significant that history was to the development of North Carolina. Neither one of us knew at the time how that history also played such an important role in shaping the world. The MV Reading and Writing Group and a collection of scholar friends from around the country that included Eva Baham, Natalie Byfield, Joanne Edey-Rhodes, Farah Jasmine Griffin, Kenneth Hamilton, Darlene Clark Hine, Dorothy Pratt, Alexandria Russell, Barbara Savage, and Deborah Gray White read and reread drafts, provided valuable critique, and shared vital information. Their support was bolstered by the South African scholars who graciously and completely embraced the project. I cannot thank Robert Edgar enough for his detailed responses and help with locating sources, particularly in South Africa, at a time when I was still unsure about what I was doing. Steven Gish generously forwarded a treasure trove of material that he had collected over the years. Iris Berger, Carolyn Brown, Judith Byfield, Dawne Y. Curry, Jill Kelly, and Robert Trent Vinson offered article, book, and archival suggestions simply because they thought that this biography was long overdue.

Usually, my friends and neighbors are sitting on the sidelines cheering me on when I am working on a project, but this time some of them became a core part of my global research community. Beverly Glover Logan and Larry Logan, for example, helped me navigate the bureaucracy of sorority and fraternity culture and offered rich historical resources as I pursued the significance of the Alpha Kappa Alpha Sorority and the Alpha Phi Alpha Fraternity in the lives of Madie and Alfred Xuma. Karen Moore offered critique and camaraderie as well as welcomed respite in my favorite North Carolina mountain town. Neighbors in Melrose Heights like Walter Prince, Sampson Hammett, Fred Easley, Mary and Joseph Gilmore, and Daisy Block and the morning walkers expressed genuine interest in my book and provided support that I can never repay.

Dawn Durante, former editor at the University of Illinois Press, was one of my biggest champions and provided assistance far beyond her customary responsibilities. Her critical eye for detail helped make me a better writer, and because of that this is a much better book. I am ultimately grateful to editors Dominique Moore, Alison Syring, and Ellie Hinton for their roles in shepherding the book to completion.

A number of others provided essential assistance with technology, a history of women's involvement in world organizations, and instructions on how to navigate the bureaucracy of federal government agencies. The names of some of them are Chuck Brown, Lori Carey, Lou Ann Parsons, and Ben Weiser.

I dedicate this book to my sister, Anita Lucinda Hendricks. She is the most remarkable person I know and, for me, represents the formidable power of Black female strength, tenacity, and perseverance that are found throughout this biography.

Introduction

When the Society for the Study of Afro-American History in Winston-Salem, Forsyth County, North Carolina, issued a call in June 1994 for community assistance with research and memorabilia for a 1995 historical calendar on Black women "who made distinctive contributions to the community between the early 1900s through 1959," Madie Beatrice Hall Xuma made the list of an impressive group of women.[1] Nearly a decade later, her name also appeared in the *Wilson (NC) Daily Times* as an educational tool for kindergarten through eighth grade students in a section called "Mind Designs." After posing the question "Is there an important or influential African-American from North Carolina whose name begins with an 'X'?" the answer was "Madie Hall Xuma, born in Winston=Salem [*sic*], was a YMCA [*sic*] founder and educator. She lived most of her life in Winston-Salem and rose to national prominence in 1941 when she overcame bitter opposition to open a YWCA for women in South Africa."[2] Several of the facts were incorrect, but by promoting Hall Xuma's activism in South Africa the feature transnationalized her story.

Hall Xuma had been propelled onto a global stage in South Africa in 1940 and by 1954 had made such an impact in the country that a representative of the Department of Bantu Education referred to her as "the mother of Africa." "Her presence in South Africa," he insisted, "has meant a new day for our dark-skinned fellow-men of Africa," and he declared, "Her name will not be forgotten in the annals of our day."[3] Indeed, more than sixty years later, South Africans still revered her. The Cape Town, South Africa, *Weekend Argus* contended in 2017, "If South Africa owes its constitutional democracy to the [African National Congress] and its heroic struggles, then the ANC owes its progressive outlook and gender sensibilities to a legion of its women cadres who, over the years, have weaved formidable foundational threads upon whose pivot this progressive culture is hinged." These women were "amongst the best minds that the country has ever nestled," and "none of them suffered fools as they formidably held their own in a patriarchal and racist society." Ultimately, they "could put any man to intellectual shame and in fact stand head and shoulders above most men." Hall Xuma was the only Black American on the list that included an impressive array of South African women like Charlotte Maxeke, Sophie Mpama, Ruth First, Ruth Mompati, Bertha Gxowa, Ellen Kuzwayo, Lucy Mvubelo, Gertrude Shope, and Winnie Mandela.[4]

Hall Xuma, however, is virtually unknown to the general public, in part because she has been ignored in much of the historical literature, particularly by American scholars. South African scholars fare far better, but they have compartmentalized nearly every aspect of her life to such a degree that they have not been able to craft a broad conceptual framework that adequately demonstrates how centered she was in the historic issues facing the world during and after World War II and the pivotal role she played in the dynamic interplay between women's groups globally after the war.[5] They have certainly cast her as a major force in the raced, classed, and gendered analysis that shaped the lives of activist women in South Africa, and they have pointed to the uniqueness of her narrative. She was a leader in the social welfare movement, represented the modern Black elite professional American woman of the early twentieth century, was the wife of African National Congress president Alfred B. Xuma, and came to be known as "An African American Mother of the Nation" in South Africa. But all of them fall short of engaging her in the kind of world affairs that activist women across the globe pursued. These included human rights, women's rights, civil rights, apartheid, and the refugee crisis, as well as questions about religion in the modern world and fears about nuclear weapons.[6]

Hall Xuma has not made it easy to capture the totality of her activism, because in so many ways she remains an enigma and does not fit easily or comfortably into any particular kind of feminist theoretical framework. She was a Black southern American woman who came of age under Jim Crow and who voluntarily moved to South Africa, witnessed the development and institutionalization of the oppressive regime of what became known as apartheid, and incurred its wrath for nearly two decades. That distinguishes her from any other Black woman in the world. Yet as Robert Trent Vinson argues, Hall Xuma embraced a traditional Black American narrative that suggested that she "felt divinely ordained to go to [sic] there and propagate the providential design narrative of African American history, likening African Americans to the biblical Israelites."[7] To be sure, Hall Xuma's religious identity was certainly tied to her sense of Black *American* superiority and guided her ideology as well as her activism in South Africa. She reveled in her Americanness, using it as the essential marker of progress, and as a devout member of the African Methodist Episcopal Zion (AME Zion or AMEZ) Church, she embraced its mission of service. But when she returned to the United States for the first time after World War II, she was alone and distinguished as *the* Black South African representative. Four years later, she even publicly self-identified as an African rather than as an American in a popular Black American magazine.[8]

Hall Xuma certainly had her critics in South Africa who argued that her focus on social welfare and emphasis on domestic skills lacked political engagement and stymied the progress of Black women and the Black community. Moreover, her cozy relationship with prominent whites called into question her loyalty to Black South Africans. Her public admission that she deliberately did not engage in politics and strongly believed that her relationships with whites were essential to Black progress only fueled the criticism. "When there is no contact between the races, one does not know what the other is thinking and they become afraid of each other," she told a reporter in 1963.[9] For her, interracial alliances were essential to Black advancement, something she had learned from her parents and from her own activism under the racist, sexist, and classed boundaries of Jim Crow Winston-Salem.

Hall Xuma had also learned that the traditional political arena such as casting ballots in elections or publicly pushing for inclusion of Black women in the traditionally male and white supremacist bastions of power yielded few if any successes for the majority of Black women. The passage of the Nineteenth Amendment in 1920, when she was twenty-six years old, a citizen, and eligible to vote, for example, did not change the overall political status for a Black southern woman like her. If Hall Xuma actually registered to vote between 1920 and 1930, she would have been one of the approximately 326 Black women and men in Winston-Salem who were successful in exercising their political right.[10] So she, like many of her cohorts, strategically devised acceptable means of activism that remained filtered through a network of female-centered clubs. In these female-centered bastions, they constructed the means to develop much-needed social welfare programs and taught themselves how to govern—learning leadership techniques such as how to conduct meetings and how to connect themselves to white female activists as a gateway to an expansion of their options. In the process, they opened the door to an acceptable gendered form of organized politicization in civic-minded public engagement.

The scholarly focus, then, on singular aspects of Hall Xuma's activism without contextualizing and analyzing the historic and life-altering eras and events in which she lived magnifies the absence of a multilayered understanding of how they all fit together. It obscures the nuanced complexities of a life that began in an industrialized South, was stymied by Jim Crow and sexism, and was influenced by the development of the largest organized Black women's club movement in American history. Affected by the wholesale migration of Black people that shaped Winston-Salem, a worldwide flu pandemic that killed fifty million people, and the First World War that highlighted America's connection to global politics, she understood the necessity of social welfare services and adequate health care and embraced the need for cross-racial alliances. Molded by one of the largest independent female organizations in the United States, the Young Women's Christian Association, she eagerly joined the global movement of women and girls in the World YWCA who sought to transform their place in the world after World War II. The move propelled her into a multiracial transnational community that made her one of the most powerful and influential Black women in the world. This biography examines how the confluence of these events, ideas, movements, and organizations shaped and centers her in Black women's history, women's history, transnational studies, American history, and South African history.

* * *

The book begins in the highly industrialized New South town of Winston-Salem, North Carolina, a place where white oligarchs ruled, a large percentage of the Black population labored in the tobacco industry for Jim Crow wages, and prosperous Blacks like Hall found educational, social, and economic opportunity. Part of a new generation of southern Black educated women who came of age as industrialization shaped the contours of a reconstructed South and the gendered expectations of women markedly shifted, Hall earned a normal-school certificate at Shaw University in Raleigh, North Carolina, and a bachelor of science degree at Winston-Salem Teachers College (now Winston-Salem State University [WSSU]). Unmarried for much of her adult life, she valued her independence, taught herself how to drive a car, often traveled alone, and vacationed in places like Cuba. Although denied the opportunity to become a doctor because of her gender, she adapted by becoming an entrepreneur, carving out a space in the business community and co-owning a dress shop with her sister.

Guided by the teachings of her mother, her African Methodist Episcopal Zion faith, and a commitment to service, she gravitated to the female-centered YWCA that promoted the social and spiritual development of women and girls. Black branches of the YWCA existed in different locations around the country by the second decade of the twentieth century, and the organization looked to expand into a city characterized as "one of the largest factory centers for colored girls and women." As a member of a coalition of savvy Black women, Hall was instrumental in the initial process of forging an alliance with white YWCA women open to the establishment of the first Black branch in Winston-Salem.[11] The Jim Crow structure of the interracial partnership demanded that the branches remain segregated and that local white YWCA administrators governed the Black branch. While the white supremacist arrangement proved to be challenging, ties to the organization afforded Black women like her the opportunity to occupy a public space and to exercise power in social, civic, and labor affairs. The activities that the YWCA advanced included services that promoted Christian principles; classes that underscored women's central roles as mothers, homemakers, and municipal domestic housekeepers; and programs to help female laborers navigate the industrial workforce. The organization also offered programs that appealed to and influenced young girls such as crafts, recreation, and summer camp. Hall was so invested in the success of the YWCA that she became general secretary of the Black branch and remained a committed lifelong member.

Fusing together her personal, professional, and reform-minded goals, Hall also played a central role in the establishment of the City Federation of Colored Women, which became the largest Black women's organization in Winston-Salem. Developed in 1926 as the umbrella alliance of Black women's clubs, the organization epitomized the successful growth of clubs among Black women, their increased interest in municipal governance, and the centrality of their role in the Black community. The YWCA was a member. When the City Federation joined the North Carolina Association of Colored Women's Clubs and welcomed the organization's president Charlotte Hawkins Brown to the city for the NCACWC convention, Black Winston-Salem club women broadened their geographical reach by linking themselves to the state and national community of Black club women in the National Association of Colored Women (NACW). The Black branch of the YWCA underscored the enormity of the shared local, state, and national alliance by hosting a reception for the momentous occasion.[12]

Hall went to New York City to pursue a master of arts degree at Columbia University Teachers College and crossed the bridge into a transnational life when she met Alfred Xuma there in the summer of 1937. He was a prominent American-trained physician, a widower, and the father of two young children. Shortly after their first few meetings, he left the United States and began a long-distance correspondence courtship with her. While only a few copies of his letters to her seemed to have survived, it is clear from her responses in an abundant number of letters to him that he regularly wrote to her about his professional work as a doctor, his international life, and his children. She in turn regaled him about her professional work as a teacher, engagement in civic welfare, service to her community, and church and family. When his overtures turned romantic, she initially resisted, seeming to delight, instead, in enjoying "virtual" travel to Europe and South Africa through his descriptions in the letters he sent and the pictures that they exchanged. Two years later, the virtual became reality. Fortified with a master of arts degree from Columbia, course work at Atlanta University School of Social Work, her Christian faith, an adventurous spirit, and a strong aspiration to be of service to the people of Africa, she accepted his marriage proposal. In 1940 a nearly forty-six-year-old Madie Hall sailed out of New York City to South Africa to marry him.

She arrived in Cape Town on May 17. The next day, she became his wife and the mother to his two young children and began a transnational journey that lasted more than two decades. Hall Xuma's marriage and motherhood began as the war in Europe escalated and he was elected president of the African National Congress. It matured under the weight of the Cold War and apartheid. As a couple, they would become two of the most powerful Black figures in South Africa and the world, but nothing that Hall Xuma had done before could have prepared her for the challenges that she faced during those early years. While she was pleasantly surprised by modern urban cities like Johannesburg, everything else about the country was different—the topography, the climate, and the people.[13] Even the language, in places where English was not spoken, proved to be a barrier. She encountered a racism and discrimination that was not as malleable as the Jim Crow she left behind and a racial classification system made up of a minority white European population that ruled and oppressed Coloureds or mixed race and the majority native Black population that baffled her. And it was a country in the midst of rapid economic changes that created major demographic shifts in population. The loss of jobs and land in rural communities upended Black life, forcing Black men and women to relocate to urban centers where poverty, overcrowding, and unsanitary conditions prevailed.

She was also an outsider in nationality and class, and for the first time in her life she felt the sting of her American elite heritage. Earning the trust and respect of many of the Black native women, in particular, proved difficult at first. Some expressed skepticism about her ability to forge a life there and doubted her commitment to Black South Africans. To them the new Mrs. Xuma was a socialite who represented the model of Black American privilege. And indeed, Hall Xuma never pretended that she was not a privileged Black American woman who enjoyed her status. After all, her father had been a prominent doctor, and her mother, who earned a normal-school certificate and taught school, had become a successful real-estate entrepreneur. In addition, her new American-educated husband was one of the most prominent Black men in South Africa and had the financial means for her to enjoy a comfortable life. "In many ways I lived better in South Africa," she remarked in an interview, because her home there was a "beautiful ten-room, modern home" and there were "four servants," which meant that she "didn't have much [domestic] responsibility."[14] Still, she possessed an indomitable spirit that assured her that she could win the confidence of elite, working-class, and rural Black South African women and engage them in a mission of service to the community.

Initially, the National Council of African Women became the vehicle. Established in 1937, NCAW members elected activist Charlotte Maxeke, who graduated from Wilberforce University in Ohio, to be the first president and focused their energies on effecting change by offering the social services Black women and their families needed. Hall Xuma's involvement in the organization quickly expanded, as she further advanced the organization's transnational linkages with the National Council of Negro Women (NCNW) that had been established in the United States by her friend Mary McLeod Bethune in 1935. But the strong desire to create her own organization to assist Black South African women pushed her to establish the Zenzele Club that advocated self-help. A female-centered space where women socialized and learned domestic skills such as cooking, sewing, and gardening to sustain themselves and their families, the club slowly gained notoriety and the membership grew. By 1950 the idea appealed to so many women that branches appeared throughout South Africa.

Hall Xuma had never publicly demonstrated a desire to engage in the traditional political arena to advance Black rights, but when her husband was elected president of the ANC, she was thrust onto a national and international political stage. Her first priority was raising money to fill the nearly empty coffers of the ANC. Then she guided her husband in the initial phase of the revitalization of the African National Congress Women's League (ANCWL), where women networked and took steps toward civic engagement. She became the president, and, not coincidentally, women also finally achieved full voting rights in the ANC. Alongside their male cohorts, Hall Xuma and members of the ANCWL challenged the South African government's oppression of the majority Black population. For example, the anti–pass law protesters who marched in the streets in 1944 included Hall Xuma, who had never publicly protested before and "was scared to death," as well as her husband and thousands of other women and men.[15] For years Hall Xuma held a distinguished place in the ANCWL, but by 1950 her ties to the ANC were severely strained and limited. She turned much of her attention to expanding the Zenzele Club's mission.

Through her political savviness, she linked the Zenzele Club to women in the United States, played a key role in the process of nationalizing the club, and ultimately propelled its globalization. She introduced her American friends to the club and gave public presentations about its mission when she traveled to America. For her efforts, she received monetary gifts and other assistance. She led the charge in integrating the organization into the all-white South African Council of World Affiliated YWCA, testing the segregationist policies of apartheid that had been institutionalized in 1948. And she played a major role in fully incorporating Black and white South African women in the World YWCA, headquartered in Geneva, Switzerland. The transnationalization of the South African Council of World Affiliated YWCA and the Zenzele YWCA linked them to a global movement of organized women's groups who insisted that the United Nations, founded in the aftermath of World War II, promote human rights and women's rights.

By 1955 Hall Xuma had become the first Black woman from South Africa elected to the Executive Committee of the World YWCA. The Executive Committee position made her one of the key figures helping to shape policies that governed the lives of more than a million and a half women and girls in World YWCA–affiliated associations in places such as Australia, Barbados, Brazil, Burma, Egypt, Finland, France, Germany, Ghana, Great Britain, Italy, Japan, Kenya, Lebanon, the Netherlands, Nigeria, the Philippines, Portugal, South Africa, Switzerland, and the United States. And it was her place on that committee and at World YWCA council meetings that afforded her the ability to take part in deliberations that shifted the World YWCA from a position of being a nonpolitical social welfare organization to a humanitarian political force in the 1950s, as members framed the organization's global response to the refugee crisis and geopolitical tensions during the Cold War.

Her extraordinary success led *Drum Magazine* to praise the broad global reach of her activism before she returned to the United States in 1963 at the height of the civil rights movement. She "founded the Zenzele Young Women's Christian Association," the article explained, "and through that organization, has helped some of South Africa's most famous women on their way to the top." Proud that Zenzele Clubs had succeeded at that "one important job" of "train[ing] women to speak and become leaders of the community," Hall Xuma boasted that many of the women had taken advantage of the World YWCA program, traveled and trained in America and other parts of the world, and brought their skills back to Africa. They included women like Mildred Mali and Edith Dlamini who studied in the United States, Victoria Mahamba Sitole who trained in England, and Edith Mkele and Phyllis Mzaidume who went to West Africa.[16] Ultimately, Hall Xuma was, the reporter of the magazine opined, "what she was—'Mummy' to the new type of woman we are seeing in our townships now; 'Mummy' to the smart social workers and new feminine intelligentsia, who will take over the leadership from her."[17]

Indeed, one of Hall Xuma's lasting legacies was paving the way for Joyce Piliso-Seroke to be the second Black woman from South Africa elected to the World YWCA executive committee (in 1975). Piliso-Seroke had been engaging with the YWCA for some time. Her mother, Maud Piliso, was among the first members of the Zenzele Club that Hall Xuma established in 1941, and she had been a founding member of the Zenzele Transvaal YWCA that emerged a decade later, demonstrating the ways in which the first YWCA generation introduced their daughters to the organization and helped set them on a path of leadership. Moreover, after ANC activist, teacher, social worker, and writer Ellen Kuzwayo became the general secretary of the Transvaal YWCA, she utilized some of the skills she acquired to be elected to the South African Parliament in 1994 as Nelson Mandela's ascendancy to the presidency of the country transformed South Africa.[18]

PART I

Winston-Salem

CHAPTER 1

The Making of
Madie Beatrice Hall

Madie Beatrice Hall recalled in an interview that her father, Humphrey Haynes Hall, first came to Winston, North Carolina, sometime between 1889 and 1890 "to look the place over" when deciding where to open his medical practice and to set down roots with his future wife, Jennie Estelle Cowan. He liked what he saw. By then there had been such an exponential rise in the Black population and unprecedented economic growth in the town that it was poised to become one of the South's most lucrative markets.[1]

Located in Forsyth County in the southern piedmont, Winston's population and economic commerce exploded after the Civil War. Prior to 1870, fewer than 500 (443) mostly white residents lived there, but the rise of industrialization brought such prosperity that by 1880, the population had jumped to 2,854, more than six times the number of inhabitants the decade before. Stimulated by the sale of leaf tobacco that began in 1872, the emergence of the Northwestern North Carolina Railroad, and the opening of Wachovia National Bank, a new era in the town's history began. Before the century ended, Winston was a New South industrial city powered by electric lights, streetcars, telephones, and at least thirteen tobacco-leaf dealers, thirty tobacco manufacturers, and four tobacco warehouses. Tobacco shipments in the month of April 1895 totaled nearly 1 million pounds, an increase of 150,000 pounds more than the year before, and leading businessmen had a half-million dollars in sales. That kind of sustained profitability and economic growth produced jobs and prospects for prosperity. Thousands were drawn to the town. Of the more than 8,000 people who resided there in 1890, 59 percent, or 4,696, were Black men and women.[2] By the turn of the century, Winston had more than 10,000 residents, and more than half were Black, making it one of the top five North Carolina cities with Black populations over 5,000. Only Wilmington, Charlotte, New Bern, and Raleigh had more African American residents.[3]

By the time Humphrey arrived, most African Americans worked in the more than twenty tobacco manufacturing plants that dotted the landscape between 1890 and 1891. Over time the number of plants diminished, and the R. J. Reynolds Tobacco Company became the largest employer of African Americans and most powerful economic engine in the town. Richard Joshua Reynolds, the owner, had arrived in Winston in 1874 and opened one of several tobacco factories the following year. His company grew rapidly, as he invested in mostly cheap Black laborers from communities in rural areas of North Carolina and in neighboring states like South Carolina, where his company heavily marketed, recruited, and chartered "special trains" to transport them to his factory. Once the workers arrived in Winston, Michele Gillespie argues, "they were often assigned the most boring and dangerous unskilled jobs at the factories," such as stemmers, graders, rollers, and twisters. White workers, on the other hand, worked in the skilled areas and were paid higher salaries. Still, with the limited economic opportunities they faced in the Jim Crow South, Blacks joined thousands of sharecroppers and farmers who migrated to the city to seek employment, where they earned far more than they could ever hope for in their rural communities.[4]

Humphrey had much in common with them. He too had come from a rural community and had first made his living from tobacco. Part of the first generation of African Americans who gained freedom after the Civil War, he was born in 1858 to Abraham and Harriet Hall. The little information available about his parents suggests that they, like their nine children, had been enslaved either in Salisbury, North Carolina, about forty miles south of Winston, or a nearby location. Denied the right to learn to read and write during slavery, neither Abraham nor Harriet had mastered either skill by 1870. Freedom, however, afforded them the opportunity to envision better futures for their children. They first built a secure economic base for the family by working the land. Abraham was listed as a farm laborer, while Harriet managed the household and poured her energies into raising the couple's children. They also stressed the importance of education. All four school-age children between the ages of twelve and nineteen were enrolled in school. Humphrey, the fifth child and the third of four boys, was among them.[5] He attended the Salisbury Colored Normal School. Literacy alone, however, did not guarantee advancement for a young Black man in a segregated southern rural town, so by the time he was twenty-two he was working in a tobacco factory.[6]

Ambition, determination, and the rise of historically Black colleges and universities in North Carolina proved to be the keys to setting him on a dramatically different path than his parents and the thousands of Black laborers who joined him in migrating to Winston. Shaw College, located in Raleigh, North Carolina, was initially established in 1865 to primarily train Black ministers. The college became Shaw University after the American Baptist Home Society provided the financial resources and expanded the school's mission in 1875. By 1882 Leonard Medical School was housed on the campus, becoming the only medical school for Blacks in North Carolina and one of the few open to Blacks in the country.[7]

The first six graduates had passed their medical exams and were licensed by the state when Humphrey enrolled in 1886. One of those graduates, Larson Andrew Scruggs had a medical practice in Raleigh and was so devoted to training Black doctors that he returned to Leonard to instruct new classes of students. While the primary faculty consisted of white doctors, for much of Humphrey's tenure at the school Scruggs presided over residents at the four-ward hospital building that had been erected during the 1885–86 school year. The hospital was fundamental to providing "clinical instruction" and "giving the student an opportunity of studying disease at the bedside of the patient and of watching the effects of treatment."[8]

Like Humphrey and Scruggs, the vast majority of Leonard graduates remained in the South, aiding in the region's development and becoming, argued Kelly Miller, a prominent professor at Howard University in Washington, DC, part of the Black "professional class" and the "missionary of good health." Of the eighteen who had successfully met the qualifications to be physicians at the medical school by the time Humphrey graduated in 1889, all but two—one who had been educated at Lincoln University before entering Leonard and moved to Philadelphia and one whose location was unknown—set up practices in the southern states of North Carolina, South Carolina, Florida, Alabama, and Virginia. And all of them became part of a distinctive club of the fewer than one thousand Blacks who had been trained as physicians in the United States. In contrast, the number of white doctors at the time stood at more than one hundred thousand, highlighting both the racial disparity and the significance of their achievement.[9]

Eight of those one hundred thousand white doctors were engaged in some form of medical practice in Winston when Humphrey arrived. Improvement in the town's health-care system had beckoned them. A hospital for white patients opened in 1887. Although the hospital closed sometime in 1891, a permanent one reopened in 1895. They even tended to African Americans whose home remedies failed or medical conditions were so serious that they required a doctor. But there had never been a health-care facility that catered to Blacks and no Black doctor until Humphrey arrived. Full of an entrepreneurial spirit and desire to provide quality service, he settled into a home in the center of town on East Second Street and operated his practice there as well.[10]

He envisioned such a promising future that he married his hometown sweetheart, Jennie Estelle Cowan, in 1890 and brought her to Winston. Nine years younger than her husband, Jennie was born in 1867 during those first few years of freedom for African Americans. She knew very little about her own mother or her father but passed on the story to her family that her mother was mixed raced and earned her living laboring for a white family in the town of Whiteville, located in the southeastern part of the state. Like so many Black women who were sexually exploited in both slavery and freedom, her mother was forced or coerced into a sexual relationship with her white male employer. Jennie was the product of that relationship.[11]

As the country entered Reconstruction after the Civil War and federal troops occupied North Carolina, white residents like those who employed Jennie's mother developed an intense fear that their valuables would be confiscated, so they, according to the story that Jennie shared with her family, enlisted the aid of "their servants" as a means of safeguarding their assets. They sent them "up to the mountains with all their jewelry and their precious things, and even money," as the "Yankees were coming through." It was on one of those sojourns that the lives of Jennie and her mother dramatically changed. "Really too weak to travel" because she had just given birth, Jennie's mother never made it to the mountain town of Asheville. Forced to stop in Salisbury because "she couldn't make it any farther," she and her baby daughter faced a grim future because the town lacked adequate medical care and did not have a hospital for African Americans. She was, however, able to secure a safe place in a Black neighborhood where minister Harry Cowan lived. Before she died, she "begged" Cowan "to keep" Jennie and to "raise her" as his child. He and his wife, Susan Horah Cowan, fulfilled her wish.[12]

Harry Cowan had been a minister for some time and was an established member of the Salisbury community. He established several churches, including Dixonville Baptist Church and Mount Zion Baptist Church, and was a carpenter and the owner of a two-story home. In 1870 fifty-six-year-old Harry and forty-eight-year-old Susan were raising three-year-old Jennie as their daughter along with two of their six children, sons Harry and Alexander. Sometime before Jennie was fourteen years old, Susan died. Harry remarried Mary Whitehead Kesler, who embraced Jennie as her stepmother.[13]

The Cowans' financial resources enabled them to send Jennie to Shaw University. Like so many young Black women of her generation, she enrolled in the Normal Department, the largest program in the curriculum, and studied to be a first grade teacher during the 1887–88 academic year. In addition to taking courses in U.S. history, etymology, English analysis and arithmetic, geography, and rhetoric she spent her spare time with Humphrey. As a couple, they made quite an impression on the campus, as they were often seen "walking across the campus holding hands." Earning a teaching position in Monroe, North Carolina, she too entered the professional class.[14]

After marrying Humphrey, Jennie relinquished her career as a teacher and embraced motherhood and domesticity. A year after their marriage, she gave birth to the first of their five children, a son named Cleo Harvey in 1891. The growth of the family prompted Humphrey to purchase his first property the following year from wealthy white tobacco manufacturers Pleasant H. Hanes and John W. Hanes and their wives for $1,500. Identified as "land known as the 'Show Grounds,'" the purchase consisted of two lots on the corner of Seventh Street.[15] In 1893 the couple leveraged the equity on the Seventh Street property by borrowing $1,200 in a deed-of-trust transaction with the Hanes brothers. They quickly increased the value of one of the lots by building their home at 125 East Seventh Street. It was at that home that the couple welcomed their second child and first daughter, Madie Beatrice, on June 3, 1894.[16]

Madie developed a special bond with both parents. She saw in her mother a woman who devoted most of her energy to her children but also found fellowship and an entrée into the public sphere in the family's religious home, Goler Memorial African Methodist Episcopal Zion Church. First established as Winston Tabernacle African Methodist Episcopal Church in 1881, Goler was one of six Black churches in Winston. It offered women like Jennie, her daughter Madie insisted, a place to engage with other women to be "active in the church and the community, looking after people who were sick or poor or needed help." Indeed, Jennie dedicated more than thirty years participating in the church's women auxiliaries. She eventually chaired the Basement Movement Club, preparing space for members to eat, directing cultural events, and raising funds for the church.[17]

Jennie believed so strongly in voluntary service that she inculcated her daughter with the same kind of commitment. Madie recounted a conversation she had with her mother when she began her "first job" and "when I got my first pay check." Her mother insisted that she "should give some of it to somebody who needs it" and encouraged her to use some of her earnings to purchase coal to warm the house of an elderly woman nearby through the winter. The lesson, however, was not simply to ensure her daughter's empathy for others; it was also a means of instructing by example. Jennie told her daughter that she would contribute to the endeavor by providing the woman with food to eat. Moreover, Jennie insisted that both she and Madie team up to ensure that the necessary repairs on the woman's home were completed.

Jennie's compassion and commitment remained such powerful lessons for Madie that she acknowledged later, "one of the greatest things she taught me" was "helping people."[18]

Madie's father, she recounted, "was so in love with me, he just thought I was an angel from heaven." Because she "was the first girl . . . he did everything to make me happy." And like Madie's mother, Humphrey engaged in the church, eventually serving on the board of trustees as treasurer, and demonstrated his support to service organizations such as the Black Young Men's Christian Association (YMCA).[19] It was, however, his passion for medicine that impressed his eldest daughter the most. She recalled, "When he had an office in the home, I was just a little girl, and I was so fond of him carrying that black bag around. And when he'd come in the house, I'd go with him to see where he was going to put that black bag down. And I watched him, he let me play around in there, sometimes he had patients, sometimes he didn't. And I was watching everything he did." The practice eventually grew so much that he moved it out of his home and into an office building on Church Street. His days were twelve hours long, and he saw patients during three staggered two-hour intervals from 7:00 a.m. until 7:00 p.m.[20]

Humphrey kept abreast of new developments and followed trends in the medical field by engaging with like-minded Black professionals in several Black medical organizations. Three of them were the North Carolina Medical, Pharmaceutical, and Dental Association (also known as the Old North State Medical, Dental, Pharmaceutical Society), established in 1887 and billed as "the Oldest Negro Medical Society in the World"; the Colored Medical Society of Forsyth County; and the National Medical Society. Serving in several leadership positions in the Medical, Pharmaceutical, and Dental Association, he was elected to the executive committee in 1907. His membership in the organization lasted for more than thirty years.[21]

While it is unclear when the Colored Medical Society of Forsyth County was established, Humphrey, supported by his wife, Jennie, played key roles in its success. Similar to the North Carolina Medical Society, members of the Colored Medical Society included a broad spectrum of medical professionals such as physicians, dentists, and pharmacists. It also engaged the wives of male members by creating the Ladies Auxiliary. At conferences members heard papers from prominent medical professionals and shared "clinical experiences of different cases," while the auxiliary of women hosted receptions and other entertainment events. Humphrey had built such a good reputation among members of the society that he was eventually elected treasurer of the organization.[22]

Humphrey's membership in the National Medical Association (NMA) illuminated his desire to broaden his local, state, and national professional association with Black physicians. Formed in November 1895 at the Cotton State and International Exposition in Atlanta, the organization's primary goal was to create a nationally unified network of Black physicians, but its aim was much more far reaching. It provided a forum for Black doctors to assemble, made available necessary literature for them to remain current, and, most important, provided an institutionalized space for camaraderie. Perhaps its greatest strength was fostering an environment that encouraged the growth of Black doctors. By 1920 Humphrey was part of an organization that had more than three hundred physicians, surgeons, dentists, and pharmaceutical doctors from multiple regions of the country among its membership.[23]

The complementary partnership that Humphrey and Jennie forged served them well as their family continued to grow, they expanded their entrepreneurial interests, and they solidified their place among a growing elite Black community. In 1897 their second daughter and third child, Edna Florence, was born. Her birth prompted the couple to leverage their Seventh Street property again with the Hanes brothers for the sum of $300. The following year, another girl, named Willie Corine, arrived. Their last child, a boy named Leroy Langston, was born in 1899.[24]

With five children under the age of ten by the turn of the century, Jennie spent much of her time caring for them and over time earned public recognition from the community for being an excellent example of a mother "able to rear a family of girls and boys" and high praise from her oldest daughter, Madie, that she "raised her children" well.[25] But Madie also saw a mother whose role in the family extended far beyond the traditional notion of Victorian Black womanhood. Jennie utilized a business intellect to earn income for the family by joining her husband in the entrepreneurial enterprise of buying and selling properties.[26] Humphrey discovered that she displayed such an adroit business acumen that he turned over the family's real-estate portfolio to her. She had become so proficient by 1914 that she looked beyond Winston's city limits, purchasing property in her hometown of Salisbury and the mountain town of Asheville. There was such promise in Asheville that she flirted with the idea of building houses on the land.[27]

Jennie's attention to the family portfolio freed Humphrey to concentrate on his medical practice and to build a separate assortment of commercial properties with various male partners. One of those ventures was with Charles H. Jones and J. S. Hill. They purchased a lot on the corner of Church and Fourth Streets from R. J. Reynolds and his wife, Katharine, in May 1909 for $3,750 and set the stage for the development of a flourishing African American–centered entertainment enterprise. During the Christmas season two years after buying the property, the Rex Theatre, which was billed as "the handsomest and most pretentious theatre for the colored race in the United

States, if not in the entire world," opened on the lot. It offered patrons the opportunity to view some of the latest motion pictures. "If there were any people in the Twin City who thought that a popular priced theatre for the colored people here would not succeed," declared the newspaper in January 1912, "they would have their opinions changed by paying a brief visit to the new Rex Theatre on Fourth street at the opening time this afternoon." African Americans were so excited by the development that they "flocked to the doors" to see the motion pictures.[28]

By the first decade of the twentieth century, Jennie and Humphrey had become thoroughly integrated into a small group of other Black professionals and business owners who had also begun arriving in the last decades of the nineteenth century and were determined to upbuild the Black community. For example, there were barbers like Crawford B. Cash and his wife, Bettie. There were also grocers, a Black undertaker, the owner of a hotel who provided a respectable place for Black travelers and lodgers to reside, and a Black dressmaker. Other Shaw and Leonard Medical School graduates also found the town attractive. They opened law offices and medical practices.[29]

In addition, Winston attracted a number of Black educators. They transformed the Black educational system. There had been some form of public education for Black children since Reconstruction, but, as in most southern communities, it was limited and crude, offering only primary grade instruction and industrial training. In the 1880s, the entire public school system was revamped and expanded and included the construction of several schools. The Winston Colored School for Black children opened with a principal and three teachers in 1884. Three years later, the Depot Street Graded School (also referred to as the Colored Graded School) was built for the mushrooming Black population.[30]

The Depot Street School became one of the signature Black schools in the state, primarily because of the arrival of educators Simon Green Atkins and his wife, Oleona Pegram Atkins. Like Humphrey and Jennie, Simon and Oleona Atkins were both North Carolina natives. He was born while the Civil War raged in 1863 in the Haywood community of Chatham County near the Cape Fear River and grew up on the same farm where his parents worked. In 1880 he enrolled in St. Augustine's Normal Collegiate Institute that opened in 1867 in Raleigh. The school's dual mission included training teachers to teach Black children and young men to become ministers in the Episcopal Church. After graduating he returned to Chatham County to teach and assisted with the establishment of the Black North Carolina Teachers' Association that began operating in 1881. In the fall of 1884, he moved to Salisbury, the hometown of Humphrey and Jennie, to take leadership of the grammar school department at the African Methodist Episcopal Zion Church–affiliated Zion Wesley Institute that was chartered as a college in 1885 and renamed Livingstone College in 1887. In 1888 he also became the treasurer of the college and by 1890 edited the school's monthly magazine, the *Southland*, that the midwestern Black newspaper the *Cleveland Gazette* noted showed "promise of being a successful venture."[31]

Oleona Pegram became his wife in 1889, and together they established a formidable partnership. She was from the coastal town of New Bern and matched her husband's desire for education and devotion to teaching. After earning degrees from Scotia Seminary in Concord, North Carolina, and Fisk University in Nashville, Tennessee, she became a teacher. Later, domestic duties and the birth of nine children shaped her world. However, they did not get in the way of her commitment to helping her husband parlay his successes into more lucrative ventures.[32]

Simon Atkins had held the position of corresponding secretary of the State Teachers' Association in 1886, and by 1890, with his wife's encouragement and support, he accepted the secretary of the Educators of Colored Youth position, where he sat on a board with some of the most distinguished national figures in the Black community, including Kelly Miller of Washington and Ida B. Wells of Tennessee. His teaching and administrative experience coupled with his national profile made him an attractive candidate to the school board in Winston that was looking to recruit someone to lead the newly revamped public school for African American children. He served as principal for several years, and his wife, Oleona, taught there. Under the leadership of the couple, the institutional footprint of the school expanded, with a library, an assembly hall, and a steady rise in the number of Black students. The couple's success at the school opened the door to new opportunities. For example, in 1892 Simon was elected general secretary of education of the African Methodist Episcopal Zion Church. It involved such extensive travel throughout the country that he decided to resign as principal at the Deport Street School.[33]

Still, because of the early work by Simon, Oleona, and the Black faculty, the colored graded school became a magnate for Black children. By 1898 nearly four hundred children were enrolled in the institution. Madie recalled that "all the black children" attended and that it was "just a block from my house."[34] They were instructed by a gendered staff of primarily Black female educators. In 1903 the seven female teachers who made up the core faculty included Amelia J. Fitts, the wife of attorney John Fitts, and Carrie Lanier, the wife of attorney James S. Lanier. In 1907 there were eight staff teaching first through seventh grades. A year later, three new teachers were hired, increasing the number to eleven. Roberta Carr, a cousin of the Hall family who boarded at their home, was among them. She and female colleagues taught the lower grades, while the principal and seventh grade teacher were Black men.[35]

The Depot Street School became so deeply embedded in the Black community that it was greatly influenced by the Black churches and became a model of support for the myriad economic and educational levels of children who attended. The school catered to family economic needs, accommodated students who held jobs that helped sustain their families, and met students where they were in their educational status. They began their day in the factories in the morning and then went to school or ended their day working after classes were dismissed.[36]

For privileged students like Madie, on the other hand, the school offered numerous opportunities for success. She excelled academically in part because her mother had taught her to read and write before she enrolled. The skills paid major dividends, affording her the ability to skip the first grade. Her mother more than likely also guided her toward the development of the artistic talent of playing the piano. The aptitude for the arts grew over time and introduced her to new opportunities. A few months before her fourteenth birthday, when she and her classmates participated in the graduation exercises in the spring of 1908, she was chosen to play a piano solo and deliver her final public presentation, titled "Success and Failure."[37]

After graduation Madie and many of her classmates remained in Winston and enrolled in the Slater Industrial Academy and State Normal School that had been established by Simon with the help of his wife. Supported by Black professionals like Humphrey and Jennie and prominent and wealthy white men who presided over every aspect of the town's development, the institution became one of the most successful educational centers for Blacks in the Southeast. The seeds of the plan had begun as early as 1886 when Simon's friend Joseph C. Price, who served in the dual roles as the president of Livingstone College in Salisbury and the North Carolina Teachers' Association, issued a call "urging the establishment of a State Institute for the training of colored teachers, as well as for the higher education of the colored youth of the State."[38]

Believing that Winston was the best place to build the institution, Simon declared, "It is impossible to have an effective public school system without providing for the training of teachers. . . . The schools in which this training is given, called normal colleges or normal schools, have been found most efficient agencies in raising up a body of teacher who infuse new life and vigor into the public schools. There is urgent need for one at least in North Carolina." He was so persuasive that local white oligarchs supported the plan, and the state legislature appropriated $1,000 for the building of a school on the condition that a matching amount was raised by the community. With the financial assistance of the John F. Slater Fund, a northern philanthropic enterprise established in 1882 that was committed to advancing Black education in the South, Simon established the Slater Industrial Academy in 1892 that evolved into the Slater Industrial Academy and State Normal School. The faculty included Cadd G. O'Kelly, Thomas R. Debman, and Humphrey Hall, who taught physiology and hygiene and earned a $50 salary.[39] Oleona also "entered into the work of her husband with sympathy and enthusiasm." Initially, she performed unspecified duties at Slater for a salary of $25. In 1896 she was teaching English, and over the years she held other positions, including assistant principal, for which she earned $200 in 1914.[40]

All of Madie's siblings would attend Slater, but she would have the most memorable experiences. She studied hard as she took courses in reading, language, arithmetic, history, geography, vocal music, drawing, science, civil government, Latin, and pedagogy. Although the school was not religiously affiliated, it was steeped in Christian doctrine. She attended devotional exercises in the chapel every day, and she also learned about a number of social reform societies and service organizations such as the Women's Christian Temperance Union that had a presence on the campus. She expanded her music skills and repertoire by taking piano lessons under the tutelage of instructor Cadd G. O'Kelly, the former dean of the Kittrell Institute Music School in North Carolina. Madie became so proficient that her musical talents were highlighted at the May 1909 commencement exercises. The large crowd that the newspaper reported exemplified "the best colored citizenship of Winston-Salem" heard her play a piano solo as part of the entertainment.[41]

Madie performed quite well at Slater, and along with her fourteen Normal Department classmates she received a Bible and her diploma at the May 1910 commencement.[42] Ultimately, her success represented the fulfillment of what her parents and their friends had built in Winston for the next generation.

* * *

The upbuilding of Black Winston and Madie's accomplishment came at a price. Between the time that she was born and when she graduated from Slater, Black success coupled with the exponential increase in the Black population intersected with the institutionalization of a form of segregation and oppression that cut across class lines and ensnared men like her father and tobacco laborers alike. White supremacy locked Humphrey out of the hospital, the only public local medical facility in Winston, because he was Black. He also could not join local organizations like the Forsyth Medical Group or gain membership in the white state and national medical associations such as the North Carolina Medical Society and the American Medical

Association, which made his membership in parallel Black organizations all the more necessary.[43]

While his success in some medical situations encouraged several white residents to seek Humphrey's medical expertise and a number of African Americans utilized his services, according to Madie, he was nevertheless also victimized by the kind of racism and discrimination that Todd Savitt argues made some Black patients refuse to patronize him "in part from a reluctance to give up traditional reliance on white doctors and from a sense of uncertainty about black physicians' abilities." This insidious notion, Kelly Miller insisted, stemmed from white supremacy's inculcation of Black inferiority to such a degree that "the colored physician is everywhere in open competition with the white practitioner, who never refuses to treat Negro patients, if allowed to assume the disdainful attitude of racial superiority."[44]

Moreover, racial animus threatened the lives of Black workers and remade interracial relationships. For example, a little more than a month after Madie was born, Walter Tuttle, a tobacco roller, was shot by a white police officer and later died of his wounds. A grand jury did indict the officer in March 1895, and he was "bound over to the court in a bond of $2,500." With the help of the sheriff and several others, he paid the bond, and in May 1895 the trial jury acquitted the officer of Tuttle's death. Shortly after the verdict, Tuttle's brother Arthur Tuttle shot a white police officer during a scuffle. The officer later died, and Arthur Tuttle was arrested and charged with murder.[45]

Almost immediately, rumors of breaking Tuttle out of jail ensued in the Black community because white supremacists reportedly discussed lynching him. Fearing for his safety, the sheriff decided to relocate him to a jail in nearly Greensboro. Distrustful of the local police and determined to keep Tuttle alive and safe, 200 Blacks accompanied him on the train ride. As news spread about what had occurred in Winston, Blacks in Greensboro mobilized, and a group of well-armed Blacks met the train when it arrived. The lynching rumors persisted, however, so Tuttle was later moved an hour away to Mecklenburg County. By the time that he was returned to Winston, African Americans had raised enough money to hire attorneys for him, and when white vigilantes reportedly planned to storm the jail and lynch him, at least 150 African Americans marched to the jail to defend him. Most of them refused to disburse even on the orders of both the sheriff and a judge. The Forsyth Riflemen were called in to restrain them. The battle that ensued between African Americans and the Riflemen resulted in the arrest of 45 African Americans and the mayor insisting on the need for a Gatling gun, a weapon first used in the Civil War that could fire hundreds of rounds in a minute, "to aid in keeping the peace of town." The gun did arrive, but the mayor never actually utilized it. Walter Tuttle was found guilty by an all-white jury and sentenced to twenty-five years in prison. The sentences for the "rioters" varied from three months to one year.[46]

The year after what the *Washington Post* referred to as "Race Riots at Winston," the landmark Supreme Court's *Plessy v. Ferguson* decision in 1896 emboldened white supremacists to cement the institutionalization of Jim Crow in Winston and cripple Black male political participation across all economic classes. It had begun as early as 1894, a year before the race riots, and escalated throughout the decade. White Democrats reduced the number of Black voters who resided primarily in Ward 3 to half that year. Black men who had been elected city commissioners, become judges in elections, and held positions on the county Republican executive committee began to systematically lose those positions.[47]

Prominent Black men tried to fight back. When attorneys James S. Lanier and A. R. Bridges, barber Junius Hawkins, and grocer Henry Neal met with a crowd at the courthouse in October 1898 and, according to the *Winston-Salem Journal*, "abused the democrats in all of the speeches and said if the democrats were elected the negroes would be disfranchised," the newspaper immediately rebuked them in an article titled "A Black Fool." "Such is the result of republicanism. Such is the reward the white men of this section get from people whom they have been paying taxes to educate for nearly 30 years and whose needs are ministered to with an [illegible] hand every winter." Ultimately, the paper asserted "that a large class of colored people here and elsewhere will repudiate such feeling and such utterances."[48]

Less than a month later, the paper issued an open letter "To The Colored People" that provided "Good Advice to the Colored Voters" on a front page that also announced that six hundred members of the Winston-Salem Democratic Club, "consisting of the very best and most influential business men, both democrats and former republicans," had unanimously agreed to change the club name to the Winston-Salem White Man's Club. Within two weeks of the announcement, the membership had risen to nearly eight hundred men committed "to ever more settle the question of white rule in Piedmont North Carolina." The *Journal* also expressed strong support for the U.S. congressional representative from Raleigh who argued that the choice was between "the White man's party and the negro party, White Supremacy or negro rule" and asked, "Which will you take? Are you a White Man or a White Negro?" By 1900 Black men like Madie's father were systematically losing their right to even register to vote because registrars refused to register them. Winston was not unique in the state or much of the South. The Democrats would sweep local elections and those in the state that year, and the wholesale disfranchisement of Blacks in Mississippi revealed the chilling signs of what was to come for Black voters throughout the South.[49]

There is no evidence that Humphrey openly challenged the denial of his political rights. Some of his cohorts like Simon Atkins did object privately, however. Writing in a letter to a minister in Salem, Virginia, "I have always regretted that universal suffrage was given to the Negroes just after the war but the efforts in our State to make the restriction apply only to colored men strikes me as being very reprehensible," Simon demonstrated an understanding of how the fragility of his citizenship rights was so closely tied to that of the Black masses.[50] But he and men like Humphrey did not retreat from the public sphere, as Glenda Gilmore suggests in her argument that "after disfranchisement of black men, black women became diplomats to the white community, just as southern progressivism flowered." Instead, they used the capital that they had cultivated with white oligarchs to assist them with developing economic and social ventures for the Black community. It was with the white male financial backing of R. J. Reynolds, Henry Fries, and William Blair, for example, that Simon developed the premier Black housing community of Columbian Heights (also referred to as Columbia Heights) in 1892, located near Slater, that grew to feature residents with "comfortable and well-arranged homes, which afford not only the means of enlarged accommodation for the school, but also a wholesome object-lesson to the students, giving them an idea of the home-life that should characterize growing intelligence in lieu of the one room log cabin."[51]

In 1899 Humphrey joined the "best colored men" like Simon and John Jones in continuing to utilize the capital of white oligarchs to embark on their most ambitious project yet, building the first Black hospital in Winston. Armed with the fact that models of the kind of hospital they proposed were already in operation in places such as Provident Hospital in Chicago, Freedmen's Hospital in Washington, Good Samaritan Hospital in Charlotte, and St. Agnes Hospital in Raleigh and that a facility was about to open in Durham, they approached R. J. Reynolds.[52] As the largest employer of African Americans, Reynolds agreed in November 1899 to "the erection and establishment of a Hospital and Nurse Training Department of the colored people of the communities of Winston Salem" on the condition that "Prof. S. G. Atkins for himself and his associates . . . can raise the sum of $5,000 for said purpose." In return he would "give the sum of $5,000 for the purpose aforesaid, provided the said S. G. Atkins and his associates shall raise for the said purpose a like sum." "I agree," Reynolds stipulated, "to give to the extent of $5,000, as much as said S. G. Atkins and his associates may raise provided this amount is not less than $3,000." All money from Atkins and "his associates," Reynolds insisted, had to be "ready for use by January 1st 1901," a little more than a year after the agreement. The proposed hospital was tentatively referred to as the R. J. Reynolds Hospital. A board of managers that included the mayor, two of Reynolds's brothers, and Simon Atkins was quickly established, and Wachovia Loan and Trust was designated as the financial repository for all donations and transactions.[53]

Local African Americans and whites were enthusiastic about the proposed hospital and the nurse training school attached to it and eagerly joined in the local campaign to raise funds. But Simon and his wife, Oleona, knew from experience that successful fund-raising for southern African American institution building often required financial assistance from northern philanthropists. So they launched a northern fund-raising tour. He lectured on the benefits of industrial education. She demonstrated the gendered face of success among Black elite southern women. An elocutionist, she performed in several venues, reciting the poetry of Paul Laurence Dunbar.[54] The combined financial yield from the local and statewide communities and northern philanthropists, however, still did not produce success initially, but perseverance finally paid off in May 1902. Reynolds matched the $3,665 that had been raised over the course of two and a half years with $1,665 in cash and the $2,000 in deeded land for the new Slater Hospital and Nurse Training School.[55]

Just before the official opening of the hospital and training school on May 14, 1902, administrative units that handled the daily operations of the hospital were approved. The interracial advisory board included Black doctors Humphrey Hall, John Jones, and the newest arrival, Frank Settle Hargrave, all graduates of Leonard Medical School, and three white doctors, Henry T. Bahnson, Samuel F. Pfohl, and David N. Dalton. Lula C. Hairston was hired to run the Nurse Training Department with an annual salary of $300.[56]

One of the most significant developments was the appointment of a ten-member auxiliary committee that included a cross-section of some of the most prominent Black women in the city. Several were the wives of Black physicians such as Madie's mother, Jennie, and physician John Jones's wife, Eliza Jones, while others were linked to educational facilities and businesses.[57] The official purpose of the auxiliary committee was to support and promote the hospital, but the auxiliary actually linked Black women to community affairs and demonstrated their vital role in the maintenance of the Black health-care system in the city. While male physicians and board members busied themselves in seeking the necessary funding and ensuring proper staffing of the hospital, the women on the auxiliary were engaged in selling the idea of the hospital to a suspicious poor and working-class community. As Darlene Clark Hine states, "It is hard to exaggerate the difficulties encountered in the attempt to dispel the fear and superstitions deeply entrenched within the black population" about medical care and hospitals in the late nineteenth and early twentieth centuries. When the hospital opened, most

Blacks became patients as a last resort. During one of the first years, for example, fifteen of the seventy-five patients at Slater were "emergency patients." Mortality rates, hovering around 11 percent, meant that at one point, ten of the ninety patients admitted died from chronic or acute diseases.[58] The work of the women on the auxiliary, then, was critically important to the success of the hospital. Their dedication ensured that a year after the formation of the auxiliary, the hospital had "bedding and linen to supply seven beds during the winter months." By the fall of 1903, the auxiliary and other Black women in the community succeeded in collecting $17 for winter fuel.[59]

The auxiliary redefined the nature of Black women's public social welfare activism in Winston. It ultimately proved to be the springboard for the development of a local Black club women's movement and offered Jennie's daughter Madie a road map on how to build female-centered coalitions and engage with the community. Over time Jennie, for example, held membership in several women's organizations after the work of the auxiliary ended and, the newspaper reported, played significant roles in "many movements started in the city."[60]

The process of developing the concept to open a hospital, raising money, and instituting administrative mechanisms to govern it was also instructive for Madie. But it was learning about the fragility of the alliance made with a single white benefactor to sustain an institution that depended so heavily on a mostly poor clientele that proved most valuable. During its entire history, the hospital never turned a profit, and indebtedness ultimately overwhelmed the beleaguered institution. As early as 1903, there was a debt of more than $200, forcing the directors to take up a collection at a meeting and the nurse to seek aid from the community. Structural difficulties also meant that there was never enough of a water supply to adequately operate the hospital. The problems became so dire that a month before Madie's tenth birthday, in May 1904, the facility that her parents had worked so hard to establish closed.[61]

The program designed to create a professional class of Black female nurses collapsed as well. Less than a year after the hospital opened, the board approved the request to increase the number of nurses and to devote $15 to "promoting a nurse training class of three members." Assistant nurse Nannie B. Allen, a Slater graduate, was hired and paid $5 a month. But the plan was stymied by myriad problems. Over the course of several years, the nursing classes were held and there were graduates, but the grand plan for the program never materialized because there was little continuity in head nurses, which contributed to the instability in the daily governance of the hospital and the program.[62]

Madie also saw how tenuous her mother's public role as a Black female activist was. Harry Cowan's health declined to the point that he moved to Winston to be with his daughter Jennie and her family. Her husband certainly played a central role in his medical care, but Jennie became Harry's primary caregiver. Moreover, public discussions about the auxiliary disappeared from the newspaper, suggesting that the auxiliary had disbanded, leaving Jennie without the organized support of women devoted to the hospital resuscitation effort. Meanwhile, Humphrey began planning a new business venture and two years after his father-in-law died had realized his dream. In March 1906, Hall Drug Company opened on East Fourth Street.[63] The business thrived. James S. Hill, then the president of Forsyth Savings and Trust, joined the lucrative venture until 1910. By then the two men had hired two clerks, Madie's oldest brother, Cleo, and Abram Henderson, to work in the business. The following year, physician William H. Bruce had become Humphrey's partner.[64]

Competing interests also encouraged men like Simon Atkins to shift their focus. He relinquished his presidency at Slater in 1904, began the process of developing a viable Black financial institution, and looked to further his career in the AME Zion Church. He first became president of the Twin City Building and Loan Association, located on Main Street. It opened in 1903 and provided mortgage loans to the Black community and stock for share-holders. He then added secretary of education of the AME Zion Church and remained in the position until 1911.[65]

In an effort to resuscitate the hospital, Cadd G. O'Kelly, the new president of Slater School, filled the vacuum. His administration brokered a deal with the hospital board that proved to be the institution's salvation, at least in the short term. It reopened in April 1905. "Colored Churches and Societies" raised $200 of the $1,690 that the hospital collected to keep the doors open.[66] And Booker T. Washington, the most prominent African American in the country, accepted the invitation to speak on Easter Monday at the Elks' Auditorium in Winston specifically "for the purpose of aiding in making the R. J. Reynolds hospital for colored people second to none in the State." A crowd of nearly eight hundred paid either 75 cents or $1 to attend the event. Separated by race, Blacks in the balcony and the three hundred whites seated on the first floor, the audience listened to William Blair, the prominent white president of Peoples National Bank, introduce Washington, who gave "one of the smartest and ablest addresses of the kind ever delivered in the State." Nearly $1,000 was raised for both the hospital and the Slater school.[67]

The problems plaguing the hospital, however, persisted. The financial deficit continued because most patients were too poor to pay for the services that they required, and the state, the county, the city, and white industrialists failed to ensure its success. Recognition of the dire circumstances prompted the majority of the board of managers at the March 1908 meeting to suggest that the best remedy "was to sell the Hospital property and move the Hospital into the city." But Simon Atkins rejected that idea, arguing that he believed that "finding relief for the Hospital at its present location" was the better solution. Within a year, he and Humphrey Hall, physician William H. Bruce, and

Francis Marion Kennedy, a teacher at Slater and cashier at Forsyth Savings and Trust Company, developed a plan to lease the hospital and the property for a five-year period from "the R. J. Reynolds Hospital Fund, known as the Slater Hospital."[68]

Many in Winston were jubilant that the hospital would reopen under "the management" of "the best colored men in the city" who "have the respect of both the white and colored people."[69] The philanthropic committee of charitable organizations, in particular, noted, "We are glad to inform our friends that the Slater Hospital is again open, and we think now, under such an arrangement as will keep it open. The need of this institution was never so much felt as during the period when it was temporarily closed." Members acknowledged, "The keeping of the hospital open for our large and increasing negro population, so many individuals of which are without the comforts and conveniences of a settled home life, is a distinctly charitable undertaking."[70]

Yet the team of prominent Black men could not stem the tide of financial losses. There were too few paying customers and too many deficiencies. Even the charity patients sent by the mayors of Winston and Salem to the hospital received a discounted rate. With poverty so rampant, only a few privileged Blacks could afford to pay $5 a week for private care or $4 a week in a public ward. And even the $2.50 to $5 required for operations was prohibitive. Between May 1909 and May 1910, the hospital had cared for only fifty-three patients and performed seventeen operations, far fewer than there had been during its first year of operation. With a total of $840.31 in receipts and $871.04 in expenditures, the deficit continued at the flailing institution. By 1912 the institution permanently closed, and African Americans would find themselves, as the newspaper reported, "put at a great disadvantage by the lack of hospital facilities."[71]

The struggle for the creation of a health-care facility devoted to African Americans had been about more than a testament to the committed efforts to upbuild Black Winston by prominent African Americans. It was also, Robert Korstad argues, a statement about how Jim Crow and systemic racism worked. Slater Hospital "withered away because neither the city nor local industrialists were willing to cover its operating expenses." The city did, however, ensure that when the contract for the new hospital for whites was finalized in 1913, a one-story annex in the back of the hospital was added for African Americans. Both were funded by city bonds.[72]

The demise of the hospital was certainly a significant blow to Madie's parents and would present major challenges to both the city and the Black community in the future. But Jennie and Humphrey had much to celebrate because Madie was completing her second year at their alma mater, Shaw University.

CHAPTER 2

"I Wanted to Be a Doctor"
Coming of Age

Sixteen-year-old Madie Hall had arrived in Raleigh after her graduation from Slater with about five hundred other students at the same time that a major Shaw University improvement campaign was under way. The president of the local Chamber of Commerce insisted that the institution's improvements would ensure that, like the city, the school's "Future is Brighter and More Assured." The impressive undertaking included the employment of thirty-one faculty, an estimated value of $171,000 for campus buildings and equipment, and the construction of a new six-bed Leonard Hospital. In addition, permits for new laboratories, a new dormitory in the Theological Department, and a central heating plant had been issued. In the end, the improvements were designed to make the school one of the best educational facilities for African Americans in the country.[1]

Shaw University already had a national reputation and attracted students from northern states like New Jersey and Pennsylvania and even some from the Caribbean island of Jamaica, but the school's administration made no secret of the fact that the improvements benefited the majority of students who resided in the region from states such as North Carolina, Virginia, and South Carolina. Shaw's president Charles F. Meserve, a white Baptist and Massachusetts native, marveled at the accomplishment of southern Black education while visiting Boston in November 1910. He told a church audience that "education among the freedmen and their descendants" in the South is "one of the most remarkable in the annals of the world."[2] That education was rooted in the Baptist denomination's tradition of intertwining spiritual leadership with Black progress. Stephanie Shaw argues that the combination was part of the mission "to cultivate or further develop a Christian (communal) spirit in the students" as well as "to instill leadership qualities in them; and to prepare them to use their training—moral, mental, and manual—to go into any community and establish themselves as useful members."[3] Instilling "Christian spirit" was such an integral part of the training that it guided the basis for the rules and regulations that governed the daily life of students. The Bible that Hall received at her graduation from Slater served her well at Shaw. All enrolled students were required to bring their own copy to the mandatory Bible class. Students also attended chapel services, held every day except Saturday.[4] Moreover, there were a number of Christian-oriented organizations on the campus. Hall first learned about the Young Women's Christian Association there and was drawn to its "female oriented social gospel" reform activism that emphasized her mother's teachings about service.[5]

Gender norms subscribed to a respectable Christian ideal of Black womanhood, dictating that female students learn proper social graces and etiquette and embrace their role as representatives of the race. All female students enrolled in domestic art and science classes for preparation in household management, motherhood, and domestic employment. They also learned the art of public speaking through the weekly meetings of the Calliopean Society that provided a gender-segregated environment to train them. Dress codes were strictly enforced, and behavior was monitored. Geographical constraints bound all students to campus to protect young Black women in particular and to minimize conflict between Black students and the white community in the Jim Crow city. Students could not visit the city of Raleigh that surrounded the institution during the school session without permission.[6]

Hall and her sixty-two first-year classmates navigated the various rules and regulations while they attended classes in the basic college preparation courses of Latin, history, geometry, English, music, and drawing that were designed to equip them with the ability to decide on an area of study in the fields of industrial, teaching, scientific, liberal arts, theological, law, pharmacy, and medical.[7] She selected the four-year teaching track and made her parents proud by sustaining the "high degree of character and scholarship" required of all students during her first two years. At the end of the second year, however, she succumbed to the influence of peer pressure by rebelling against her parents' educational aspiration for her. Because "all the girls in my class were getting just normal school diplomas so that they could teach" and fearing that she "would be the only one left for the third year," she argued, Hall refused to complete her junior and senior years, graduated with a normal-school certificate, and returned home. Her mother was so deeply disappointed in her decision not to pursue the four-year degree that Hall remembered she "worked me so hard, she made me wash and iron and cook and scrub and do all kinds of things." While laboring under the exhaustive weight of tedious domestic work, Hall wisely decided to "go back to Shaw and get those other two years."[8]

Hall, however, did not return to the university, because when "I finally made up my mind that I'd rather go back to college and as I was getting ready to go," she was offered a teaching position in her hometown. Luckily for her, she had passed the state teachers examination after she graduated from Slater because her mother encouraged her "to take the examination just to see how good I was in education." She "ranked very high in the list" but was too young to teach in the public schools at the time. Now nineteen years old, she "forgot about Shaw and started teaching."[9]

Hall joined a "Splendid Corps of Teachers" who began their professional careers in the eleven public schools of the merged cities Winston and Salem in 1913. With a Black and white student population estimated to be between four and five thousand students, four schools were dedicated to the education of Black students and seven to white students. They included Depot Street School, Oak Street School, Columbian Heights School, and the newest institution, Woodland Avenue School, where Hall began teaching second grade. She had at least one longtime friend, Zula Patterson, a former Colored Graded School and Slater classmate, on the faculty of six women and had known the principal, Robert W. Brown, most of her life.[10]

Woodland may have been the newest school for Black children, but the facility and the environment in which Hall and her colleagues worked were not only unequal but inadequate as well. As the Black population had grown, more students were crowded into limited classroom space, and the schools had fewer resources and teachers than white schools.[11] With twelve classrooms, Woodland had more than any other Black school, yet the number of Black children attending the school quickly outstripped the capacity. That was because in the decade between 1903 and 1913, the number of Black and white children attending school nearly doubled in the cities of Winston and Salem. As a result, by 1917 student prospects for success were grim because 50 percent of white children and 60 percent of Black children were classified as underachievers and in grade levels far lower than their age bracket.[12]

The statistics grew so alarming that the board of commissioners solicited aid from professors at the University of North Carolina at Chapel Hill, the premier white public educational institution in the state, to examine the causes and suggest remedies for the social, economic, industrial, and educational needs of Winston-Salem and Forsyth County. Published in 1918, the report presented a bleak picture. It criticized the organizational structure of the administration of the school system and, more important, revealed the systemic persistence of racial inequality between Black and white schools and teacher salaries.[13] "The buildings are not well located in relation to the homes of the children whom they serve," the report noted. For Black students, in particular, the buildings were severely lacking, because "in one case two buildings are used for a single school unit, and in another case one building serves also to house two years of high school work. There is no separate unit for instruction in high school subjects for colored children." Black students failed in far greater numbers than their white counterparts. According to the authors, "*three* out of every *five* colored pupils fail to be promoted each year." Attributing some of the failures of the system to "irregular attendance," the report also cited "a long series of causes" that included "poor health, contagious diseases, crowded rooms which does not permit teachers an opportunity to give the necessary individual attention to pupils, insufficient teaching apparatus, etc."[14]

There were also far fewer Black teachers than white. Of the 142 teachers in the school system, 106 were white, while only 36 were Black. They worked with more students but earned less than white teachers. Of the five white graded schools examined, teachers taught an average of 36 students. In the four Black graded schools, teachers taught nearly 60 students. The discrepancy meant that the 11 teachers at Depot School taught 767 students. The 7 teachers at Oak Street taught 448 students, and the 7 at Columbia Heights instructed 333 students. Woodland Avenue School, with its twelve classrooms, had 11 teachers and 633 students. All of them were female and Black.[15]

Hall, nearly twenty-four by then, was one of the most seasoned, having been at the school for at least four years. Her seniority did little to offer advancement or financial incentive because "the white men principals are the most favored class of school officers in the system in regard to salary," wrote the authors of the report. Demonstrating their own bias in favor of male superiority, they drew a clear demarcation along gender lines, declaring, "All of the principals in Winston-Salem should be men" regardless of race. Pointing to the distinct benefits of male leadership and the inadequacies of female leadership, the report noted, "The administrative supervisory duties of a school principal can almost always be better carried out by men teachers than by women teachers. Not only do men exert a stronger influence over the pupils but they can, as a rule, secure better co-operation and they have less jealousy and opposition to contend with among their women teachers."[16] Moreover, in a random sampling of twenty-five comparable cities, Winston-Salem ranked at the bottom of teacher salaries. The overall average salary for teachers was $500. But for Black teachers, the annual average of $300 compensation was far below that of white teachers. The highest salary for a Black teacher was $446.25, more than $200 less than the highest-paid white teacher.[17]

A year after the report was released, postwar Winston-Salem moved to modify and transform the school system. Leaders adhered to several of the report's recommended remedies for improvement, such as hiring strategies that included the appointment of health and attendance officers to monitor the well-being and absence of students and a business manager and additional clerical staff. Higher salaries and regular salary increases were instituted to attract competent teachers. Curriculum changes in schools were implemented to provide the best chance for students, particularly Black students, to succeed. Better facilities to equip classrooms with modern technologies and an improvement in recreational areas such as playground began. All were to be financed with the $800,000 in school bonds.[18]

Even with all of the improvements, the problems that Black women faced in the teaching profession remained because the number of African Americans arriving in Winston-Salem continued to increase and Jim Crow continued to reign. Still, teaching was one of the most respected professional jobs for Black women in the community and in the South. It certainly provided secure employment and a steady income, but the profession was also one of the few occupations that engaged Black women in public affairs and encouraged Black female leadership. Hall's status as a teacher played a significant role in her participation in the annual Emancipation Day celebration festivities in 1916. A national tradition held by African Americans across the country, the one in Winston-Salem attracted a large crowd, showcased a celebratory parade that began at Woodland Avenue School, and illustrated the steady progress of African Americans since slavery through the portrayal of prominent historical figures and decorated floats that highlighted the link between the public education system and the premier Black industrial school in the city, Slater Institute. Once participants arrived at the courthouse, there were music, recitations, an address by prominent Howard University sociology professor Kelly Miller, and a poetry reading by Hall.[19]

Her selection to read poetry at the Emancipation Day celebration had also been bolstered by her prominent place in the city's growing artistic community. After she began her career at Woodland, she participated in what the newspaper hailed as "the greatest musical event in the history of the colored people in North Carolina." Held in the Slater Chapel on a Friday evening in December 1913, it featured a number of local singers and musicians as well as those from historically Black colleges such as Howard, Fisk, and Shaw regaling the audience with a combination of classical renditions of Wolfgang Mozart, Frédéric Chopin, Robert Schumann, and Eduard Shütt and jubilee melodies like "Swing Low, Sweet Chariot." One of the organizations responsible for the production was the Twin City Mozart Society.[20] Credentialed by the piano skills that she had cultivated in childhood and enhanced in music classes at Slater and Shaw and her independent study with a teacher from Europe (German teacher W. D. Darken), Hall had by 1915 earned a prominent place in the organization.[21]

Records of the Twin City Mozart Society remain scarce, but the organization seems to have been part of an international Wolfgang Amadeus Mozart movement that emanated out of his birthplace, Salzburg, Austria, in the late nineteenth century. Memphis, Tennessee, boasted of a Mozart Society as early as 1883, and more than one hundred female vocalists in the New York Mozart Society performed at a garden party at the White House for First Lady Helen Taft in 1911.[22]

Performances by the Twin City Mozart Society of Winston-Salem first appeared in newspapers in 1910, shortly after Hall graduated from Slater. The group highlighted the talents of a broad section of members from the religious and educational communities and often held their programs in welcoming institutions such as Slater and Black churches. The productions were grand, like the seventy-five singers and musicians who performed at St. Paul Methodist Episcopal Church for a concert in October 1910. Slater hosted another event a little more than a week later. Advertised as a concert for all citizens of the city, whites were encouraged to attend by reserving seats. Under the leadership of the dean of the music school at Slater, fifty singers sang "beautiful jubilee songs as sung 40 years ago" to the mixed-race audience.[23] By 1912 the society had expanded its repertoire and become so popular that the group played the central role in producing "A Classical Soprano Contest," a "Grand Concert," and a "Great Jubilee Concert."[24]

For Hall, however, the love of music was only one of the reasons she enjoyed being a part of the group. The all-male quartettes were matched by a female quartette. Her former classmate, good friend, and fellow musician John Diggs often played the piano as well, and the organization embraced its philanthropic role in the community. Part of the funds generated from tickets sales for a 1912 event was to support the Black YMCA. When the Women's Christian Temperance Union held a fund-raising meeting at First Baptist Church in April 1915, the primary goal was to raise enough money to establish a "lunch room" that would "include employment office and sleeping rooms for the women and girls passing through the city and those seeking employment" as well as a nursery and kindergarten. The Mozart Society rendered the music on a program that was so woman centered that one of the "very interesting feature[s]" was the "female quartette" that was led by Hall.[25]

Membership in the Mozart Society certainly bolstered Hall's musical talents, but it was her directorial debut of her first cantata in the fall of 1917 that cemented her place as one of the most prominent creative cultural figures in Winston-Salem. The three-act cantata *Jepatha [Jephthah?] and His*

Daughter that portrayed the Hebrew Bible story of a father who makes a vow that ultimately meant sacrificing his own daughter promised such "a record breaking" audience and monetary profits that a professional management team coordinated the production and event. Held in Greensboro at the Grand Opera House in September 1917, it included a cast of sixty singers. Nearly six hundred Blacks and whites paid between fifteen and fifty cents to attend the elaborate event. Community interest in Winston-Salem was so high that many traveled by a "special train" that left Union Station at 5:50 p.m. to take them to Greensboro for the Monday show. It was such a resounding success that there was a "special request" that the event "be repeated at the colored graded school chapel" a few weeks later in Winston-Salem to again benefit the AME Zion Church. On October 8, the auditorium at the school was "completely filled" with a Black and white audience who came to enjoy a smaller and shortened version of the cantata directed by Hall and Janie Thornton.[26]

Cantatas were not new to the city. The Department of Music at Slater boasted in its 1910 catalog of establishing a chapel choir with "the best singers for the purpose of studying choral music and rendering cantatas and operettas from time to time." As a former student there, it was not surprising that Hall chose that medium to showcase her directorial debut.[27] But the production held other possibilities, too. Hall had seen Black elites like her parents cultivate relationships with prominent whites all of her life, and the cantata as well as the kind of classical music and jubilee songs generated by the Twin City Mozart Society provided another vehicle in continuing that linkage.[28]

African American music and performance certainly engaged prominent whites with the Black community, but Hall understood that it was mostly short term and provided few long-term benefits, so she and some cohorts mapped out a strategy to align themselves to prominent activist white women and advance organized social welfare programs for African Americans. Sometime between 1916 and 1917, they initiated informal private contact with local white YWCA members to inquire about establishing a Black YWCA in Winston-Salem. The white YWCA women, Hall and her cohorts learned, "had been talking about it and they were so glad that we came."[29]

Among the prominent members of the white YWCA was Katharine Reynolds, the wife of R. J. Reynolds. She played a central role in the establishment of the local white YWCA in 1908 that, like the national YWCA, with its one million members in nearly every state, primarily focused much of its energy on young single white female laborers. In addition to assisting with housing and employment, they organized YWCA clubs in many of the factories, including R. J. Reynolds Tobacco. That was why R. J. Reynolds "made a matching pledge of five thousand dollars" to ensure the success of the organization, ultimately sealing the bond between the YWCA and the industrialists who employed the women they served. Moreover, his wife, Katharine, held several leadership positions. The first was as vice president, and by 1916 she had been elected president. Under her leadership, the membership stood at eight hundred, and in April 1917 the organization opened a new YWCA building that the newspaper declared "stands and will stand as a monument to their generation."[30] "The influence and usefulness to the community" of the YWCA, the newspaper insisted, was without parallel, with an abundant number of programs that "covered every department of Religious, Domestic, Educational, Physical and Social life" and offered "a homelike atmosphere and home privileges not found elsewhere in the city" for young single migrant and vulnerable women laboring in many of the factories.[31]

The meeting that Hall and her cohorts engineered with white women paid dividends, because four months after the opening of the new white YWCA building, members of the Institutional Department of the Reynolds Temple Colored Methodist Episcopal (CME) Church announced in the newspaper the formation of a Black YWCA and welcomed any Black woman who could pay the monthly fee of twenty-five cents to become a member. More than likely, this was actually a YWCA Club or what was commonly known as a Blue Triangle Club rather than a branch, but the formation of the organization through members of Reynolds Temple Church was no accident. Located in a new African American housing community being constructed by R. J. Reynolds, the membership had a vested fidelity to both Reynolds and his wife, Katharine.[32]

Interest was so high that by the time the first meeting was held a little more than a week later at the Colored Day Nursery on Seventh and Vine, sixty-seven women had joined the coalition. Hall, an early proponent, was probably among them. They moved quickly to elect a slate of officers and appointed a board of directors and a board of trustees.[33] The following month, a public call was issued for "All colored women interested in the Y. W. C. A. work" to meet at the Depot Street School. Ruth Reed, the general secretary of the white YWCA, was to "lecture and give some important advice on the work being undertaken by the colored women." Two months later, a "mass meeting" was held again. This time Reed did not come alone. She was accompanied by Adele Ruffin, a trained African American member of the national YWCA staff.[34]

Ruffin had recently been appointed the national YWCA field supervisor for the South Atlantic region. Her impressive résumé included attending Norfolk Mission College in Virginia, teaching at several normal schools in the South, and serving as the general secretary of the Phillis Wheatley branch of the YWCA in Richmond, Virginia, before joining the national office. Her job required extensive travel throughout the region to strengthen the links between the YWCA and Black women. It was hazardous work for a Black woman. Forced to ride in Jim Crow train cars with few or limited accommodations, she was often refused access to restaurants. Constrained by "an undercurrent of race prejudice which is dangerous," she recognized that only "one mistake means tragedy." In spite of the dangers, Ruffin was a passionate, committed, and vociferous proponent of the YWCA. Insisting a decade later that "the Y. W. C. A. is an authority on the needs of women," she argued that the organization was such a major force in Black women's lives because "it aids in the fellowship of women, through women by women and with women. It is one of the most substantial institutions of the world where womanhood is given the opportunity of giving to the world those principles that are for the advancement of the universe, and for the improving of Christian principles."[35]

Ruffin's presence at the meeting in November 1917 strongly demonstrated that both the local and the national white YWCAs were interested in facilitating the development of a relationship with Black activist women, but America's entry into World War I interrupted any significant advancement of the plan. It lost steam and sputtered, but the idea for an official branch did not die.

* * *

World War I ended in November 1918, but the global influenza pandemic that gripped the world upended Hall's life and that of many of the people in Winston-Salem. As the *New York Times* reported in October, the "Spanish influenza now has reached epidemic proportions in practically every State in the country," and "in spite of all efforts by Federal, State, and local authorities the disease has spread rapidly and the death toll has been high in most parts of the nation." When the pandemic finally ended, the number of people who had died in the United States was 675,000.[36]

Winston-Salem was not spared from the ravages of the disease. The directive by local officials for people to remain indoors and warnings about mingling and congregating virtually shut down the city. Economic losses were staggering because businesses halted operations. Schools and churches closed their doors as well.[37] But nothing could stem the tide of those suffering from the disease or dying from it. The small Alexander Hamilton Ray Hospital for African Americans that opened in the wake of the demise of Slater Hospital was not equipped to provide necessary services. Moreover, R. J. Reynolds died just before the pandemic in July 1918 and, as "probably . . . this state's wealthiest citizen" and the person who "largely built a city and brought prosperity to an entire section of North Carolina," donated $120,000 for the construction of a Black hospital. It seems, however, that the pandemic halted any promise of construction beginning on building the institution.[38] Without a viable Black hospital and not enough beds in the segregated building on the campus of the white hospital, the city woefully lacked the skills, personnel, and institutional facilities to meet the needs.

By late October, city alderman sought assistance from the Red Cross to help open two emergency hospitals. The Hanes Emergency Hospital was designated for whites. And with the cooperation of various individuals, groups, and companies, including Simon Atkins, teachers at Slater and the city schools, as well as a number of white women and the telephone company, the Depot Street School became the site of the sixty-bed Depot Street Emergency Hospital nearly overnight (within twenty-four hours). Black physicians Alexander Hamilton Ray, John R. Henry, and John C. Williamson staffed the hospital. Head nurse Flora Belle Johnson supervised the five assistant nurses. Two registrars and two orderlies also worked at the facility. All were supervised by a white physician.[39]

While "a great deal of suffering was lessened and lives were no doubt saved" because of the opening of two hospitals, the toll on the citizens of the city revealed the devastating cost of the epidemic. Nearly 160 people died, 45 African Americans and 114 whites. Fifty-nine percent had been in the prime of their lives, between the ages of fifteen and forty. The death toll was gendered, afflicting a higher number of women than men, 88 women to 71 men, and more single than married people. Residential location also played a role in who died and who lived. Most of the dead were from Northeast Winston and Southwest Salem, areas where "most frequently that workers from the Health Department would find all or nearly all the members of families sick and almost invariably in ill vented, poorly lighted insanitary houses."[40]

Hall's family had little in common with many of those who lost their lives, but they were afflicted anyway. Her relative Reverend Robert B. Hall, who had been a minister at Union Baptist Church in Columbia, South Carolina, suffered so severely from influenza that he quickly succumbed to pneumonia. He never recovered and died in October 1918. She was also sickened by the disease. She survived, perhaps because her father was a physician and she and her family had the financial means and social connections for her to terminate her employment at Woodland and recuperate outside the city. Her parents sent her to Miami, Florida, to rest.[41]

Initially, she planned to remain in Florida for only a month, but after recovering from her illness she first pursued an opportunity to go back into the classroom in a local Black public school. Lured by the fact that one of the teachers was forced to quit because of the sudden death of her mother and because her father insisted that as his only child, she "come home and keep house for him," Hall was asked to replace her.[42] At the home where she boarded, Hall met Mary McLeod Bethune, a seasoned educator and activist who was best known for establishing Daytona Educational and Industrial School in 1904. The school had become such a success that it was the four-year high school of Daytona Normal and Industrial School. Moreover, Bethune had played an integral part in the development of the Southeastern Association of Colored Women's Clubs. Elected the first president, she led the organization in its quest to assist Black girls and promote interracial cooperation.[43]

In a recollection of one of her first interactions with Bethune, Hall noted:

> One day I came in from school and I stopped in the living room, opened the piano, started playing and singing and she was upstairs and heard it. She came down and she saw who it was playing and she said "why didn't you tell me you could play the piano?" I said, "well you didn't ask." So, she said "how would you like to come up to Daytona to my school, I need a pianist. I've got one—a woman who is head of the music department but she's gone off with the glee club. They've gone to California." I believe she said California or Boston, or somewhere with the glee club raising funds for the school and she says uh, "I don't have a pianist when she's gone." So, she said "if you come up to my school and do the playing for us I would appreciate it very much and make it well worth your while."

She accepted Bethune's invitation to be a member of her faculty.[44]

Bethune was such a major influence in her life that Hall declared that she "loved" her primarily because she had "made it all on her own." Awestricken by Bethune's drive to improve opportunities for her students, Hall applauded her tenacity and praised her for being "a go-getter." There was no better evidence of that than when business tycoon John D. Rockefeller visited the school during a Sunday vesper service where children sang Negro spirituals and Bethune used the opportunity to successfully solicit a very large donation from him.[45] There was also a more personal connection between the women. Bethune provided care to Hall after she had an operation. "She took me over to her house," Hall remembered, "and looked after me as if I was her own daughter. I never forgot that."[46]

Florida may have offered Hall respite and safety from the pandemic, but it could not shield her from the underlying racial tension that simmered in Winston-Salem. Regional newspapers such as those in southern states like Florida and Georgia and national newspapers like the *New York Times* highlighted what the *Winston-Salem Journal* declared was "the event [that] will go down in history as one of the most unfortunate and meaningless tragedies that has ever occurred here." What began a week after World War I ended and in the midst of a global pandemic on Saturday, November 16, far surpassed the racial event of 1895 and underscored the city's place in the national debate about race, justice, and mob violence.[47]

According to Jim Childress, a white man, an armed Black man attacked him and his wife, Cora, as they were walking to a nearby store. He shot Jim in the stomach and head, forced Cora Childress to go with him, and had most likely killed her. While a critically injured Jim Childress was rushed to the hospital, a group of citizens, led by the police chief and sheriff, scoured the area for Cora Childress's body. She was not dead when they found her, but she was in a "very serious nervous condition." When the police chief asked if she had been "offered any violence," she said yes. She also said yes when the sheriff asked her if the assailant "had accomplished his purpose." According to the newspaper account, she didn't scream or call for help because, she explained, "he would have killed me afterwards if I had not pleaded so with him to let me live to see my three children again."[48]

The following day, Sunday, November 17, a Black man who reportedly migrated from Durham and had been living in the city for only a few weeks was arrested for carrying a concealed weapon. Because he was described as having "borne a good reputation, had been industrious, and had spent the greater part of time in his room" and because his weapon did not match the one used in the assault on Jim and Cora Childress, the police did not believe that he had any connection to the crimes. But police arrested him anyway. That same day, a number of Black women and men attending a United War Work Drive at the courthouse encountered a crowd of hundreds of white people in front of the jail who wanted justice for Cora Childress because they believed she had been raped by her Black assailant. Two witnesses later testified in Superior Court Records that several in the crowd also shouted, "We are the Invereness Cotton Mills crowd, and we've came after the nigger" and "We want that nigger; we're going to lynch him!"[49] Some five hundred surged into the building, according to reports. Several in the crowd had guns, and at some point one of them fired, seriously wounding a white prisoner. Apparently believing that the Black prisoner had been the one shot, the mob left the building. But after learning that the wrong prisoner had been shot, the mob, now much larger, doubled back and returned to the building.[50]

The mayor summoned the Home Guards (a form of National Guard for cities) to join in the fight to guard the jail and surrounding area. The agitated mob's attempt to push past the police and Home Guards failed. But outside mob members began yelling, looting stores and businesses, and shooting randomly. Meanwhile, the governor ordered Home Guards from Greensboro and soldiers stationed at Camp Polk near Raleigh and Camp Greene in Charlotte to assist. Firemen turned water hoses on the mob in an attempt to disperse them. In the ensuing melee, five people were killed: a firefighter, a young white girl who was watching the events from a window, and three African Americans. At least twenty-five were injured, including several members of the Home Guards.[51]

Troops were stationed throughout the city, including in a Black neighborhood for the protection of the Black citizens residing there. By Tuesday the city was calmer, and only one hundred soldiers remained. A week later, Monday, November 25, all the soldiers were gone. There were subsequent arrests and recriminations, and Cora Childress never did identify her attacker or say that she was raped.[52]

What occurred in Winston-Salem was not an anomaly. It was part of a national violent trend. Even after the United States entered World War I in April 1917, a race riot in East St. Louis, Illinois, raged for nearly a week in July, killing nine whites and dozens of African Americans and causing thousands of dollars in damages. At least twenty people lost their lives in the August 1917 Houston, Texas, race riot. Some of those among the dead were soldiers and police officers. To be sure, for much of the period between the summer of 1917 and 1918, violent racial disturbances lessened considerably, but in the immediate aftermath of war, soldiers returned home, the pandemic raged, and racial tensions resurfaced. Winston-Salem became one of the earliest ominous signs of the massive racial violence that would ultimately erupt in the country during the Red Summer of 1919.[53]

Yet Hall never publicly commented on the incident at the time or in her interview decades later. Of course, she might not have remembered it, or her silence highlighted how the complexities of the racial relationship forged between elite Blacks and whites in the late nineteenth century continued to shape those relationships in the twentieth century. For example, in the aftermath of the riot, the "leaders of the best colored people of the city" quickly issued the statement that "it is our duty to correct the impression that seems to have gone abroad that there is bad feeling between the races in Winston-Salem, and out of which feeling there was developed a race riot. The fact is," they contended, "Winston-Salem has had no race riot. There has been no lynching in Winston-Salem." While acknowledging that the situation had been horrifying, they were convinced that the altercation and subsequent deaths highlighted class distinctions more than racial differences. "The best white people of Winston-Salem," they insisted, "have taken special pains to commend the leaders of the best colored people of the city for the stand they have taken on law and order." In the end, they concluded, "The history of the past will bear out the truth that nowhere in North Carolina is there a better race feeling than we have in Winston-Salem."[54] And a year later, in the aftermath of the Red Summer when Simon Atkins updated the public in an article titled "Many Changes among the Negroes in Line of

FIGURE 2.1. Madie Beatrice Hall in 1921. Courtesy of Winston-Salem State University Archives, C. G. O'Kelly Library.

Steady Progress," the *Winston-Salem Journal* praised his acknowledgment of "the co-hesiveness of relations between the two races in Winston-Salem as opposed to the frictional conditions in Washington, Chicago and ther [*sic*] cities where less amicable relations obtained."[55]

Discussion about the riot also receded as attention turned back to more pressing health concerns. The second outbreak of influenza that gripped Winston-Salem during the winter season of 1919–20 was far less severe than the pandemic in the fall of 1918, but Hall must have worried about her family. Officials reported that in February alone, 5,000 had the flu, 350 had pneumonia, and 63 whites and 77 Blacks had died. They urged people to combat the disease by getting the proper nutrition, "avoiding worry," getting enough sleep, and staying away from public venues. As a precaution, theaters and schools were among the places that closed. Even churches curtailed Sunday services. The coordinated emergency effort to contain the disease involved the Health Department, the Red Cross, and Black real-estate broker and drugstore owner Charles H. Jones, who offered a building on Maple Street for housing a temporary Black hospital. The Jones Hospital was aided by physicians in the Colored Medical Society that included Humphrey Hall as one of three doctors on the medical staff.[56]

By mid-March 1920, the city was in recovery. As a precautionary measure, some schools and businesses remained closed, but meetings resumed and by the fall athletic programs in the public schools did as well. Hall came home sometime between 1921 and 1922.[57]

The time away had been transitional for her. She left Florida and accepted a position to work with the newly established Black YWCA in Lynchburg, Virginia. The time spent in both Florida and Lynchburg proved to be quite valuable, as she mapped out new avenues of activism and thought seriously about her professional career. She flirted with the idea of giving up teaching to enter the flourishing field of social work, but by the time she arrived back in Winston-Salem, she was sure she wanted to be a doctor. The desire had been fueled as much by her father as it was by her friendship with a Black female doctor in Columbia, South Carolina. She became so consumed by the idea that decades later she still struggled to find the words to describe her feelings about it. "I just wanted—it was in me," she concluded.[58]

Her father, however, was insistent that she could not be a doctor. In response to her pronouncement, he said, "No, no. No girl can be a doctor." It was a blow to her, and so was the fact that the lack of resources, mismanagement, and indifference from philanthropic foundations had forced the Baptist Home Mission to close Leonard Medical School in 1920. The strong-willed Hall, however, moved forward with her plan anyway. She "wrote to Howard University for admission there in the medical school" and, she claimed, "was accepted." Her brother Leroy, who had just graduated from Livingstone College, was also destined to enter Howard, so she approached her father once again, asking if "'I'm accepted and Leroy is accepted. Why can't I go?' He said 'Leroy can go, but not you.'"[59]

Humphrey's rejection of his daughter's desire to train to be a physician not only dashed a dream but also revealed the raced and gendered reality of a young Black woman's life. Tormented by the encounter with her father, the memory still remained fresh in her mind more than sixty years later, but time and age had altered her perception. In her eighties, she came to view his refusal to allow her to go to medical school as less of a penalty for being female and more as his way of protecting her from the travails of the medical profession. Black women certainly did face severe disadvantages and problems in the profession. As Darlene Clark Hine noted, more than 550 physicians had graduated from Howard University by 1900, but of that total only 25 were Black women. The small number of Black female graduates forced a number of Black women who wanted to earn a medical degree to migrate north. Matilda A. Evans and Eliza A. Grier, for example, graduated in 1897 from the Woman's Medical College of Pennsylvania that first opened in 1850. In 1898 both returned to the South and earned their medical licenses in South Carolina. Evans, however, stood out for having "considerable hospital practice" and because when "she stood the examination before the State board of medical examiners," she "surpassed many of the male applicants, white and colored." Evans was such a professional anomaly that one state newspaper opined, "A woman doctor is somewhat of a novelty in this city and a colored one is an unexpected innovation in the medical profession."[60]

Evans used her medical school hospital experience to open Taylor Lane Hospital and Training School for Nurses in Columbia and became known, according to the *State* newspaper, as "South Carolina's Brainiest Negro." When Taylor Lane was destroyed by fire, she opened St. Luke's Hospital and Training School for Nurses. She also centered herself in the medical profession by becoming a member of the National Medical Association and in the state medical community of the Palmetto Medical Association. As a result of her local, state, and regional success, she garnered numerous accolades. They included being elected the second vice president of the Palmetto Medical Association in 1906 and sixteen years later taking the leadership position of the association as president.[61]

While is it unclear whether Hall ever met Evans, she did develop a close friendship with one of her protégés, Ruth B. Carroll, and seems to have been greatly influenced by Carroll's achievement. Born in 1885 in Greenville, South Carolina, she was the daughter of prominent minister Richard Carroll. Interest in medicine led her to begin a career in public health as a nurse at Evans's Taylor Lane Hospital in Columbia. At some point, she decided to become a physician. Whether Evans played a role in her decision to enroll in Meharry Medical College in Nashville isn't clear, but their early working relationship in the hospital and Evans's unwavering commitment to her profession as a physician suggest that she may have mentored Carroll and been as determined to increase the number of Black female professional physicians as she was to the training of Black female nurses. When Carroll graduated from Meharry in 1908, she was one of only three females. She first earned her license in Georgia and joined a practice in Waynesboro. Pulled back to South Carolina, Carroll passed the state medical exam in 1909. In 1913 she had joined a practice with Matilda Evans and was specializing in "Diseases of the Chest."[62]

Bolstered by Carroll's success, Hall questioned the patriarchy that limited her professional opportunities. She and Leroy had attended the same public schools in Winston-Salem, her intellect matched or exceeded his, and she had the same passion for medicine that her father, whose "mind was always on medicine," possessed. Yet because he was male, after Leroy graduated from Slater, he would enroll in three different college and university programs on his quest to becoming a doctor. He graduated from Livingstone College in Salisbury, North Carolina, in 1922 and afterward briefly attended Howard University. He then enrolled in Meharry Medical College in Nashville, earned his medical degree, passed the state exam, and was licensed to practice in North Carolina in 1927. In a last-ditch effort to persuade her father to change his mind, Madie Hall attempted to enlist her mother's help. The attempt failed, so she went back to teaching.[63]

* * *

The gendered, raced, and patriarchal world in which Hall lived may have thwarted her effort to become a doctor, but postwar and postpandemic Winston-Salem's entrance into an unprecedented economic boom offered her other possibilities. The city had become a place, Black reporter Hoyt A. Wiseman of the *Winston-Salem Journal* declared in 1923, where "our people have almost reached the point when their every need can be supplied within the race" and the leading place in the state where "the increasing prosperity and progressiveness of our race [is] showing quite so clearly."[64] Indeed, the Black community boasted of numerous new Black businesses. One of the crown jewels was the Lincoln Theatre. Called a "palace within itself," the theater, located on Church and Third Streets, opened in April 1924 and was hailed as "the handsomest and mose [sic] exquisitely furnished theatre for colored people south of Washington." The seating capacity of twelve hundred attracted a number of major figures, including Marcus Garvey, the leader of the Universal Negro Improvement Association, an organization first established in Jamaica in 1914, set up operations in New York City in 1916, and spread throughout the country.[65]

North Carolina was fertile ground for the organization. The state had the fifth-largest number of southern members of the UNIA, and Winston-Salem had three UNIA divisions.[66] So when Garvey arrived in the city on Sunday, September 21, 1924, "every available foot of space was occupied" in the Lincoln Theatre by a crowd of fifteen hundred to two thousand that included members of the UNIA African legion and Black Cross Nurses organization. The elaborate program included speeches, singing, poetry, and a collection for the UNIA and for Garvey who was out on bail from his conviction for mail fraud in June 1923.[67]

Winston-Salem was also a city that had the largest number of "weekly wage earners" that a YWCA report estimated stood at 25,000 in 1920.[68] Much of that progress was driven by the consumer demand for cigarettes and the prosperity of R. J. Reynolds Tobacco Company. Between 1904 and 1914, the number of users had doubled, jumping from 3.4 million to 6.9 million. By 1919, however, it had risen to 53.2 million after the company initiated a marketing campaign for Camel cigarettes. In 1914 a half-billion Camels sold, and by 1917 that number had jumped to 12.3 billion. The market share was 40 percent during the World War I years. By the end of the decade, the R. J. Reynolds Company had made "Prince Albert the world's most famous brand of smoking tobacco and Camel cigarettes, the most famous brand of that kind." Ultimately, the city of Winston-Salem was the leader of tobacco manufactured products in the world.[69]

To be sure, most Black tobacco and mill laborers, women and men, as well as domestics remained exploited by Jim Crow rules, poor pay, and poverty, but large numbers of African Americans also found economic opportunity and class mobility. For those reasons, thousands continued to migrate there. When the Census reported its findings in 1920, the population had more than doubled that of the combined Winston and Salem in 1910. The 48,395 residents eclipsed Charlotte's population by more than 2,000, making Winston-Salem the largest city in North Carolina. While African Americans were no longer the majority, their numbers had jumped by more than two and half times those a decade earlier. Nearly 21,000 African Americans resided in the twin cities. The majority were female and between the ages of eighteen and forty-four. That demographic, particularly those with professional jobs and the discretionary income available for purchasing consumer goods, was a key reason Hall invested in a joint dressmaking partnership with her sister Edna. Like her older sister, Edna had been teaching for some time but longed to move into another profession. Together they intended to capitalize on the fashion-conscious desires of modern twentieth-century women.[70]

In March 1924, the two women opened the "modernly equipped fashion shop" Hall & Hall in their father's building on Patterson Avenue. Advertising that their merchandise was tied to the fashion capital of New York, their store specialized in "millinery, dressmaking[,] beading, hemstitching and plaiting [or plaiting or pleating] of all kinds." In staking their claim to customization, they had become part of what Wendy Gamber refers to as "craftswomen" who "took pride in mastering delicate fabrics, fashioning original creations, and cutting garments that fit," a tradition that was fading fast in the 1920s.[71]

Opening a millinery and dressmaking shop in an age when "department stores had won a decisive victory" over "self-employed craftswomen" exhibited self-confidence, an acute understanding of a unique niche of the feminine fashion industry in the city, and a marketing skill set that catered to and attracted a particular clientele. The sisters certainly were aided in their endeavor by the rise in the number of those entering the Black middle and upper classes in the city and their personal, cultural, and educational connections with women from the community and the church such as Roberta Carr and Josephine Kyles.[72]

Carr fashioned a model of new Black womanhood. Records suggest she was Madie Hall's cousin, the oldest among the eclectic mix of young women in the Hall household, and began boarding with the family when she enrolled in Slater. A 1906 graduate, she became a teacher at the Depot Street School. Over time she became so integrated into the Winston-Salem community that she attended social events with Jennie and Humphrey Hall and many of the old-guard Black elite such as Crawford B. Cash.[73] After teaching for nearly two decades, she then decided shortly before or soon after World War I to abandon the profession for a post as the cashier for the local branch of the North Carolina Mutual Insurance Company that billed itself as "the oldest, Largest, Strongest Negro Insurance Company in the World." She was such an integral part of the company that her name appeared prominently in newspaper advertisements. Carr's own business sense and her affiliation with the company encouraged her to engage in economic affairs of the city by working with the local branch of the National Negro Business League. Believing that the organization was "second only to the Christian Church," members like her strategically centered financial skills and business knowledge into their lives. She purchased her first property in December 1912 for $175. Then in 1926, Jennie and Humphrey Hall sold her a lot for "One hundred Dollars and other valuable consideration."[74]

Josephine Kyles and Hall had much in common and may have crossed paths during the time that Hall worked in Kyle's hometown of Lynchburg, Virginia, after the war. Born in either 1900 or 1901 into an aristocratic family, she was the mixed-race daughter of Alphonza or Alfonsas, a merchant, and Olinda Humbles and the granddaughter of Adolphus Humbles, who became a prominent businessman, landowner, and strong supporter of the Virginia Theological Seminary College (now Virginia University of Lynchburg). Kyles graduated from Oberlin College in Ohio in 1923. Like Hall, she developed an interest in music and played the piano. Active in social welfare work, she served as secretary in the YWCA at Hampton Institute in Hampton, Virginia. In June 1926, she became the third wife of native Virginian and prominent fifty-two-year-old bishop Lynwood Kyles, who presided over the AME Zion Blue Ridge Conference, in an elaborate ceremony. After the wedding, the couple returned to Winston-Salem, where Bishop Kyles had been residing since 1923.[75]

Carr and Kyles would have found the experience and services that the Hall & Hall boutique offered for specialty pieces far more pleasurable than what the retail department stores like Rosenbloom-Levy, with its assortment of ready-made fashions, offered. But department stores were not the only competition for the sisters. There were nearly two dozen dressmakers and businesses that offered fashion-related businesses in the city directory in 1926. Nearly half of those independent dressmakers were Black, and by 1927 there were fifteen Black dressmakers listed among thirty-seven Blacks and whites who advertised themselves as dressmakers.[76]

Hall and her sister, however, had something that most other independent entrepreneurs did not, a community with a vested interest in their success. As the sisters were "the daughters of Dr. and Mrs. H. H. Hall, who are well known in the state," and as "graduates of the Slater state normal school," the *Winston-Salem Journal* highlighted the centrality of their family connection and educational pedigree. But when the *Journal* announced that this "Fifth Avenue Fashion Shop" would be run by two women who had connections to the "fashion schools" in New York that "specialized in their particular line," it recognized them as elite entrepreneurial women. Theirs was a business that catered to women who expected "24 Hour Service" along with professional expertise. Ultimately, the newspaper declared, "The friends of the girls will be glad to see the splendid work that is about to be done by some of the local talent," and "The work of this shop will be watched with an eagle eye."[77]

The sisters poured their energy into making the shop a success. Their mother and other relatives helped. When Hall, Edna, and their mother as well as cousins Roberta and Emma Carr and Jennie Carter embarked on a long-distance car excursion during the late summer of September 1924, it was a vacation and shopping excursion for their entrepreneurial pursuit and Willie's upcoming nuptials to Harold Kennedy, the son of Francis Marion Kennedy, one of the partners in the coalition effort to save Slater Hospital in 1909 and the third president of Slater School from 1910 to 1913, that played a role in where the group of women traveled. They visited Baltimore, Washington, New York, and Philadelphia, spending time with relatives and friends and visiting the garment district and fashion houses. Two months after they returned home, in November 1924, Willie and Harold married in an elaborate evening ceremony at Goler Church that was described as "one of the grandest weddings to take place in this city in years."[78]

For the sisters, the intimacy of the custom business proved to be an entrepreneurial success. Hall & Hall was so commercially lucrative that by 1926, both women devoted all of their energies to the business. The hours, however, were taxing, and as owners and managers, catering to the desires of customers was demanding. Nearly two years after opening the business, Madie Hall suffered from such exhaustion that in January 1926, she "decided to take a needed rest for about five weeks." She first traveled to Miami, Florida, to visit with friends. Then she took her first trip outside the United States, boarding a ship to Havana, Cuba, to be the guest of some friends who resided in the Caribbean country.[79]

Only ninety miles from Florida, Cuba had been part of the diasporic transnational destination of Black Americans for decades. Like Hall, writer and artist Langston Hughes viewed the island as a place of respite and creativity. Business interest also beckoned African Americans to the Caribbean and South America. Robert S. Abbott, the editor and publisher of the *Chicago Defender*, highlighted Havana, the last stop of his trip from South America before he and his wife, Helen, returned back to New York in 1923. Abbott rhapsodized about the city's "many beauties" and expressed the promise of the place as a tourist destination, remarking that "maybe one day her source of greatest income will be the thousands of American tourists who come fleeing the frost and chill of the North."[80]

Abbott's musing had gained some momentum by the time that Hall went to Cuba because more American steamship companies expanded the number of ships offering passage to passengers, as "railways funneled travelers on their way to Cuba to Miami, Key West, New Orleans, and other southern ports where they boarded steamships to the island," Frank Andre Guridy argues. But it was Pan-American Airways that made Cuba an international destination. Pan-American first flew from Key West to Havana in 1927. Eventually, the airline established Cuba as "a hub of its Latin American operations," essentially broadening linkages in the transnational relationship between Black Americans, Afro-Cubans, Latin America, and the world.[81]

A refreshed Hall returned home from her sojourn to Florida and Cuba in February. She immediately went back to laboring in the dress shop and by the following year had added caretaking responsibilities to her duties when her mother had a stroke. Seeking the restorative health benefits of the spa oasis in Hot Springs, Arkansas, Hall and her mother left Winston in early April 1928 and enjoyed several weeks of camaraderie and healing.[82] The caretaking responsibilities consumed much of her time, so she and Edna ultimately abandoned their joint enterprise, but Hall continued in the business. This time, however, she was the sole proprietor, and there did not seem to be the same kind of fanfare that Hall & Hall received. Relocating to a building that the family had purchased at 305 East Seventh, she simply advertised in the city directory.[83]

Hall also turned her attention back to expanding her engagement in the arts and the church. Prior to her mother's illness, she had directed an Easter cantata at Goler and won high praise from a reporter who was impressed with the "very beautiful drama" in part because of the "oriental costumes" the participants wore. Hall's penchant for showcasing elaborate costumes and mixing the drama of the arts with religion was driven by her strong belief in the utilization of various kinds of educational methods to engage her audience.[84] Her production of the *White House Mock Wedding* might have been more subdued than the colorful cantata, but the message was far more poignant and instructional. A fictional bourgeois aesthetic, the production demonstrated Black patriotism and reflected African Americans' triumph, however briefly, over the racist and discriminatory contradiction in their lives. In the refashioned marriage of a son of a president and the daughter of a senator, the play examined American politics through the raced lens of an all-Black cast performance before a Black audience in a segregated Black church. While southern Black women had been granted the right to vote in 1920 with the passage of the Nineteenth Amendment, they, like Black men, continued to be denied equal political rights and remained marginalized in American society. But in this play, African American women and men centered themselves at the highest level of American politics. Cast members became the wedding participants and the officials who gathered at the wedding of the Black son of the Black president and the Black first lady.[85]

Another mock wedding generated so much excitement that the newspaper advertised it as "one of the most elaborate church affairs of the year." The audience drawn to the presentation of *Queen's Wedding* at Goler witnessed the talents of a skilled director and musician. The paper highlighted those attributes as well as Hall's long history of involvement "in civic movements" and her prominence as the "daughter of Dr. and Mrs. H. H. Hall." The colorful costumes that adorned the "beautifully dressed" choir of seventy-five who sang and marched down the church aisle to witness the wedding of the prince standing beside his queen bride enthralled the audience. The featured duet performed by a violinist and Hall on the piano did, too. She welcomed the support of the community in making the production a grand success. "I wish to thank the characters taking part in the Queen's Wedding and the citizens who rallied to the cause," she announced in the *Journal*.[86]

She became such a significant force in the cultivation, development, and execution of musical and dramatic productions that she was appointed to a committee made up of a cross-section of churches in the city that sponsored the biblical play *Hagar*. The elaborate production with a cast of two hundred portrayed the book of Genesis narrative of the Egyptian slave Sarah who became the surrogate to give the patriarch Abraham a son. In addition to her work on the committee, Hall took on the role of Sarah. Declaring that "the drama was one of the best seen in this section in years," the newspaper praised Hall for being "at her best."[87]

"Women Are Awakening"

Shaping the Parameters of Black and White Alliances

The Black YWCA in Winston-Salem finally opened while Hall was recovering from the pandemic in Florida, and by the time she returned home the organization had become a central hub of the Black community. The groundwork for success that had been guided by the early connection that Hall and a number of her cohorts had initiated with local white YWCA women had been fueled by the national YWCA's establishment of the War Work Council program in June 1917. The program engaged an unprecedented number of women in war work and quickly advanced the YWCA's activism among Black women and girls:

> War conditions brought to the front the deplorable lack of facilities for amusement for the more than million colored girls in this country. These girls are a fact in society which has been largely neglected and the emergencies of the war brought even greater problems to them than to white girls. In the sections where such work was most needed prejudice against the colored race was often the strongest. The difficult housing problems in communities near camps and large cantonments were accentuated through segregation. Colored girls looking for rooms in a strange city were usually compelled to take quarters in the squalid sections. It was equally difficult to secure adequate headquarters for the Young Women's Christian Association work, as decent, well lighted buildings were seldom rented to the colored, even north of the Mason and Dixon line. Then, too, colored girls and women were entering the field of industry for the first time, without an industrial background, not understanding their relation to men and women already in the industrial field, their responsibility to each other or toward their employer.[1]

Black activist women like Hall had long been aware of the "deplorable lack of facilities" for Black women and girls in Winston-Salem. In 1910 the Census reported that there were 4,019 Black females in a total population of 17,167. A decade later, in 1920, the Black female populace had more than doubled to 10,503, or nearly 22 percent of the 48,395 residents.[2] And the numbers kept rising over the next decade. While Charlotte regained the title of the largest city in North Carolina in 1930, the population of Winston-Salem jumped to more than 75,000, and the 17,893 Black females made up nearly 24 percent of the population. Moreover, the largest number of them were in their prime working years, between the ages of fifteen and forty-four.[3] They often lacked adequate housing, were unskilled, and could find only low-paying jobs in the tobacco industry, the hotels, and laundries that dotted the main business district and as domestics in the homes of the wealthy. R. J. Reynolds was perhaps their largest employer. Of the more than 6,000 women laboring for the company, estimates suggest that some 60 percent were Black by 1921 and steadily climbed during the decade.[4]

The national YWCA's commitment to incorporate Winston-Salem's Black female populace into the organization became part of a long-term strategy to increase its membership and expand the numbers of its more than 24,000 Black members nationwide. Although the city was still reeling from the pandemic, the process moved swiftly when several African American YWCA workers from the national YWCA office were dispatched to the city.[5] Juanita Saddler was one of them. A native of Oklahoma, a graduate of Fisk University, and a former teacher, Saddler was tasked with meeting with women and girls who worked in the factories and helping them develop YWCA clubs or Blue Triangle Clubs.[6] The unique YWCA symbol of the blue triangle recognized that there needed to be "a unified plan of club work for young girls in the Y.W.C.A. to meet their increased needs for spiritual guidance, wholesome recreation, and opportunities for service." And the primary objectives of the clubs were "to give girls through sound, natural activities, the habit, insight, and ideals which will make them responsible women, capable and ready to make America more true to its best hopes and traditions."[7]

The Black women who had been waiting for more than a year in Winston-Salem for this historic moment were so enthusiastic about developing the first YWCA clubs that at the end of the first month, Saddler had been engaged with 150 girls and had persuaded several to become leaders in the group. The attendance was so large that the schoolroom where they began meeting proved insufficient. After she appealed to city officials for better facilities, the Day Nursery then became the main headquarters. Two months later, "a special girls' worker," referred to as a "recreation secretary for colored people," arrived to organize clubs and plan activities. Discussions about opening a recreation center quickly began.[8]

When Saddler presided over a meeting at the Odd Fellows Hall on a Sunday afternoon in January 1919 to move out of the club phase and toward officially organizing the Black branch, Ruth Reed, Adele Ruffin, and nearly 100 women joined her. Reed laid out "the association's purpose and plan," while Ruffin discussed "the relation of the colored branches to the national organization."[9] The relationship fit a pattern of white female supremacy that had been adopted by the national YWCA in 1910 of favoring local white YWCAs as the "central Associations" with direct ties to the national and bestowing on them the power to determine if a Black "branch" would be organized. The success of the endeavor rested on the "combined three premises" that Nancy Robertson argues were necessary for the proposed establishment of any Black YWCA in the South: "The first was that the 'best elements of both races' needed to work together. Second, in doing so, they would promote mutual understanding and harmony and ease racial tensions. And finally, these efforts could be carried on within the confines of a segregated society."[10]

It was not a new approach to race relations among women in the city. Before Hall began her teaching career at Woodland School, Black teachers throughout Winston-Salem had one of their first large-scale encounters with white civic-minded women. Developed in cities throughout the country in the first decades of the twentieth century, the beautification and cleanliness campaigns attracted some of the "most public spirited" and powerful white women to form a branch of the Women's Civic Improvement League in Winston-Salem in 1908. Appointed by the board of alderman, the group was initially led by Kate G. Bitting Reynolds, the wife of William N. Reynolds and the sister-in-law of R. J. Reynolds. Dedicated to the cause of city beautification, the group worked diligently for years, planting flowers, removing trash and debris, and eliminating unsightly signs. Distressed by the lack of sustained progress, they complained in 1912 that the city had systematically failed to enforce city ordinances and sanitation regulations, so it remained a dirty, polluted, and unsanitary place. As a remedy, the group lobbied aldermen to expand their efforts and to initiate a clean-up campaign in the Black community.[11]

To assist them, they enlisted the aid of educated Black women, particularly teachers. In early March 1913, one hundred Black women, Black ministers, and a committee from the white branch of the Civic League gathered at First Baptist Church to create the first Black branch of the Civic Improvement League. Lenora Sills, who facilitated the meeting, laid out the administrative relationship between the Black and white leagues and set the racialized parameters of the two organizations. "The new colored league will be an adjunct of the Woman's Civic Improvement League," the paper announced.

It has been organized "in order to carry on the improvement work not only in the districts occupied by the colored people but to interest the colored people in better conditions and have them carry on the work among their own people."[12] Interest among Black teachers was so high that after Sills was invited to a meeting on Wednesday, March 12, 1913, to discuss forming a Black "sub-organization" school branch of the Civic Improvement League like that among white teachers and students, "practically every colored teacher in the city" attended. Unlike the broader campaign that targeted neighborhoods citywide, Black teachers and their students directed their attention to school grounds. "It would be," the newspaper explained, "the cleaning up of the class rooms, keeping the desks perfectly neat and clean, putting flowers in the windows and beautifying the grounds, where there are grounds that can be beautified."[13]

By May the successful alliance of Black and white Civic Leagues advocated together for the "beauty of homes and surroundings[,] better health conditions and more sanitary premises." There was so much enthusiasm among African Americans that within a few days of organizing the branch of Black teachers, nearly five hundred Black residents "signed cards agreeing to whitewash their homes and premises."[14] In one day, the Sanitary Department broke a record in the amount of trash collected. "More trash," the newspaper proclaimed, "was hauled away from the city yesterday than on any other day in the history of the city." Ultimately, the paper concluded, "the campaign promises to be the most successful in the city's history and as a result Winston-Salem will be more beautiful as well as healthier and more sanitary."[15]

Inspired by their success, Black and white Civic League members continued their joint activity throughout the summer. At the end of May, they convened at the Depot Street School "to discuss civic league problems." At a later meeting with nearly one hundred Black women in attendance, Sills and the group decided to hold a "public mass meeting of the colored people so that the men would be in attendance."[16] In the end, Black women's work with the league had not only gained them entrée into the world of white female activism but also proved to be a means of accessing power in the racist and sexist Jim Crow environment. A more complex and sophisticated kind of arrangement with local white YWCA women guided by the dictates of a nationally institutionalized women's organization afforded them the opportunity to make further advances.

Black women were so excited by the promise and meaning of the new YWCA that the Colored Day Nursery on the corner of Seventh and Vine Streets where "the children of the laboring women who are employed in the factories are kept during the day for a very small cost" proved inadequate. The branch temporarily moved to 717 North Depot Street (later renamed Patterson) near the R. J. Reynolds factory. Then at a Tuesday-evening meeting, "team workers and friends" of the Black YWCA collected $678 of the $2,500 campaign launched in April 1920. By 1923 the organization had finally found a permanent home on North Chestnut Avenue.[17] It was, a YWCA report revealed, "located in the heart of the industrial section and has the financial support of a number of employers." Described as "a barn-like building created out of a warehouse," the branch provided "splendid facilities for recreation of large groups."[18]

One of the first official events of the newly formed Black YWCA was a joint vesper service with the Phyllis Wheatley Home on a Sunday evening in the summer of 1920 that the newspaper described as a "program [that] showed the work done through these organizations for colored women and girls." The paper praised both groups for their "co-operation" and for "doing the best service possible at this time." But recognizing that even the combined efforts of the two organizations could not meet the needs of Black female laborers, the paper called their joint efforts "inadequate" yet remained steadfast in its assertion that tackling the problem was "much strengthened by the union of forces and promises much for our future in this line."[19]

The cooperative efforts demonstrated between the two institutions had taken time and a realization that together they could do far more for Black women and girls than separately. Established about the same time, each had a similar mission, to help Black "girls and women who come to our city and are likely to fall into the hands of the demon of society," but the method of organization and governance differed significantly. The Phyllis Wheatley Home had been the brainchild of the Phyllis Wheatley Association, a club developed by Black activist women in 1916. Hall probably was a member of the club, but she vehemently disagreed with the creation of the home because it conflicted with her vision of creating a small space financed by local churches for domestics to congregate and integrate themselves in the community and, most important, because she believed that it lacked the necessary institutional financial resources to succeed.[20]

Hall lost that debate to advocates like Lena B. Neal, who had built an impressive résumé for the decades that she had resided in the city. Born around 1863, Neal first began integrating herself in the community when she became a teacher at the Colored Graded School and honed her social welfare and fund-raising skills as a member of the Ladies Auxiliary for Slater Hospital as she worked alongside Hall's mother, Jennie. Then when she saw a lucrative business opportunity as the Black population rose in the city, she left the teaching profession. Earning income from the boarders who lodged in her home on Depot Street and Vine, she had a front-row seat to the drama unfolding because of Black migration. As the Black population spiked, so did the number of boarders whom she housed. Between 1910 and 1920, they more than tripled, jumping from a little over ten to more than thirty.[21]

Aided by the national wave of Black women who had been memorializing Phyllis Wheatley, the first Black female published author in the United States, in various forms since at least the 1880s, Neal tapped into the historical success of a national Black female activist brand. The first Phyllis Wheatley Club had appeared as early as 1892 in St. Paul, Minnesota, and quickly spread.[22] Many of the clubs, particularly those in urban centers, also began to develop and operate Phyllis Wheatley Homes as members became, Chicagoan Elizabeth Lindsay Davis noted, "more and more interested in a problem that was assuming alarming proportions that of colored women coming into the city, many of them from the best families in other States, and finding it impossible to secure a congenial environment in which to live or desirable employment by which to support themselves." The homes provided shelter, clothing, and education for migrating Black women. Some also acted as employment bureaus, assisting with the location of jobs.[23]

The effort to establish the Winston-Salem home that began in the summer of 1918 influenza pandemic attracted white women from both the Civic League and the YWCA. League member Lenora Sills made brief comments at a fund-raising rally, and white YWCA board members disseminated information and "valuable suggestions" because of their "similar work" among white girls.[24] The rally generated $500 and a gift of a land lot valued at $500, but the women fell short of the goal of obtaining the $10,000 to purchase a mortgage-free ten-room house that was "situated on an improved street with street car accommodations and every modern convenience."[25]

Neal and members of the association, however, were so determined to establish a housing facility for Black women and girls that they decided to take on a mortgage, enlist the aid of more than a dozen Black churches, and model their home after one located in Cleveland, Ohio, where the board of directors was interracial with Blacks and whites. More significantly, association members maintained that while the home's primary purpose was to "offer protection to the young colored girls coming to the city looking for employment," an equally important role was as a "place those who may want to employ such girls as are in the home [to be put] in quick touch with them." To facilitate that exchange, "An intelligence department will be maintained by the home for the purpose of giving accurate information to prospective employers about help available thru the establishment."[26] The gamble paid off, and by 1920 the Phyllis Wheatley Home was fully operational at 707 East Fourth Street. For about two dollars a week, young women found room and board, laundry services, and a matron who maintained the facility and protected the young women who resided there.[27]

But Hall had been right about the long-term impact of the lack of institutionalized guaranteed financial resources. Like Slater Hospital, the home struggled for sustainability from the beginning. The Black community rallied behind the home, but their contributions in cash and other resources were not enough to sustain the home, so the Phyllis Wheatley Association, led by Neal, resorted to placing constant appeals to the white community in the newspapers. While publicly supporting the home, white YWCA women privately expressed uneasiness with the appeals, as evidenced by the damning indictment of the Phyllis Wheatley Association from the national YWCA that could only have originated from the white Winston-Salem YWCA. The organization argued that the association and the home were "handicaps" and that the association was "using the name of the Y. W. C. A." primarily for "raising money."[28] Nevertheless, the Black YWCA and the home became so intertwined that the home began operating as *the* unofficial hostel for Black women. The YWCA stationed a traveler's aid at the home who provided lodging recommendations to "traveling women and girls" and helped locate suitable lodging "when there is no space at the Phyllis Wheatley Home."[29] And when the organizations held a joint meeting at the YWCA in late August 1920, it was clear that the membership rolls of the two groups overlapped. At least two members of the YWCA and the Phyllis Wheatley Association held senior positions in both. Mrs. C. A. Williams chaired the finance committee at the YWCA and was the treasurer of the Phyllis Wheatley Association, while Mrs. M. A. Patterson chaired the house committee of the YWCA and served as president of the Phyllis Wheatley Association. More significantly, the Black YWCA interchangeably became known as the Phyllis Wheatley YWCA, the "colored" YWCA, and the Chestnut Branch YWCA.[30]

The strong alliance between the two organizations ultimately encouraged Adele Ruffin to return to the city in June 1920 to set up a "conference in Winston-Salem on the matter of merging the Phyllis Wheatley Association, which is really a boarding home, with the branch for colored women and girls." Challenged by the fact that "all Young Woman's Christian Association officers are new," she wrote, members "agreed that this is the logical time for such a merger." The discussion had been induced primarily by "community impatience with financial appeals" and secondarily as a means of reviving the agenda of the Phyllis Wheatley Association, which, they argued, had demonstrated a "lack of progress."[31] The merger, however, did not occur. Either the Phyllis Wheatley Association members rejected the attempt to strip them of their autonomy and refused to merge with the YWCA, or, more than likely, the two groups reached a compromise. Still, the home remained the "unofficial" Black counterpart to the white YWCA housing facility.[32]

* * *

By the time Hall had arrived in Winston-Salem from Lynchburg and reengaged in the community, the Black YWCA had a solid foothold in the community. She embraced it and contributed her wealth of experience and expertise to the branch. That experience included what she had learned in her administrative position at the newly organized Phyllis Wheatley YWCA in Lynchburg, Virginia.[33] Like the Black women in Winston-Salem, there was urgency among prominent Black Lynchburg activists such as Hall's friend Anne Spencer in creating a safe space for Black women and girls during the war. Joined by a coalition of women, Spencer began the process of forming the same kind of Blue Triangle Club in 1918 that Winston-Salem did. Adele Ruffin, a familiar figure to Hall, was the liaison between the Black women and the white YWCA branch members who had formed their branch in 1912 to determine if a Black club would be formed. Several times a month, Ruffin met with both groups, and her successful negotiation led to the official formation of the Blue Triangle Club. For two years, the Lynchburg Blue Triangle Club operated successfully, so members expressed interest in organizing an official branch. To further their cause, the women again contacted Ruffin to seek her guidance, and by 1920 the Lynchburg Phyllis Wheatley Branch YWCA was born.[34]

Hall immediately began her job as the "special worker" for the Girl Reserve. From 1920 until June 1921, she played a key role in overseeing the implementation of one of the YWCA's signature programs for girls. To meet the needs and desires of a postwar modern generation of young women and girls, she helped usher in the new push for girls to embrace work, recreation, fellowship, and religion. She taught a multitude of recreational skills, including dancing, and encouraged the girls to explore nature by taking them on picnic outings. The program became so popular nationally that Young Men's Christian Association representative Channing H. Tobias insisted it was "probably the outstanding feature in the Young Women's Christian Association program." And indeed, between 1920 and 1925, the number of members in the program jumped from 80,000 to 192,000 and many churches "were encouraging the growth of the national organization of girls." So many southern states embraced the program that by 1933, 16 percent of the Girl Reserve Clubs could be found in the region.[35]

In Winston-Salem, nearly 200 Black and white girls formed the nine different groups organized in elementary schools, high schools, and the R. J. Reynolds factory. The Black community had such a vested interest in the success of the Black branch's program that when the YWCA initiated the "finance campaign" in June 1922, the minister at St. Paul Methodist Episcopal Church insisted that the YWCA's history as a national and international organization devoted to the success of girls and young women was so "well known" by Christian workers that there was no need to repeat it. But he argued, it could "be summed up in the slogan and purpose of the Girl Reserve: 'To face life squarely' and 'To find and give the best.'" "If Winston-Salem through an organization can help its girlhood and young womenhood [sic] adopt this slogan and purpose as its code of conduct," he concluded, then "its worth to the town can not be measured in material terms and its work should receive the hearty support of those who are interested in the bringing of the Kingdom of God into the life of our city." The nearly 60 community members who pledged to assist with the campaign included Hall's father, Humphrey Hall.[36]

When the members of the Girl Reserve appeared in the fall of 1922 at the annually held "colored Piedmont fair," they demonstrated their "embroidery work and sewing." Three years later, the group was showcasing its "first recognition service" to the community.[37] Members took field trips to Camp Betty Hanes that the YWCA established in 1925 "to promote the moral, physical and mental better of colored girls." Located in Clemmons, North Carolina, on the Georgia Mebane "plantation," just outside of Winston-Salem on the Yadkin River, the camp afforded girls the opportunity to participate in several different types of recreational sports as well as athletic games like volleyball. They also took classes in music, art, and the study of nature.[38]

Hall championed the branch's commitment to making it a learning and training center. The branch offered a course in elementary French under the auspices of the Educational Committee; a class in "civics and current events" of state, county, and city governments; and a class for teachers that provided "splendid training for teachers and prospective teachers as well as those who wish to learn fundamental facts about the Bible and child study." She supported the classes in dressmaking and helped propel the music programs. She also encouraged the growing list of cooking, gardening, embroidery, crocheting, and manicuring classes; the health education exhibits; and the recreational sports such as basketball and volleyball offered to girls. A ten-day cooking course presented by Josephine Bell of Nashville, Tennessee, captivated attendees. Bell, a regular on the national YWCA circuit, embodied the essence of instructing women on the modern techniques of home economics. "All housewives and persons interested in cooking are invited to attend these classes," the YWCA's advertisement announced. While the main goal was instructing women on how to prepare meals, other goals included the creation of a feminized space that was welcoming and fun.[39]

Perhaps one of the most important services at the YWCA building that Hall championed was the creation of a library for Black patrons. Since, the newspaper reported, "there is no public library in the city open to this group of citizens and that a large number of the homes from which they come have a very limited supply of books of any sort," Black YWCA women initiated a "book shower" in 1920 to fill the void. With the goal of filling the organization's shelves with donated books, members planned to lend them out to the community. Their perseverance led, six years later, to the institutionalization of a "colored branch of the Carnegie Library" by the city's library system. In August 1926, the librarian at the white main Carnegie Library assured the Black community that "there are a number of good books on the market by negro authors and it is planned to place many of these on the shelves of the library that the local negroes may learn of the accomplishment of their fellowmen." She insisted that they would be "only the best books" that would include authors such as Benjamin G. Brawley, William S. Braithwaite, Charles Chestnut, Frederick Douglass, W. E. B. DuBois, Paul L. Dunbar, Robert R. Moton, William H. Shepard, Booker T. Washington, Phyllis Wheatley, and Carter G. Woodson. However, she concluded that there would be "no book placed in the library that will cause racial friction."[40]

Opened in February 1927 and named the Moses Horton Branch in honor of George Moses Horton, an enslaved North Carolina poet who published his first book of poems, *Hope of Liberty*, in 1829, the library was overseen by YWCA members. "A large number of persons" attended and browsed the "splendid collection of books covering practically the entire field of literature." Eager for the opportunity to read books by Black authors and about Black people, "numerous people who visited . . . made reservations for books."[41]

Moreover, the YWCA building itself became a "central meeting place" for multiple organizations. The National Negro Business League often met there, and the community attended recitals in the facility. The YWCA and the YMCA occasionally joined forces to provide educational, recreational, and cultural events. And the members of Hall's home church, Goler Memorial, held services there for four months in the fall and winter of 1929 and 1930 while the church was being renovated.[42]

Hall was so committed to the Black YWCA branch that she joined the governing administration in April 1927 as the general secretary. While insisting that she had not been "trained" for the position, she had by then built quite a résumé of professional and administrative experience. She had, of course, worked at the Lynchburg branch, been elected vice president of the local Woman's Community Service League, and established a critical national network through her association with Mary McLeod Bethune, who was elected president of the National Association of Colored Women in 1924.[43] And more important, Hall embraced the position and guiding principles of the northern and southern Black and white members of the Continuation Committee of the Interracial Conference of Church Women who in 1926 insisted "that interracial action must be preceded by interracial thinking." They denounced "forced housing segregation," calling it "unspiritual and un-democratic"; "urge[d] that preventive measures against lynching be adopted"; and contended that "in view of the limitations of opportunities for Negro women in employment we suggest that groups of women be encouraged to become aware of conditions in industry and in other forms of employment in their communities and states." "Interracial committees of church women," the committee determined, could wield enormous power in "their communities" through programs in organizations like the YWCA by "securing provision for recreational opportunities for Negro children through playgrounds and organizations for training, culture and team work, such as the Scouts, Camp Fires, Girl Reserves and Hi Y's."[44]

One of Hall's first official acts was to ensure that five members of the branch's Girl Reserve attended the YWCA conference held in Kings Mountain, North Carolina, where one hundred participants gathered. And when she announced that the two-week summer retreat at Camp Betty Hanes would be July 15–29, she insisted that "the rates were being made low enough so all the girls in the community wishing to take part may be able to do so." The community strongly supported her efforts by providing cars to transport participants to the camp.[45]

During her tenure, Hall also initiated an aggressive membership drive "to reach every girl and woman of this city" during the week of January 22–28, 1928. That included "those who have never joined the Association" and "those who are already registered as members but have not renewed their membership." Competing for prizes for signing up the most new members, YWCA women fanned out across the community, visiting with individual women and girls and soliciting aid from organizations and churches. Nearly two dozen churches embraced the representatives, the membership drive, and the mission of the YWCA, providing time for various YWCA representatives to speak "in the interest of this Christian institution for women and girls." Josephine Humbles Kyles highlighted that Christian link between the YWCA and the church when she told the members of First Baptist Church "that the 'Y' was giving to the church in helping girls and women to find Christ and to better their conditions in life." Hall, on the other hand, underscored the centrality of women in the work of social welfare when she declared to the Mount Calvary Baptist Church congregation that "a new day is dawning and the women are awakening to their task of service."[46] Indeed, "a new day" had dawned among organized Black women in Winston-Salem. There was so much interest in women's activism that during Hall's tenure, the Black YWCA had one of its most profitable years. "The Young Woman's Christian Association, under the direction of Mrs. Jane Thornton Melton, who has headed the board of management for the past two years, and through the efforts of the secretary, Madie B. Hall, and associates, the accomplishments have been remarkable," the *Journal* noted in February 1928. The praise was certainly warranted. Three hundred new members had joined the organization, and there had been an "increase of the work at the 'Y'" as well as "the effective program that is being put over with the present group of workers."[47]

The administrative position also engaged Hall in one of the most politicized debates of the era. Women had moved into the labor force in unprecedented numbers during and after the war, which encouraged the YWCA to create the Industrial Department. It aided employers and government officials by sharing research and generating surveys. More important, the department provided critical support to female workers by monitoring and documenting working conditions and disseminating information. To aid in local efforts, the national YWCA appointed an industrial secretary who supervised the development of Industrial Clubs in local branches and monitored their progress.[48]

Winston-Salem proved to be fertile ground for the work. By 1927 nearly seven thousand Black women and girls were employed by R. J. Reynolds Tobacco Company, as Louise Leonard, the national industrial secretary of the YWCA, noted in an October visitation report. Some of those female laborers actively engaged in the YWCA Industrial Clubs and, like their white counterparts, found the union movement that had a foothold in the southern industrial sector enticing. Groups like the Tobacco Workers International Union of the American Federation of Labor had set up shop in the city in 1919 and remained embedded in the Black and white communities over the next decade. The TWIU, which joined an array of local unions in coalescing under the umbrella of the Central Labor Union of Winston-Salem, negotiated contracts and even offered "unexcelled funeral services" to African Americans. In 1924 the Woman's Auxiliary of the Central Labor Union was established. Union membership promised the prospect of earning "equal pay for equal work, regardless of sex." Jim Crow, however, crippled any gains that Black women might have obtained.[49]

Pay inequities and racism persisted, but TWIU's initiation of an aggressive recruitment campaign in the Black community helped solidify Black female loyalty. Months before Hall departed from her post as general secretary, in January 1928, the TWIU opened a branch on Patterson Avenue (formerly Depot Street) in the heart of the Black community and near one of the largest

R. J. Reynolds Tobacco Company plants. The move created "great alarm" for the company, as the new national industrial secretary, Eleanor Copenhaver, wrote. That was in part because African Americans had begun to demonstrate "more willingness to come out for the union than the white workers" against a company that at the end of 1929 had $120 million in assets.[50]

Publicly, Hall and other Black YWCA women remained silent on the union and labor issues in a concerted effort not to antagonize the largest employer of African Americans in the city. But after nearly a decade of studying the gendered and racial aspects of the labor market and the impact on Black female laborers, Black YWCA women privately demonstrated "a sympathetic interest in the strike situation reflecting so many of their own people."[51] Their sympathy and what some perceived as an "aggressive industrial education" policy drew swift criticism from prominent men and employers in the community and forced Copenhaver into the uncomfortable position of denying that the YWCA was aggressive or was in any way connected to communists. In her 1930 report, she noted that "the Y. W. C. A. has never been in any sense radical."[52] But the die was cast. At various times, the YWCA continued to fend off the "radical" label throughout the early years of the Great Depression.

When female laborers who regularly used the facilities at the Black YWCA decided in March 1935 to invite Louis Austin, labor activist and editor of Durham's Black newspaper the *Carolina Times*, to discuss the ways to "organize and raise wages and standard of living," they found themselves on the receiving end of the coercive force of the white male oligarchy. Austin had been a presenter at the YWCA in 1932 and was well known in the city. Then he had given "an impressive address" titled "The Contribution the Negro Press Has Made to the Progress and Development of the Negroes of This Country." But when he came three years later to present his message about Black laborers organizing and demanding higher salaries, the city moved swiftly and decisively to squelch Austin's visit. Striking at the heart of Black women's effort to tie laborers' advancement with the progress of the Black community, Robert Korstad notes that "the chairman of the Community Chest threatened to withhold funds from the YWCA and other agencies" if the women insisted on holding the meeting. The women rescinded the invitation, capitulating because of their fear of retribution in both the workplace and the community of which they were a part.[53] Black YWCA women may have been coerced into withdrawing their invitation, but they did not remain quiet. They, however, did not approach the chairman of the Community Chest or the oligarchs who controlled the companies. Instead, they complained about the strong-arm tactics of business leaders to local white YWCA women like Jane Skinner, the general secretary, and national staffer Annie Kate Gilbert. It was such a heated issue and so alarming to Black women that both Skinner and Gilbert commented in an interview and in notes on "the question which had been raised by some of the Negroes with the Joint Committee in regard to a union meeting which had been called off but which was to have been held at the Phyllis Wheatley Branch." Labor issues in the city remained concerns for Black workers and YWCA members for some time, but protests grew louder as the politics of the city, state, and federal government changed and opened the door to advancements.[54]

Hall remained a committed and active member of the Black YWCA even when her leadership role ended. She represented the YWCA in the National Negro Business League's nationwide effort to document the number of Black businesses. Founded by Booker T. Washington in 1900, the league was developed to encourage and foster economic opportunity and to provide business networks for the Black business and professional community. Hundreds of affiliated chapters were established throughout the country, including in Winston-Salem. Directed under the assistance of Tuskegee Institute, the nationwide survey campaign was a gargantuan effort that necessitated the cooperation of various business arenas, including builders and contractors, tailors, hairdressers, barbershops, bakeries, schools, restaurants, merchants, ministers, doctors, lawyers, undertakers, druggists, and women's and men's clubs and organizations.[55]

Hall was elected to serve on the YWCA board with seven other women for a year in 1929. And when the Girl Reserve Department sent out a call for "all girls of all ages" to attend a meeting at the YWCA in the winter of that year to form a "glee club" of singers to inspire artistic skill and creativity, Hall was the natural choice to chair the department. With her skills as a musician and director, she was certainly the best-trained and most qualified member.[56] "Officials of the 'Y' work," the newspaper announced, "were very anxious to have the girls form this club." Through the club, officials intended to envelop as many girls as possible into the program. There were membership campaigns that rewarded the girl who garnered the most memberships. There were also celebratory ceremonies to recognized the girls' achievements that included parents and friends.[57] In addition, Hall participated in fund-raising efforts to provide resources for girls to attend a summer conference. She helped direct an elaborate production that was "considered to be one of the best ever rendered under the auspices of the local 'Y.'" The large cross-racial audience enjoyed the combination of comedic show, fashion exhibition, and children's presentation.[58]

Significantly, Hall's willingness to join with other Black and white women to confront the lingering racial concerns that continued to plague the YWCA fostered a new kind of agency. Although the national YWCA created the Council on Colored Work in 1921 that highlighted racial practices and policies, the racial landscape throughout the South reinforced the power structure of white domination and Black subordination to such a degree that both the individual and the collective experiences of Black and white women bowed under its pressure.[59] To address the issue, Hall accompanied Jane Maxwell and a large group from Winston-Salem to attend an interracial YWCA conference in Charlotte in January 1930. After they returned to the city, Maxwell reported, "This was the first conference of its kind in this section and indicates the long step that has been made in advancing a mutual relationship and better understanding racially. The high ideals that are fostered by the Y.W.C.A. centers in the developing of a spiritual sympathy and interest that motivates better human understanding. No race, creed, color or locality limits this process, but because of tradition it necessitates a slow, steady development. Our women have awakened to this fact and the reaction has been deliberate, spontaneous, but not spasmodic. And whenever an opportunity presents itself, in some way, to establish a new line of thinking, with new groups, it is accepted."[60]

The flowering of Black female agency against Jim Crow, however, met resistance. The reaction of the white Winston-Salem branch president at the Detroit convention in April 1931 signaled how intransigent racism remained among YWCA women. Bleeker R. Bahnson, the president of the white YWCA, became more agitated by the "interracial social gatherings than about the textile resolution" that highlighted the treatment of Black workers being discussed.[61] Jane Skinner wrote in 1932, "We decided we would work toward the suggestions made in Constitution for City Associations, that is, to have the chairman of committee at the Colored Branch sit on like committees at the Central Association and of course we look forward to the time when the chairman of the branch can be on our board of directors. Racial prejudice being what it is and the situation in Winston-Salem being what it is we cannot of course put this into effect at once."[62] And after a presentation "on interracial affairs" at the white branch in Winston-Salem, members were so incensed that they insisted "that the forward work which had been done in Winston-Salem was destroyed by such a speech." Their complaint to the national office forced Annie Kate Gilbert, secretary of the National Services Division, to travel to the city to quell their anger. She later wrote that in her meeting with Skinner, the chairman of the Industrial Department, and the chairman of the Girl Reserve Department of the white branch, they pointed out several key issues, including that they "wished they knew where the National Board felt it was going on interracial matters." While emphasizing that they certainly "did not believe in the social equality," they, however, "were convinced of their obligation to work on matters of common concern such as opportunities for education of Negro children." Still, they "resented the attack on the South" by one of the speakers, "when the same attack so far as facts were concerned could have been made on any section of the country (this without any doubt will militate against immediate future progress in several southern communities)."[63]

Some of the persistent consequences of white supremacy could be seen most clearly through the lens of the YWCA's work among the most vulnerable populations in the city. After the mayor "issued an appeal for the jobless to report" in mid-November 1930, more than 2,800 unemployed citizens registered. African Americans made up more than half that number. While the mayor may have surmised that "Winston-Salem was much more fortunate than the general feeling had indicated," many in the Black community were alarmed because by the following week, the numbers of unemployed had increased significantly.[64] Those who were unemployed had risen to 3,200, which included the names of 170 additional Black women and men. The disturbing numbers forced members of the Black branch of the YWCA to express "grave concern, being well aware of the suffering existing because of no income." General secretary Jane Maxwell noted that "our associational program has always included an employment office, with an active employment and industrial committee to serve as resources for our unemployed girls and women," and "We are anxious for the women and girls of this community to feel and know that their interests are ours, and their unhappy state is shared, until relief is reached."[65]

To meet some of those needs, the branch dispensed with its traditional Thanksgiving dinner as the Depression deepened in 1932 and replaced it with providing more than three hundred families and individuals with "baskets filled with flour, lard, sugar, rice, grits," and "plenty of vegetables." Hall, while working along with Jane Maxwell and Olivia M. Hampton, in particular, earned high praise for the effort. "Miss Madie B. Hall, the daughter of Dr. Hall, one of the oldest doctors in this community," the newspaper announced, "worked with the two secretaries to carry out this wonderful mission of aiding others at this time." The program was such a successful achievement that "never before in the history has such a remarkable program been carried out as this one for the people." Ultimately, the paper surmised, "The Young Women's Christian Association at this time is to be commended for the work that they were able to put over at this time."[66]

Members of the YWCA also heightened their interest in maintaining a connection to the Community Chest that had been established in 1923 as a philanthropic effort to serve the needs of citizens in the city. Hall, for example, joined one of the "teams" of a group who was "realizing the vital need of social and welfare institutions and having a genuine desire to lend whatever aid possible in the furtherance of these organizations" in 1931. Led by physician

William H. Bruce, the group held a mass meeting and outlined a plan to develop a "colored drive" to assist the Community Chest with meeting its goal of raising $130,000. African Americans had a major stake in the campaign's success because a little more than 30 percent, or $40,000, of the funds were to be "spent in the support of organizations being operated for the colored citizens of this community." They included the Memorial Industrial School that housed orphans, the YMCA, Travelers' Aid, and the YWCA. Everyone was instructed to "give what you can to aid this great worthy cause of humanity."[67] As the Depression deepened, however, the intricate ties between white male oligarchs and the Community Chest heightened concern among YWCA members to the point that they proposed that the man who presided over the Chest be replaced by a trained social worker because he seemed far more interested in furthering the interest of the businesses linked to the Chamber of Commerce rather than pursuing the goal of the Chest, which was to assist those in need.[68]

Poverty concerns, race issues, and labor problems persisted for YWCA women, but, imbued by the Christian spirit of the organization's mission and the common commitment to social welfare, Black and white women continued to work together and instituted myriad programs that included providing tutoring, supervising playgrounds, campaigning to clean up poverty-ridden areas of the city, and promoting health and hygiene. Black and white Girl Reserve committees held meetings together, and both branches promoted "prevention rather than treatment of disease" by implementing Negro Health Week, a national movement that had been introduced in 1915. Among myriad other programs, there was a plan to have a white female physician educate Black girls about their health. The two doctors in Hall's family contributed their services to help. During the first week of April 1932, her father and brother Leroy joined with other doctors in holding free clinic hours to provide much-needed medical care.[69]

* * *

By 1926 the Black branch of the YWCA was only one of many Black women's organizations in the city. With their overlapping interest, a group decided to coalesce them under an umbrella organization. As a result, the City Federation of Colored Women was born. The inaugural meeting was fittingly held at the Black branch of the YWCA. Hall was elected chair of the Program Committee and found herself joining a slate of officers that included Oleona Atkins and her cousin Roberta Carr. President Mary L. Hairston was convinced that the time was ripe for this army of Black women to affiliate with regional and national Black female networks in the North Carolina Association of Colored Women's Clubs, established in 1909, and the National Association of Colored Women's Clubs, organized in 1896. Her first presentation to the group was fittingly titled "Why It Is Necessary to Join the Federation."[70]

One of the first major fund-raising events sponsored by the City Federation was the play *Go Slow Mary* at the Lincoln Theatre. Performed in November 1926 in an effort to fund "the many needs for an establishment for the protection of womanhood and to reform girls who have gone astray," the play captivated the community. "No play has received so much advertisement as this play," the newspaper proclaimed. Billed as a "farce comedy," the play featured thirty-two-year-old unmarried Hall cast as Mary, the wife of Billy, who was, at the time, unemployed. The play situated the upper-class couple in a floundering marriage consumed by the weight of the monotony and complications of married life and presented the tension between the traditionally prescribed feminine domestic role of women and the masculine professional role of men in modern society. The "domestic bickering" that arises originates because of the question of whether it is easier "keeping house or earning a living in the business world." The wife is convinced that her role, bound by the spatial boundaries of the household, is more difficult, while her husband argues that his public role in the capitalist world is much more challenging. In the end, Billy realizes that he is not cut out to keep house, and his wife, Mary, discovers that "it was better for a woman to demand the respect of home training and the perfection of a well-kept home than to engage in a pursuit that was far beyond the duty of womanhood."[71]

The play entertained the attending crowd. *Go Slow Mary*, the paper proclaimed, "was dramatized by one of the best trained group of local players ever to appear on the stage." Moreover, Hall and her costar earned high praise. "The playing of [C. L.] Harris and Madie B. Hall," the reviewer wrote, "was considered by many the equal to that of any player seen on the stage in years." The play proved so successful and profitable that the YWCA sponsored it again in May 1927 at the Lincoln as well.[72]

A year after it was established, the City Federation had become such an integral part of the NCACWC that the state organization held its spring 1927 conference in Winston-Salem. Charlotte Hawkins Brown, the president of the NCACWC and a longtime YWCA member, presided over the Saturday, April 23, meeting at St. Paul Methodist Episcopal. On Sunday morning, she was the guest speaker at the Congregational Church worship service, and during the Sunday-afternoon meeting held at Goler Memorial Church she spoke to a standing-room-only audience.[73] Members of the City Federation and the YWCA participated in every aspect of the program. The YWCA hosted a reception for the group of visitors, and members spoke at the conference. Hall became one of three women on the press committee to ensure widespread coverage of the event. And the Phyllis Wheatley Association opened the Phyllis Wheatley Home to visitors.[74]

The City Federation's bond with the NCACWC fostered a strong and unique link with members of the NACW. When a number of members of the City Federation had not received their issues of the NACW's *National Notes* journal that they fervently read, for example, they did not hesitate to request that Hall, in her capacity as general secretary of the YWCA and an officer in the City Federation, inquire about the delay. She wrote directly to her friend Mary McLeod Bethune, then president of the NACW, in November 1927 and asked Bethune to "look into" the matter.[75]

Hall had built such a successful activist life in Winston-Salem that she earned praised in 1931 for being a part of "some of the leading doctors and men and women of all vocations" who had been educated at Shaw. The group included her father and his generation of male cohorts who had shaped the social, cultural, and economic progress of the Black community. In other words, she secured a place among the "best colored people" and "leading black citizens" in the city.[76]

Hall utilized that clout during the growing economic despair at the beginning of the Depression. In 1932 large numbers of African Americans engaged in creating urban farms by planting vegetables in the spaces around their homes. In addition to responding to the pressing need of food, many also had begun to embrace a city-beautification project that had been so successful before World War I by expressing an interest "in flower gardens as well." There were so many of both kinds of "allotted plots" that minister Harry C. Jones was appointed the head of the city vegetable-garden project, and Hall, an avid gardener and member of the Garden Path Flower Club established in 1931, became the director of the flower-garden project.[77]

A few months after she was appointed director of the flower-garden project, she hosted one of the social events of the season for the eighty guests who arrived in the Hall family backyard. The party celebrated the culmination of a commitment to both combating poverty and hunger and the transformation of unattractive yards in Black neighborhoods into beautiful cultural spaces. She named hers "Shady Rest Garden" to highlight the pleasures of cool comfort from the August heat and a place of relaxation and escape. In addition to flowers, it contained a rock garden and a lily pool with fish. Shady Rest was, the newspaper opined, "a scene of exquisite beauty."[78] Like her garden-club members, she believed that flower gardens played a crucial role in alleviating the emotional turmoil inflicted by economic devastation and the despair of living in blighted communities.[79]

She became so well known throughout the state for her expertise and advocacy of home and city beautification that she assisted with the establishment of the State Federation of Garden Clubs of North Carolina at North Carolina A&T State University in Greensboro in 1935. The members could think of no better person to be elected the first president of the organization than her.[80]

She had also been propelled to state prominence by her musical talents. For example, on a Sunday afternoon in March 1933, thousands of people crammed into the Charlotte, North Carolina, Armory Auditorium to be a part of the Negro Music Festival to hear a "melody of negro spirituals" from a "chorus of 300 negro singers." Anticipation for and interest in the festival had been so great for the first presentation on the previous Monday evening that for more than two hours, fifteen hundred African Americans and one thousand whites enjoyed, the *Charlotte Observer* proclaimed, "the most elaborate negro music festival ever attempted in this part of the south." The Sunday encore drew an even larger crowd than the first. Two thousand Blacks and two thousand whites sat in the auditorium. The Negro spiritual that so enraptured both Black and white audiences was punctuated by the featured talent of two Winston-Salem natives, soprano Vivian Bright and her accompanying pianist, the "well-known musician" Madie Hall.[81]

PART II

New York

CHAPTER 4

The Bridge between Jim Crow and Apartheid

Hall balanced her activism and string of successes with difficult personal losses during the early years of the Great Depression. She lost her mother in August 1930 when Jennie suffered a second stroke and died at the age of sixty-two. The telegrammed condolences from all over the country demonstrated how prominent a figure she had become. Mourners filled Goler Memorial AME Zion Church to remember her as a "a wonderful example of what it means to live a clean and pure life" and as "a peaceful neighbor, Christian worker and community builder." She would be the first of the immediate family to be buried in Evergreen Cemetery.[1]

Her eldest brother, Cleo, died in March 1931. Records about what happened to him remain limited, but Hall noted in an interview that he had suffered from epilepsy. Like his sister, he had been well educated, attending Slater, a school in the neighboring town of High Point, and Biddle University (now Johnson C. Smith University) in Charlotte. Perhaps because of his ailment, he remained close to his parents and spent his early years working as a clerk at his father's drugstore.[2]

Three months after Cleo's death, her father was hospitalized in the segregated Black wing of City Memorial Hospital. After his discharge, Hall became his primary caregiver. Humphrey rebounded and over the next several years enjoyed his medical practice partnership with his son Leroy and actively engaged in a number of activities, such as becoming treasurer of the Negro Social Service Council. Established as an umbrella organization for myriad Black social welfare agencies such as the YWCA, the YMCA, and the Phyllis Wheatley Home by the mayor between the fall and winter of 1931 and 1932, the organization benefited the Community Chest and provided aid to African Americans. Hall worked closely with her father in an effort to raise money. She was one of the directors of a fund-raising pageant and acted as mistress of ceremonies at the program. Perhaps Humphrey's most significant enterprise was his participation in the June 1934 ceremony honoring his good friend Simon Atkins's retirement as president of the Winston-Salem Teachers College. Atkins had been in such poor health that he could not attend the event and died only a few weeks after at the age of seventy-one.[3]

Hall also embarked on several new ventures of her own. One of the most consequential was becoming the secretary to Josephine Kyles, the vice chair of the Woman's Home and Foreign Missionary Society. In that position, she accompanied Kyles to the AME Zion conferences and learned far more about the global reach of women's evangelical work and the importance of mission societies at home and around the world.[4]

The Woman's Home and Foreign Missionary Society had been established in 1880 because, Bettye Collier-Thomas argues, "male clergy failed to raise adequate funds to support mission programs in Africa and other foreign stations," so "it became clear that without the substantial involvement of women the denomination would not be able to mount a successful program." From the beginning, the all-male General Mission Board maintained control of the Woman's Home and Foreign Missionary Society, "required that two-thirds of the money raise" by the organization "be sent to the general treasurer for foreign work," and refused to allow the Woman's Society to hold its own conference. Women in the organization fought hard for autonomy for years. Their persistence finally yielded success nearly five decades after the creation of the organization when the Woman's Society held its first conference in 1928. The price of the organization's success was the concerted effort "to circumvent the advance of lay women and assure episcopal involvement" on the AME Zion–Woman's Home and Foreign Missionary Society's executive board by the appointment of bishops' wives as supervisors.[5] In spite of the oversight, the victory gave women of the church a segregated gendered vehicle through which they could engage in programs that mattered to them.

Kyles emerged as one of the most prominent members. Her interracial inclinations coupled with her keen interest in the gendered face of AME Zion missions in Africa, in particular, captured Hall's attention and respect. An early proponent of interracial cooperation and alliances, she had been a presenter at the first National Interracial Conference of Church Women held in Pennsylvania in September 1926 and the following year became a member of the Church Women's Committee on Race Relations.[6] Kyles had also joined in a speaking presentation at a missionary meeting held at Goler church with A. Lucille Alleyne, a native of North Carolina, the wife of Bishop Cameron Chesterfield Alleyne, and a missionary in Africa for four years, on a Sunday afternoon in January 1928. She and her husband also hosted Bishop

W. W. Mathews and his wife in their home in 1931. Elected a bishop in 1928, Mathews had served some of his supervisory post in Liberia, Africa, the first AME Zion mission established in Africa in 1876, by leading in the effort to establish schools and churches throughout the area.[7]

Hall's second venture proved to be key to opening the door to a new life. After attending a Thursday Bridge Club meeting and conversing with one of the members, she decided to return to school to finally obtain her bachelor's degree. Although she had crafted a successful career with the two-year normal-school certificate that she earned at Shaw University, she nevertheless had been deeply troubled by her awareness that "my father and mother wanted me to finish college." She also recognized how the transformation of the work environment for Black women during the Depression limited her employment opportunities because she was afraid that if she went "out there looking for a job," one of "the first things they'll ask me" would be whether she had a college degree.[8]

When she met with Francis L. Atkins, who had become the president of Winston-Salem Teachers College after the retirement and subsequent death of his father, Simon Atkins, she first expressed her strong desire to "go back to college," but she made it clear that she did not want "to go back to high school" in the process. After examining her transcript, Atkins told her that she had enough credits to satisfy "a year and a half" and did not need to go back to high school or repeat all of the first two years of college courses.[9] Her reentry into college coincided with the state's interest in expanding and enhancing the level of education of Black teachers. Largely a secondary school for the nearly two decades since it was established, Slater had been tapped by the state to become one of the key training institutions for Black teachers largely in part because of Simon Atkins's success of utilizing philanthropic donations for the construction of new buildings and the improvement of classroom space and shifting the program's pedagogical methodology from the traditional curriculum that offered mostly rudimentary high school–level courses with additional teaching instruction to one that included college-level courses. Between 1917 and 1918, Simon Atkins successfully lobbied the state legislature for an appropriation of $10,000 and initiated a citywide campaign that yielded $25,000. The improvements to the campus, the institutionalization of a concentration on the mission of training Black teachers, and the convenience of having Columbia Heights School as a laboratory for students to learn how to teach provided the incentive to remove *industrial* from the school's title. As a result, the state accredited Slater as a normal school in 1920. Over the next five years, the school continued to improve and advance. In 1925 Slater received an official charter from the state and was renamed Winston-Salem Teachers College.[10]

Under the leadership of Francis Atkins during the Depression, Winston-Salem Teachers College maintained its status as a central hub in the campaign to "upgrade the teaching profession by requiring more stringent conditions for certificate." As a result, the college enjoyed tremendous growth, visibility, and prestige. It had a four-year academic curriculum and an enrollment of more than four hundred between 1935 and 1936. Twenty faculty taught in fourteen classrooms, capital assets were $634,612, and the library contained six thousand bound volumes and more than eighty magazines and periodicals.[11]

Hall enjoyed the fruits of the college's growth as a student in the bachelor of science in education program and at the age of forty-one delighted in the experience. Like a young college-age student, she engaged in extracurricular activities. Serving as vice president of the Dramatic Club, she continued to perfect her acting and directing ambitions. An honor-roll student, she exhibited an intellectual curiosity that highlighted her scholastic ability.[12]

Focusing on her studies, however, became far more difficult when her father was injured in an automobile accident in October 1935. He suffered for several weeks and died on November 9. Recognition of his prominence and service during the more than four decades that he resided in Winston-Salem was displayed by the two thousand mourners who gathered at Goler for his funeral. And his lifelong commitment to developing "a better feeling among members of both races" ensured that a member of the African American Twin City Medical Society and a white representative from the Forsyth Medical Group were among the list of speakers.[13]

The death of her father thrust Hall into the two new roles as head of the family and the executrix of an estate that included the family home on East Seventh Street and a number of residential and commercial properties along with tenants and land to manage and maintain. She juggled those obligations along with her course work. She also added a new job with the Federal Works Progress Administration (WPA), one of the most sweeping New Deal programs in the Franklin Roosevelt administration, to her busy life.[14] The federally appropriated funds given to states provided jobs for thousands of Black and white North Carolinians who took advantage of the state-run program between 1935 and 1940. While many of the workers were men, women found some success in the program. In the state of North Carolina, during the first half of May 1936, for example, a newspaper estimated that nearly 41 percent of the workers hired by the WPA were women and that far more of them held jobs classified as semiskilled, professional, and technical than men. As one of those "unemployed teachers who were without professional opportunity" and fortified by her pursuit of the State Primary Certificate and the BS degree at an accredited institution, Hall found employment for two months, from the end of April to the end of June 1936, as the supervisor for the WPA's County Colored Teachers Project of Forsyth County. Working fifteen hours a week, she earned a salary of $42.50 every two weeks.[15]

That summer of 1936, she earned a State Primary Certificate Class "A" and graduated with the BS degree.[16] The wages from the WPA coupled with income generated from several properties left to her and her siblings by her parents ultimately minimized financial concerns as the Depression worsened. But it was the financial investments that her father gave to her that provided the opportunity for her to pursue the master's degree. It changed her life.

With a renewed interest in teaching and a desire to gain as much insight as she could into the methods and pedagogy of the education profession, she applied to Columbia University's Teachers College in New York. The decision to apply to a northern school had been born out of Jim Crow laws and customs that forced those African American like her to migrate north for advanced study. Stymied by the lack of available master's degree programs in Black educational institutions and barred from admission to white colleges and universities, many determined their future by leaving the state.[17]

When Hall arrived in New York for fall classes in 1936, she was welcomed by longtime friends physician Charles Talmadge Kimbrough and his wife, Alva Cash Kimbrough, as well as Max and Susie Yergan. Charles graduated from Slater a year after Hall in 1911 and then attended the AME-supported Kittrell College in Vance County, North Carolina; Biddle University (now Johnson C. Smith) in Charlotte; and Lincoln University in Pennsylvania. He earned his medical degree from Syracuse University in New York and was recognized in Winston-Salem as "one of the leading doctors of the country." Alva was the daughter of Crawford B. Cash and the sister of Hall's friend Faye Cash. While still living in Winston-Salem, she had assisted Hall with one of her major productions.[18]

The Kimbroughs resided on West 145th Street in Harlem in an affluent Black professional area and were part of a tight-knit aristocratic Black community. Alva led a busy social life as the vice president of the Physicians Wives' Association and as a member of the Les Jolie Huit Bridge Club. In addition to playing bridge and socializing, club members also provided assistance to those in need by donating goods and services to several charitable organizations. Charles spent his leisure time playing tennis, often participating in tournaments. As a couple, they attended numerous parties and teas and appeared on the society pages of the *New York Amsterdam News*.[19]

Hall had known Max and Susie Yergan for at least twenty-five years. Both North Carolina natives, Max was from Raleigh and Susie was from Salisbury. They attended Shaw University at the same time as Hall, although Max was in the class ahead of her and Susie in the class behind. Max engaged with the YMCA at Shaw, and after attending an international convention in 1916 he had a conversion and committed himself to foreign missions. As had been the case for Hall, Susie developed an interest in the YWCA. She taught at Shaw for several years after graduating and then married Max in Salisbury in 1920. The following year, he became the YMCA's secretary to Africa, and the couple moved to South Africa. They were based at the South African Native College at Fort Hare (known simply as Fort Hare). During his two-year leave as YMCA secretary in the spring of 1927, he visited Winston-Salem and "delivered stirring appeals" about "the opportunities of the American people and those of their fellowman in South Africa." Ultimately, he called on his Winston-Salem Teachers College audience to "help to bring about such a force that would teach those 10,000 miles away the principles of womanhood and manhood." The Yergans returned to Africa at the end of the leave but traveled back to the United States years later. Susie continued her engagement with the YWCA and was honored along with women from Palestine, Turkey, Korea, Japan, and Uruguay at an international tea sponsored by several individuals and organizations that included the New York Lexington Avenue branch of the YWCA in April 1934. Two years later, Max resigned from his position in the YMCA, and the couple returned to New York in 1936.[20]

Max may have left South Africa, but he continued to be engaged in the country's politics. After joining forces with concert artist and actor Paul Robeson, he helped establish the International Committee on African Affairs. Yergan's commitment to supporting Black South Africans, in particular, was most visibly demonstrated in his promotion of the All-African Convention that had been established to combat the passage of the Native Bills and to defend Black rights in South Africa. He became the secretary of external affairs and was in attendance, along with Eslanda Robeson, Paul Robeson's wife, when the second convention convened its meeting in 1936 in Bloemfontein, where hundreds of delegates gathered to demonstrate their opposition to the disenfranchisement of Black Africans and racial discrimination in the country.[21]

Max's initial flirtation with communism congealed around the same time, as he grew increasingly angry and worried about the fate of Black South Africans. Support from a small but committed group of prominent African Americans who believed that a successful future for Black Americans could be found only in the race-neutral communist system certainly played a significant role in his transformation. They included Robeson as well as John P. Davis of the National Negro Congress, organized in 1936 to fight for a broad spectrum of equal rights for African Americans, including fair employment and housing. And like many of them, he found camaraderie, encouragement, and sustenance when he visited the Soviet Union in 1936.[22]

Embraced by the well-connected Kimbroughs and the globetrotting Yergans, Hall enjoyed an eclectic mix of people and cultures. They and the dynamic milieu of the city linked her to the world. Even during the latter years of the Depression when poverty and hardship continued to take a toll, New York remained urban, cosmopolitan, and populated with multiracial and multiethnic people from many different countries. Hall firmly planted herself in that global community and in the process transformed the trajectory of her life.

As one of the best institutions of higher learning in the country, Columbia University Teachers College played a pivotal role in that transformation. By the time that she arrived at the university, thousands of students were matriculating in the graduate program in Teachers College.[23] Situated between the cross-currents of the emerging needs of the managerial and professional workforce that had evolved out of industrialization and progressivism, Teachers College became a central part of the development and creation of pedagogy for teachers in the United States. In New York City alone, Richard Glotzer argues that "between 1900 and 1910 high school enrolments quadrupled to 50,000 and continued to rise, creating pressures for access to advanced training of all kinds. Elite institutions like Columbia remained socially selective, although most recognised the benefits of tightly controlled meritocracy. The result was a broadening of public vocational and technical education as well as the expansion of higher education for the masses. Teachers College, Columbia, of course played an important part in this process." Teachers College earned the reputation of being "an egalitarian institution concerned with public education and its related specialisations" that was "committed to a meritocratic admissions policy."[24]

Increasingly, the institution became recognized as a center on "national issues," because by 1920 the faculty was not only engaged in "projects in many regions of the country" but involved in international ones as well. With funding from the Rockefeller Foundation, the International Institute, created in 1923 at Teachers College, was "to establish an intellectual centre for the comparative study of education and offered the colleges' growing number of international students a congenial social and intellectual environment for their studies." By the end of the decade, Canadian and South African students were part of the institute's program of study. It was aided by the efforts of such philanthropic organizations as the Phelps-Stokes Fund and the Carnegie Foundation whose interest in national and international education had grown more intense after World War I as more students from various countries throughout the world enrolled in Teachers College for training. Moreover, because faculty, administrators, or former students of Columbia or Teachers College held key positions in major philanthropic and missionary organizations and had strong personal, ideological, and scholarly connections to the international community, international students found a welcoming environment to study and live both at Teachers College and in New York City.[25]

Former students of Columbia as well as faculty also focused on Black education in the Jim Crow South. Alumnus Thomas Jesse Jones, who received his PhD in sociology, held a researcher position at Hampton Institute from 1902 until 1909. He quickly began compiling comprehensive data that detailed the status of Black southern education. In 1917 he published his analysis in *Negro Education in the United States*. By 1919 he had acquired the position as the Phelps-Stokes Fund's educational director, playing a key role in further shaping education for Blacks in the South. He would also develop an interest in Africa, as the Phelps-Stokes Fund's Educational Commission for East Africa and West Africa took shape in 1922 and 1925, respectively.[26]

Mable Carney, associate professor of rural education at Teachers College, spent time studying Black educational institutions in the South in 1924 and developed a course called Negro Education and Race Relations that annually attracted hundreds of students from different races and countries. Moreover, Carney also extended her interest in Africa. She visited the continent in 1926 as an emissary of the British Ministry of Education and the International Missionary Council. When she returned to the United States, she established the Negro Education Club in 1927. At least fifty students took part during the academic year, and it was so popular in the summer term that three times that number joined the group. One of the main projects of the club included inviting prominent speakers to present in various types of venues. "The club," Richard Glotzer argues, "served not only as a focal point for the college's black students but also as a sort of social science laboratory for whites interested in race relations." Carney developed a particular interest in the comparison between South Africa and Black education in the United States. So attracted to the idea, she "too would become a key figure in Carnegie work, fashioning her teaching and famed field trips to Harlem into an innovative and hospitable environment for international students, including African students."[27]

Four years after her foray to Africa, Carney joined a cross-section of distinguished Black and white scholars and administrators of local and state agencies and institutions in a series of lectures under the auspices of Teachers College that was held during the winter and early spring of 1930. From January through April, leading national presenters Agnes Donohugh, Franz Boas, James Hardy Dillard, Samuel L. Smith, Nathan C. Newbold, Jackson Davis, John Hope, and W. E. B. DuBois discussed Black education.[28] A similar series that began six years later demonstrated the continuing ties between the Teachers College, Black and white educators, and leading activists. Like the earlier version, the focus was primarily on African Americans, but the regional context shifted to a discussion of northern Blacks.[29]

Many of the students attracted to the Negro Education Club as well as Carney's classes, methodology, and interest in Africa expressed their own views about the role that Teachers College played in assisting with race relations in the report "Some Things Teacher College Should Do to Promote More Wholesome Attitudes and Better Relations toward Negroes" that was compiled in May 1937. Hall was completing the first year of her studies when the document appeared, but it is unclear whether she was one of the students directly engaged in its development, was a member of the Negro Education Club, or was in any of Carney's classes. But because of the small percentages of Black students in attendance in Teachers College and Carney's significant influence in the college, it seems certain that she participated in some key way in the robust educational atmosphere.[30]

That educational atmosphere spilled over into her residency at the non-profit residential International House located on Riverside Drive on the Upper West Side. The institution had been established in 1924 with $3 million donated by the John D. Rockefeller family to promote understanding between students from around the world. Designed to be a "world home" in a cosmopolitan city, the International House tethered itself more to communities of the world than to America. Records on the time that Hall spent there were unavailable, but the 1933–34 manual for the institution emphasized that the goal "is the improvement of the social, intellectual, spiritual and physical condition of men and women students, without discrimination because of religion, nationality, race, color, or sex, and from any land, who are studying in the colleges, universities and professional schools of the city of New York." Of the more than five hundred students who resided in the facility, only one-quarter of them were American.[31]

Like Teachers College, the International House nurtured Hall's intellectual curiosity. For a $7 fee for the academic year and between $185 and $320 for a room, she joined more than two hundred women living at the facility. There was a smorgasbord of activities catering to a wide variety of interest that included vespers, socials, and excursions to introduce residents to the city and surrounding areas. There was also the mission of creating "the fine spirit of friendliness and fellowship" among residents. To meet that goal, the house promoted the "Sunday Supper" that lasted for several hours on Sunday evenings. It began with a reception in the Great Hall, touted as "a friendly meeting and gathering place of the House," at 5:30 and then proceeded to the Assembly Hall that could seat a thousand for dinner. At 6:00 p.m., one of the residents said grace in their "native language." Afterward, the participants listened to music and enjoyed a presentation from a "distinguished" speaker "from this and other lands, who speak on outstanding world problems."[32]

Hall became intimately immersed in other cultures through the "National Nights" that were "arranged to give opportunities to different nationals to present the customs, manners, music, art and culture of their countries." Visual aids helped her physically see the geographical landscape of the countries. For eight weeks on Wednesdays, residents gathered in the Assembly Hall to view onscreen the "natural beauties of different countries." She participated in "a miniature World Assembly" through the International Student Assembly that discussed world affairs at meetings held five times a month. And she found the opportunity to engage in intellectual discussion with a wide variety of people from across the globe about topics of importance to her in the "Interest Groups" that met twice a month.[33]

The International House also had a history of hosting events and programs about African Americans and the Black diaspora. For example, the Harmon Exhibit of Fine Arts featured work by Black artists at the house in January 1930.[34] And on Sunday, July 25, 1937, physician Alfred Bitini Xuma, who had arrived in New York in June, gave an "illuminating" presentation in the auditorium on "conditions in South Africa."[35] American educated, Xuma had earned degrees at Tuskegee University, the University of Minnesota, and the Medical School at Northwestern University and had strong ties with white intellectuals such as Mabel Carney and with African American and South African activists like Max Yergan. He had also built quite a reputation in South Africa among Blacks as well as white Europeans. Seven years before he appeared at the International House auditorium, he had spoken at the Conference of European and Bantu Christian Student Association in South Africa in a speech titled "Bridging the Gap between White and Black in South Africa." At the beginning of the speech, he implored his audience "of Christian students in a Christian country" to "ask ourselves whether the practices of our country between White and Black are in keeping with our profession of the Christian faith?" Toward that end, he declared, "The educated African is our hope, our bridge. He is an asset that responsible and thinking white South Africa cannot afford either to ignore or to alienate without disastrous results in the long run. He should be brought into close contact and co-operation with the thinking European. He must be consulted in all matters affecting the African community. It is he, and he alone, who can best interpret the European to the African, and the African to the European."[36]

While a copy of his speech in the auditorium at the International House is not available, Hall must have been quite intrigued by his presence. She probably learned that his broader ideological framework about Black and white interracial relations shared striking similarities to her own. And through him she must have seen the intersectional parallels between her own activism, previous work on the AME Zion's Home and Foreign Mission, engagement with missionaries who had given presentations at her church on Africa, and the exploration of South Africa through articles such as "'Colour Bar' Voted Down in South African Mines" that appeared in the *Star of Zion* informing readers about the oppression of Black mine workers in country.[37]

When she was introduced to him for the first time at the event, Hall engaged with a man who intellectually excited her and was, according to the general manager of an academic cap-and-gown company, "rather meager," at a height of five feet, five inches, the same height as she.[38] He was equally enthused with the introduction and seemed so charmed with her that he shortly thereafter began writing her. While most of his correspondence to her is absent from archived papers, her letters to him reveal much about their initial interactions with each other. On International House stationery on August 2, 1937, she wrote:

> Dear Dr. Xuma,
> Thank you for your letter today. I am answering immediately because you said you would be leaving very soon.
> Tuesday at 2, p.m. I have an appointment with one of my instructors so I'm sending the information in this letter today.
> I shall probably be in New York City until about 6 or 7 of Sept. as I am planning to take the intersession. Then, home for 2 wks—back to New York for regular fall session last of September.
> I wish it were feasible to get in a word with you now but I see that is impossible under present arrangements—however, since I will be here the 23 of Aug., give me a ring or drop me a line when you return.
> Hope you'll have a safe trip. Looking forward to your return,
> I am
> Sincerely yours
> Madie B. Hall[39]

Their encounter had been pleasant enough that she volunteered her services to obtain some sort of information for him, revealed her schedule, and asked him to contact her when he returned to New York. But there still was a formality to the letter. In her closing, she signed the letter with her full name.

Meanwhile, as Hall enrolled in intersession courses, Xuma embarked on the final leg of his three-month search for funding for programs to assist Black South Africans. He had already covered hundreds of miles reacquainting himself with people in Minneapolis–St. Paul, Chicago, and St. Louis, Missouri, who had helped him when he was a student in the Midwest more than a decade before. He also made trips to Detroit as well as Mount Vernon, Iowa, and Wilberforce University in Ohio. At the conclusion of his travels, he met with representatives in the Carnegie Corporation and the Milbank Memorial Fund as well as Mabel Carney, who had assisted him with compiling a list of perspective donors.[40] By the time that Xuma returned to New York, Hall was completing her course work for the intersession, and he was preparing for a second presentation at the International House. This time, though, it was in his position as vice president of the All-African Convention. He along with D. D. T. Jabavu, the president of the organization, had been invited by the International Committee on African Affairs, founded by Yergan and Robeson, to help highlight "the ruthless exploitation of the people and resources of Africa; repressive legislation of the most destructive type, and the growing poverty and misery of Africans" on September 7, 1937. Xuma's topic, "The Basis of Repression in South Africa," was to "lay the foundation" and "show the inevitability" of Jabavu's presentation, "Africans an Modern Politics." Six hundred people attended the event. Hall was one of them.[41]

She and others in the audience heard, according to Xuma's friend Roy Wilkins, the assistant secretary of the National Association for the Advancement of Colored People (NAACP) and the editor of the organization's magazine *Crisis*, a bold and instructive analysis of white domination and Black oppression in another part of the world. Writing in the *New York Amsterdam News*, Wilkins declared that "THE DARK BROTHER in America is so accustomed to visiting the wailing wall and complaining about his treatment at the hands of his white fellow-citizens that often he fails to note that, of all the dark people in the world—living in countries dominated by whites—he is the best off." While arguing that "this is no excuse for whites continuing lynching, disfranchisement and various forms of exploitation," he nevertheless insisted that "it is a fact and a blessing we do not appreciate until we have occasion to compare our lot with that of our dark brothers, say in South Africa."[42] Describing Jabavu and Xuma as "brilliant native South Africans" who presented a "picture" of "the life of the native in South Africa" in such "simple, stark language" that it must have "stunned" those in attendance, Wilkins juxtaposed the racism and discrimination in the southern United States with that of the oppression of Blacks in South Africa. For Black South Africans, he insisted, "Nothing in Mississippi is as bad. North Carolina and Virginia would be a heaven for a South African native. Even in Georgia and the Scottsboro state of Alabama a South African native would have a picnic compared to his present lot in his native land." "For South Africa, a huge, rich country, has been literally stolen from its native and taken over by whites" although "there are only two whites for every six natives, but so completely have the natives been shoved into slavery that their numerical advantage means nothing."[43]

In a searing portrait of the conditions in South Africa, Wilkins contextualized the policies that would ultimately be institutionalized as apartheid a decade later. Forced to carry a pass, refused passage on public transportation, and denied admission to professional schools in South Africa, men like Xuma had been compelled to leave his country to be educated. "In Johannesburg, where my good friend Dr. Xuma hails from and practices medicine," Wilkins wrote, "a native may not ride on the trolley cars. Now, Dr. Xuma, educated at Tuskegee, the University of Minnesota, Marquette, the University of Chicago, Edinburgh and Vienna, is probably, by any fair ranking, among the first hundred leading citizens of his city. Culturally his is perhaps superior to 99 percent of the whites. Yet because of the color of his face he must either walk or use his own car."[44]

Amid the bleakness, however, Wilkins argued that there was still hope in South Africa, because "although the natives are beaten down they are by no means whipped. From among them are arising leaders." "Strange as it may seem," he opined, "from among the whites there have come forward men and women who see that the present order cannot go on. Beginnings are being made toward honest and self-respecting interracial action against the evils all about. Young white people like many young white people in Dixie are refusing to swallow all the old bunkum about natives. Progress is unbelievably slow when compared to this country of ours (and ours seems to us to be the last word in slowness), but it is being made."[45]

Wilkins called on progressive Black Americans to defy the white South African government that refused to allow Black Americans to visit the country because they "don't want American Negroes around teaching their natives by example and lecture how to be discontented." The inability to travel to the country necessitated new methods of "agitation." He suggested that the Pan-Africanist idea of "black people of the world getting together and helping one another" be instituted to assist South African natives. Rejecting the popular notion that white philanthropic funds be used to educate Black South Africans, he instead suggested that with their intricate and long-term ties, American Blacks themselves should create "a fund [that] could be raised to provide scholarships in this country for young natives to prepare them to go back to their people." Wilkins not only removed white control and input but also linked an exceptional Black American narrative to the "late lamented Garvey movement." Black American agitation for justice would be transferred to another country to shape a civil rights movement and ultimately policy. Also, he connected the movement to one of the most powerful Black institutions in the nation, the Black church. If church missionary departments, he postulated, "could chop off a part of their missionary funds and bring a young man to America in another twenty years the pressure of these young trained leaders from this and other countries would force a different destiny upon South Africa."[46]

The church had certainly played a major role in shaping his friend Alfred Xuma's life. The seventh child of Mnuzana Abraham Mangali and Nkosekazi

Elizabeth Capase, Xuma was born in 1893 in the remote Transkai of South Africa. His family of Xhosa-speaking farmers abided by traditional customary law. When his parents adopted Christianity, they joined the Wesleyan Methodists, were baptized, and became Abraham and Elizabeth Xuma. Neither of them learned to read, but his father became a preacher and counseled members of his tribe and many in the Wesleyan Methodist Church for a half century. If his father was "handsome, aristocratic, dominant," then his mother epitomized all of the qualities of femininity. She was, Xuma noted, a "quiet, reserved dignified matron of the family."[47]

Xuma worked hard on the family's farm while also earning an education at an Anglican school located five miles from his village. He then entered Clarksbury Training Institute, a Wesleyan mission school, to became a teacher. He eventually became a principal. Influenced by a number of Africans who had studied in the United States and his own desire to access training in a professional career, he looked beyond the geographical borders of South Africa. With permission from his parents, he applied to Booker T. Washington's Tuskegee Institute. Once accepted he left South Africa and sailed to New York City in August 1913. With several other African friends, he then boarded a train that traversed a southern route to Alabama. He did well at the school, ranking third in his class, and was chosen to speak on the "problems of poultry raising" at the commencement and installation ceremony of Robert Moton as the new principal after the death of Washington. After he graduated in 1916, he and one of his friends endured some tough times. As Xuma recounted, "Our financial means, which we shared, were so limited that before I finally got employed in the same foundry [in Birmingham], I had to walk around most of the night to keep from sleeping and sleep most of the day to keep from eating, and what little I ate was often so stale from cheapness that it was almost unfit for human consumption." In spite of the challenges he faced, he decided to remain in the United States to seek advanced degrees.[48] But he, like Hall, found that the Jim Crow South would not accommodate his aspiration, so he migrated to the Midwest.

Xuma left the region at the same time that a massive number of southern Blacks were fleeing the oppression and violence of Jim Crow for better social, political, and economic prospects in midwestern and northern cities. He relocated in St. Paul, Minnesota, and for the first time in his life, he was in a distinct numerical minority. Unlike urban centers such as Chicago, Detroit, New York, and Philadelphia that beckoned the vast majority of southern Black migrants, St. Paul's Black population remained minuscule in comparison to the number of whites. By 1920 the city had a population of 234,698, but only 3,376 were African Americans. The predominant white conclave, however, did not deter Xuma from his mission of pursuing a bachelor of

FIGURE 4.1. Alfred Xuma actively engaged in the University of Minnesota campus life. He was a member of the Webster Literary Society and is pictured here on the end of the back row in the upper right-hand corner. The all-male organization was established in the Agricultural College in 1916. Members studied oratory and debate by presenting papers and debating students from other colleges and universities. Image courtesy of Historical Papers Research Archive, University of the Witwatersrand, South Africa, and description of the club courtesy of the University of Minnesota Archives, *Gopher Yearbook 1919*, 340, and the *Minnesota Daily* student newspaper, January 12, 1917, 3, and March 15, 1918, 3.

science degree at the University of Minnesota's College of Agriculture. In 1917 he was admitted to the program and over the next three years immersed himself in campus life and the small Black community in the city.[49]

Xuma joined the Alpha Phi Alpha Fraternity, the Webster Literary Society, and the campus Young Men's Christian Association. Cementing a bond with Black American men, he became a charter member of the Alpha Xi Chapter of the Alpha Phi Alpha Fraternity, the first Black male fraternity in the United States, and served as the chapter's first associate editor of the organization's journal *Sphinx*. The Webster Literary Society had been established in the College of Agriculture the year before Xuma arrived on the campus. The society debated other college students and presented papers on issues of the day such as one titled "The Prohibition Movement" and addressed farmer concerns in papers called "The Fertility of Soils" and "Gathering Maple Sap."[50] In the Black community, he engaged with young men like Roy Wilkins, who had resided in St. Paul since 1907 and probably attended St. James African Methodist Episcopal Church, where Xuma taught Sunday school.[51]

He earned his BS degree in June 1920 and enrolled in the University of Minnesota's Medical School. Poor academic performance, however, led to his dismissal. After working several odd jobs on the campus, he relocated to Chicago, found a job as a shipping clerk at the Methodist Book Concern, moved into the YMCA, and enrolled in the Lewis Institute (now the Illinois Institute of Technology), taking French and physics from February until August 1921 to shore up his academic credentials for readmission into the University of Minnesota. But even after his success at Lewis, the university denied his readmission. He then applied to several medical schools throughout the Midwest and the southern historically Black institutions Meharry Medical College in Tennessee and Howard University in Washington. He was admitted to two. Choosing to remain in the Midwest, he enrolled in Marquette University's School of Medicine in Milwaukee, Wisconsin, in the fall of 1921, where he took courses in physics, chemistry, zoology, genetics, bacteriology, and botany. Financial pressures, however, continued to plague him, and even his work as a house servant for a wealthy family was not enough to cover his expenses. In 1923 the lack of funds forced him to end his studies at the university. He eventually left Milwaukee and moved back to Chicago with the hope of enrolling in the medical school at Northwestern.[52]

The completion of the two years at Marquette coupled with strong recommendations from Evelyn Riley Nicholson, the president of the Woman's Foreign Missionary Society of the Methodist Episcopal Church, and the YMCA eventually earned him a coveted spot in the junior class at the medical school at Northwestern University in 1923. Charitable donations and hard work kept him there. After the highly sensationalized article "College Goal of Ex-Savage Near Failure" appeared in multiple national newspapers and characterized him as a student "at the end of his third year in Northwestern university medical school" who had "no money with which to finish his course and obtain the coveted diploma" was published, Xuma gained much sympathy for his plight. The newspaper article embraced the primitive Africa narrative that had shaped American views of the continent. Painted as a child who had "roamed the African wilds with tribesmen," "saw his people engulfed in an age of appalling savagery," and "saw his own blood relatives subjected to torture by witch doctors seeking to drive out devils," Xuma's background confirmed negative perceptions of the "dark continent." But conversion by missionaries to a more civilized way of thinking and living stimulated young adult Xuma. He developed "a vision" that included "study[ing] medicine," going to the United States, and "return[ing] to minister to his needy people." The completion of his vision, however, was in jeopardy. While desperately pursuing his degree in the United States, he "has gone hungry for two or three days at a time" and now lacked the financial means to complete the degree to help his people. The newspaper appeal drew sympathy and donations from those like E. B. Hodge of Grand Rapids, Michigan, who wrote "Enclosed is $15, which please accept as my small contribution toward the fund which I hope has been started to enable Mr. Alfred Xuma to finish his last year in his studies as medical missionary that he may be the better fitted to return to minister to his African brothers."[53]

The minimal cost and his strong support of the YMCA allowed Xuma to find a home at the Wabash Avenue YMCA. There he immersed himself in his studies and earned good grades. By all accounts, he performed well, projecting a "pleasing personality" and actively engaging in the program. His allegiance to the YMCA encouraged him to present a lecture at the YMCA Assembly at Northwestern in November 1924. After completing his course work, he graduated in 1925 and then interned at City Hospital in St. Louis, Missouri, to earn his medical degree in June 1926.[54]

The following year, Xuma informed the dean of Northwestern that he had kept himself professionally engaged since graduation and leaving the United States. Writing that he had "passed the examination for the diploma of the Royal College of Physicians and Surgeons at Edinburgh" and performed "operative gynecology and surgery in Hungary," he told the dean that he had finally returned home to South Africa after nearly fourteen years.[55] Xuma's success, however, could not protect him from the racially discriminatory system. The South Africa that he returned to had institutionalized many of the segregationist policies that began before he left. The majority Black population had been stripped of their rights to reside in the city, lost their ability to own property, and been denied most of their political rights. Even Xuma, with his American education, could not escape the onslaught. Denied the position as superintendent of the Bridgman Memorial Hospital in Johannesburg, a financial venture of the American Board of Missions, about which he had written the Northwestern dean, he refused to move to rural areas as deemed more appropriate by white officials and opened his own practice in the suburban conclave of Sophiatown, Johannesburg.[56] Thus, his return to the United States a decade later had some urgency for him. Determined to play a role in shaping the future of Black South Africans, he was looking for aid from white and Black American acquaintances and friends.

Xuma's sojourn in the United States in 1937 had also been a personal mission. He was a lonely man whose wife and the mother to his two children had died three years before. He had married Amanda Priscilla Mason in October 1931. Announcements of their nuptials in prominent Black American newspapers highlighted their standing in both countries and the geographical intersection between Blacks in the United States and those in Africa. Mason was a Liberian of American descent and, like Xuma, had spent more than a decade acquiring an education in the United States.[57] She attended Wilberforce University in Ohio around the same time that Xuma was enrolled in the University of Minnesota. Steven Gish, Xuma's biographer, suggests that the two may have met in the Midwest while both were attending "one of the many international Christian student conferences" held in the region. And,

FIGURE 4.2. Alfred Xuma with his medical degree from the University of Edinburgh, Scotland, United Kingdom. Courtesy of Historical Papers Research Archive, University of the Witwatersrand, South Africa.

indeed, Amanda joined the Wilberforce University YWCA, served as president of the organization from 1918 to 1921, and was one of three delegates sent to Des Moines, Iowa, in 1919 to attend a student-volunteer convention that hosted thousands. As one of three speakers at a session on Africa at one of the local churches, she urged "American Negroes of character and education to come to Africa to teach their brethren anything and everything that tends toward civilization." An outspoken advocate of her home country and the continent of Africa, she noted in 1920 that she "wish[ed] that more of

FIGURE 4.3. Amanda Mason was the president of the Wilberforce University YWCA from 1918 to 1921 and is seated in the center on the front row, third from the right or left above the "W.C." Under the insignia blue-triangle banner "Body, Mind, Spirit" the branch had been operating on the campus for twenty-six years when this photograph of the officers was taken. Image courtesy of Historical Papers Research Archive, University of the Witwatersrand, South Africa, and description of the organization courtesy of the Wilberforce University Rembert E. Stokes Library Archives, *Wilberforce Forcean Yearbook 1921*, 42, 123–24.

the educated American Negroes would realize the fact, that the redemption of Africa depends upon the tiny Negro Republic, 'Liberia.' When Liberia shall have been developed and its influence felt throughout the continent, the 'Black Man' shall come into his own. Africa is truly the land of beauty, wealth and prosperity." Before she graduated from Wilberforce in June 1921, she had garnered so much recognition that at a service held the Sunday before the graduation ceremony, she was given "a fund of fifty dollars" and memorialized with the establishment of an Amanda Mason Club. Members of the club "pledged themselves to forward means to assist Miss Mason in her work" in Liberia.[58]

By the time she and Xuma were engaged, she was headmistress at the Industrial and Literary School for Girls in Freetown, Sierra Leone, that was under the auspices of the African Methodist Episcopal Church. The couple settled in Johannesburg and had daughter Elsie Elizabeth Nozipho and son Alfred Howard Mtutuzeli. But shortly after giving birth to their son, in April 1934, she died.[59] Xuma was devastated by the loss, but, buoyed by his parents' support, he became determined to find another partner like Amanda. He sought references and advice from friends who were familiar with prominent female members of America's Black elite. He wrote to Max Yergan in November 1936:

> All is well with the children except the absence of a tender and guiding voice of a mother. But I feel that it is in Providence's plan to provide them with some one [sic] who will fill the gap that the departure of their late mother left. That some one [sic] will have made a great contribution to Africa if she assisted in developing in these little ones those ideals which my late wife and myself had for them. . . . I greatly feel the need of a partner and the inspiration she will be in my little efforts to serve my Africans.

Max would be one of the key contacts in his search, and so were Susie Yergan and several other American-based South African friends that included Eva Morake and Mayme Sims.[60]

The friends initiated an earnest and intense search for potential candidates. Max had provided at least one name for Xuma's "personal matter" as early as 1935 but was deliberately vague about his choice. Telling his friend, "With regard to the person in New York whose name I first mentioned to you and about whom you correctly understood me as being very much impressed I am frank to tell you that I consider that person a very splendid person indeed, and it was for that reason that I was so emphatic in what I said," Yergan then asked, "I wonder if you wish me to take the liberty of writing there?" In 1936 Morake submitted the names of three women—the first was a principal in Philadelphia, the second was the daughter of the secretary of a mission and a teacher, and the third was "near white but a nice girl" whom she met at the Y. Even after providing him with the names, she told him that he would "make a better choice when you get over," because, she concluded, "it is always best to see." By February 1937, Xuma still had not found a suitable mate, but his friends were still hopeful that they could help. Yergan noted at the end of a long letter that month that he and his wife often thought of Xuma and his "existing family and we think of the other member who, I hope, will be soon and satisfactorily found. I hope I shall have something soon to write you on this matter, but it may be just as well to await your arrival here and then I can be of any help possible to you." At the end of May 1937, Xuma left

South Africa for his three-month sojourn in the United States. He may have met some of the women on the list of prospects during his stay, but by the time he boarded a ship headed to London on September 15, 1937, to enroll in a public health course in the School of Hygiene and Tropical Medicine at London University, Hall had moved to the top of the list.[61]

* * *

Hall was still at home in Winston-Salem when Xuma left the country and more than likely dealing with her duties as executrix of the family estate. One issue in particular had kept her busy the entire time that she was enrolled in Teachers College. On November 19, 1936, only a few months after she arrived in New York, one of the family's rental properties that had been constructed before 1913 caught fire. Unfortunately, Versal Johnson, one of three tenants who resided in the building, died in the fire. The tenants, including Johnson's representative, sued Hall and her siblings "to recover for personal injuries and wrongful death alleged to have been caused by the negligence of the defendants in failing to furnish proper means of escape from fire in a building owned by the defendants." Their lawyers argued that a statute passed in 1923 required the owners to provide at least two means of escape from the building that the building did not have. The court battle lasted the entire first year of Hall's time at Columbia and remained an issue when she first met Xuma in 1937. Shortly after she began her fall session of classes in late September 1937, the court refused to uphold the tenants' demand and issued a judgment against them in October. The tenants, however, refused to be thwarted in their desire for compensation and appealed to the North Carolina Supreme Court. For six more months, Hall and her family remained embroiled in a battle with the tenants. The ordeal finally ended on June 15, 1938, when a judge ruled "the judgment of nonsuit must be Affirmed."[62]

By the time the favorable judgment came, she had already celebrated earning a master of arts in elementary education in February 1938, resettled in Winston-Salem, obtained a short-term teaching position at Winston-Salem Teachers College, and begun a correspondence relationship with Xuma. Hall's responses to him strongly suggest that he initiated the transatlantic connection, as his first letters appeared when he was attending school in England.[63] In a letter dated June 10, 1938, she noted that two letters from him had arrived, "the last a few days ago," and that she "was very glad" to have heard from him. Signaling that the two had been corresponding for some time before, she confessed that his "first letter was misplaced somewhere so I did not have the London address" and had sent her letter to his South Africa address in the hope that it would be forwarded to him in England. The rapport the two had developed encouraged her to tell him that she had "been resting since I came home in February except for six weeks when I taught at the College here before Commencement June first." In this prologue phase of the introduction, she told him that she was "not a lady of leisure" and that "I work hard all the time." As a result, she stressed that there was "not even a vacation in sight this year."[64]

Her personal passion for gardening and her role as an advocate for Black children also became prominent topics. "I have planted a late garden (vegetable)," which was unusual for her because, she explained, "I love flowers and heretofore I have put a great deal of my time growing them, but this season I decided to try my luck with vegetables." She was also pouring her energy into a project that was "the thing that is nearest to my heart," a government-sponsored nursery for Black children. "Working like a Trojan," she wanted to ensure that the government's efforts to create a nursery for Black children in the city would be successful. "We have several kindergartens privately owned and one supported by the Missionary Board of one of the white churches here," she acknowledged, but insisted that "we need one supported by the Government." Before she closed the letter again with her full signature, she suggested that he might be interested in reading the clipping that she enclosed from the local newspaper that highlighted "the progress of the Negroes in this city including a new hospital to be opened about the first of July."[65]

For months they had navigated phases of the relationship through correspondence, but the inherent challenges proved too much for Xuma's romantic impulses, so while in the process of completing his written examinations for the diploma of public health, he began making plans to travel back to the United States as soon as July again to seek resources for Black South Africans and to visit with her. In turn, she responded, "I shall be mighty glad to see you" and inquired, "About what time do you expect to reach North Carolina" because she "want[ed] to be at home" when he arrived.[66] Whether she comprehended the meaning and nature of his gesture to return to America or was simply being coy remains unclear, but what followed in their correspondence exposed the complicated details of the awkward and inconsistent first steps of what would become their transatlantic courtship.

At the outset, the courtship was beset by a number of issues. The first was the interest and investment from friends whom Xuma had charged with assisting in his search for a wife. A few weeks after he told Hall that he was returning to the United States to see her, Susie Yergan wrote to him about a woman who worked at Tuskegee with whom she had "a long chat one evening about which time I told her much about you. She seemed to regret that she had not had the opportunity to meet you. I am sorry myself because I am more convinced than ever that she is a person you ought to see while here this time."[67]

The second was distance. Xuma was so troubled by the ocean and miles between them that when his plan to travel to the United States did not materialize, his abject disappointment inspired him to rush forward with two proposals in late July 1938. The first was for her to visit him in South Africa. The second was for her to marry him. Both demonstrated an irrational vivacity from a man who prided himself on his judicious logic. Completely besotted, however, he threw caution to the wind and lurched ahead. He enclosed photographs, or snaps, as they referred to them, of his home country in his letter, perhaps in the hope that she might be enticed. And, indeed, when she responded on August 8, 1938, she told him, "I received your letter and the lovely snaps. They are very, very lovely" and noted that his "letter was most interesting" and "made me feel like catching the next boat to South Africa." He had clearly unearthed or revived something in her, but she was also stunned and dismayed by the suggestion that she should marry him. She bluntly responded, "I am indeed grateful for all the things you have offered me for a prolonged stay in South Africa but you see I am only interested in a career, not marriage." "When I told you I was interested in your country," she continued, "I meant that I would like to come over and work in some way that would be helpful to your people there. There are several reasons why I cannot marry now. If you still think there is something that I can do in South Africa please let me know—what, how and when." Then she offered him the opportunity to see her on her terms when she planned to travel to Europe the following summer. "Perhaps," she suggested, "I can extend the trip to South Africa."[68]

Xuma refused to be discouraged by her terse reply and escalated his expressions of desperation to see and marry her. Hall, on the other hand, retreated, but she continued the correspondence. Maintaining a polite posture, refusing to engage in any kind of romantic discussion, yet relaying details about her busy life and vacillating between referring to him as Dr. Xuma and Alfred (eventually settling on Alfred), she remained steadfast in her lack of interest in his marriage proposal. In her August 26, 1938, letter she told him that she had "only a few more days now for leisure and then for 9 long months of grind—happy ones I hope for I dearly love children," because she was now teaching at Kimberly Park School where several of her cohorts had been working for some time. She also noted that her social calendar was full—visitors from Florida who had been there for two weeks and "a round of entertainment both here and out of the city." With so much activity, she lamented, "I am almost completely exhausted."[69]

Xuma, who seemed to have been overpowered by his emotions, however, persisted. He told her about another plan to come to America. This time, she vehemently discouraged him from coming and made her feelings for him clear. "From your letter I understand you are making or hope to make the trip to America solely to see me. I would not [she underlined this three times] have you incur that expense to see me unless you come of your own accord. It would not be fair to you nor my American friends (male) of whom I am particularly fond—especially one—and I am sure I could not give you all of my time." Expressing deep concern about his insistence on changing the nature of their relationship, she wrote, "I thought in the beginning we were only to be casual friends. I would be interested in your work and you in mine. I am sure we could get along nicely in a platonic manner but as far as romance goes I am not particularly interested."[70]

Hall's blunt dismissal of his marriage proposal came in spite of the fact that she apparently knew about the search for a companion that had been launched by him and several of his friends. She even wondered whether the search in particular had complicated her relationship with her friend Susie Yergan, whose marriage to Max Yergan was so troubled that they had separated. "Mrs. Yergans [sic]," she noted, "has not written to me since she left New York last fall. I can't understand 'why.' I sent a letter to her in Arkansas but she never answered." Believing that Susie had such a vested interest in Xuma's search for a wife, Hall speculated that Susie's silence stemmed from the relationship that she had developed with Xuma in the past year. "I hope she wont [sic] think our friendship will keep her from being friends to us also," she lamented. Moreover, she added, "If they [Susie and Max Yergan] have relatives or friends in whom they would like for you to become interested it might be well to consider them because as I told you in my last letter marriage does not enter into my mind yet." While she could understand why he might be "upset at this stage of the game about my writing," she was happy to continue the correspondence, "as often as you care to have me write—if my writing helps you in any small way." "The only thing," she adamantly insisted, was that he "understand clearly is that romantically I am not interested in you but platonically I am" (also underlined in the letter three times). Since her feelings had been openly expressed, she believed that they could "enjoy a beautiful friendship that can and will bring to both of us true happiness."[71]

Her emphatic refusal to consider his marriage proposal at what was considered advanced age for a woman could be perceived as an anomaly or as a presentation of a far more complicated portrait of the choices that educated Black women born in the last decades of the nineteenth century and the early decades of the twentieth century believed they had. Hall embraced certain conventional norms of elite African American women, but she also eschewed others. Clinging to her own freedom as a single woman while engaging in a transatlantic friendship with a man whom she wanted to offer only her companionship and adventure, mostly from afar, were two of them.

CHAPTER 5

"If I Had Wings I Would Truly Fly Over"

The Courtship

Writing to Xuma from her "sick bed" in November 1938, Hall announced that the family home on East Seventh Street that "was really too large for only two of us now" had been sold and that she was in the process of "building a 5 room cottage in another section of the city for one sister and myself." They planned to move in around Christmas.[1] However, in addition to reporting that she had finally recovered from the terrible cold she contracted in the fall in a subsequent letter on New Year's Day 1939, she told him the delayed completion of the cottage on Cameron Avenue meant that she and her sister were not moving in for another week. The delay did not dampen her excitement, though, about her return to the classroom "for the second half of the year's work." Expressing a deep love of her students and a renewed interest in a profession that she had once grown weary of, she insisted, "I have enjoyed working with the little folk—experimenting and trying out all sort of things with them—I have 40 of them directly under my care" and declared, "I love them all."[2]

The New Year's Day letter also revealed, for the first time, that Xuma had become a topic of conversation in her family. When Hall noted that her brother Leroy, a member of the Alpha Phi Alpha Fraternity, was so impressed by Xuma's stature that he wanted to know if he was "the same 'Xuma' who is a member of the 'Alphas' of London, Eng," she affirmed her family's interest in who Xuma was and in the transatlantic relationship they had developed. Xuma's Alpha Phi Alpha Fraternity connection to Leroy through his charter memberships at the University of Minnesota and the London chapter earned in August 1938 mattered to her and seems to have contributed to her move toward a new kind of intimacy with Xuma. Apparently with Xuma's encouragement, she began dispensing advice and opinions about personal family matters. His deep concern about how much time he had spent away from his children while in America and in Europe earning his educational degrees and how his absence might have affected them moved Hall to respond, "I know you are happy to be home with your children and that they are glad to have you home. I think, however, it was good for you to leave them while they were quite young than to wait until they have grown up, say to adolescence."[3]

Moreover, Hall began a serious flirtation with the idea of a visit to South Africa. Motivated in part by the arrival of a catalog that Xuma ordered on her behalf from the University of Witwatersrand, she declared that she was looking forward to being able "to take my time and read thru it" and that she was "especially" happy about looking at "the courses that would interest me." But there was also her appreciation for his "invitation to visit Sunny So. Africa." So giddy at the prospect, she teased, "Some day you may look out and see an old familiar face knocking at your door—then you will be surprise [sic]—ha! ha!"[4]

By the end of January, Hall's inquiries about his children had escalated, and she demonstrated a curious interest in his deceased wife, Amanda. She also moved past the flirtation of a visit to South Africa to actually putting a plan in motion to travel to the country. She wanted to know his "wife's maiden name and from what town in N C did she come from?" "We have," she told him, "at least 7 or 8 teachers in this school alone from Wilberforce University," where Amanda had attended school.[5] And, significantly, she was "trying to get all of my business arranged this year so that I shall be free to be away from home for a while. In fact I am still anticipating a trip to Africa more and more. You write to me such grand ideas and happenings there that if I had wings I would truly fly over to see and enjoy some of those things." Concluding the letter with "Write when you have a little time and tell me more about Africa," particularly, she noted, "it[s] social, economic and industrial life."[6]

As the relationship between Hall and Xuma advanced, Xuma apparently withheld that information from the friends he had enlisted to help him find a wife. When a fellow Alpha Phi Alpha Fraternity member in Savannah, Georgia, inquired about Xuma's children in February 1939, for example, he "hope[d] they shall get a kind and understanding step-mother." He assured Xuma that he was doing a good job of "going about it properly—taking your time and looking the land over for your own companionship, too," and insisted that he believed Xuma would "make the right choice" in the end.[7] By then Hall had clearly become his choice, and the sudden rush of emotions that she displayed in March because of the nearly monthlong delay of the delivery of one of his transatlantic letters clearly upended any pretense that she wanted to remain in a platonic relationship with him. She was so distraught by the time that she received his letter, she confessed, "I have wondered and wondered what could be wrong." "Somehow," she continued, "I look for a letter almost one a week and when I fail to receive it I feel that something must be wrong, but they say no news is good news." And revealing that Xuma had again sought her advice about his children's education, she lamented that "I, too, wish your children were here, or I, there."[8]

All the signs now suggested that they were at a crossroads and moving toward something far more consequential than friendship. At one point, she announced, "Who knows, things may turn out our way yet—lets [sic] hope and wait a little while longer." In the meantime, she assured him, "Things are shaping up for me nicely here." She and Edna were anticipating company as her brother Leroy and his wife, Eleanor, were in the process of building a new house across the street. She expected that "by fall . . . we shall be happily domiciled together and in easy reach of each other." With her family in close proximity, she could "feel better leaving home with my brother close by to see about our little home and my two sisters and little nephew."[9] Requesting that he tell her "more about some of the things you would like for me to help in there," and offering to "brush up on some things that I have either forgotten or have never known about," she had clearly made the decision to go to South Africa. She was also quite interested in taking courses at the University of the Witwatersrand. "When I get out of school this summer I hope to spend more time on my music. Would there be time for some courses at the University? You know I believe in progress. I must keep mentally progressive and ever on the upward march."[10]

Hall's attraction to Xuma and anticipation about a trip to South Africa had gained such momentum that the slowness of transatlantic airmail weighed heavily on her. When the letter that Xuma had penned in February did not arrive until the second week of March, she announced, "Your letter February 21st reached me a few days ago" and again admitted that she "was worried a while because I could not hear a word from you." Imagining the worst, she "thought perhaps you were ill or something was wrong." This time something was indeed wrong. His daughter's health crisis had forced him to take the drastic step of removing her from school. Very concerned about the situation, Hall sympathized with him by noting, "I am so sorry you had to take the little girl out of school but her health comes first regardless of education. If I were there now her education would not be interrupted but could continue despite the fact she is being kept from school." Moreover, she emphatically declared, "I have definitely made up my mind to come to Africa—perhaps as soon as early fall (Sept or October) if everything works out as I want it to work." She then requested that he give her some pointers about how to navigate the geographical logistics of travel on "how to get to So. Africa," asking whether it is "necessary to go to London or to Europe for that matter."

She also demonstrated that she had been reading about and exploring the history of the country and demanded to know if it was true that "it is hard for American Negroes to get into So. Africa."[11] Whether Xuma answered her question remains a mystery, but he might have told her, Robert Trent Vinson argues, that white South Africans had been limiting African American access to South Africa for some time, as they "strained to create a 'white South Africa' that included the banning of African American peoples and images and the general subjugation of American Negro residents."[12]

A little more than a month later, Hall accepted Xuma's marriage proposal, on April 21, 1939. "Every time he'd write me a letter, he'd ask me, and when I answered, I wouldn't mention it," she remarked in an interview decades later. But when he asked her once again in the letter that probably arrived on April 8, "Will you marry me?" and simply "signed his name, that's all," she finally acknowledged her own feelings.[13] In remembering why she decided to marry him, she insisted that it was primarily driven by her strong Christian faith and recalled how a dramatic scene unfolded on a day when she was working at school as she grappled with her response. Over "two or three hours; I'd write a while, I'd get down on my knees and I'd pray a while. I said 'Lord, tell me and show me what to do, this is a very crucial moment in my life.' And the third time I did that, when I got up off my knees, as plain as I'm talking to you right now, I heard, 'Go, and I'll go with you.' And that was it. I put that in the letter 'Yes, I'll marry you.'" When Xuma received her reply, "he was so happy" that he quickly sent her "a cablegram" and told her that he would "make the arrangements; don't worry about anything."[14]

Time and distance certainly shaped Hall's version of the story. For a deeply religious woman like her, there is no doubt that her Christian faith played a pivotal role in her decision, but to solely rely on that narrative decenters her in explaining the vital role that her own desires played. A far more accurate account of the dynamic force that shaped her decision was revealed nearly four months after she agreed to be Xuma's wife. She admitted to him that for the past two decades, she had "longed for the opportunity to get into Africa," essentially confirming her centrality to crafting her own destiny.[15]

Hall also accepted his proposal for several other reasons that encouraged her to move forward quickly and write on April 21, 1939, "I resigned my position yesterday." Pleased that "things are coming along nicely . . .," she was "working feverishly now getting things in shape so that I can soon be ready to come to So. Africa." She had initially "thought it would be better to spend another year on this side," but after some contemplation she came to the conclusion that she would "definitely . . . be ready by Sept or Oct. this year." That eagerness stemmed from the fact that she "was glad to know that there would be no desire of yours to prevent me from living my own life. I couldn't live any other way—for to be free mentally and otherwise is the greatest part of my personality. I have enjoyed comfort and independence. I have been happy and free all of my life—to cramp me now means death to me—but I do trust you and do feel that somehow I shall be happy there in So. Africa with you. I am willing to sacrifice, if the sacrifice is not too hard."[16]

Then there was the revelation that although she "had excellent chances to marry" before, she "never accepted, waiting I suppose for something that would make me very happy." Now, she believed, the "time has come" because "my education is what I have wanted it to be—time has also brought many experiences along lines of accomplishments etc. I really think the time is ripe for me to marry." And finally, she reiterated what her mother had instilled in her long ago about service to the community. So steadfast in that commitment, she concluded, "If you think sincerely and definitely that I can serve there and that I, too can grow personally—I am willing to accept."[17]

Now, nearly forty-five years old and eager to fulfill a dream, Xuma's marriage proposal seemed to offer a chance, at last, to realize her own decades-old aspiration. But the emotional, political, and economic process of dismantling her life and moving to a new home nearly nine thousand miles away would not be easy. At various times, she alternated between demonstrating a smorgasbord of emotions including strength and vulnerability, confidence and apprehension, and peace and anxiety. Early on in the process, she discovered that she had no idea how to get to South Africa and was a bit uneasy about traveling such a long distance alone. "Don't forget to tell me how to get to So. Africa," she reminded her future husband. Demonstrating a vulnerability that she had not before, she told him, "You see, I have never crossed the ocean before and I will be a little bit nervous but <u>brave</u>, ha! ha! ha!" And, for the first time, she closed her letter with the romantic gesture "Love Madie."[18] Still, two weeks later, while reaffirming the declaration that she had "definitely decided to cast my lot with you," she did not profess romantic love for him as the reason. Instead, she wrote, "Maybe I can be of _some_ service there." Her dedication to service, however, did not mean that she was without apprehension. Repeating some of what she had written in the April 21 letter ("I think I told you in my last letter that I resigned my position as teacher here for another season"), her letter in May revealed a woman who needed confirmation from him that he still wanted to marry her. That vulnerability was certainly compounded by the fact that Xuma was unable to return to the United States to see his new fiancée, meet her family, and properly make the formal announcement of their engagement because he could not get out of South Africa.[19]

Still, they moved forward with their plans. Responding to his request for information that he needed for submission to South African authorities, she listed information about her age, family and education:

Age—1900 June 3 born in Winston-Salem, N.C.
parents, Dr. and Mrs H. H. Hall—both deceased.
two sisters—one brother—Teacher elementary
M.A. degree—Columbia Univ—1938. B. S.
Teacher's College—Winston-Salem, N.C.

And, she added, "You may say that I desire to make So. Africa my home through my married relationship with you."[20] Most of the statistics were accurate, but there was a glaring omission and an even more flagrant discrepancy. She did not mention her older brother, Cleo, who died in 1931, and she had shaved off six years on her date of birth. Now thirty-nine years old, Hall crafted a fictitious account of her age that followed her for much of her life and has often confounded scholars.

As the process slowly moved forward, a far more assured Hall appeared in later correspondence. She began making her own travel arrangements and thought that it was time to formally announce her engagement to family and friends. She decided to "make inquiries about sailing direct to Cape Town from New York" and planned to use her own money to pay for the trip by "sell[ing] a piece of property that will give me the necessary funds for passage." Using the venue of "the formal opening" of her brother and his wife's new home in August for the public announcement of their engagement, she asked if he would send the engagement ring by then.[21]

As the school term came to a close in June, she seemed energized, restless, and resolute. After complaining that she was "dead tired" and disinclined to fill her summer "teaching children and adults piano and organ music," she had been inspired while listening to the radio by "a very interesting talk on South Africa by a Mrs. Hughes, I think, who has only recently returned from Cape Town." She expressed her excitement that a woman was engaged in "looking over the mission fields for the A.M.E. Church." She had also grown keenly interested in whether he had "started negotiations yet relative to my coming over" because she was "getting all keyed up over the expected trip there." She was so "keyed up," in fact, that when she explained that her supervisor wanted to discuss future work with her, she planned to turn her down. "You see," she declared, "once I make up my mind to do a thing I never turn back. It takes a long time to plan something—but once that is accomplished, I move on. Nothing they can offer me will make me alter my course now—only You can say—don't come then I'll remain over this side."[22]

In her new role as his fiancée, she assured him that she loved children and predicted that she would "get along beautifully" with his daughter and son, took special interest in the design of her engagement ring, and continued to keep him abreast of travel plans. After visiting a jeweler in town to examine rings, she told Xuma that she wanted one with "one large square stone (diamond) either with smaller diamonds or sapphires on either side of the band" and "made of white gold." Including a detailed diagram drawing of the ring, she was guaranteeing that he would not make a mistake, and she made it clear that she wanted the same kind of quality jewelry that her father had given her when she graduated. It was a "very pretty ring" made of yellow gold with seven diamonds clustered together. She was also busy applying for a passport, reiterating that she was born on June 3, 1900, and that she was "39yrs" old.[23]

No longer suspended between the anxiety about leaving the United States and the desire to begin an adventure that she had longed for, she freely confirmed that melding the lives of two nearly fifty-year-old professional adults was in many ways like a corporate merger. Success depended more on genuine affection, sound negotiation, and shared values than a display of youthful romantic love, although she freely demonstrated affection toward him in her letters now with phrases like "The wind blows like fall now, Soon that same wind will blow me to you."[24] At the same time, she also emphasized the importance of bargaining. Underlining "Now about negotiations" in her June 25 letter, she sent a clear message to Xuma about her fundamental role in the process. What followed was the affirmation of an astute businesswoman who had "already started things on this end—passport, etc." and consulted with a friend who had "toured several countries about a year ago" about "how to go about securing the passport." And to quell her concern about traveling such a long distance alone, she initiated the conversation about the possibility of companionship for the trip in the form of an AME minister and his wife on what she referred to as her "adventure."[25]

While her independence and confidence were the driving forces behind her ability to launch the negotiation phase with Xuma, it was the economic dynamics of the Depression that pushed the two of them into renegotiation. Arguing that "everybody wants what we have for nothing," she was unable to secure a good price for the property that she put on the market to pay for the trip. Refusing to "sell so cheap" and unwilling to abandon her adventurous plan, she turned to him for assistance. Accepting his earlier "promise to send me the money to make the trip with," she saw no ambiguity between relying on his financial acumen and insisting on her independence because her short-term dependency reflected the smart economic decision of a businesswoman.[26] For her it would have been unwise to sell a valuable land asset in such an undervalued economic market, even for personal gain.

Equally proficient and professional when describing the kind of wedding she wanted, she began a letter near the end of June, "Now about the marriage." She believed that they should "wait until I get to Johannesburg for that. I imagine I will be dead tired from such a long trip and therefore will need rest so instead of marrying at Cape Town I shall wish to end the journey first there maybe a quiet church wedding or something of that sort. I don't [go?] for spectacular—doings—people, quiet, unobtrusive, is the thread that runs through my entire life." Her critical characterization of herself led her to tell him, "You'll find me plain, easy to get along with, cooperative and congenial."[27]

By early July, the enormity of her decision to marry him and move to South Africa again played havoc with her emotions. The cool proficiency and professionalism receded as she gave voice to her chaotic feelings. As if she finally realized the magnitude of the move that she was poised to make, a wistful Hall "wonder[ed], Do you ever think of me—so many thousand miles away?" and confessed that "I think of you often—what you are perhaps doing—, to children—home—friends—everything." And, she seemed to just now realize how little she knew about him and his customs, so for the first time she asked him a question about his religious affiliation and was far more interested in the details of his marriage custom. After noting that she was a Methodist, she expressed curiosity about why there had to be two marriage ceremonies—the first at Cape Town soon after she was scheduled to arrive and the second in Johannesburg. "Does that mean you have two marriage performances? One legal; the other religious," she inquired. She also wanted to know whether it was necessary to "have a big wedding at Church like they do here in America or does one simply go to the church and be married by a priest or preacher?" In the end, the astute negotiator became so malleable that she agreed to "leave it to you to settle—whatever you do or wish will be alright with me."[28]

In mid-July, she was distraught because she had not heard from him. "I have waited and waited for a letter from you for such a long time. I am wondering what on earth can be the matter. It was June when I heard from you last. I have thought all kinds of things—Are you ill—the children—has something gone wrong? Tell me, the suspense is too great!" she admonished. The lack of correspondence from him created uncertainty at a critical time when she needed unwavering assurance. Moreover, as more of Xuma's American friends learned of the impending marriage, some seemed to have determined that Hall was not the most suitable candidate. One major detractor was Hall's friend Susie Yergan who corresponded often with Xuma.

Her relationship with Hall, however, seems to have taken a dark turn. "Have you heard from Mrs. Yergans [*sic*]?," she asked Xuma on July 15, 1939. She had heard from Susie—receiving a letter the week before—that heightened Hall's suspicions about an attempt to sabotage the marriage. "I am wondering if she has said anything to you to discourage you in this marriage." She noted, "There seems to be an underlying current in which she pushes you forward at the same time she seeks a retreat." Revealing that this was not the first aggrieved incident that she had with Susie, Hall recounted, "Once in New York (before I met you) I had an opportunity to go to So. Africa thru the A. K. A. sorority on a fellowship exchange (an African woman coming to America and an American going there) when I volunteered to go—she raised objections—I wonder now why? In my letter from her she has prefaced her 'go forward' with a negation—Is it possible that she does not want any other star to shine as brightly as the 'Yergans'?" For some reason, she continued, "She seems to think I will not like it in Africa—She did—<u>why can't I</u>." Moreover, she assured him that "I lived in Southern Florida for two or three years and I loved it there. I can adapt myself almost anywhere."[29]

Clearly perturbed by Susie Yergan's response to her impending marriage, she blamed much of Susie's disposition on the slow and painful dissolution of her marriage. The Yergans' difficulties had begun at the same time that Max embraced communism and questioned the role of Christianity. At one point, he argued that "communism offers to Christianity its supreme opportunity as a force for social regeneration." Bewildered and hurt, Susie found herself adrift. By 1936 the father of her three children had become a stranger. They subsequently separated.[30] For a while, she left New York and relocated to Arkansas to teach and then moved back to North Carolina to be the dean of women at her alma mater Shaw University. Friends rallied around her. Most tried to keep in contact, but Susie's responses to them were sporadic. Still, Hall made an effort. For a weekend in March, Susie was scheduled to visit with her in Winston-Salem but canceled because of "pressing duties." Hall had even planned to visit Susie at Shaw in the winter of 1939, but months before Susie's circumstances and appearance had declined so significantly that Hall reported, "A friend of mine, who lived across the street motored to Raleigh to Commencement at Shaw Univ." and "saw Mrs. Yergans [*sic*]. He [assume that this is referring to Max] was suppose to come to Raleigh the next week to file suit for divorce. She is very unhappy—quite thin and discouraged." Moreover, she continued, "The work is hard there also. Too, her mother is an invalid at Salisbury. Susie must furnish the finance for her. It is a pitable [*sic*] situation." For the most part, she told Xuma, "People don't like the way he has treated her." But she argued, people also "blame her for some of it," saying, "She has not kept up with the times in some of her ideas." Ultimately, Hall expressed more sadness than anger about their mutual friend. "She is really pitiful," she concluded, "and worries quite a deal about him." The couple did not legally dissolve the marriage until nearly a decade later, in 1945.[31]

With only a few months to successfully meet the target departure date of October 15, 1939, the personal turmoil surrounding their mutual friend soon took a backseat to the more pressing issue of dismantling her life in America. It was far more complicated than either she or Xuma could have imagined. First, there was the bureaucratic negotiation of permission from South African officials for her to enter the country. Xuma initiated the legal processing of Hall's application to move there by writing to D. L. Smit, the secretary of native affairs, in Pretoria on July 5, 1939, inquiring about a transfer of property deeds and a permit for his "fiancée—Miss Madie B. Hall an American citizen of North Carolina, U.S.A."[32] After being granted an interview with Smit on the morning of July 11, he left nothing to chance. Quickly sending a follow-up letter that same day to Smit, he reiterated "the information and details concerning my fiancée":

> Miss Hall, a daughter of the late Dr. and Mrs. H. H. Hall, was born June 3rd., 1900 in Winston-Salem, North Carolina, U.S.A.
>
> She was until recently, when she resigned her post in preparation to coming to South Africa, a teacher in the Public School at Winston-Salem, North Carolina. At one time she was secretary of Y.W.C.A. She received her training first in her home town where she took her B.S. degree at the Teachers' College. She also holds the degree of Master of Arts from Columbus [sic] University, New York City.
>
> As a Public [sic] servant and one whom I know to be held in high esteem by the community, I have no doubt that good testimonials as to her character and standing could be had from responsible public officials and citizens in her city, as well as from her teachers at Columbia University.
>
> As to the deposit of £50 which may be required by the Department of the Interior, I wish to state that, as a Medical Practitioner of about twelve years standing in Johannesburg, I have assets in the form of fixed properties unencumbered, and could also give a Banker's guarantee, my Bankers being the Barclay's bank (D.C.& O.) Commissioner Street East Branch, Johannesburg.
>
> I hope this information is sufficient and adequate enough to guarantee the issuance of the permit for Miss Hall to enter this country at the earliest possible time.
>
> Yours faithfully,[33]

Unaware of Xuma's interview and letter to Smit and of the letter that he had written to her on July 14 explaining all of it, a frantic and impatient Hall sent a hastily worded cable on July 18 that simply said "Cant hear from you cable. Trouble. Love Madie."[34]

Permission to leave the United States as an American citizen was the second major hurdle. If she was to travel in October as planned, she needed to obtain a passport fairly quickly. Nine days after sending the cable, she reported that she had "formally" applied for her passport and spoke to a "steamship agent" about travel to South Africa. The monthlong trip would begin in New York City and end in Cape Town on November 15.[35] Travel, however, would be impossible if she didn't have the necessary funds to pay for the trip. She still had not received money from Xuma, who, it seemed, did not have the cash readily available. Impatient with him for the oversight, she testily wrote, "Now Alfred you will to have to send me the fare as you promised," because "I am getting everything ready and when I hear from the agent no doubt he will want a deposit or something. Please send the fare as soon as you can possibly do so." Perhaps regretting her earlier testiness, four days later she asked him to "send the money whenever you think to meet" the October 15 deadline and, after discovering that he had a cold, encouraged him take care of himself. And she signed the letter with the salutation, "Love for yourself." The money finally arrived in late September.[36]

Then there was the complication of separating herself from family and her obligations. Hall had, for most of her adult life, played a central role in the family dynamics. She had cared for her mother when she was ill, stepped into the mothering role for her younger siblings when her mother died, and took care of her father as he aged. She even helped raise her sister Willie's son, Harold Kennedy Jr., born in 1926. Assisting Willie seemed all the more necessary because by 1930 Willie's husband, Harold Kennedy, was no longer in the home. Presumably to supplement her income as a teacher, Willie opened her home to boarders. Five lodgers, two women, a sixteen-year-old girl from Virginia, and two men, lived with her and her three-year-old son. The four adults taught in the public schools, while the young girl was unemployed.[37]

Additionally, when Hall's father died, she assumed the dual roles as head of her family and the family business. She took both seriously. So when Xuma pressed her about making the trip to South Africa earlier, she told him that she was "sorry" that she "cannot get away before 15 of October." Her reason, as she had noted "in the previous letter," was that the completion of her "brother's home [was] being delayed because of bad weather and it will be Sept now before they will be able to move in." Problems with tenants delayed the trip as well. "I am having some trouble with tenants. I had to see a lawyer today about one," she continued. Her goal was "to get leases signed for protection both for them and us." Ultimately, she "hope[d] everything will turn out to everyone's great satisfaction so that I will not have any worries while away."[38]

By early September, the frenetic pace of the couple's transatlantic maneuvering slowed considerably, and everything finally seemed to be falling into place. On July 20, 1939, Smit indicated "that the South African Legation at Washington should be authorized to grant a visa to Miss Hall to enter the Union," provided that "suitable certificates of character to the Immigration authorities" as well as a payment of £50 accompanied the application. The confirmation and stipulations concerning Hall's entry into South Africa arrived on September 6: "Miss Madie Beatrice Hall will be allowed to enter the Union in order to marry you. She will be admitted on temporary permit carrying a deposit of £50, subject to the marriage taking place in the Union within two months of her entry." Also, she had received her American passport, and her engagement ring had arrived.[39]

Other challenges, however, were brewing. The first one appeared when Hall noted that she had been anxiously "waiting for some word from the travel agent" whom she had given "details more than two weeks ago." The second concerned the engagement ring. While the Customs Bureau at Washington had been in contact with her and forwarded it to the Winston-Salem Post Office, she and her attorney learned after arriving to pick it up that they "would have to pay 65% of its value which is $140" (worth $2,623.48 in 2021) to possess it. After some discussion between the authorities and her lawyer, the postal authorities indicated that she needed to correspond with Xuma "to see if you thought it would be worthwhile to pay the $140.00 duty or have it returned to you." He had thirty days to make the decision.[40] But Hall could not resist seeing the ring before she and her attorney left the post office. Afterward, she reported to Xuma she was "tickled pink." "It is gorgeous, too, divine!; I love it," she exclaimed. Then she playfully remarked, "I can see that from now on I shall not hesitate to have you make selections for me, Ha! ha! ha!" She was equally intrigued by the post office staff's interest in the ring, her, and him. She noted that "the entire post office force must have had a peek at that ring," and thought that "they were a little surprise[d] at a Negro woman claiming it." So curious about the man who had sent the ring, "They asked all kinds of questions about you. I was delighted to answer them to be sure. I told them a great deal."[41]

On August 24, she told Xuma, "I am getting ready now to make the trip." "With my passport secure and the ticket still in the making I am getting a few clothes together. My books, etc., I shall send separately from my luggage. You have a typewriter so I dont [sic] think I'll bring mine." But there was a war brewing. "What about the war scare?" she asked him. "From this point it looks much like they are going to fight." Recognizing that her travel plans would be affected, she complained, "Of course I shall have to go through England. That will hold me a little long on this side won't it?" Still, she was determined to "go forward with plans as I have made them."[42] That, however, was not to be, because Germany invaded Poland in September 1939. "I am at a loss what to do," she wrote to him on September 22. Declaring, "We had things under control until Britain and France declared war," a deflated Madie lamented, "I was supposed to have sailed on the 5th of Oct, Normandie to Eng—thence to So. Africa on the Union Castle. Now it has developed that the U.S. government has recalled all passports and that American citizens cannot go to countries that are at war unless on very urgent business. Any way I would undertake to go would finally land me at So. Africa and since that nation has declared a state of war I would not be permitted to go. I am very sorry!! The only thing I can do now is to wait and hope that everything will soon be over."[43] The wait would be a long one as the scale of the war escalated.

In the meantime, the two of them made the best of it and continued their long-distance engagement through correspondence. She used her time to update him on the status of the money and the ring that he had sent her. She deposited the money for payment of the trip in the bank but offered to return it to him. Because she felt that it "was too much to pay the Government," the ring had been returned to him. The delay in her travel also offered her the chance to tell him how she wanted to spend her time in Africa. Interested in some kind of work with juveniles, she had discussed the matter with her neighbor, a juvenile officer in the city.[44]

She showed much more restraint than she had with Susie Yergan when he reported that some of his friends thought that she might "mistreat" his children. Shocked and baffled, she quickly dispelled the accusation and asserted, "I have never mistreated any child. . . . I love them too dearly." He could, she insisted, "rest assured that should anything like that ever happen I shall be ready for an insane asylum. So lets [sic] don't worry about such things. They are inconsequential." She reasoned that she had "a duty to perform and with my eyes set toward that goal I must go on until I feel that life has been well spent for humanities' [sic] good." More important, she continued, "Children have always been in and out of my life. I raised my sister's little boy from birth—my mother died soon afterwards—he is now 12 yrs. She has never had the care of him. I have taught school several years—always primary—never above 3rd grade—although I've had opportunity to teach in High School and at the College—but my preference has been little tots of whom I am genuinely devoted and sincere. So you can believe me when I say your children will not in the least be mistreated—not by me."[45]

Nevertheless, Hall was idle for the first time in her life. She had quit her job so lost both her professional identity as a teacher and the daily routine of working with children. To remedy that, she and Xuma decided rather quickly that she would be wise to engage in some kind of promising activity that would be beneficial to her and to him in South Africa. In one of the few surviving notes from Xuma to her, he wrote in a cable on September 29, 1939:

> Darling,
> Don't worry. Better safe than sorry. Try enter Atlanta School Social Service. Valuable preparation.
> Love Alfred[46]

A little more than a week later, she cabled him, "Accepted atlanta [*sic*] university will write you from there im [*sic*] quite happy although disappointed about trip, Madie." Using the money that he had sent her for the trip to South Africa, she hurriedly packed, located lodging, and moved to Atlanta. Two days after sending the cable, on October 11, she was a student at the Atlanta School of Social Work at Atlanta University. Xuma's connections and money "paved the way" for her quick entry, but it was her own intellect, tenacity, and resolve that pushed her to succeed.[47]

The Atlanta School of Social Work's training of Black social workers dated back to its establishment in 1920. Under the direction of sociologist Edward Franklin Frazier from 1922 to 1926, the Atlanta School adopted a yearlong curriculum in 1924 that included courses in "casework, human behavior, social investigation, physiology, home nursing, community organization, play leadership, social problems, and fieldwork." Five years later, the curriculum was driven by "courses specifically dealing with the Black experience in America" such as "1) the techniques of community work among Black people; 2) industrial problems of Black people; 3) the conduct of social surveys in Black communities; 4) housing problems of Black people, and 5) recreational problems of Black people."[48] With the introduction of sociology and research courses, the school became the first to be accredited by the American Association of Schools of Social Work in 1928. From the time that it was established, scholar Cynthia Neverdon-Morton argues, "The graduates were employed throughout the United States as district agents and executives in 'colored' departments of associated charities, as probation officers, as Urban League officers and assistants, and as welfare workers in industry, church social service departments, the YMCA and the YWCA." Ultimately, "The graduates' activities firmly established the formal framework for social work in the black community."[49]

From the moment Hall entered the program, she planned to transnationalize her training because both she and Xuma knew that her work in the program would serve the Black people of South Africa. Delinquency and the training of Black social workers in South Africa had emerged as a major topic in 1939, and Xuma was a significant figure in the discussion. After a meeting of the Continuation Committee on Bantu Juvenile Delinquency in Johannesburg on July 24–25, 1939, that included representatives from municipalities and South Africa government departments like Native Affairs and Public Health, an invitation to Xuma from G. Ballenden of the Non-European and Native Affairs Department to attend a subsequent meeting being held on September 13 ensured that he would become an integral part of the deliberations. While the war severely limited the Native Affairs Department's direct participation in the committee's work, the group continued to conference, discuss juvenile delinquency, and, most significantly, plan the development of a "training school for social workers among the Non-Europeans." Moving toward that goal, the American Board Mission in South Africa invited him to be part of a board committee overseeing the establishment of a school of "curriculum and housing of the training school" in October.[50] Hall assisted him in his role by supplying him with the most current information she learned in her courses and through her research on juvenile delinquency and training for social work. Her instructors were fully aware that she was far more interested in "information and materials—all that I can get" than grades. Beyond the requirements for the university, she was "writing to Washington for as much material as I can get on delinquency; dependent defective and neglected children," one of the main highlights of her term paper. And she asked him, "What other immediate <u>needs</u> do you have there that you think I should get information on?"[51]

Her course work, fieldwork, interactions with leading scholars in the field, and the library at the university also afforded her the opportunity to engage in the pursuit of knowledge, something that she had always enjoyed. Reporting that she was "Quite Happy," she immersed herself in her work. Taking a full course load that included Principles of Case Work, Problems in Child Care, Social Statistics, Medical Information, and Group Analysis, she attended classes three days a week, on Monday, Wednesday, and Friday. She also engaged in "field work" at the local Urban League three days a week, on Thursday, Friday, and Saturday.[52] The fieldwork interested her the most. "This semester I am working with groups—women and girls—next semester case work," she told Xuma. She was "very anxious" to start the case work because she had "never had an opportunity for personal contacts before." She thought that she would be "very happy (after I receive the training) to know that through my efforts, tact and knowledge I shall be entrusted to try to make adjustments for people who need that type of thing." In the end, her commitment and devotion to the training were because *she* was "thinking seriously in terms of Africa and what I can bring that may help my people there."[53] Her immersion into social work for the good of her "people there" compelled her to explore intellectual perspectives on conditions for Black South Africans. In the course of her study, she read *Africa* magazine, discovering "late books written by distinguished authors and synopsis of the same." The scholars varied in their views. "Some give 'glorying' accounts of the conditions and improvements made in So Africa; others were not so good," she told Xuma. So concerned about some of the "not so good," she asked Xuma, "Is it true that you people are on reservations 15 to 20 miles away from the city proper with no sanitation, lights, water and etc?" Expressing her shock, she stated, "I thought you were on the outskirts of the city but within city limits like most of the southern towns in this country. I knew there were problems there but not to that extent."[54]

The shock did not deter her from the commitment she had made. Instead, the realization of how such limited opportunities shaped the lives of Black South Africans encouraged her to proceed with her process of shedding some of her personal possessions in preparation for her life of service. One of the key areas of the preparation for her mission was the way in which she thought about clothing. For a woman who had once owned a sophisticated dress shop and loved fashionable dress, the declaration that she would "do well to bring one" trunk with her since she was "try[ing] to be sensible in all undertakings" had to be difficult. "Clothes," she argued, "don't mean so much after all," especially because she "only want[ed] to be presentable—for all occasions." That meant that her "'fussy' days" were now "gone," replacing the "days when I was interested in spectacular things." The cleansing of herself of those desires meant that she could "appreciate the real honest-to-goodness things that are seemingly worthwhile."[55] A missionary had been born.

As the war dragged on and further delayed her trip, she tried to maintain her composure but found it far more difficult than she had expected. "I am so anxious for the war to close and normalcy return so that I can still make the trip to you safely," she wrote Xuma in one of her last letters in the year. Eager for reassurance that they would eventually be together, she implored him to "write and tell me about the plans you had made for me before the war started."[56] She just couldn't stop thinking about the war, though. Admitting that she was so "war conscious these days," she "listen[ed] to the radio for all types of war news. Also read all the papers available." And she worried particularly about Germany's proximity to South Africa: "This a.m. I see Germany is operating near South Africa. Too bad! Are the people there much concerned?"[57] The people in South Africa were concerned, but Xuma was devoting most of his time to ensuring that his bride-to-be could come to South Africa soon. Time was of the essence, so he moved quickly. On March 21, 1940, Xuma made a payment of $410 to the Atlanta University School of Social work through the American Board Mission account for her.[58] A week later, he wrote to L. Brink in the Department of Interior about "re-authorising them to grant visa to Miss Madie B. Hall to enter the Union. The matter is of greatest urgency, as the boat is likely to sail any date now."[59]

In early April, Hall ended her studies at the Atlanta School of Social Work after learning "from the United States government that if I could be in New York in two weeks time, there would be a ship that I could take." Everything moved quickly thereafter. The authorities "were making all the arrangements," primarily because "at those times [of war] you couldn't tell the position of ships and what ships were in and where—when they were going and things like that." The urgency and secrecy meant that she had little time to bid her family and friends a final farewell, finalize some financial matters, and pack. Listed in the Census enumerated on April 25, 1940, as the head of a household that consisted of both sisters Edna and Willie and her nephew, Harold, she was assured that her family would remain intact in spite of her absence. The close presence of Leroy (listed as Le Roy in the Census) and his wife, Eleanor, across the street fortified her assurance as well. And with the transaction of a piece of property that involved a trustee of the Winston-Mutual Life Insurance Company and her sister Willie completed, she finally felt satisfied with the dismantling of her American life.[60]

But there was still an annoying interest in her relationship with Xuma. Louise Ballou Gow, the American wife of Francis Herman Gow, a prominent South African American-educated African Methodist Episcopal minister, was the latest. She, unlike the others, however, did not attack Hall but instead sounded the alarm about Xuma. Writing from Richmond, Virginia, on March 26, 1940, Gow noted that she "would very much like to talk to" Hall, since she had learned "that you may be going out to marry Dr. Xuma." She was so concerned that she cautioned Hall, "Look around you carefully first before you marry. Things are very, very different from here and you may not like it." The long-distance courtship between Hall and Xuma, Gow implied, had not been under the best circumstances for her to acquaint herself properly with Xuma. Advising her to take a year of "courtship" while in South Africa, she would have a better chance "to know your future husband." "I would advise this to anyone marrying here or abroad but particularly abroad!" she insisted.[61]

Gow assured Hall that she was not a "busy body"; rather, she was "a kind, soft-hearted young woman" with fifteen years of marriage behind her. "This is the first time in my life that I've written a letter like this—but there is so much at stake," she declared. Duty bound to warn Hall about "what others express to me but dare not write," it was clear that she had gathered a great deal of information about Hall. Gow described South Africa as "a delightful country" and noted that "there is a great opportunity for service." She knew that Hall was a teacher and admired her accomplishments, but Gow also surmised that it might not be enough to sustain a marriage to Xuma. "Now I hope that you're a strong-willed, self reliant girl who is able to stand up to a man," she stated. "If you can do that then I'd say go because Dr. Xuma is a fine young man." But she warned that if Madie demonstrated weakness and dependence, then she would not be happy because Xuma was "a tyrant, an autocrat. There, it's out! We all know it."[62]

Gow may have deemed Xuma an autocrat, but Hall saw him as a man who was so sympathetic to her emotional fear of making the long journey alone that he supplied her with the name, address, and telephone number of Ruth Cowles, a nurse with deep ties to South Africa, to be her travel companion. A white American with a home base in Los Angeles, Cowles, who listed missionary for the church as her occupation in 1930, had been on a year's leave and was making plans to return to South Africa.[63] With Cowles's contact information in hand, Hall headed to New York City where she had first met Xuma and began focusing on passage to South Africa.

* * *

When she arrived in New York as a guest at the home of longtime friends Charles and Alva Kimbrough, the city's elite Black society demonstrated quite an interest in her, who she was marrying, and where she was going. The popular Black newspaper *New York Amsterdam News* dubbed her a "popular socialite-teacher from Winston-Salem, N. C." The article essentially disconnected her from her long-term and skillful devotion to building organizations that assisted the Black community and deprived readers of learning about her passionate dedication to helping poor and troubled girls. She was simply the woman whose "destination is Johannesburg where she is to become the bride of Dr. Alfred B. Xuma, a leading physician shortly after her arrival there on May 18." To be sure, the article was not completely inaccurate. Hall indeed embraced her socialite life, attending teas and socials and playing bridge. Even her time in New York added substance to the claim. Friends and acquaintances held a number of social events, including the one at the Les Jolie Huit Bridge Club where she was among the "specially invited guests." It was one of the social events of the year. Many of those who attended accompanied her on board the Holland America line ship *M. V. Zaandam* that was destined for Cape Town, Singapore, and the Netherlands East Indies on Saturday, April 27, 1940, for a "delightful party" hosted by Charles Kimbrough.[64]

Hall must have fondly remembered the gaiety of the event as the ship pulled out of New York Harbor and embarked on its twenty-day voyage across the Atlantic. She must also have been pleased that Ruth Cowles was among the passengers joining her on a journey to a new continent, country, and life.[65]

PART III

South Africa

CHAPTER 6

"I Had to Do Something for Women Here"

On Thursday, May 16, 1940, the last day of the trip on the *Zaandam*, the twenty-seven passengers dined on a multicourse "farewell dinner," and on the following day the ship pulled into Cape Town Harbor. Hall and several other passengers disembarked.[1] For a moment, she wondered if she would recognize Xuma since the last time that she had physically seen him was in the fall of 1937. Ruth Cowles's presence certainly provided comfort since she could rely on her to identify him, but neither of them was prepared for what happened next. First, Xuma was not among the crowd at the dock waiting to greet her. Second, Cowles had booked passage on a train and was anxious to leave but quite worried about Hall being left by herself. Although Hall was very worried that Xuma was not there, she assured Cowles that she would be okay and instructed her to leave. But she really was not okay. Standing alone on the dock in an unfamiliar country, she was overcome with the feeling that she had made a terrible mistake.[2]

As she was trying to come to grips with her predicament, a staff person at the dock approached her with the news that Xuma had phoned and revealed that he had been in a car accident. He assured her that Xuma was not hurt, that he expressed concern about her, and that he "asked one of us to go out and get you and take you in—that you were probably alone." She followed the staff person inside, where she received tea and cookies. By the time Xuma arrived, she claimed that her doubts about him had faded, and she finally felt that "everything was alright." Still, the initial meeting between the two of them must have been quite awkward and grew more so when she discovered that because of the late hour, they could not be married until the next day. As a result, Hall's first night in South Africa was spent with her fiancé securing overnight accommodations for them in a hotel.[3]

The calamitous new beginning for the couple continued the following day. Around ten thirty in the morning, they went to the government offices in Cape Town to register and marry in a civil ceremony. It took far longer than anticipated, so the subsequent church wedding that Xuma had arranged could not begin until sometime near noon. When they finally arrived at the church, there "wasn't a single person inside." Xuma explained to her that many of his friends, patients, and acquaintances in the area had been waiting for them, but they were mostly "working people" who "took their lunch hour to come to the church," and because "we were so long coming they had to go back to work." Remarkably, neither she nor Xuma was deterred in committing their lives to each other. The minister united them in marriage in the empty church, and afterward Hall decided to direct her own postwedding production by playing the "Wedding March" and "Oh Promise Me" while her new husband sang. In the end, "it was," she asserted, "a beautiful thing."[4]

Afterward, they embarked on a sightseeing tour "all around Cape Town" and had lunch at the hotel. They departed from Cape Town early the next morning and headed to Johannesburg on the train. Upon arrival they toured Johannesburg before Xuma finally took Madie Hall Xuma to his home at 85 Toby Street in Sophiatown. His new wife met her eight-year-old stepdaughter, Elizabeth, and her six-year-old stepson, Alfred Jr., for the first time. Xuma then began preparations to introduce her to his community and the rest of his family. He first invited guests to their home for a "Welcome Supper (In honour of Mrs. A. B. Xuma)" on Monday evening, May 20. Days later the announcement of his marriage appeared in the nationally distributed *Bantu World* newspaper. Xuma then took Hall Xuma to meet his family in the Transkei. His brother Ben led the celebration in welcoming the "Mother of Assemblies" to the family.[5]

Determined to integrate his new bride into his social network, Xuma quickly began introducing her to a number of his friends, such as Black South African Mina Soga, the president of the National Council of African Women, and white Europeans Ray E. Phillips, a minister and prominent figure in the YMCA, and his wife, Cora Phillips, an activist in the YWCA, as well as John David Rheinallt Jones, the head of South African Institute of Race Relations, developed in 1929, and his wife, Edith Rheinallt Jones, a member of the NCAW.[6] He also ensured that she was welcomed into the Black community. The "Welcome reception" held in her honor took place in the Doornfontein suburb on a Sunday in August and included speeches from some of the most distinguished women and men in the area. By the fall, she was in great demand. For example, in October 1940 she was the featured speaker at the home of Edith Rheinallt Jones where the Bantu Nurses Association had a meeting. She spoke on the familiar topic "What Negro Women Are Doing in America."[7] In November the Johannesburg and District Sunday School Union invited her to be the speaker for the organization's convention for Sunday-school workers. The group expected her to give a talk called "The Dawn of Religion in the Mind of the Child" or some other title that reflected "something on the religious influences that are, or may be, exerted upon the mind of the pre-school child." Later that month, she shared the podium with two other presenters for the Daughters of Africa meeting held at an AME church in Alexandra Township.[8]

Also among the list of growing public engagements was Hall Xuma's presentation at the Wilberforce Library Society. Established in 1905 by the former alumni of Wilberforce University in Ohio in the United States Charlotte Manye Maxeke and her husband, Marshall Maxeke, the Wilberforce Institute in Evaton provided educational and training opportunities to Black South Africans and emphasized Black self-help and self determination. Alfred Xuma had a vested interested in the school's success and became a member of the board of trustees in 1933. So it was quite fitting that his new bride, who espoused the self-help philosophy as well, informed the friendly audience about the "the American Negro and his progress." In the presentation, she argued that the "tragedy" of American slavery "did not lie in the fact that the slave worked long hours; that he had too little of food and clothing; that he was often flogged or even that he was sometimes sold away from his family." Rather, "The tragedy lay in the fact that from infancy he was so conditioned and trained by precept and the collective expectation of his world that he came to believe in his own inferiority and to accept his servile status as a matter of course." Freedom, she insisted, offered African Americans the means to prove self-worth, "to pull himself up" and throw off the shackles of servitude and the emotional scar of inferiority.[9]

Publicly Hall Xuma presented a picture of confidence, but privately she was struggling to acclimate to her new home. The transition had been so difficult that years later, she admitted, "I think I must have cried for three months after I arrived." Everything about her life there was different. She endured the indignity of being "called 'Annie,' like all African women were, by young shop assistants" and found that "there were no facilities for 'us' in the city. No cups of tea, no place to rest, no light lunches." The treatment and lack of services were "hard to accept," and so was the fact that some of "her township neighbours were suspicious of her American origin."[10]

However, retreating from public life or giving up on her marriage to return to the United States did not appeal to her, so she continued to cultivate a circle of Black and white female friends and utilized the tools available to her to acclimate to the country. She applied to the master's program at the University of Witwatersrand in social studies as a means of learning about the people, the history, and the customs. Informed, however, by the registrar that the program "has not yet been formally approved by the Senate" and that she needed to make an appointment with the department head to discuss the matter, she changed her major and entered the anthropology program instead.[11] Writing to her friend Anne Spencer in Lynchburg, Virginia, that the courses were "very interesting and most helpful in trying to understand the life and customs of the African people," she also had an eye to investigating the linkages between African Americans and Africans. She hoped that when she returned to the United States, she would "have been able to do some research that will throw some light on the connection between the African music and the Negro Spirituals."[12]

As Hall Xuma made steady progress toward adjustment, her husband engaged in a busy schedule of his own in his medical practice and a multitude of other endeavors. They included an array of speaking presentations, a physician position at the Crogman Community Clinic, board membership on the South African National Council of YMCA–proposed School of Social Work that would specifically train non-Europeans social workers, and membership on the executive committee of the Bantu Men's Social Centre that had been offering recreational and cultural space to Black youth and the Black elite since it opened in 1924.[13] More important, Steven Gish argues, "Among the African community, Xuma's political stock had risen steadily since his return from the United States and Europe in late 1938. He had come to be admired by more than just the handful of individuals who led the major African political organizations. Africans from all over the Witwatersrand—and beyond—increasingly began to look to Xuma for inspiration and leadership in 1939–1940."[14]

His most important opportunity to fulfill that mission came when Stephen Oliphant, a member of the western Cape branch of the African National Congress requested Xuma's permission to place his name in nomination for the presidency of the ANC in May 1940, a few days before Hall Xuma arrived in Cape Town. Xuma had affirmed his commitment to the nomination verbally, and less than a month after his marriage he responded to Oliphant's request for a written statement of acceptance to be nominated, affirming that he had "no objection in allowing my name to go forward as your candidate for the presidency of the African National Congress" and signaling that his wife supported him. He won the three-year president-general post vote at the December meeting in Bloemfontein, and his ascendancy to the presidency of the ANC moved him from being one of the most prominent Black men in South Africa to being the most powerful Black political figure in the country. And as Xuma's wife, Hall Xuma was thrust into the national and international spotlight as part of the "unofficial 'first family'" of Black South Africa.[15]

Previously known as the South African Native National Congress, the ANC had been around for nearly three decades by the time Xuma became the president. Established in 1912 in Bloemfontein and renamed the ANC in 1923, the organization's primary mission was to fight the white South African government's institutionalization of systematic discriminatory policies that oppressed Black South Africans. The organization's strategies, tactics, and successes continue to be debated by scholars, but by the 1930s an ineffective and conservative ANC leadership caused the membership to suffer a sharp decline and inactivity threatened the existence of the organization. As a result, Xuma's wartime leadership faced staggering challenges. The ANC financial coffers were virtually empty. Accustomed to a weak central leadership, many of the branches refused to abide by his directives initially. Xuma met that defiance with resolve. Fueled by his own personal encounters with racism and discrimination, he was determined to use the ANC as the vehicle to reshape the direction of Black life in South Africa. For example, on his way to the ANC meeting in Bloemfontein in December, he was pulled over by a white police officer, who demanded to see his pass. During the encounter, the officer slapped him. Xuma filed charges against the officer, who was fined.[16] The fine, Xuma knew, would neither remedy nor stop the unrelenting white racism, but a strong Black political organization similar to the NAACP in the United States might. With that goal in mind, he implemented an organizational structure and launched a fund-raising drive that included the solicitation of grants and the initiation of publicity and recruitment campaigns to increase membership. Under his guidance, the organization embarked on a goal of signing up a million members in 1942 that included young people and women.[17]

Hall Xuma found an opportunity to utilize her husband's ANC presidency as a vehicle through which she could assist him and build a strong coalition of Black activist women. In the summer of 1943, she launched a campaign to help put the ANC on sound financial footing. The fund-raising enterprise mimicked the popular productions that she had showcased in Winston-Salem and brought to life the speech that she had given before the Wilberforce Library Society. She wrote, produced, and starred in the extravaganza *American Negro Revue (The Progress of a Race)* that initially ran two nights in June and two nights in July 1943. As the master of ceremonies, her husband headed a production that shared remarkable similarities with the popular early-twentieth-century publication *Progress of a Race; or, The Remarkable Advancement of the American Negro, from the Bondage of Slavery, Ignorance, and Poverty to the Freedom of Citizenship, Intelligence, Affluence, Honor and Trust.*[18] Her adaptation included eight scenes and opened with "History of the Race" and a musical chorus singing "Tis Moro" and "Danny Boy," followed by a solo of

"Love, Here Is My Heart." Scene 2 featured act 1, or the "Slavery Scene," that highlighted Black life in the southern United Sates. Blacks were captured and sold where the vast majority lived and worked on plantations. It was not until after emancipation that true "Family Life" for African Americans emerged. In scene 4, act 2, the fictitious family that she created bore some similarities to her own. There was a postman father, a housewife mother, a dentist son, a dressmaker daughter, and a young daughter and son who went to school. Scene 6 featured a soloist singing the Negro spirituals "Deep River" and "Lord What a Morning," and a chorus sang "King Jesus Is a'Listening." The show ended with "Noted Personages of the Afro-American Race" that included scientist and inventor George Washington Carver, actors Paul Robeson and Hattie McDaniel, and U.S. congressman Arthur W. Mitchell.[19]

The first showing was such a hit that the flyer for the second performance at the Bantu Men's Social Centre was "By Public Demand." Moreover, patrons were encouraged to book early, because one hundred people were turned away at the last show. Still, in his critique of the production Maurice Cohen complained about its length, remarking, "Some items were somewhat on the long side. For instance, the mannequin parade featured too many models." In response Hall Xuma highlighted her understanding of the racialized politics of the country by pointing out to him, "Africans cannot go home from an evening's entertainment just when they like, due to curfews and pass regulations. For that reason, the show was prolonged where otherwise it would have been cut." On the other hand, white minister Ray Phillips, the head of the two-year-old Jon H. Hofmeyr School of Social Work, and his wife, Cora, who saw the first show never mentioned the length and thought the production was "making an excellent contribution to an understanding of Negro and African Life on the part of both South African Europeans and Africans." Other whites and Blacks agreed with their assessment. Ticket sales were so high that Hall Xuma bragged to Anne Spencer that the four shows "brought us in the handsome sum of £300 nearly $1500 in American money" and "more than justified us for our efforts in trying to do a little bit for the people."[20]

With that kind of success, she decided on a third showing. As excited by the prospect as she, her husband requested that city hall be the venue for a Sunday production in Kimberly in mid-December. Unfortunately, neither city hall nor the Sunday date was available, but when the ANC annual conference was moved from Kimberly to Bloemfontein, the show was repeated in Bloemfontein on the two nights of December 14 and 15, 1943. This time, though, it appeared to have been less profitable. When the receiver of revenue in Bloemfontein notified the Xumas that because "they failed to apply for Exemption in respect of Entertainment for Tax" within the four-day time

FIGURE 6.1. Madie Hall Xuma began raising money to replenish the nearly empty coffers of the African National Congress soon after her husband was elected president of the organization. This is an advertisement for the second presentation of the extravaganza *American Negro Revue* that she produced and directed. Her picture appears in the upper right-hand corner. Courtesy of Historical Papers Research Archive, University of the Witwatersrand, South Africa.

window for the performances, they were liable for the license fee and the entertainment tax and were to remit them promptly, Xuma tried to get an exemption on the grounds that the show was performed for the ANC "for no personal gain" and that the organization had actually "lost money in the promotion." He insisted that he was using ANC "reserve funds" to pay the tax and the license but still hoped that there would be "reconsideration" about the order for repayment because it was "a heavy blow on this charitable organization."[21]

The lack of profit or the unexpected interaction with the segregationist government did not deter Hall Xuma. The broad press coverage and semi-success of the *American Negro Revue* overrode any concerns she might have had about pushing forward with a different kind of second production. This one resembled the religious Easter plays that dramatized the biblical messages that she had so often showcased in Winston-Salem. Marc Connelly's play *The Green Pastures* that also became a popular film featured an all-Black cast playing biblical figures, including God, Noah, Moses, Adam, and Eve. It toured throughout southern states like North Carolina and earned high praise. The Sunday *Raleigh News and Observer* headline about the film, for example, screamed "Hollywood Turned Heaven Loose for This Picture." The industry, author Paul Harrison wrote, "waited five years before anybody could make up his mind to film the magnificent fable. To be sure, the entire south had received it with cheers, except one town in west Texas. And publications which never in their histories had printed a picture of a Negro took down the barriers for this play, because it presented the type of Negro for whom most southerners hold a real affection." The *Franklin Times* in Louisburg concluded, "Now, at last brought to the screen with a cast of 800, Marc Connelly's Pulitzer Prize–winning play seems destined to arouse more widespread interest than any other film production in a decade." And, indeed, cities throughout the state clamored to show the film. The "Premier Showing" accompanied by "Hall Johnson's Famous Negro Chorus Singing 25 Spirituals" opened on Sunday, July 12, 1936, in Raleigh. R. B. Harrison, who appeared as "De Lawd" in the play that toured the country, gave a presentation at Guilford College in Greensboro, and the film version began playing in the city on August 12, 1936.[22]

There was also controversy about the film version in particular. During Hall Xuma's first term at Columbia University in New York in the fall of 1936, numerous articles appeared in both the *New York Times* and the *New York Amsterdam News* recounting serious concerns. A number of places in the world were also banning it. The Toronto Board of Motion Picture censors banned its showing in theaters because it was "sacrilegious." It met a similar fate in Port of Spain, Trinidad, but strong protest and an appeal forced the board's decision to be overturned because "Negroes, contending the original decision of island censors was prompted by racial prejudice." The London film censors were so conflicted that they deliberated for five months about the fate of the film showing. They ultimately came to the conclusion that unlike the play that was banned in 1931 for "impersonation of the Deity on stage," the film could be shown.[23]

Hall Xuma ignored all of the controversy even as the South African government demanded that she do something that she never had to do in the United States when she produced a show—ask to be granted permission from the Department of Interior. Her formal letter of request, however, proved not to be enough. She had to "furnish this Department with a copy" of the play before a decision could be made.[24] After she submitted the play, the Department of Interior concluded that "the Minister has, in terms of Section 9(1) of Act No. 28 of 1931, decided that as the play is calculated to give offence to the religious convictions or feeling of a section of the public, he is unable to agree to the presentation thereof."[25] As Iris Berger notes, the decision not only rested on the declaration that it was an affront to "religious convictions," but, more significantly, revealed the clear understanding that the "South African authorities correctly perceived the political implications of blacks appropriating Biblical legend." Like she had done in the production of *White House Mock Wedding* that placed African Americans at the highest echelons of American government, Hall Xuma's production of *Green Pastures* would have positioned Africans as the supreme Christian authorities in an environment where white Europeans demonized them daily. This was not lost on government officials. For the first time since she had arrived in the country, she faced the force of a government resolute in its determination to "silence potentially subversive ideas."[26]

* * *

The fierce pushback from the South African government coincided with major shifts in the demographic movement of the majority Black African population. The loss of land through segregationist policies such as the Natives' Land Act of 1913 coupled with the hunt for employment encouraged an unprecedented number of rural Africans to migrate into urban spaces, which contributed to the erosion of family structures. The institutionalization of racial segregation in some areas also pushed Black Africans into specifically defined spaces and transformed urban centers like Johannesburg. Accurate census figures are difficult to obtain for the number of Black residents who resided in the city before 1950 when the total population had swelled to more than 910,000, but one source suggests that in 1946 more than 387,000 Blacks lived in the city. While the vast majority were men, nearly 140,000 of them were women. In the small western areas that included Sophiatown, where Hall Xuma and her family resided, 54,000 Black Africans, 3,000 Coloureds, and 1,500 Indians were packed into the confined space. Poverty and crime plagued the overcrowded area. The Xumas were one of the few residents who owned their property, as home ownership stood at only 2 percent by 1950.[27]

The Black women and girls who migrated to the town looking for work were often single with few resources and no access to adequate housing. Most lacked adequate education as well as appropriate recreational outlets and the resources and tools to advance the trajectory of their lives. In Winston-Salem, Hall Xuma had utilized the Black YWCA in coordination with the white YWCA to address some of those issues. The YWCA in South Africa, however, had no official Black branches, so she first looked to Mina Soga and members of the National Council of African Women as the vehicle to become actively engaged in social welfare. Established in 1937, the primary purpose of the NCAW centered on tackling social welfare issues such as education, health, children, vocational training, and the home. The mission attracted women throughout the area to the organization. By January 1940, for example, in Johannesburg alone, eighty-five clubs affiliated with the NCAW.[28]

Longtime activist Charlotte Maxeke was elected the first president. By the time that Hall Xuma arrived in South Africa, however, Maxeke had died (October 1939), and Soga had taken the reins of the NCAW. Educated at a private Presbyterian mission school, Soga became a teacher and was a strong supporter of church missions in Africa.[29] Soga welcomed Hall Xuma in part because of her friendship with Alfred Xuma but also because Hall Xuma served as a key figure in solidifying the link between Black South African women and Black women in the United States. Hall Xuma's friend Mary McLeod Bethune had established the National Council of Negro Women in 1935 and had already extended the transnational reach of the organization to South Africa when she contacted Soga in 1940 about forging an alliance between the NCAW and the NCNW. In the letter, Bethune noted, "We should like very much to have the National Council of African Women become a part of the National Council of Negro Woman–incorporated so that together we could work for world freedom for all women." Ultimately, as Grace V. Leslie argues, Bethune's outreach to the NCAW demonstrated her belief "that the NCNW's fight against racism and sexism transcended national boundaries."[30]

Hall Xuma's presence in South Africa centered her in that fight and helped promote Bethune's interest. In July 1941 when the NCAW held an interim meeting in Port Elisabeth to discuss a number of administrative issues that included the logistics and fund-raising efforts for the Johannesburg conference scheduled in December 1941, she joined white European member Edith Rheinallt Jones in taking the lead of a local committee of nine women. The two leaders had the "power to add" to the committee and ask delegates "to pay a Conference fee of which the amount would be settled when hospitality arrangements were further advanced."[31] Moreover, for the December 1942 conference, Soga wrote to her friend Alfred Xuma, asking him to "allow your dear wife to attend our conference which starts on the 16th December to the 19th" rather than accompany him to his ANC Conference. "Please don't decline," she begged. "You know that this part of the country is very ignorant—white & black alike, and it would be a treat for them to see an American Negress *so* polished and educated. It will enthuse your African sisters and change the attitude of some Europeans toward us & make them see what we can be, given the opportunity." To facilitate her goal, Soga wanted Hall Xuma to be a keynote speaker at the conference because "Our woman-hood need a push up & they must see a model of their own flesh & blood or should I say—colour?"[32]

The NCAW may have presented itself as promoting racial uplift, but the organization's history of aligning with prominent white European men and women like Rheinallt Jones engendered both praise and criticism. On the one hand, the interracial cooperation that linked the NCAW to institutions like the Jan H. Hofmeyr School of Social Work that had been established in January 1941 won high praise. Supported by the South African National Council of YMCA and funding from other private sources that included the Carnegie Corporation, the school was headed by Ray E. Phillips. One of the members of the committee who worked with Phillips and oversaw the development of the school was Alfred Xuma. The need for the school was so great that the *Bantu World* editorialized, "The impact of Western civilization upon us has uprooted us from the anchor of the ancient life of our race, and thus created social problems that can only be dealt with by trained men and women. It is absolutely essential that at this stage of our development we should have the guidance of men and women with expert knowledge."[33]

The first educational facility in South Africa to focus specifically on provid-ing professional social work training to Africans, the Hofmeyr School was first located in the Bantu Men's Social Centre. Its primary objectives shared remarkable similarities with the kind of training that Hall Xuma had under-taken at the Atlanta School of Social Work. In the early planning stages of development, student attention was directed to three areas of service in the two-year program of study. The first were recreational facilities, such as boys and girls clubs, and community centers. The second was in welfare reform, such as probation officers and child-welfare investigators. The third was to create a professional force of career secretaries for organizations such as the YMCA, YWCA, and social centers and sports clubs. Students often performed their fieldwork in places like the Bantu Men's Social Centre and the NCAW.[34]

On the other hand, the interracial coalition raised questions about the dominant role of white women like Rheinallt Jones. Even Soga, on occasion, found herself interrogating Rheinallt Jones's motives. But there was also concern about the economic and educational class of the members of the NCAW as well as their lack of political engagement.[35] Hall Xuma, in particular, invited harsh scrutiny. A nonnative American-educated Black woman, she acknowledged an interracial affinity that symbolized for some a clear lack of understanding the nuanced intricacies of South African white supremacy and the kind of paternalism it espoused. Boasting in later years that she had both Black and white friends in North Carolina and that in South Africa the overwhelming majority of her friends were white, most of whom "were people at the top," she appeared out of step with the struggles of the majority of Black South Africans. And, in what appeared to be a lack of interest in learning a native language, she seemed unwilling to immerse herself in native South African culture because she viewed herself as their superior. While most South Africans spoke English, they took pride in holding on to their native language. Her husband's language was Xhosa. According to Hall Xuma, however, she inquired about learning the language, but it was her husband who saw no value in the idea. He told her that it would be a "waste of time" because "every African you meet speaks English."[36]

In the end, Hall Xuma made no apologies for her race, class, nationality, or ideas, but the scrutiny must still have been unnerving. Americans Max and Susie Yergan had faced similar criticisms during their time in the country. A primary complaint against them was that Susie and Max "did not socialize with the African staff at the college [South African Native College or more commonly known as Fort Hare], tried unsuccessfully to enroll their children in the segregated white school in Alice, and never learned Xhosa, the language of the Africans among whom they lived for more than twenty years."[37] Hall Xuma's marriage to a prominent native Black South African may have provided her with more legitimacy, but it could not completely shield her. One researcher found that in some cases, "simple folks are afraid to receive her in their home" because of their own embarrassment about "how poorly I am furnished." Another woman (Beauty Selela of the Vaal YWCA) revealed that when she and several other women first met her, they "were a little afraid when we heard that she was American, because we thought she was of a different culture." But, she added, "In those days we were feeling very inferior. . . . But Mrs [sic] Xuma made us feel comfortable about being ourselves. . . . She brought light to black women."[38]

As a Black woman of privilege, Hall Xuma believed, as her parents had taught her, that the Black elite was key to moving the Black community forward, so she ignored the disapproving assessments and continued her engagement with the NCAW. More significantly, the year after she arrived in the country, she decided that she "had to do something for women here" so began the process, activist Ellen Kuzwayo argues, "to develop women she did not know, women whose language was completely strange to her," by inviting several to her home. They, by Black South African standards, were privileged women whose ranks as teachers, church workers, and housewives set them apart from the masses and in many ways mirrored the club women in Winston-Salem. She quickly won them over. By 1941 the group had formally established the Zenzele Club, elected Joanna Mabuza the first president, and adopted the motto "Lifting as We Climb" of the National Association of Colored Women's clubs as theirs.[39]

Like the NACW, Hall Xuma wanted the club to be active in the community, in large part because she had been haunted by an encounter with a woman from Sophiatown when she first arrived in South Africa who asked her "to read a letter" that she had. Hall Xuma discovered that the letter was not written in English, so she told the woman that "she'd come to the wrong person because the letter was in one of the African languages." The woman refused to be thwarted in her endeavor and encouraged Hall Xuma "to hurry and learn the language so that I could read the letter for her." Saddened that the woman lacked the education to be able to read, Hall Xuma in turn told the woman that "she should hurry up and learn to read" on her own. The encounter made such an impression that she "made up her mind to do something about the local women—something to encourage them to stand on their own feet instead of depending on other people too much." The Zenzele Club became the vehicle.[40]

Hall Xuma did not create a new idea with the formation of the Zenzele Club, but she did revitalize a self-help thread that had been familiar to Black women for nearly two decades. Some form of Zenzele or "help yourself"/"self-improvement" clubs had been operating since the 1920s in mostly rural areas with a focus on self-improvement and community development. For example, Florence Jabavu, the wife of the D. D. T. Jabavu, established the African Women's Self-Improvement Association in the town of Alice in 1927. Florence Jabavu's primary goal was to educate rural women about the practical skills necessary to maintain their homes and communities. Cooking, sewing, farming techniques, and hygiene headed the agenda of the organization. Others would follow a similar route. Charlotte Maxeke promoted Black women's affiliation with homemakers' clubs in Johannesburg, advocated for the preservation and stability of the family, and advanced the idea of planting vegetable gardens. Black American women like Susie Yergan also engaged in the self-help movement. She established the United Home-Makers Club before she and her husband, Max, permanently left South Africa. The goals were quite similar to and affiliated with the African Women's Home Improvement Association.[41]

Like the NCAW, the class and professional status of the members in the Zenzele Club branded it "a select society." The club certainly served a particular niche and became so popular in that classed circle that within two years, the number of members jumped from six to more than thirty. The group held regular monthly meetings and initiated a number of activities. Hall Xuma revealed the role of the club in a letter to Anne Spencer in 1943 as primarily a means of teaching women essential domestic skills. At the gatherings, she noted, "We learn all sorts of things such as cooking, sewing, handcrafts, and the like." One of the most enjoyable aspects of the club for her was teaching the women about gardening. "Only yesterday at our monthly meeting I was surprised to hear the members asking for guidance in flower gardening," she wrote. Since spring was near, she continued, "We are therefore planning a trip to a nursery where we can get expert help along that line." The group also held workshops and public forums. For example, in February 1943, Hall Xuma inquired about utilizing classroom space at the Anglican Church Mission in Sophiatown for a function on a Sunday at the end of March for that purpose.[42]

Over the next decade, ten affiliated branches were established. In addition to Sophiatown, there was a Zenzele Club in Orlando by 1947. The one in Witbank began operating in 1948. The organization met on alternate Saturdays, and the membership rose from eight to twenty-four. Some of the activities in the club included "a Cake Bazaar" and demonstrations in how to make "scones with sour milk, biscuits and even home-made condensed milk" as well as earrings and brooches. The Johannesburg branch was even more active than the Witbank branch. In addition to demonstrations in baking, embroidery work, earrings, and brooches, members over time learned how to arrange flowers and ferment juices. "Refresher Courses" for all of them were provided in various locations. Members also raised funds for a Christmas party by giving a concert at the Bantu Men's Social Centre and by holding a silver tea.[43]

Another critical aspect of the club was the institutionalization of linkages with Black American women in the NCNW. Hall Xuma continued to receive some of the same kind of material that the NCNW sent to the NCAW long after she first established the Zenzele Club in 1941. She, in turn, shared the material with Zenzele Club women, acknowledging, "It really is an inspiration to our people here to know and learn about the Negroes overseas. These articles coming through are very helpful to me for I am able to show them and tell them of current news about our people there [in the United States]," she acted as the liaison between the club and the NCNW and sustained transnational ties.[44]

Zenzele branch members developed strong emotional ties to Hall Xuma and appreciated her foresight and interest in their success. One Johannesburg branch member had been so inspired and enriched by the club that she wrote, "It is rather difficult for a member like myself to be able to say just howmuch [sic] she has gained from Johannesburg Women Zenzele Club, yet on the other hand it is equally ungrateful for me to fail to mention just howmuch [sic] the club has improved me." The club, she continued, "has improved me Socially and mentally. It has removed inferiority complex in my person. It has taught me to work cooperatively. It has enabled me to depend on myself regarding Home management. It has taught me to rely on myself when duty calls."[45] Betty Motsepe also expressed her appreciation: "I feel that it is my duty to express my appreciation of the work you have done for us. When I joined the Zenzele Club I did not know any of the things you taught us. I feel that all the time that I spent every Saturday attending the meeting brought me a bit amount of knowledge which I can fit in my life."[46] The Witbank and Minaar branches were especially "grateful to her for her inspiration and very wise guidance." They thanked "her for her untinted [sic] faith in the ultimate independence of Africans and particularly the faith she has displayed in the totalindependence [sic] of the womanhood of this continent."[47]

In addition to the Zenzele Clubs, Hall Xuma made inroads in other ventures as well. She promoted "pen friendships" and became a member of the Homemakers Club to bridge the gap between rural and urban communities. The information available on the two is limited, so it is unclear whether her association with them had some connection to the Zenzele Clubs or was independent of them. They both, however, were quite popular. After Hall Xuma apparently posted an advertisement in the *Bantu World* about the development of the "pen friendships" program in 1947, responses from Vredefort in the Orange Free Province, Johannesburg, and East London revealed keen interest in the endeavor. One teacher whose hobbies were tennis and reading noted that she had only "my school work, church work and all interests mentioned" to occupy her time, but since she found it "boring to listen to the radio month in & month out," she thought that she would "try Penfriendship [sic]." A man from Johannesburg noted that "I would like to have pen friends as I am a motor mechenic [sic]" and wondered if he "would get an advisor in such a course."[48]

Variations of the Homemakers Club had been operating for some time, and they continued to have broad appeal among women interested in learning about patchwork, beadwork, and hosting tea parties. The main branch that

Hall Xuma belonged to was located in Johannesburg, but there were others in Roodepoort, Evaton, and Vereeniging. The club held exhibitions, awarded prizes, and convened at an annual conference. Hall Xuma cemented her place among Homemakers Club women and was so popular that she was elected the acting secretary for the 1948 conference.[49]

On the surface, Hall Xuma's activism seemed to be solely wedded to social welfare and uplift, but she could never completely be divorced from politics in a country where every act of self-preservation or advancement in the Black community was a political assertion of opposition to racism and discrimination. But her politics was subtle and nonthreatening and initially flowed through the partnership she shared with her husband. Her influence on him could be seen very early in his ANC presidency. During his presidential address in December 1941, for example, he told conference members, "Do not mind being called agitators. Let them call you any names they like but get on the job and see that matters that vitally require attention, Native Health, Native Food, the treatment of Native Children and all those cognate questions that are basic to the Welfare of South Africa."[50] Arguing that the social and economic welfare needs of Black Africans were intertwined with the ANC's agenda ultimately resulted in the organization's membership resolving "That this Conference recommends to the parent body the necessity of reviving the women's sections of the Congress in terms of the provision of the Constitution. Further that women be accorded the same status as men in the classification of membership. That the following means be made to attract the women (a) to make the programme of the Congress as attractive as possible to the women, (b) a careful choice of leadership."[51] The resolution was certainly historic, but entrenched ideas about gender roles in the male bastion of the ANC refused to yield initially, so it took another two years before the organization passed the resolution (December 1943) and recognized that, burdened by race and sex discrimination, African women faced "special disabilities and differences" and "peculiar problems" that were unique to them. While the resolution did not revolutionize or upend the contested gender dynamic within the ANC, women did gain equal voting power with men.[52]

Women's ability to vote empowered Hall Xuma, as she became the first African American president of the African National Congress Women's League. The empowerment, however, did not look on the surface like political engagement, either. Under Hall Xuma's leadership, the actions and work of the women in the ANCWL often mirrored those of her Zenzele Club, blurring the lines between them to such a degree that critics suggested she had so wedded Black women to "fund raising and catering" that she did little to advance the political influence of women of the ANCWL. She certainly played into the criticism when she insisted in interviews that "she persistently avoided anything to do with politics" or "stayed out of politics."[53]

In spite of her repeated denials, she was mired in the gendered, raced, classed, economic, and national politics of the country. In a draft of a May 1944 keynote address to a Bloemfontein audience, she declared that Black unity was the only means of progress and layered it with the names and entrepreneurial successes of Black American women. God, she wrote, understood America represented "a superior environment" that was more "civilized" than the original homeland of Africa and that African Americans "had to be put thru a period of slavery so that he could learn true adversity and hardship." From the depths of that misery, she insisted, they emerged as "a great spiritual force and . . . a united nation." "Nothing," she proclaimed, "is gained or won in isolation," because "to be a great force you must become united."[54]

Although African Americans still had not quite made it to the "promised land," they were headed in that direction because those Blacks who were educated after slavery "didn't wait for another race to pull him up, he set about to do it himself," and "he in turn set out to teach his brothers and sisters and they when they became educated taught others. This is how to moved [sic] along so fast." "So rapid was there [sic] advancement in those few years," she boasted, "their rise has startled the world." As proof, she insisted that African American women and men had enjoyed success in nearly every profession. Among the enterprises established by African Americans, a list she seems to have retrieved from an encyclopedia or history text, she pointed to two thriving entrepreneurial beauty-culture industries founded by Black women. Poro Manufacturing Company, located in St. Louis, Missouri, had been the brainchild of Annie Turnbo Malone. Its plant, she noted, had "modern appliances at a cost of $250,000." The other was Sarah Breedlove, who adopted the name Madam C. J. Walker after marrying Charles J. Walker. The Madam C. J. Walker Manufacturing Company began operating in Indianapolis in 1910. For Hall Xuma, Walker's enterprise demonstrated success, in part, because when she died in 1919, her estate confirmed her commitment to the uplift of the Black community by donating thousands of dollars to charity.[55]

By portraying America as a more conducive and progressive "homeland" for African Americans, she challenged elite Black South Africans to embrace their duty and responsibility to their community. "I find that in this country some of the more fortunate people among our group who have had the opportunity to get and [sic] education, whether it be a degree at a college or university or trade or vocation draw off from the masses and become a class within themselves," she wrote. "If we are going to take that attitude my friends," she insisted, then "we shall not get anywhere as a race. God has given you this opportunity so that you can better serve your fellowman. He has said in the scripture He who would be greatest among men must be the servant of all. We cannot serve if one draw ourselves from the masses. We must give to them and share with them some of the things we have learned ourselves."[56]

Ultimately, it was her husband's forceful push that opened the door for her to broaden women's public activism in the political struggle. When Alfred Xuma sent a formal letter to prominent men soliciting the formation of ANC branches in March 1944, he wrote, "I am also urging the organization of the women into the African Women's League of the Congress," because "without the women we cannot go far."[57] Moreover, in a similar letter to female leaders, he centered women in the discourse about the future of Blacks in South Africa by stating, "The freedom of the African people from oppression and disabilities will depend upon all men and women doing their part." That could be accomplished, he argued, only "by organizing our people into a strong organization for women and through which we may speak." Assuring them that Hall Xuma joined him in his certainty that both the presence and the activism of women were critically important to issues that faced families in the country, he demonstrated his unwavering faith in his wife's leadership. "My wife and I request you to organize the women," he wrote, "so that they can play their part for the abolition of Pass Laws, for better education and feeding of African children, for better wages and houses for African people so that we also can develop good family life like other races." The letter ended with a promise that he and his wife "will visit the area to set up your branch and also for the enrollment of your members."[58]

That same month, Jellicoe Ntshona announced to Xuma that the Western Province Regional Committee had formed an Anti-Pass Committee in Cape Town and scheduled a protest in April 1944. Xuma made plans for him and Hall Xuma to attend. He instructed Ntshona to "take pains to properly organize this meeting so that it be attended by people that matter and people that can influence public opinion" and suggested that "a reasonable group of men and women" meet him and Hall Xuma as they disembarked from the train. They should all have "banners directing attention to the meeting at the City Hall." In the end, though, it was his concern about the marginalization of women in the protest plans that forced him to tell Ntshona, "Do not leave the women behind in any of these meetings."[59]

At the anti-pass conference held May 20–21, 1944, in Johannesburg, Xuma and Hall Xuma were among the five hundred who attended. They participated in discussions about creating anti-pass petitions and circulars that would be distributed throughout the country and about planning a mass demonstration in August. Xuma emerged from the conference as national chair of the anti-pass campaign, and he and Hall Xuma joined the other twenty thousand anti-pass female and male marchers in the streets of the city as the conference ended on a Sunday afternoon.[60]

The couple's unified determination to increase female membership in the ANCWL did not wane during their entire tenure. Three years after the anti-pass march, for example, Xuma responded to an invitation to address the Itireleng Bakgatla Young Women's League (which also seems to be spelled "Itereleng Bakgatla") by writing, "I am interested in your suggestion and my wife is also interested because the African National Congress authorised her to try to organise the African Women's League, the Women's Auxillary [sic] of the African National Congress."[61]

Hall Xuma's presidency of the ANCWL proved useful in other ways as well. When she submitted her application to attend a Social Workers Conference in August 1944, she appeared unsure about whether she would qualify for entry. Ray E. Phillips told her, "The Committee is not too strict in insisting on definite Social Work Organizations being represented only." The best strategy for her to gain access, he suggested, was for her to "apply either as University student of Social Science or as head of Womens [sic] Section of the Congress."[62] His recommendation underscored how significant her role as head of the ANCWL was as a means of integrating herself into the professional community, expanding her knowledge, and advancing women's engagement.

* * *

American interest in the race relations in South Africa never wavered during the war. That was due in part to the Xumas' connections in America and to Black media outlets focused on the continued oppression of Blacks and people of color around the globe. Black newspapers like the *Negro Star* of Wichita, Kansas, for example, reported that Jan Smuts, the prime minister of South Africa, was seriously considering reversing a policy that denied conscripted Black Africans to "bear arms" as the war dragged on, highlighted riots that had erupted in the country because of unfair labor practices and poor pay, and noted a suspension of pass laws in some large cities.[63] The NAACP's journal *Crisis* wrote about Black South Africans who were "turning out thousands of rounds of ammunition a day" to assist with the war effort. And then there was the article "South Africa: A Case for the United Nations" that declared, "The 'worst place in the world' for black people is South Africa, where two million whites hold six and one-half million natives in slavery." L. D. Reddick, the author of the article, linked the authoritarian regime of South Africa to that of Germany and Italy and determined that even when African leaders like Alfred Xuma, D. D. T. Jabavu, G. S. M. Timkulu, and S. B. Ngcobo "condemn the political domination of their people," they were hampered by the minuscule number of seven white liberal Parliament representatives assigned to speak on behalf of millions of native Africans. "It should be remembered," Reddick concluded, "that South Africa and her statesmen are eager to play leading roles in world affairs. Is it too much to insist that those who aspire to influence the peace terms for other nations should first demonstrate their fitness at home? South Africa must not be allowed to annex, as she wants to the African Protectorates of Basutoland, Swaziland and Bechuanaland." He urged the United Nations to "take up the case of fascism in South Africa" and demonstrate to the world that "what President Roosevelt said is true: *that the Four Freedoms and the Atlantic Charter apply to the whole world*."[64]

The article, as it turned out, had been part of a strategically choreographed plan of transnational protest against the South African government initiated by the Council on African Affairs, the new name of the International Committee on African Affairs, in New York. It laid out the strategy and grievances in the "Bill of Rights and the Atlantic Charter from the African's Point of View" that was developed by an ANC coalition committee of twenty-eight members from a wide variety of organizations, associations, and institutions. Adopted at the December 1943 Bloemfontein ANC conference, the document became the mechanism of alerting the world about the persistence of oppression in South Africa.[65]

Keeping the plight of Black South Africans in the news throughout the war made Xuma's trip to America at the end of the war far more forceful and newsworthy. He boarded a plane in Johannesburg on October 21, 1946. After arriving in the United States, he found lodging at the YMCA on West 135th Street in New York, filed a Foreign Agents Registration with the Federal Bureau of Investigation (FBI) in the Department of Justice as required by the act of 1938, and reported in his statement that his purpose was to speak to officials at the United Nations about his opposition to the South African government's annexation of Southwest Africa.[66]

The NAACP and several other organizations welcomed his return to the United States. On November 8, he along with South Africans H. M. Basner, a member of the South African Senate for Africans in the Transvaal and Orange Free State provinces, and H. A. Naidoo and Sorabjee Rustomjee, representatives of Natal Indians, attended a reception at the headquarters of the Council on African Affairs. Among those present were chair Paul Robeson, executive director Max Yergan, W. E. B. DuBois, and members of the NAACP and the Urban League. On November 17, the council sponsored a protest meeting at Abyssinian Baptist Church, where Xuma, joined by a contingent of speakers, spoke to a crowd of three hundred people. And on

November 21, the council took the protest to the South African Consulate in New York, where the group picketed.[67]

Xuma was also awarded the certificate of merit at the African Academy of Arts and Research's "One World" dinner at the Hotel Capitol in New York on November 22 and was one of seven speakers that included Charlotte Hawkins Brown and W. E. B. DuBois. He took part in a discussion in the Schomburg Collection at the New York Public Library that was hosted by W. E. B. Du-Bois and L. D. Reddick on November 26 and joined a large contingent of international guests at a function given by Estelle Massey Riddle, the former president of the National Association of Colored Graduate Nurses, and members of the National Negro Council and Alpha Kappa Alpha Sorority.[68] He also strategically lobbied the United Nations while South African prime minister Jan Smuts was there. His success ended with the United Nations' rejection of South Africa's request to annex territory in Southwest Africa and highlighted the world organization's concern over the oppressive racial policies inflicted on non-European South Africans.[69]

After Xuma returned to South Africa in late December, he and Hall Xuma resumed their busy lives. They also hosted prominent American sociologist George E. Haynes in their home during his monthlong visit in February 1947 as he worked on behalf of the World's Alliance of the YMCA.[70] Then they began preparation for Hall Xuma to travel to the United States for the first time since she had left in April 1940. Unlike Xuma's whirlwind six-week tour, hers would last for nine months. Reconnecting with family, friends, and acquaintances and dealing with family business matters were top priorities. The letter that she had received from an attorney in April 1945 about the sale of family property in Reidsville required immediate attention.[71] Telling him that she did not receive the letter until June 14, 1945, she agreed with the sale of the property, instructed him to give her portion of the money to her sister Edna, and notified him that she would be "coming home now that the war is over" so she would be there to "look after our property in person."[72]

In the seven years that she had spent in South Africa, Hall Xuma had made a remarkable transition. She had arrived in the country in 1940 as a single woman who did not have children and who had no deep personal connection to anyone other than Alfred Xuma. She had since become a wife and a stepmother, created the Zenzele Club, took leadership of the ANCWL, and in the process become one of the most admired and powerful women in the country among Blacks and whites. With assistance from her sister-in-law who lived with them, Hall Xuma raised a son and a daughter devastated by the death of their mother at very young ages. By the end of the war, they were eleven and thirteen, and she had been virtually the only mother that they had ever known. The children embraced her, and she reciprocated. Her daughter, Elizabeth, who was a student at Lovedale when Hall Xuma decided to return to the United States, for example, penned a letter to "Mummy" that wished her "a pleasant journey" and the hope that she "arrive safely at America."[73]

Hall Xuma had acclimated to the environment and the people so well that her two years of anthropology classes at Witwatersrand encouraged her to write a collection of stories about African children. Submitting a request to Charles Scribner and Sons editor Alice Dalgliesh, who had been recommended to Hall Xuma by a former Columbia University Teachers College professor, she asked if Dalgliesh "would consider reading some of these stories and let me know if they have any value for young children particularly in America."[74] Because she already had "two books on the list about Africa," Dalgliesh noted that there was no room to "do another one just at present." She did, however, suggest to Hall Xuma that because "it is very difficult for you to handle the stories at long range," she should consider hiring the agent in New York that she recommended.[75] A book by Hall Xuma does not seem to have ever been published, but the exchange with Dalgliesh revealed America's ongoing interest in Africa and Hall Xuma's desire to become an author and influence the dissemination of information about African children.

More significantly, Hall Xuma had developed meaningful long-term personal relationships. Like her daughter, "My dearest Mummie" was how Zenzele Club member Esther Mohlabi greeted her in the letter she wrote on August 18. So distraught about Hall Xuma's scheduled trip to America, Mohlabi lamented that the "departure is a blow to us" but wished her "a successful journey." She "also hope[d] that when you return to us one day, we shall continue in the same spirit as we did in the past. It is not easy to loose [*sic*] such a prominent person like yourself. I must say, that you have uplifted the social standard of our S. African women. I believe your image will haunt us during your absence."[76] Betty Motsepe, another Zenzele member, wished her "a pleasant journey" and a wonderful vacation. Motsepe was especially looking forward to her return "so that we will also gain from your ties to America as you will bring new ideas back with you."[77]

CHAPTER 7

"Prominent South African Woman Arrives in New York"

Hall Xuma boarded the Pan American flight to America on August 21, 1947. The next day, the *New York Times* reprinted an announcement dispatched from Pretoria, South Africa, about her imminent arrival in the United States under the headline "Mrs. Xuma on Way Here." While primarily highlighting her marriage to Alfred Xuma and the fact that, like her husband's visit the year before, her trip "coincide[d] with the General Assembly of the United Nations," the article also underscored her leadership among South African women. It cited her presidency of the ANCWL and noted that she would attend the International Council of Women (ICW) Conference in Philadelphia.[1]

The Black press also demonstrated a keen interest in her. After she settled at Hotel Theresa in Harlem, reporters from the nationally distributed *Chicago Defender* and the New York–based *People's Voice* set up a series of press conferences. The *Chicago Defender* portrayed Hall Xuma as the same kind of socialite she had represented before leaving the country in 1940. There was no real article initially about her or why her presence in the United States was so important. Instead, readers gazed at a stand-alone photograph with a descriptive caption underneath. Surrounded by symbols of Africa, she was the "AMERICAN WIFE of African physician" on "an extended visit" in the United States. Wearing a "necklace and bracelet" made "of Zulu beads," she seemed to have cooperated with the effort to paint her as more of a socialite than a political figure. She stood looking directly into the camera with her left arm and hand resting on top of "a handsome Kaross, a farewell gift made of several skins including a leopard's," and the right hand holding a "gorgeous ostrich plume." The cost of the plume, the caption stated, equaled about forty dollars in U.S. currency, but "Fifth Avenue, New York, would ask much more."

Three weeks elapsed before the *Defender* published an article that articulated Hall Xuma's substantive remarks about how things were "growing worse for all non-whites" in South Africa.[2]

The New York–based *People's Voice* where her friend Max Yergan was a prominent staff member, on the other hand, headlined its article "Prominent South African Woman Arrives in New York." For the politically leftist paper, Hall Xuma symbolized the postwar fusion of the burgeoning African American civil rights movement, global Black oppression, and the Cold War assault on freedom.[3] In that role, she instructed readers about the racial hierarchical divisions of "Europeans, colored people, Indians and natives—or South Africans," the problems that the majority non-European population faced, and the ways in which the "different regulations set by law . . . keep them from uniting." She told readers about the ways in which the government's strategy and tactic of segregation shaped the lives of the nine million Black majority, two hundred thousand Coloured, and two hundred thousand Indian populations. Under the white/European minority, they were separated in every arena, including recreational facilities, social spaces, employment, and education.[4]

She also painted a world of two distinctly different Black South Africas. One was located in rural areas where "the natives live in reservations," and the other resembled a major urban city in the United Sates. "The tribes" of "the natives" who "are considered Bantus" embodied more traditional, unrefined, and remote areas of South Africa, while the urban city of Johannesburg, where she and her husband resided in "a beautiful, large home," represented modernity. The Bantus may have made up the majority of the Black population, she insisted, but the group of "professional and highly cultured residents" who lived in her community symbolized the contemporary face of Black South Africa. Although still a small group, she lamented, the professional and cultured Black South African often eschewed intimate interactions with the Bantu and primarily mingled with "their more successful racial brothers."[5]

It was a triumphant postwar return of a citizen of the United States and a successful solo debut for the first Black American female dignitary from South Africa. She embraced that dual status and took them with her to Philadelphia two weeks later as she spent three days immersed in the ICW conference held at the University of Pennsylvania from September 5 to September 12. She wasn't the only person from South Africa attending the first ICW conference, held since 1938 and the first one convened in the United States since 1925. White European women from the National Council of Women of South Africa had also sent a delegation. More than likely, Hall Xuma interacted with them because of their link to the NCAW. She also engaged with her friend Mary McLeod Bethune, other members of the National Council of Negro Women, and many of the one thousand delegates from more than twenty-five nations who attended the conference.[6]

Revealing a new kind of women's international activism, Leila J. Rupp argues, the ICW was emboldened by the postwar conference theme "The Power and Responsibilities of Freedom." Delegates followed a historically gendered pattern of highlighting a social welfare agenda. They called for better housing and health care in addition to demands for adequate child care and equality for women around the world. It was, however, their discussions "condemning war, aggression, and crimes against humanity and demanding a more active role for women in national government and the United Nations" that grabbed global activists like Hall Xuma's attention and demonstrated the significant role the conference played in the expansion of women's roles in the international sphere.[7]

The bold agenda stemmed from the fact that the United Nations had already taken a lead in promoting universal human rights and becoming a global advocate for women. The process had gained momentum the year before, in February 1946, when the French delegation submitted a proposal for women's participation in UN conferences in London and former first lady Eleanor Roosevelt read "An Open Letter to the Women of the World from the Women Delegates and Advisers at the First Assembly of the United Nations." In it she argued that women had "performed so notably and valiantly during the war," and for that they had been rewarded with "seventeen women representatives and advisers, representative of eleven Member States," who were "taking part at the beginning of the new phase of international effort." She and the other women were hopeful that "their participation in the work of the United Nations Organization may grow and may increase in sight and in skill." More significantly, she urged "governments of the world to encourage women everywhere to take a more active part in national and international affairs, and on women who are conscious of their opportunities to come forward and share in the work of peace and reconstruction as they did in war and resistance." In the end, there was no vote or any official action taken, but UN officials took notice and so did women around the world. Like Hall Xuma, many of the delegates attending the ICW conference in Philadelphia planned to attend the United Nations while in session in New York.[8]

The ICW and the United Nations were not the only organizations activist women turned to in their effort to reshape the international landscape. For example, the Women's International Democratic Federation, founded in Paris in 1945 (at the International Congress of Women Conference), put forth the primary objectives to end fascism, maintain world peace, promote child welfare, and campaign for equal rights for women.[9] One of the groups attracted to the WIDF agenda was the NCNW. For the November 26–30 Paris meeting, the NCNW sent a delegation that included Charlotte Hawkins Brown, Vivian Mason, and Thelma Dale. As president of the NCNW, Mary McLeod Bethune argued that being a part of the historic conference provided a useful means "to integrate our women, Negro women, in a great mass movement where they can learn to articulate and take action to obtain economic, political and social justice." Being part of the WIDF was one of the tools helping to "form ourselves into a solid phalanx like the women of Europe are doing, and fight forthrightly and consistently for a reconversion of American democracy and life."[10] In November 1946, the NCNW demonstrated its investment in the WIDF by pushing one of the organization's recommendations—appealing to the United Nations to use its influence in protesting the production of the atomic bomb. Members believed that a diplomacy that encouraged "win[ning] agreements rather than arguments" proved far more effective.[11]

The World Young Women's Christian Association, headquartered in Geneva, joined the chorus of women's groups pushing for the global expansion of women's interest. Rooted in the establishment of the YWCA in Great Britain that began operating in 1855, the World YWCA was born in 1894 with the intent to unify YWCAs worldwide and to spread both Christianity and social welfare to women and girls around the globe. It had been so successful that by the time the organization celebrated its fifty-year anniversary the year before the war ended, it claimed associated branches in nearly fifty countries, with more than a million and a half women and girls. Many of those branches had been severely affected by the war, so as a long-term part of the celebration the World YWCA launched a fund-raising campaign for "a special Reconstruction Fund of $80,000" to assist with rebuilding, providing training, and dispensing aid to women and children.[12]

That forward thinking enabled the American YWCA, one of the largest and wealthiest affiliates, to send emissaries to war-torn countries and raise money to finance rebuilding just months after the war ended. For example, the organization sent a representative in January 1946 to Germany to represent the World YWCA in assisting "women in displaced persons' assembly centers" and dispatched the head of the foreign division and a member of the national board to investigate YWCAs and their work in a dozen countries devastated by the war. Moreover, in March 1946, the organization initiated a campaign to raise more than $2 million for its Reconstruction Fund that was "designed to give leadership training to women in thirty war-effected countries." It was, the chair of the committee insisted, "one of the most important undertakings ever launched by women of America for women overseas." To ensure a broad interracial coalition effort, Dorothy Height, a member of the

Black YWCA National Board and an affiliate of the NCNW, was appointed to direct the Reconstruction Fund campaign among Black women.[13]

American affiliates also championed the changes that set the World YWCA on a new course at the World YWCA conference in Hangchow, China, in 1947, the organization's first conference after the war. It broadened its "Christian Task" and over the next decade, according to the then secretary for South and East Asia, Elizabeth Palmer, committed to the shift from the "non-denominational" and "interconfessional" religious ideals to "conscious ecumenical thinking—when real thought has been given to what it means to individuals to belong to an Association which brings members from different confessions together and what it must mean to the Association to have that kind of membership." As a result, the World YWCA expanded its membership base by embracing "members of different Christian churches" and committed to opening up opportunities for the development of more branches across the globe.[14]

A significant outgrowth of those changes included tackling the conundrum of systemic racism within the organization's own ranks. The World YWCA may have been ideologically transnational, but Black women like longtime member Hall Xuma found themselves adrift from the organization while in places like Africa because of the haphazard and problematic way the World YWCA had initiated efforts among Black diasporic women. Extension YWCA work, similar to the Blue Triangle Clubs in the United States, had begun in places like Ghana as early as 1899, but formal affiliation with the World YWCA would take another fifty-six years. Even Elizabeth Palmer acknowledged, "In 1947 you could count the people from different parts of the world other than the USA and Europe" on the World YWCA Executive Committee or even on the staff.[15] But the World YWCA was committed to changing that. The Mutual Service subcommittee proved to be the organization's means of reshaping the World YWCA's relationship with Africa in particular. The early purpose of the committee was to begin the process of surveying the area for future expansion of the organization on the continent. Marianne Mills was the first to be dispatched there after the China conference.[16]

The World YWCA's commitment to Africa did not occur in a vacuum. It came on the heels of the American YWCA's adoption of "The Interracial Charter" in 1946 that linked the rise of racial tensions to the polarization of the postwar world and prompted the three thousand YWCA delegates in Atlantic City, New Jersey, to pledge that "wherever there is injustice on the basis of race, whether in the community, the nation or the world, our protest must be clear and our labor for its removal vigorous and steady. And what we urge on others, we are constrained to practice ourselves." As one of the first organizations to desegregate in the United States, the YWCA's decision proved to be in the vanguard of the budding civil rights movement among Christians, Channing Tobias of the YMCA surmised. "I think it is a great step forward in Christian, Human relations," Tobias noted, and "I think it will have a salutary effect on the YMCA, which has been slower in recognizing the importance of making sacrifices wherever necessary in order to live and operate according to Christian principals." The *Chicago Defender* declared the charter "a forthright expression of the Christian and democratic intent of the YWCA; and it is believed will set the tone for other organizations which presently follow a policy of racial segregation, if not down right racial exclusion."[17]

Hall Xuma finally arrived in Winston-Salem on Monday, September 8, and for the first time in seven years embraced her family, friends, and Goler church congregation. Then she launched a speaking tour designed to forge relationships with the city's Black religious institutions. Invited by the Women's Society of Christian Service, she spoke at the Sunday-morning 11:00 o'clock service at Mt. Pleasant Methodist Church on September 21, 1947. Her talk was titled "The Local Church and Its World Vision."[18]

Her campaign was short-lived, however, when "Dr.," as she affectionately referred to her husband, requested that she return to New York for two reasons. The first was for her to be the South African representative for the dedication of the Africa House that provided meeting space for African students in the United States. The president of the African Academy of Arts and Research who had found himself profusely apologizing to Xuma for not being aware of his wife's arrival date and not having prepared a reception for "the wife of one of our foremost Africans" rectified his gaffe by contacting Xuma and inviting Hall Xuma to the opening of the Africa House on Sunday, October 12, 1947. Insisting that she was important to the cause because she had "helped in a most significant manner to cement a greater friendship for us with South Africa and set the stage for command and respect for the entire continent and also the work we are endeavoring to do through our program in this country," he clinched the couple's allegiance and ensured her appearance.[19]

Supported by gifts from Haile Selassie of Ethiopia, the government of Haiti, and others, the house, located on West 140th Street, reflected a broad coalition of international diasporic interest and cooperation. There to celebrate the event along with Hall Xuma were dignitaries from Haiti, the Gold Coast, and Liberia. She was the lone woman on the main program.[20] "When I think of the African student and scholars presenting themselves in the grand [?] in which they did this event," she noted in her opening remarks, "my heart is filled with joy. I wonder if [?] Americans can go to other sections of the world and have such fine impressions." Then as the envoy who "brought greetings from South Africa," she told the large crowd gathered there:

> South Africa is one of the worst countries when it comes to race relations. Almost everything there is under white control. When the South Africans try to expand in any direction, he always encounters the whites. In 1940, I set about organizing women's groups. Today, more than ten such organizations exist with their programs geared toward cultural, educational and home economic interests. When the African woman refused to carry passes, they were threatened with being jailed and accepted the challenge. Today, the women who were unified in their fight are not compelled to carry passes. It is in this light that we should come to realize that in unity there is strength.[21]

She praised the African Academy of Arts and Research for "accomplishing a great deal in interpreting Africa to the American people" and told the audience, "I am happy that I was invited to visit with you today and to learn that you purchased this beautiful building, known as AFRICA HOUSE. This is a challenge to us in Africa. I shall carry this challenge back with me. I assure you ladies and gentlemen that there will be an Africa House in South Africa."[22]

The following Thursday, October 16, she fulfilled Xuma's second request by heading to the UN Assembly gathered at Lake Success, New York, from September 16 to November 29, 1947. She was most interested in the status of South African prime minister Jan Smuts. The crushing defeat for Smuts that had erupted in 1946 with a contingent made up of her husband and Indian leaders continued to make waves at the meeting in 1947. The South African Indian delegation that attacked Smuts for the government's repressive record had gained the strong support of India, a country whose leaders demanded that the United Nations "block the persecution of the Indian minority in the Union of South Africa."[23] Smuts's defiant refusal to adhere to the United Nations' recommendation against the annexation of Southwest Africa encouraged the *Chicago Defender* to declare it "the first test case of the power of the General Assembly over nations which fail or refuse to carry out its recommendations." Ultimately, Hall Xuma could report back to Xuma that the majority of delegates rebuked Smuts's rejection of placing the territory under UN trusteeship.[24]

Her unscheduled reappearance in the city was greeted by Black elites with excitement. One of them threw an elaborate event that included serving a six-course dinner to honor her and a businessman from Bermuda. Her friends Alva and Charles Kimbrough were among the guests who attended and basked in the conversation about "customs and traditions in Bermuda and South Africa" and viewed the two movies *Americans All* that promoted South American countries and links to the United States and *King Solomon's Mines* that detailed the experiences of a cast that included Paul Robeson searching for riches in South African diamond mines. For the occasion, one newspaper reported that she appeared "radiant in a ballerina creation fashioned by Mary Richardson out of black net picturesquely embroidered with black straw." Guests were quite interested in the fact that "the material, made in Europe but brought here from Africa by Mme. Xuma, is an exact copy of the pattern worn by Queen Elizabeth when the Royal Family visited Africa recently."[25]

In the weeks that followed, she embarked on a full schedule of presentations, such as the twelfth annual National Association of Negro Business and Professional Women's Clubs convention held at the YWCA in New York City, in other cities nearby, and in Newark, New Jersey.[26] Then, as she made her way down the Eastern Seaboard, she also stopped in Washington to honor Bethune's invitation to attend the NCNW's twelfth annual conference. Convening November 10–14 at a meeting that was described as an "All-Out Attack on Race Problems," the contingent of international women included Hall Xuma and six hundred delegates. They also demonstrated their understanding of how intertwined race and global politics were by issuing a call for international peace. Elizabeth "Bess" Truman, President Harry Truman's wife, held a reception at the White House for delegates, and on the last day many attended the International Night that showcased representatives from twenty-five different embassies and presentations from speakers like the UN representative from Liberia.[27]

When Hall Xuma finally arrived in Winston-Salem shortly after the conference, she shared Thanksgiving dinner with her brother Leroy and his wife, Eleanor, and reacquainted herself with family and familiar places and spaces. On her calendar, she scheduled an array of teas, breakfasts, lunches, and dinners with friends; an appointment with the hairdresser; a meeting with her garden club; and time for bridge. Then she finally celebrated Christmas with her siblings.[28]

As the new year unfolded, she enjoyed the success of a personal quest to be inducted into the Alpha Kappa Alpha (AKA) Sorority, the first Black women's sorority in the United States. Founded in 1908 at Howard University, the graduate Phi Omega chapter was established in Winston-Salem in February 1924. Committed to service and community advocacy, Hall Xuma considered the organization both "elevating" and "worthwhile."[29] And, indeed, in the years since she had been in South Africa, the sorority had awarded an annual scholarship at Winston-Salem Teachers College. All of the members had joined the YWCA, and the organization provided the opportunity for one girl to attend YWCA camp and one boy to attend YMCA camp. Financial donations to the Community Chest supported the tuberculosis campaign and helped Black children receive examinations and immunization during Negro Health Week. Perhaps one of the most noteworthy projects of the sorority was the development of the Maude Young Ray room at Kate Bitting Reynolds Memorial Hospital for African Americans that had been built in 1938 with a financial gift from William Neal Reynolds, Bitting's husband and the brother of R. J. Reynolds. The room memorialized one of the founders of the AKA chapter who had died.[30]

On Saturday evening, January 24, 1948, she was initiated in AKA by Rachel E. Diggs, her friend, bridge cohort, and head of the AKA chapter (called Chapter Basileus). Many of her fellow "sorors" welcomed her in the organization with personal notes. The sentiments from Nell B. Wright and Mary Henry embodied a triangular transnational connection between the sorority, Hall Xuma, and South Africa. Wright hoped that her membership in AKA would provide the "strength to continue your noble work with the girls and women of South Africa," while Henry wanted her to "spread the spirit of Alpha Kappa Alpha from here to South Africa."[31]

Hall Xuma's mission to educate as many people as she could about Black South Africans, particularly women and girls, encouraged her to blanket the area throughout the winter and spring. She visited nearby Salem College, a school for girls founded by the Moravians, and spoke to students at Kimberly Park School, where she once taught. She also went to the local YWCA and by late January had become such a celebrity that WTOB, one of the popular radio stations in Winston-Salem, hosted her on one of their Saturday broadcasts on January 31, 1948. Afterward, she began a weeklong lecturing tour across the area on February 26. The first stop was in Wilson, North Carolina, where she gave an interview to the local paper and a Sunday presentation at an AME Zion church on February 29. Then she went to Mt. Olive, Goldsboro, and Burlington. Her final stop was Durham, where she was a guest of the Daughters of Dorcas, the oldest federated club of Black women in the city. Established in 1917, the group's primary purpose was to ensure quality health care for African Americans. Lyda Moore Merrick, the daughter of leading physician and businessman Aaron M. Moore, who founded Lincoln Hospital, was among the prominent members and Hall Xuma's longtime friend. When she returned home to Winston-Salem, she spoke to more groups at Goler, St. Paul Church, and Winston-Salem Teachers College before she once again left for the Northeast.[32]

Her first stop was Philadelphia, where she spoke to the Business and Professional Women's Club. The next day, she and her cousin Roberta Carr Farmer became the houseguests of some friends in Annapolis, Maryland, and enjoyed several social events that included a three-course dinner party and a Delta Pi Omega chapter of the Alpha Kappa Alpha Sorority reception. Invited by the National Association of Colored People of Anne Arundel County, she delivered a presentation on Thursday at Mt. Moriah AME Church. She also joined a cast of speakers that included three women and three male ministers in the second of a three-day event at Morgan State University in Baltimore on Saturday, March 20. Referring to it as "Religious Emphasis week" in her date book, the theme was titled "Religion in Action."[33]

When she arrived back in Winston-Salem, she seized on the theme as Easter services approached. Devoting most of her Sundays in April to the cause, she spoke to a cross-section of denominations that included Moravians as well as the Baptist and Christian churches.[34] In the end, the sheer volume of presentations coupled with the cost of travel, she intimated to Josephus Coan, who had been an African Methodist Episcopal Church missionary in South Africa during World War II, left no time or personal funds for her to attend the AME conference.[35]

In the waning days of her time in North Carolina, Hall Xuma played bridge and attended a drama tournament, book-club gathering, garden-club meeting, and YWCA mother-daughter banquet. Members of the garden club were so excited to have her there that they threw a party in her honor. Equally inspired by her success, her alma mater Winston-Salem Teachers College featured a picture of her in the May issue of the *T.C. Alumni Bulletin*.[36]

She also spoke to the congregation at First Institutional Church, addressed the members at the North Carolina Federation of Negro Women's Clubs in Statesville, and was honored at a dinner hosted by a friend in High Point, North Carolina, on Saturday, May 15. Ten women, including Jane Melton, Lillie Turner, and Minnie Clark from Winston-Salem, joined her in celebrating her status as "a delegate to the UNO at Lake Success, N.Y." and as the "president of the African Women's League of 4,000,000 women." It was the last major event in North Carolina. After a visit to the Blue Ridge Mountains, she left Winston-Salem for the last time on Tuesday, May 18.[37]

The following day, she was in Brooklyn and then in Philadelphia on Friday, May 21, where friends threw her a theater party on Saturday evening and a "'Bon Voyage' breakfast" the following morning. In Baltimore by Sunday afternoon, she attended a tea held at the YWCA by the Delta Sigma Theta Sorority. Her final presentation in the United States was at a school for delinquent girls on Monday, May 24. Returning to New York, she boarded a flight to South Africa on Thursday, May 27.[38]

The nine-month trip had been both personally and professionally rewarding. Returning to the United States as *the* representative of South Africa made her a transnational figure and enabled her to profit from her celebrity. She

Mrs. Madie Hall Xuma '36 on her first visit to this country after living in Johannesburg, South Africa for nearly eight years. She is a native of Winston-Salem and is representing South African Women at the United Nations. She plans to return to Africa in June.

FIGURE 7.1. This is a photograph of Madie Hall Xuma in the Winston-Salem State University *T.C. Alumni Bulletin* (1948). The description underneath captured the essence of her post–World War II transnational life as a resident of Johannesburg, South Africa, a native of Winston-Salem, North Carolina, and a representative of South African women at the United Nations in New York. Courtesy of Winston-Salem State University Archives, C. G. O'Kelly Library.

notated that the funds she collected "For Africa" had generated nearly $856 (approximately $9,528 in 2021) from churches, organizations, public schools, colleges, individuals, and even Black female small business owners like hairdressers.[39] If the investment of time and labor had yielded such remarkable financial returns, then the long-term alliances with Black American women were incalculable. Members of the Business and Professional Women's Club in Philadelphia were so enthralled by what she told them about the creation of and work with the Zenzele Club that Madison Hill, the national president of the organization, told a reporter that some of the members decided to form an American Zenzele Club of their own. The Daughters of Dorcas members in Durham were also impressed. Believing that "the club motto 'Lifting As We Climb' refers to people not only in Durham, but wherever human uplift is needed, and can be promoted by means of the somewhat meagre resources of the club," they "reached far away into Johannesburg, South Africa to help our sisters in Mrs. Madie Hall Xuma's community."[40]

* * *

Hall Xuma reunited with her husband at the Johannesburg airport on Saturday, May 29. Although saddened by the fact that she missed seeing her nephew Harold graduate from college by just a few days, she was happy to be home to be able to celebrate her fifty-fourth birthday on Thursday, June 3, with her husband.[41] Zenzele Club members were excited by her return as well. At the Johannesburg branch, where Madie was acting secretary, members demonstrated their admiration for her devotion "to collect the very latest ideas on the artistic side of House-Craft etc., etc." for the benefit of the club and held a reception in her honor. The Zenzele Clubs of Sophiatown and Roodepoort also planned a reception, "displaying a right royal Welcome" for her. And the Homemaker's Club celebrated her arrival with a party.[42]

All of the celebrations were eclipsed by the national election in South Africa that had occurred on May 26, 1948. Jan Smuts and the United Party may have won the popular vote but lost enough seats in Parliament to ensure victory for the National Party to usher in a new kind of oppression for the Black majority. While the win had not been expected, it was not entirely a surprise, either. The Australian newspaper the *Sun* reported in 1947 that the unification of African and Indian discontent in South Africa had reinforced the "Color Fight" to maintain white supremacy. Moreover, one journalist insisted that the "UNO's treatment of South Africa has made the Union's white population more bitterly anti-colored than ever before."[43]

Led by the xenophobic fears of the white minority, the National Party promoted white supremacy and blamed the rise of Black African protest and crime on the increasing number of rural Blacks who had flocked to the cities seeking employment. To address what they perceived as an alarming crisis, the party had proposed a form of complete racial segregation that strictly controlled Black African movement and employment yet ensured the necessary and steady labor pool required for production and growth. The repressive policy known as apartheid appealed to white Afrikaner voters who sought to institutionalize a kind of oppressive racism and discrimination that would transform the lives of all Black Africans for nearly fifty years. Both Xuma and Hall Xuma would engage in the struggle for Black equality but in uniquely different ways and with very different outcomes.

In October Alfred Xuma met with a small coalition of ANC and All-African Convention members that included his friend and president D. D. T. Jabavu to discuss plans to combine the membership and resources of the two organizations by merging them into one. In their statement "A Call for African Unity," they concluded, "The situation constitutes a challenge which cannot be ignored by the African people," and "The primary necessity in meeting the challenge is unified action on the part of the African people." Therefore, 116 ANC delegates, 30 All-African Convention delegates, and 50 unaffiliated attendees met at the December 1948 conference to discuss and solidify the union. Dissension within the group, however, disrupted the merger and set the ANC on a new course. A powerful coalition pushed for far more confrontational calls of action. Over the next year, Xuma's presidency of the ANC was embroiled in a contentious struggle for power. Before the December 1949 ANC annual meeting, ANC Youth League members Nelson Mandela, Walter Sisulu, and Oliver Tambo demanded that Xuma endorse their "Programme of Action" campaign of mass action and civil disobedience. His refusal to agree to the Youth League plan dominated the meeting held December 15–19 so much that after Xuma gave his presidential address, so many members wanted to voice their concern about his leadership and the "Programme of Action" that by the time that adjournment arrived, more than a dozen people still had not had a chance to speak. One of the members who did opined that "Congress stood in dire need of a re-orientation of policy and a departure from the beaten track of speeches to which he had listened for the past 15 years." Another argued, "It was imperative that Congress, as a National Liberation Movement, should set itself a goal, an ideology towards which every member should strive," that "can only be found in the doctrine of African Nationalism and the instrument with which to achieve this ideal could be none other than Boycott." Even the remark by Xuma's friend Minah Soga of the NCAW that her organization "believed in commanding rather than demanding justice" could not stop the inevitable. Xuma's nine-year tenure as head of the ANC ended when James S. Moroka was voted in as the new president.[44]

In spite of his defeat, Xuma remained a member of the ANC and for a short while served on the ANC's Executive Committee. He and Hall Xuma also continued to be so popular that South African Edmund Mlotywa wanted to monetize their celebrity by marketing their images. He wrote to them in March 1951 "for permission to print your pictures on 'NECK-TIES' to be worn by African people as a symbol of honour and respect for the very fine role which you have both played towards the betterment of your people." He insisted that the neckties would "inspire a feeling of self-respect to our African people and thereby promote loyalty to their leaders" and hoped that the couple would give their approval.[45] It is unclear whether permission was granted or the neckties were ever printed.

The change for Hall Xuma drastically altered her life. Her leadership and much of her engagement with the ANCWL ended as well, so she focused her attention on developing ways to expand the scope of the Zenzele Club, an organization that she had established independently of her husband. Embarking on a mission to desegregate the YWCA in South Africa, she moved out of Xuma's shadow. She "approached the two YWCAs already in communication with the World YWCA, the Associations of Durban and Port Elizabeth, with a view to calling a conference" and in the process set herself on a new national and international course.[46]

Branches of the YWCA among white/European women had first begun in 1886 in Cape Town and by 1904 had spread to Pietermaritzburg, Port Elizabeth, Durban, and Johannesburg. Offering Christian fellowship and housing to European girls, each of the locations shared similarities with the mission of YWCAs throughout the world. In 1905 the creation of the National Council of the YWCA centralized the administration, and in 1908 the organization affiliated with the World YWCA. Disagreement over policy changes to the basis of membership in the World YWCA in 1931, however, divided the South African coalition. The National YWCA withdrew from the World YWCA but continued to operate. The Port Elizabeth and Durban branches decided to remain affiliated with the World YWCA, and in 1951 the two coalesced into the South African Council of World Affiliated YWCA. The two different white YWCAs coexisted in South Africa for several decades.[47]

The South African Council of World Affiliated YWCA had embraced the World YWCA China meeting policy and implemented some programs among Black women, but the process was slow and crippled by racial tensions and government rules. Elizabeth Lester, the general secretary of the Durban YWCA, explained in a letter to Helen Roberts, the general secretary of the World YWCA, in August 1949 that there had been efforts among Black South Africans as well as Coloured and Indian women and girls, but heightened racial divisions stymied any sort of cohesive YWCA campaign in the country. "About Johannesburg and Dr. and Mrs. Xuma," Lester wrote, "I have gathered from Press cuttings lately that the Bantu people are not as ready to co-operate as once they were. They want to go off on their own pattern. That, of course is what we want; to help them to help themselves." Still, she concluded that "it is of the Will of God and a part of his plan that we have to contribute in our day and generation to the breaking down of these race barriers, and to the giving of our very best to our fellow citizens, irrespective of race and colour." The following month, the Board of Management of the Durban YWCA reported, "All members were in agreement that work should be extended among Bantu women" and "that the proposal to send an Advisory worker from the World's Association to South Africa for two years is a good one." But there continued to be serious concern about how government policies would impact the organization's plans to build a Bantu-Hostel and ultimately forced Lester to conclude, "Life in S. Africa is most complicated today, and I should think it is the most difficult place to carry out our Y.W.C.A. purpose." But, she asserted, "Still, in many ways we try."[48]

Part of that trying entailed welcoming Carrie Meares as the World YWCA advisory secretary to South Africa for a two-year period in 1950. A native of South Carolina and member of the national board of the YWCA in America, she had held a number of positions in the YWCA over the years and was eager to get to work. But even she found it far more difficult than expected. In her World's YWCA Project for South Africa report in 1951, she expressed "an urgency about these times in South Africa which seemed almost unparalleled. It was a time when the purpose and program of the YWCA seemed to have in it the elements of such great hope—in a land so full of despair." For two years, she acted as the liaison between Hall Xuma as the newly elected president of the Zenzele Clubs in 1951; Agnes Neilson, president of the Durban YWCA; and Mrs. V. F. Paterson, president of the Port Elizabeth YWCA, with the development of a Coordinating Committee to facilitate the process of forging links between the Black Zenzele Clubs and the white YWCAs.[49]

Initially, the work with the Zenzele Clubs was seen as an "extension program" of the Durban and Port Elizabeth coalition, but the program inspired such a heightened level among club women that enthusiasm grew. The Black women in Johannesburg who first met on June 9, 1951, quickly fortified their ties to the YWCA by electing a leader and developing rules. Phyllis Mzaidume was elected president. She presided over a cross-section of twenty-three women and shepherded the group through that first crucial meeting. The group decided to convene a second time and set an agenda that determined that the cost of membership dues would be five shillings a year, set a plan in motion to send two delegates to the Coordinating Committee meeting, and embraced a long-term service project.[50] It was because of that kind of interest and success, along with cooperation from Neilson, Paterson, and Meares, that Hall Xuma believed that the long-term future of Zenzele Clubs was bound to the World Affiliated YWCA. A trip back to the United States and two invitations from the World YWCA to meetings in Europe and the Middle East reinforced that belief.

The second trip to the United States was quite different from her first. This one had been hastened by her sister Edna's long-term illness. Suffering for at least a decade with such severe hypertension and other infirmities, Edna had been hospitalized for a short time during Hall Xuma's visit from the fall of 1947 to the spring of 1948 and even required an operation in January 1948. Three years later, her condition had deteriorated to such a degree that she was hospitalized again. Summoned home, Hall Xuma boarded a Pan American flight headed to America on April 1, 1951. By the time she arrived in Winston-Salem, Edna had been discharged from the hospital. However, in the letter she wrote to her husband in June 1951, she reported that her sister still had not fully recovered.[51]

Edna's health remained a concern for the duration of her trip home, and so did her own fear about flying as a result of the crash of "that airliner— Flight 151—the same plane I came over on" several weeks after she arrived. Originating in Havana, Cuba, the last week in April, the plane was en route to Miami when it collided with an American navy plane practicing maneuvers, crashed, and killed forty-three people while Key West beachgoers watched in horror. Hall Xuma was "heartbroken" about the loss of life and announced to Xuma, "It is really terrible!" and insisted, "They must get everything fixed before I come back."[52]

The anxiety over the crash coupled with Edna's illness and what may have been her own lingering signs of menopause took a toll. Nearly fifty-seven years old now, she had "started the treatment" and, though feeling somewhat better, was still plagued by "dizzy feeling sometimes." The summer weather compounded her misery. Far more acclimated now to South Africa's seasons and temperatures, Winston-Salem was baking. At "over 100 degrees," she noted that sleep eluded her at night because it was simply "too hot."[53]

In spite of her emotional anguish and own ailments, she worked feverishly to alert as many Americans as she could about the racist system of apartheid that she had now lived under for three years. The continued interest of Black Americans concerning political developments in the country helped propel her cause. Two months before she arrived in the United States, the six-year-old cultural and entertainment *Ebony Magazine* had waded into the global political realm with the article "The World's Most Prejudiced Nation." Opining "In America it is called Jim Crow; in South Africa it is *apartheid*. But anywhere in the world it still is the same doctrine of racial superiority, of keeping people apart because some who are light complexioned are allegedly superior to others who are dark. In the Union of South Africa this dogma has reached its zenith with *apartheid* the guiding principle of state. Under the hand of Hitler admirer Prime Minister Daniel Malan, South Africa rates as the most prejudiced and most undemocratic country in the world today."[54]

Hall Xuma carried that theme to the annual North Carolina Federation of Negro Women's Clubs convention in Shelby.

Her mission, however, wasn't simply a discussion about oppression. Hall Xuma was also there to remind her audience about her work in the "uplift of the native women" and to solicit their help in furthering the cause. Black South African women, she would argue, had embraced the rapidly spreading organizational development that she had begun with the first Zenzele Club and enjoyed the international connections made with Black women in the United States. More important, with her assistance the World YWCA had entered South Africa and begun making significant inroads with Black women.[55]

Throughout the summer, she traveled to places like New York City and Chicago, touting a similar message. In Chicago she also joined Lydia DePriest, the sister-in-law of former U.S. congressman Oscar Stanton DePriest, in a tour of the *Chicago Defender* newspaper plant and again posed for a photo for the newspaper. This time, however, it was simply a head shot of her and very little commentary.[56]

By mid-August 1951, she was back in North Carolina presenting speeches as the "missionary from Africa" when she joined a number of religious dignitaries who spoke at the AMEZ Women's Conference held at Goler Metropolitan AME Zion Church. Guided by the theme "Mid-Century's Challenge to Christian Missions," she stood before a crowd of three thousand and enlightened them about the centrality of service in the work of missions. Two weeks later, she was one of a host of speakers that included the Liberian ambassador and a bishop from India at the Lott Carey Baptist Foreign Mission Convention in Durham where two thousand delegates heard her message.[57]

Businesswomen like beauty culturalists, also known as beauticians and hairdressers, demonstrated a particular affinity to her because of the broadly defined context of her mission of assisting Black South African women. The beauty culturalist industry had become such a powerful institution in the postwar period that members used organizations, schools, and transnational partners like Hall Xuma as the vehicles to empower women in economic marketplaces around the world. Tiffany Gill argues, "Just as African American beauticians visited Europe to legitimate their standing in the industry, black women from Africa and the diaspora came to the United States to be validated as stylists and educators in their respective countries. Most came to be educated in African American beauty schools before returning to their respective countries to open their own salons and schools."[58] Hall Xuma had no interest in opening or operating a beauty shop, but she was vested in transporting Black American women's ideals of beauty to South Africa.

For many Black American women, the bond forged with their hairdresser was sacrosanct. She, like Black women all across the country, had maintained a standing appointment with a hairdresser for much of her adult life, so one of the first things she did when she arrived in New York in 1947 was make an appointment to get her hair done. She subsequently continued to schedule a hairdresser appointment in nearly every city she visited. The personal visits quickly intertwined with the professional because so many Zenzele Club women had requested that she purchase pressing combs, a tool that when heated made kinky hair straight, for them. On each of the two trips to the United States, she gladly filled those orders. She also enrolled in a beauty culture course so that she could demonstrate how to use the product properly and teach the newest techniques of hair grooming and hairstyles to the women. The entire enterprise, Hall Xuma argued, had as much to do with the political and economic machinations of South Africa as it did with appearance. The politics of being Black and female with kinky hair under South Africa's oppressive regime required the use of every tool available, she insisted. While Black women could not change their skin color or gender, they could modify their hair texture and possibly alter the trajectory of their lives. "A native with hair traated [sic] and styled may be identified as colored (a mixture)," and in the process "avoid some discrimination," she told a reporter. Ultimately, assuming the textured characteristic of mixed-raced women's hair, she believed, elevated Black or native women from the bottom rung of the racial stratification system and offered them the prospect of better economic opportunity.[59]

She was not alone in her assertion. Tiffany Gill suggests that for Black women in the United States, "In the 1950s and 1960s, hair that was styled to release or straighten the curl pattern was the only acceptable way for African American women to wear their hair. For whites to see black women with their hair in its natural state was considered feeding into negative stereotypes of black women as unruly and undeserving of respectable treatment."[60] So when Hall Xuma flew out of the Idlewild Airport in New York on October 1, 1951, she ensured that straightening combs were being sent to Black South African women.

She first traveled to London to enjoy time with her son, Alfred, who was completing his last years of high school there. Then she went to Switzerland, where she met with administrators and staff at the World YWCA headquarters in Geneva before going to Beirut, Lebanon, as a guest for the twelve-day World YWCA Council meeting held every four years. She joined Mrs. H. D. Brunt, the "official" corresponding affiliated South African delegate. Brunt, along with the nearly two hundred other delegates from sixty-two countries, participated in discussions that determined the future of the organization. While Hall Xuma was a visiting observer, her physical presence at the meeting was such an extraordinary event for Zenzele members that they had initiated a fund-raising campaign to help ensure that she could attend. When she finally arrived home on November 14, she told a reporter for the *Bantu World* that it had been a "wonderful" trip and that she "would not have missed it under any circumstances."[61]

Moreover, she had heightened Black American interest to such a degree that *Our World Magazine*, a nationally distributed periodical that catered to an African American audience, featured her in December 1951. Under the caption "IT HAPPENED IN OUR WORLD: African emissaries, following the pattern of globe-trotting Americans, come here to see our democracy at work" cemented her place among the most iconic figures in the world. Those featured included Kwame Nkrumah, prime minister of the Gold Coast, speaking to Walter White of the NAACP; a group from Nigeria conversing with Eleanor Roosevelt, the former first lady; and others from various countries in Africa who had ties to America. But unlike all of the others, Hall Xuma's photograph stood alone, and her inclusion accentuated the complexity of the race, gendered, and transnational facets of her life. The only woman among the "African emissaries," she was also the only one identified as "Winston-Salem born" who "calls herself an African." The fact that she embraced a South African identity continued to make her an enigma on the world stage.[62]

It was that enigmatic personality that Margaret Hathaway engaged with when she replaced Carrie Meares in 1953 as the new World YWCA advisory secretary to South Africa. Born in Salem, Oregon, Hathaway had been familiar with and immersed in service and mission work for much of her life. Her role model had been her mother, Agnes E. Shephard Lewis, who dedicated her life to service. Before Lewis died in 1946 at the age of sixty-eight, she had been actively engaged in her Presbyterian church and served as president of the YWCA board in Portland, Oregon. Hathaway, a graduate of Willamette University in Salem, Oregon, followed a similar path but broadened her geographical reach much further than her mother ever could. While married to Willis Hathaway, a secretary of the YMCA, she spent time in China under the auspices of the Presbyterian Board of Foreign Missions and taught history and music courses. After his death, she committed much of her energies to the YWCA by steadily working her way up in the organization. Serving as an administrator at the YWCA in Long Beach, California, she later moved to a position on the National Board of the YWCA's Defense Service Department before joining the administrative staff of the World YWCA.[63] Hall Xuma and Hathaway forged a close bond and together committed themselves to transforming racial consciousness among women in South Africa and ensuring the institutionalization of a viable YWCA program among Black women.

Hathaway reported to South Africa in early February 1953 and found such a vibrant and committed movement of Black women that even she surmised,

"The most hopeful area of work is among African women." And, indeed, the Zenzele YWCA of the Transvaal had been created in 1952. It operated out of a room located in the Jan Hofmeyr School of Social Work.[64] Enthusiasm among Zenzele members for the YWCA movement had also fueled activity and an increase in the number of branches. During the early months of 1952, for example, each member of the Johannesburg branch sold between five and ten tickets to raise funds for their silver tea. The Zenzele YWCA in Brakpan organized a concert to raise money to sponsor a refresher course. Hall Xuma and her husband joined the president of the organization for the event that included prayer, speeches, and music by the Zenzele choir. Moreover, interest in the concept encouraged such phenomenal growth of the Zenzele YWCA idea that before the year ended, five branches in Johannesburg, Benoni, Germiston, Nigel, and Springs had become part of the South African Council of World Affiliated YWCA. The power of the coalition was reflected in the central question on the first page of the newsletter (or Program Exchange Sheet) distributed in the fall of 1953. "Where is everybody going?" was the main question on the front of the newsletter; "To the Exhibition in Bethlehem!" was the response. Hosted by the Zenzele YWCA of the Transvaal in October, delegates from various clubs gathered there to be inspired, review the year's projects, and develop plans for the year.[65]

By the time the exhibition was held in October, the oldest Zenzele Club developed by Hall Xuma had been operating for more than a decade and had impacted the lives of a new generation. Margaret Hathaway informed the World YWCA that one young woman from Piet Retief, located about two hundred miles from Johannesburg, who was "the daughter of an old Zenzele member," was "urged by a young teacher to write to Mrs. Xuma to ask more about this Zenzele YWCA of which she had heard." The young woman noted that "when she heard about this movement she realized if they could only get in touch with us it would be a way they could grow and feel related to other women outside their community." The interest of women like her led to the development of nine new Zenzele YWCA branches by 1954.[66] Moreover, Hall Xuma's success also inspired other women on the continent. For example, she received an invitation from women in the Gold Coast (now Ghana) to visit so that she could help them develop their own clubs.[67]

As more Black women eagerly joined clubs or sought ways to create new Zenzele YWCAs, the ambitious alliance forged between Black African and white European YWCA women showed unsettling signs of teetering under the weight of isolation and apartheid. After meeting with a group of seven women that included Hall Xuma, Cora Phillips, and Margaret Hathaway, Agnes Neilson told Hathaway, "At the tip of this continent where we are so isolated not only from the rest of the world but from each other, we need to be more closely tied to the World YWCA." Hathaway could do little at the time about the relationship with the World YWCA, but she did contact the World YWCA and asked that the organization provide her with a car so that she could visit women throughout the area and ensure that they got to know each other.[68]

That proved to be far more difficult than she imagined because of the Group Areas Act of 1950 and the pass laws instituted by the government. The Group Areas Act that had divided the country into segregated geographical areas and determined where, when, and how long any group could be in a particular place meant that many Black YWCA women could not attend the multiracial group meetings that were held in locales like Durban.[69] And as early as 1952, some cities had begun to enforce a requirement that Black African women obtain permits or passes to be in certain areas. Before the decade ended, Black women, like Black men, throughout South Africa were forced to carry passbooks. They did not, however, do so willingly. Women demonstrated in towns and cities across South Africa, often joining the Federation of South African Women, established in 1954, in mass protest or burning the passbooks. As a result, a number of them were arrested and fined.[70]

Black women and their families were certainly impacted the most by the laws, but Hathaway quickly discovered that apartheid's policies didn't just ensnare Black women. As she tried to maneuver the area, she complained:

> As a "white" I could not go in and out of African townships without a permit. I called on the senior government officer of African Affairs in Johannesburg who agreed to give me one for weekdays and working hours of 8 a.m. to 5 p.m.; but I explained to him I might as well give up for most of the African women who I had met were working. Therefore if we were to develop a YWCA programme and meaning among women, such leadership—if available—would be voluntarily after working hours and at weekends. Fortunately he granted me an unrestricted permit which opened the way for me to experience the quality of African leadership.[71]

If "crossing the colour bar" had not been easy for Hathaway, then even for Hall Xuma, a Black American whose life had been shaped by the racism and segregation of Jim Crow and the oppression of apartheid, it was far more difficult. Living under both Jim Crow and apartheid, she was one of the few Black women who understood the gendered dynamics and politics of global white supremacy, so when the European National Council of Women of Benoni invited her to speak at their February 1953 branch meeting, "she told the appreciative European audience that she would readily welcome invitations to a common platform where women of both races would come together and discuss differences and assert their influences to bring about harmony among races." Then she insisted that "she had dedicated herself for service not for any particular race but for all people."[72] The comment highlighted her insistence that as a woman and a Black woman, she was the embodiment of the kind of activist who represented the interest of all women and at the same time exposed the paradoxical world in which she lived. Hall Xuma had been fighting for the rights of Black women all of her adult life, yet for this audience of white women she felt compelled to proclaim her allegiance to the advancement of *all* women, regardless of race, to both appease them and gain their support.

The paradox was not lost on her, as she demonstrated in her remarks about how a history of systemic sexism and racism had shaped and impacted the lives of Black African women and their families. Arguing "No race can rise if the women folk are left behind," she insisted that under the traditional rules of African life, women could not thrive. The inequality stymied their progress. Moreover, the arrival of Europeans challenged the livelihood of rural Africans by disrupting and in many ways destroying the Black family and the community that sustained it. Forced to move to urban areas, Black men left rural communities and their families in droves. Many African women also fled to find work, again challenging the fundamental dynamics of the family and forcing Black women into specific types of labor that exploited them.[73]

The picture that she painted, however, was not completely bleak. A number of women, Hall Xuma boasted, had triumphed over adversity. They found success through education in positions as "a teacher, social worker and a nurse" and in the process were "awakening" to the possibilities in their lives. These accomplished Black South African women, she told the audience, were assuredly "following the steps of their Afro-American people who have advanced."[74] For her, the assertion, while steeped in her own beliefs about African American superiority, was an important affirmation of Black African women's power, influence, and tenacity.

CHAPTER 8

A Transnational Nexus
The World YWCA

When the YWCA Coordinating Committee met in Port Elizabeth in March 1954, Hall Xuma was one of a cast of fifteen women determining the future of the YWCA's interracial alliance. The group wrestled with a full slate of issues that included a debate about the emblem design for the YWCA badge and the price to charge when marketing the product and a discussion about plans to develop a clear operating budget and ways to secure future funding. They also underscored the dates for leadership-training workshops at various branches as well as made preparations for their first national conference the following year.[1]

More significantly, the meeting marked a critical juncture for the organization because it began navigating the transition from a theoretical ideology of interracial cooperation to implementing the process of forging a unified national body. The Black and white attendees whose lives had been shaped by white supremacy and six years of apartheid policies shared a common bond as South African citizens but little else. Six years of apartheid rule had systematically stripped Black South Africans of their citizenship rights. Mixed marriages were outlawed in 1949; the 1950 Group Areas Act that determined where Blacks and whites resided also banned several publications dealing with race relations between 1951 and 1952; the Population Registration Act in 1950 set up the mechanisms for determining the racial categories of citizens that subsequently led to the legal classifications of White, Coloured or Native/Bantu; the Reservation of Separate Amenities Act segregated parks, beaches, and restrooms; and the Bantu Education Act of 1953 set up separate educational facilities for Blacks, withdrew state subsidies to the mission schools (the primary avenues for the education for Black children), and ultimately prohibited Blacks from attending white schools by establishing separate colleges and universities for Black Africans, Coloureds, and Indians.[2] And the government's weaponization of passports and visas as a means to limit Black citizen's mobility also escalated. A chief in Southwest Africa who was invited to speak before a UN committee in Paris during the 1951–52 session and to preach at a church in London, for example, was denied a passport for both. A sixteen-year-old boy who won a scholarship to a school in Kent, Connecticut, in 1955 could not attend because "the police were not prepared to grant him the required certificate of character," so he suffered the same fate as the chief.[3]

Hall Xuma and her husband were not immune. When Alfred Xuma submitted applications to renew the couple's passports to travel to Liberia in 1953, the Department of the Interior rejected them and refunded the deposit. While their applications were later approved, it was clear that they had become targets.[4]

The tensions that lay uneasily between committee members boiled over when it became clear that white women lacked a real understanding of the racial and cultural context of the majority Black population's lives. The use of the "Zenzele" moniker associated with Black branches mystified many of the white YWCA women present and smacked of separation rather than unification. Cora Phillips, who had been engaged with Black Africans for much of her life and assisted her husband with the development of the Jan Hofmeyr School of Social Work, took the lead in pointing out the practical and cultural reasons for the name. She told the group that it was the Zenzele Club members who initiated the request "to be affiliated with World's YWCA," and after a positive response "they began to take steps to register." When they began that process, "a problem arose in finding a name for Registration because the local YWCA in Johannesburg which is not affiliated with the World's YWCA movement was already registered. They, therefore, took the name Zenzele YWCA of the Transvaal which had special significance for members in that area and which distinguishes it from the YWCA of Johannesburg." It was a defining moment that opened a dialogue between Black and white members to speak about similar concerns in other cities and branches. In the end, the committee embraced the diversity of its membership and unanimously concluded, "If for some groups the word Zenzele has special significance for their club it may be used, just as other clubs may choose other names, but all are members of the Young Women's Christian Association."[5] That collective decision bridged the divide and promised to make the organization one of the most powerful vehicles representing the multiracial interests of women and girls throughout South Africa.

The decision also propelled the momentum to shift from the status of a "corresponding relationship" with the World YWCA to a "Category B," or an organization working toward full affiliation that as Coral A. Haley, president of the South African Council of World Affiliated YWCA, noted would enhance the way in which "we relate ourselves to the World's YWCA." The group had already been busy drafting a new constitution and was in the process of making revisions before it was sent to the branches for review. Completing the task as quickly as possible, Margaret Hathaway argued, was essential "if we wish to have our Constitution submitted for approval prior to the World Council Meeting in 1955." "As we are now in a Corresponding Relationship we are eligible for only one voting member," but "hoping for fuller representation and participation in the next World Council Meeting," after completing the constitution, "we then could be recognized for change of status." For the best reference on how this worked, Hathaway told the group to look to Hall Xuma who had attended the Beirut Council meeting where she witnessed firsthand "the change of status for the Burma Association."[6] Her attendance at the Beirut conference and her meeting with World YWCA officials in Geneva certainly made her a valuable asset on the committee, and so did the fame that made her the leading Black female voice internationally.

Hall Xuma had indeed become such a prominent figure in the global community of the YWCA that she was invited in 1954 to give a speech at the centennial celebration of the YWCA in New York City in April 1955 and to attend the World YWCA quadrangle meeting in London that September. Apartheid policies, however, threatened to thwart her ability to attend both. She submitted her passport application to South African authorities in November 1954, nearly five months before her planned departure on April 6. A month later, she received notification of receipt of her "Application for Permission to Travel" from the Witwatersrand Divisional Naturalization Staff and told to make an appointment and to "bring with you your identity papers, such as Aliens Registration Book, Motor Driver's Licence [sic], Income Tax Assessment or latest balance sheet and documentary evidence of fixed property." It took nearly four months of negotiation with authorities for her to obtain permission to travel. While the consul general of the United States in Johannesburg signed and stamped her American passport on February 16, 1955, the South African government made the process of authorizing her foreign travel far more difficult. At one point, her husband was forced to "put up a banker's guarantee as requested by the Department of Native Affairs" to secure her a reserved seat on the plane. When that failed, he utilized the limited vestiges of his stature as a statesman and wrote to the secretary of the interior, who ultimately intervened. The whole ordeal finally ended when she received the passport on Saturday, April 9.[7]

The Xumas' difficulties did not occur in a vacuum. Personally threatened by the Native Resettlement Act of 1954 that gave the government the power to take the property of Africans, forcibly remove them from their place of residence, and relocate them to other townships, the Xumas' found themselves at a crossroad. Their community of Sophiatown became one of the first casualties, so to save their home they engaged in a public national and global battle with the South African government.

Even before the act was approved, Alfred Xuma had helped form and subsequently headed the coalition of property owners in the western areas in the development of the African Anti-Expropriation and Ratepayers Association and Proper Housing Movement in 1951. At a meeting before the Ad Hoc Committee on the Removal of Non-Europeans from the Western Areas in October 1952, he complained that there were no Black African representatives on the committee, that the reason for the removal was because of the "commercial value of these properties," and that the entire policy was part of a larger attempt to "dispossess" Africans "of land ownership to facilitate undisputed control, subjection and white domination." And in 1954 Xuma discussed the South African government's removal plan on broadcast journalist Edward R. Murrow's CBS program that was televised throughout the United States.[8]

Then in 1955, he and Hall Xuma sat down for an interview with the Associated Press. The content of their interview circulated in American newspapers and on television and radio from coast to coast as well as in Canada. Under headlines like "Johannesburg Shift Catches N.C. Woman," "Negro Couple of Johannesburg Facing Ruin in Race Struggle," "South Africa Negro Couple Defies Mass Removal Order," "They'll Come and Take Us Then Destroy This Home as Others," they painted such a dire situation that after receiving a letter from Alfred Xuma, Willie Kennedy, Hall Xuma's sister, told him on March 15, 1955, "It was indeed a surprise to hear from you after all these years. I must admit I was a little frightened. Judging from the papers, radio, magazines, and television, things look awfully dark over there and I have been plenty worried." She also expressed concern about whether "Madie will be able to come home next month" and appeared so uneasy about the situation that she suggested he should "consider coming over here" as well.[9]

Willie had reason to be worried. As a couple, Xuma and Hall Xuma expressed their joint rage over the government's resettlement scheme and their "long struggle to stir African Negroes into political wakefulness." Together they "vowed not to sell their home voluntarily to the government," although they "expect[ed] to be expropriated and then removed forcibly." But Hall Xuma also used the media forum to issue her strongest personal public rebuke of the South African government. She angrily attacked the country's racially stratified system by highlighting the peculiarity of her status as an African American and non-European. Complaining that she had "been ordered off streetcars reserved for nonwhites in Johannesburg because, being an American, I am not always regarded as what they call a 'native.' And I've been ordered off streetcars reserved for whites because I am a Negro. Very often I have to walk." Ultimately, she insisted, "color prejudice in South Africa is far worse than anything she ever encountered in America's Deep South."[10]

While linking the two oppressive regimes, she also articulated a fundamental distinction between them. Under Jim Crow, there had always been, in her view, a malleability, particularly for prominent and prosperous African Americans, that was absent from apartheid. The sentiment was shared by others whose American citizenship could not save them from the wrath of apartheid. For example, Black American newspapers had earlier cited the kind of "anti-Negro laws" in South Africa that forced actors Canada Lee and Sidney Poitier to become "bonded servants" of the white American director in 1950 while they were making a film in the country. Although the two men found "some moments of respite" from Alfred Xuma, who "offered them hospitality and camaraderie," they had no other recourse so "accepted the terms," reported the *New York Amsterdam News*.[11]

Fellow Black club women in the North Carolina Federation of Negro Women's Clubs also found Hall Xuma's plight disturbing. In the article "Apartheid" that appeared in the *Federation Journal*, members were reminded that Hall Xuma had "described the political and social situation that was distressing the South African native people" in her earlier visits and that what concerns she "expressed then have very sadly come to pass; for over the radio, through television, and newspaper reports have come to us describing the removal of the native people to a segregated town." "To Dr. and Mrs. Xuma," the organization declared, "our club women express their regret that such useful persons are forced to give up a comfortable home and pleasant surroundings. As they face what must be a most painful situation, we wish them to know that over here we are thinking of them and praying that God may overrule all their unhappiness and displeasure for His eternal good. The world is not standing still. Truth, justice and right have always conquered and will conquer over there; For God moves in a mysterious way[.] [']His wonders to perform' and 'He standeth now within the shadows, keeping watch above His own.'"[12]

When Hall Xuma arrived in New York City in late April 1955, the situation in South Africa remained a potent topic among the four thousand YWCA delegates who attended the opening of the twentieth triennial conference. The conference was characterized as "Democracy in action" by the *Atlanta Daily World* and the *Pittsburgh Courier* because "Colored women from all over the world played a significant role in all program spots, workshops and mass media." Hall Xuma, in particular, drew quite a bit of attention. Recognized as the "Lone South African," she "stressed the part played by African women in present day life" in South Africa. Telling the audience, "We have no money or no buildings but great Christian spirit," she also declared, "I would not change places for the spirit of the women is indeed great in South Africa."[13] The meeting had been so exhilarating and she had been so well received that she bragged to her husband, "People literally engulfed me on the platform after the meeting was over. Photos were taken and many autographs signed by me." "It was my day!"[14] The meeting also offered her the chance to network with philanthropic organizations. She found the discussion with a representative from Phelps-Stokes Fund in New York promising because there was an indication that an increase in the donation of "funds for South Africa" might be forthcoming.[15]

She arrived in Winston-Salem feeling good about what had transpired in New York and elated by the developments she saw in her hometown. "The Medical Society of N.C. is being integrated very fast these days. In fact, integration is becoming a thing in America," she wrote to Xuma in May.[16] To Margaret Hathaway a few weeks later, she declared, "Integration of schools especially in the South is engaging much attention now. Some of the people want to go on with it and give it a trial; others, the die-hards, are fighting tooth and nail to upset it." Some of those "die-hards" in Winston-Salem were "trying to put up two more High Schools for Negroes in Negro areas to force the people to attend rather than admit them to white schools." While no one was certain "what the outcome will be," she was absolutely "sure the NAACP will fight it" if schools were not integrated.[17] She was, of course, right about the NAACP and those segregationists who refused to bow to the winds of change or the *Brown v. Board of Education* decision by the Supreme Court in 1954. The battle over desegregation continued for years.

The contrast in her exhilaration over the slow demise of Jim Crow in America and her fear of being removed from her home in South Africa was cause for both celebration and despair. On the one hand, she saw African Americans "building beautiful Ranch houses here. Went to see two yesterday here in Durham. One especially cost $65,000 not including furnishings. On 2 acres of land. It is a show place in Durham."[18] On the other hand, she was certain that "the time for persecution of the Xumas has arrived" and that the couple's forced removal from their home of fifteen years was not far away. Determined to keep their spirits up, however, she opined, "We'll take it gracefully, however, & not panic. Somehow, I feel *God* will work out everything in a just manner."[19]

Coping with the racially schizophrenic international worlds in which she inhabited, however, proved far more difficult for her because Edna, ravaged by the onset of encephalomalacia, a form of brain damage, for two years, died on September 15, 1953. Still gripped by pain and sadness, the family was still mourning her absence two years later.[20] There was such melancholy that Hall Xuma lamented to Xuma, "Its [sic] so sad to be here without Edna." So she arranged to stay with Leroy and his wife, Eleanor, across the street from the cottage that she and Edna had once shared. The decision also offered her nephew, Harold, and his wife, Annie Brown Kennedy, who had put down roots in Winston-Salem and opened their own law firm, and their twin boys some much-needed space. Together the family supported each other while they also dealt with the rapidly deteriorating health of their uncle, who lived in Salisbury.[21]

The sudden death of Mary McLeod Bethune compounded her grief. Bethune had suffered a heart attack and died in the middle of May at the age of seventy-nine. She had been a friend and role model and had dedicated so much of her life to the Black community and to the country. Their thirty-five-year friendship had been forged in Florida, grew out of both of their commitments to activism and service, and linked them across two continents because of their shared view about Black women's global engagement.[22]

The emotional weight of her sadness coupled with fears about her life in South Africa manifested in her body to such a degree that physical symptoms appeared less than a month after her arrival in the United States, when she had "a piercing pain running from my neck along the right side around my right breast." She made an appointment with a doctor, who diagnosed it as neuralgia and told her to take vitamins. She later reported "feeling better" but recognized that the cause of her complaint was probably because she was "run down and need a long, long rest." She told Xuma that she was "getting the rest I need—Sleeping and eating," but in reality she ignored her own personal promise to turn down all speaking engagements. For most of the time she remained in the country, she was in constant motion, seemingly in an attempt both to outrun her emotional turmoil and to shape the narrative about what was happening to Black South Africans. She delivered the keynote for the Women's Day Program at Grace Presbyterian Church on "Woman [?] a Force in History" and spoke to her sister-in-law Eleanor's class of students who had been learning about South Africa. She was "asked to speak at the 'Y' Association (white)" because "they want to know about our activities in S.A." and appeared on a "*panel convention* at the local YWCA, both white and black," where she "spoke for South Africa" just as she had done in New York. Her presentation was so compelling that she insisted, "Many of the white girls told me I spoke so convincingly they were wondering if they too could not go to South Africa and give service." She agreed to be a guest at the Shaw University commencement and made plans to be the speaker at the university's alumni dinner. She also joined in the festivities when host

Lyda Merrick of Durham threw a party in her honor, spoke on the radio, and appeared on television, commenting "about the general characteristics of the Country."[23]

Perhaps because of the circumstances under which she left South Africa, the separation from her husband had also been far more taxing on this trip. She missed him so much that she lamented on May 23, 1955, "It is really lonesome to me without you." Although she noted, "It is nice to be at home to meet so many of my friends," she insisted, "I belong with you for happiness and real joy."[24]

When she boarded the train headed to Washington in early July, she was emotionally and physically exhausted, but she still visited with friends there and then rode with her sister Willie and others as they drove to New York, where she was to depart for Europe. Try as she might, however, she could not outrun her fears. Her concern, in particular, about her status in South Africa had escalated to the point that she asked Margaret Hathaway in late May, "What shall I do when I leave New York? What passport shall I show? American when I leave and S. A. when I arrive in Geneva? I am beginning to start to worry all over again, I had such a hard time getting out of South Africa." Ultimately, her concern forced her to schedule an appointment with the South African consul immediately after arriving in New York. He reassured her about her ability to reenter the country and told her, "I could quote him if any trouble comes up regarding entry into South Africa."[25] His words alleviated some of her fear, but she was well aware that she was at the mercy of the Afrikaner, who as the *New York Times* opined in June 1955, "has now consolidated its grip on the Government so strongly that it ought to be able to remain in power for years to come."[26]

* * *

Only after leaving the United States did Hall Xuma confess that she had been "overworked in America" and "was very happy to get away."[27] Geneva provided a neutral space between the grind of public life in America and the thoughts about repression in South Africa. She lunched with Lilace Reid Barnes (the outgoing American president of the World YWCA), dined with others, and spent days in meetings at the Crêt-Bérard center in Puidoux, Switzerland, with representatives from all over the world, including American YWCA staff like Dorothy Height. And when she and Margaret Hathaway left Geneva for a four-day stop in Paris, she enjoyed the anonymity of strolling the streets and watching people. "Americans," she opined, "are leaving for Europe & other places abroad by every means of transportation everyday— especially Negroes. Many conferences are being held in Europe by them." It was an exciting discovery for her, and so was the fact that she heard "Southern

FIGURE 8.1. After leaving the United States in July 1955, Madie Hall Xuma traveled to Geneva, Switzerland, Paris, France and then to London to attend the World YWCA Council Meeting held at Royal Holloway College, September 1–16, 1955. Three hundred delegates came from Europe, North America, the Middle East, the Caribbean, Latin America, Asia, Australia, and New Zealand. She was the first Black woman from South Africa elected to the World YWCA Executive Committee at the meeting. She is pictured here with Irene Pictet, the new treasurer of the Executive Committee. Courtesy of World Young Women's Christian Association Archives, Geneva, Switzerland.

brogue from the U.S.A. as well as Chinese, Japanese & others as one strolls down Ave De Champs Elysees."[28]

When she and Hathaway arrived in London on Friday, August 19, they settled in at the Montague Hotel. After checking on her son and visiting with some friends, she went to the World YWCA Council being held September 1–16. Agnes Neilson joined her and Hathaway there as the South African World Council representative for the centennial year of the founding of the YWCA in Great Britain. The conference drew the largest audience ever at Royal Holloway College. Three hundred delegates came from the Middle East, Europe, the Caribbean, Latin America, North America, Asia, Australia, and New Zealand. Sixteen hailed from various countries in Africa. Representatives from world organizations such as the United Nations Edu-

FIGURE 8.2. Madie Hall Xuma (*on the left*) enjoying tea with two of the delegates who attended the World YWCA Council Meeting at Royal Holloway College in England in September 1955. Courtesy of World Young Women's Christian Association Archives, Geneva, Switzerland.

cational, Scientific, and Cultural Organization (UNESCO), World Council of Churches, and World Alliance of YMCAs also joined them. Delegates spent long days working on revisions of the constitution that would formally "give the movement a mandate to cooperate with other bodies and international organizations" and brainstormed about ways to increase the number of "trained members to carry on the work" of the YWCA because everyone attending understood "the importance of personal contact, especially with people of different countries and the necessity of awakening interest and a sense of responsibility."[29] In the evenings, delegates found the time to engage with people from other countries by attending various parties. Hall Xuma and a member from Texas hosted one of them. Their party, however, specifically welcomed camaraderie and respite "for all of the Negro members at the Council," including those from "the West & East Coast" of Africa. It signaled how much the two women understood the need for Black enclaves in an organization in the midst of racial transformation.[30]

FIGURE 8.3. Madie Hall Xuma (*on the right in a coat*) on the lawn with delegates who attended the World YWCA Council Meeting at Royal Holloway College in England in September 1955. Courtesy of World Young Women's Christian Association Archives, Geneva, Switzerland.

The South African Council of World Affiliated YWCA and Hall Xuma were triumphant at the conference. The final version of the constitution that had been submitted to the World YWCA in April 1955 was officially recognized with the Category B classification that members sought. The significance of the occasion was not lost on the World YWCA. The organization declared that it represented a remarkable demonstration of unity across race lines, as "the Bantu and the European communities of South Africa stood shoulder to shoulder and spoke with one voice."[31] Hall Xuma played such a critical role in the process that she was elected as one of the nineteen members of the World YWCA Executive Committee. It was a pivotal moment for her and the World YWCA. She became the first Black woman from South Africa to earn a place on the committee. So elated with the honor, she boasted to Xuma, "Congratulations are being showered from everybody and I believe they are genuine." "They seem," she continued, "so appreciative of the work I have done in South Africa."[32]

Moreover, the World YWCA finally reached its goal of incorporating far more women of color. Along with members from the United States, the Netherlands, Burma, France, Japan, Great Britain, Switzerland, Australia, Germany, Egypt, Canada, and Finland, representatives from Brazil, Barbados, Ghana, and the Philippines were elected to the Executive Committee for the first time. Newly elected representative Nita Barrow from Barbados commented on the "slow and painful" transformation of the image of the World YWCA: "That image was of white, wealthy, ladies of leisure, meeting during the day: of 'white hair and white faces.' The change was from an organisation 'that did *for* people, to one in which people were partners.'" That partnership was on full display at the end of the conference for "a centenary service of thanksgiving and dedication" held in St. Paul's Cathedral for a crowd of two thousand.[33]

As a new member of the powerful Executive Committee that administered over the organization, Hall Xuma attended her first business meeting September 17–19 at the British YWCA. Four-year appointments to the four subcommittees—Finance, Secretariat, Mutual Service and Extension, and Affiliation—were made; two consultative groups were created, Social and International Questions and World YWCA Publications; and finally the president and officers of the World YWCA organized consultative groups for the four pressing areas of ecumenical, leadership, youth programs, and membership and refugees. Hall Xuma's appointment to the Mutual Service and Extension Subcommittee, led by Clarabell Ba Maung Chain from Burma, and the Publications Consultative Group, led by Olive Standen from Canada, set her on the path to becoming one of the most influential Black women in the world.[34]

Membership on the Executive Committee over the next four years allowed her to gain intimate insight into the internal machinations of how the federation of the World YWCA functioned, become familiar with its global reach, and engage with women whose lives, language, and culture differed from her own. Most of the $104,200 (equal to $1,016,531 in 2021) budgeted expenditures for May 1956 to April 1957 came from national affiliates across the globe, but there were donations or other contributions that totaled $34,100. Interest generated $4,100 and publications $3,500. The bulk of the expenditures, $58,800, went to salaries and insurance, while $10,500 was paid for costs associated with the Executive Committee, such as travel and lodging expenses to ensure that all members could afford to attend meetings.[35]

For an organization with more than a million and a half members guided by the bold agenda of "social welfare on a universal basis" to "help people become self-supporting," the income was quite modest, which is why the success of the World YWCA depended so heavily on both a devout belief in the *federation* concept and an adherence to the Christian mission of service. Hall Xuma witnessed firsthand how wealthier associations in places like the United States, Europe, and Australia bankrolled staff and projects in other parts of the world and how those with less money expressed their gratitude and contributed what they could to the sustenance of the federation. For example, an important update on the meeting's agenda was the report about the "Priority 'A' List" inherited from the previous committee to raise $5,000 to assist the YWCA in Jordan and "to find support through Mutual Service towards the budget of $6500 which the World YWCA has provisionally underwritten" for South Africa. Branches in Malaysia, Denmark, and Belgium had already contributed $452 toward the Jordan branch. Japan had given $500. The American branch was looking for ways to add $500, and branches in Australia, Lebanon, the Netherlands, Germany, and Finland planned to help.[36] Voluntary cooperation across the globe to meet the needs of a world community proved to be one of Hall Xuma's most valuable lessons and useful tools during her tenure on the committee.

After the meeting, Hall Xuma flew back to South Africa and wrote an article for the *Bantu World* declaring that the World YWCA Council was "one of the most stimulating and interesting Council Meetings the World's YWCA has ever had." While she noted that "it was a relief to be home again," the newspaper opined, "Like her famous husband Mrs. Xuma just never has time to rest." Indeed, by the time the article appeared in print, she and Agnes Neilson had already engaged in a series of leadership-training workshops to inform members about their experiences at the British conference.[37] More significantly, Hall Xuma had been elected the first Black president of the of the South African Council of World Affiliated YWCA and was preparing to join three hundred members from more than forty urban cities and rural areas who were heading to Durban for a continuation of the centennial celebrations.[38]

Holding the dual positions as the president of the South African Council and membership on the World YWCA Executive Committee propelled her popularity. For the *World Y.W.C.A. Monthly*, she symbolized the nexus of the two organizations. In the picture featured in the magazine, she stood in the center of executive planning delegates of the South African Council of World Affiliated YWCA who had met in Johannesburg in April 1956. The article noted that this was their first meeting since official admission as an organization into the World YWCA.[39]

The dual demands on her were enormous, but with the assistance of her two friends Cora Phillips as secretary and treasurer and Margaret Hathaway as executive secretary, she successfully led a South African Council that included a sprawling amalgamation of Black, white, and Coloured associations

FIGURE 8.4. This photograph of the South African Centenary Conference of World Affiliated YWCA was taken in Durban in 1955. The more than three hundred members who attended the three-day conference represented thirty-six communities. Seated on the front row left of the aisle (*left to right*) are Victoria Mahamba Sitole, Durban YWCA staff member; Mrs. Sharp, board member of Port Elizabeth who was formerly president of South African Council of World Affiliated YWCA; Miss Moase, Port Elizabeth general secretary; Mrs. E. Lebona of Bloemfontein, who was one of the trainees in USA at the Leadership Training Project; and three members from the Wentworth YWCA club located in a Coloured suburb in Durban. On the front row right of the aisle (*left to right*) are Madie Hall Xuma, the newly elected president of the South African Council of World Affiliated YWCA; Mrs. Swainston Harrison; and Mrs. W. H. Haley, retiring secretary and president of the South African Council of World Affiliated YWCA. Courtesy of World Young Women's Christian Association Archives, Geneva, Switzerland.

that stretched across sixty cities and rural communities in nearly every region of the country. They spent a great deal of time traveling to those branches, engaging with members, and giving speeches. Hall Xuma's most poignant moments, however, were with the Zenzele YWCA of the Transvaal, the first group of Black women to become integrated into the YWCA organization. The branch hosted the conference and exhibition in December 1956 at the end of her first year as president. Delegates from forty-eight clubs and associations attended the conference that the newsletter proclaimed "will surely go down in history as a high point in our work together." Discussion groups about leadership, membership, programs, finances, and future steps were led by Hall Xuma and others. There was also a collection of ten pounds for

FIGURE 8.5. In this photograph of the South African Council of World Affiliated YWCA National Board in 1956, Madie Hall Xuma, the president, is standing in the center with a hat and glasses on. The photograph was the first taken of the group since the organization's official full admission into the World YWCA and was featured in the *World Y.W.C.A. Monthly* publication in December 1956. Courtesy of the World Young Women's Christian Association Archives, Geneva, Switzerland.

Cora Phillips to send to the World YWCA for the Hungarian Relief Fund directed at refugees in that country. In addition, Hall Xuma was the keynote speaker at the annual Transvaal Zenzele YWCA meeting in July 1957.[40]

Moreover, her achievement reached far beyond South Africa. She was a symbol of progress and success for Black YWCA women in other African countries. *Ghana Today*, for example, reported in July that when she visited the country in her role as president of the South African Council of World Affiliated YWCA, a local branch threw a party in her honor and provided her with a souvenir as a gift.[41]

Under her administration, the South African Council YWCA focused on the World YWCA programs of social welfare and self-support. Members directed most of their energy to tackling some of the issues that rural women faced by essentially operating like a social service agency. There were myriad educational courses, homemaking-skill demonstrations, recreational activities, religious services, musical programs, clubs for young teens, and various community service projects. All of it required both volunteers and funding. Members eagerly committed themselves to serving their communities, and the World YWCA remained steadfast in providing staff, money, and other resources in a place where Elizabeth Palmer, the general secretary, acknowledged the work was "difficult" but concluded that she "cannot think of any part of the world in which it seems to me more important for us to be trying to carry out our purpose." To that end, the World YWCA assisted with negotiating with the USA YWCA in the appointment of another staff member to South Africa when Hathaway was slated to leave for Rhodesia in 1958 and called on the coalition of Australia, Canada, and New Zealand to contribute financial support for the staff.[42]

Still, the global needs far exceeded the resources of the World YWCA, so the organization was limited by how much it could provide on a long-term basis. The "precarious" nature of the South African Council finances Hall Xuma and Cora Phillips revealed to Elizabeth Palmer meant that "our present funds come largely from contributions of well disposed friends and bodies outside of the YWCA."[43] And, indeed, Hall Xuma and her husband had been cultivating those relationships with "friends" in the United States and soliciting their aid years before she was elected president of the South African Council. In 1954, for example, Alfred Xuma appealed to a New York philanthropist who had set up a foundation in South Africa and appointed him and his wife as the "agents" disseminating financial resources. When he requested the use of funds in December 1954 for "a medium-sized X-ray machine for doing chest and bone work gratis for my type of patients who cannot afford the usual $15.00 fee for examination," he also requested funds for the "the Zenzele YWCA." But he insisted, "Of the two projects . . . the Zenzele YWCA requirements are greater and more pressing although the X-ray scheme is also aimed at greater and more effective service to the needy." He was

> particularly interested in continued and increased financial assistance to the Zenzele YWCA movement which has rapidly and spontaneously developed into a national organization with equally increased financial needs for its maintenance, development and direction. What is most important about it is: It is the most outstanding movement among African women for the development of character, healthy leadership and stability of the home, but the membership though willing is largely poor and unable to be self-supporting. It will always depend on outside generosity for its continuence [sic]. At present, it maintains an office and an executive Secretary for the Transvaal only but a budget of about £750 or about $2000 per annum, £500 or about $1350 of which is a private grant for the next two years only.[44]

The United States remained a fertile financial resource for the YWCA because three years later, Hall Xuma and Hathaway were seeking funds from Riverside Church in New York City. In one of the updates that they sent to the congregation about the South African Council, they expressed their appreciation for "gifts" and expressions of "personal interest" to the Riverside community. Boasting that "our membership is growing and we now have little YWCA groups in over 60 communities and rural areas," they were happy to report "that increasingly the program is developing among the teen-agers and young adults." But they worried about how the theme of the World YWCA Membership Day, "My Task in Family Life Today," could be implemented in such a "challenging" area like South Africa. With ample housing throughout the country in short supply, they could only hope, they lamented, that what they were able to achieve brought them in "this Christian fellowship which links us with each other not only in this vast country but with you also in the outside world."[45]

The end of Hall Xuma's term as president of the South African Council did not diminish her popularity or clout. When the NCAW announced its "Coming of Age Conference" in celebration of its twenty-one-year history in 1958, it was her stature as the first Black president of the South African Council and as the most prominent member of the Zenzele YWCA that they invited her to write one of the "Congratulatory Messages" to appear on a poster advertisement. For the organization that embraced her when she first arrived in South Africa, she wrote, "On behalf of the Zenzele Young Women's Christian Association I wish to congratulate the National Council of African Women for attaining its twenty-first birthday and for the services which it has rendered to the African community during that period. To have been able to stay together and work together through that period is an indication of wise and able leadership as well as devoted and loyal following. I wish the council long life of continued service to the upliftment and advancement of the African peoples."[46]

Hall Xuma also continued to vigorously promote exchange and leadership programs for young Black African women. For example, after completing trips to Denmark, Sweden, and Switzerland in 1958, she inquired about a fellowship for formal leadership training in Sweden for a YWCA member who could invest "two years of service to the YWCA."[47]

Her extensive travel and work on behalf of the World YWCA Executive Committee prompted the *World* magazine to call her the "Great Union ambassador" when she embarked on a monthlong trip in July 1956 that ended in Geneva for an Executive Committee meeting. On the way there, she scheduled a three-day stop in Uganda to "look over YWCA work" in the country and stayed in Kampala, where she was the guest of South African–born Ugandan Legislative Council member Pumla Ellen Ngozwana Kisosonkole.[48]

When she arrived in Geneva this time, she presented the portrait of a seasoned activist. Deliberative in her thought process about issues, she either made a motion or seconded them on numerous occasions and genuinely embraced the intergenerational and globalized context of the World YWCA's mission. At the July meeting, she played a key role in legislative decisions that pointed to the committee's commitment to engaging in social and international issues and intertwining the agenda of the World YWCA with other international organizations. Several of the decisions involved ensuring that the World YWCA maintain a relationship with the International Labour Organization because it was "in view of the direct interest of the World YWCA" and sponsoring a seminar with the National YWCA in India at the same time that the UNESCO general conference was being held. Hall Xuma strategically "moved" "that a seminar, sponsored jointly by the World YWCA, the National YWCA of the USA, and the National YWCA of Canada, be held in New York, at the time of the session of the UN Commission on the Status of Women, in the Spring of 1957." She supported the institutionalization of "one day a year" to "sacrificial giving towards the World YWCA Mutual Service Programme" for contributing to "Standards of Living, Technical Assistance and Aid to Development" for YWCAs around the world.[49]

On her a return trip from Geneva, Hall Xuma made two stops. One was in Portugal and the other in Liberia. The Portugal trip seems to have been, like the stop in Rome on her way to Geneva, part of a personal quest to see the world, but the stay in Monrovia, Liberia, reflected her positions as both a South African and a World YWCA dignitary. She was there as the guest of the minister of the interior.[50]

The business conducted at all of the World YWCA meetings between 1955 and 1960 demonstrated how engaged Hall Xuma was in navigating the challenges to the organization and to politics on the world stage. The postwar refugee crisis that had been expected to abate after the war, for example, had instead continued to grow. YWCA associations, individual members, and their families had been impacted and devastated so much by the effects of displacement, housing, shortages, and poverty that the Executive Committee determined that the World YWCA was "the only women's organization doing any extensive international refugee service" and was thinking carefully about how to commit more staff and resources to places like Germany, Yugoslavia, and Trieste, Italy.[51]

Displacement coupled with the expulsion of thousands of people from countries at war internally and externally, particularly women and girls, and social and international issues remained topics in 1958 for the Executive

Committee, and so were concerns about encouraging leadership training, embracing younger members, and the Christian mission of the organization. That was why there were two meetings in the fall that year. The World YWCA Consultation of the Christian Task of the YWCA, held from October 30 to November 6, preceded the Executive Committee's meeting November 9–22, 1958.[52] More than thirty-three women and men from twenty-one countries attended the consultation. To facilitate discussion of "the last paragraph of the Functions of the World YWCA and two Paragraphs in the Preamble," four groups examined four issues:

1. The YWCA's role in providing Christian Education for its members;
2. The understanding of a commitment to Christian unity;
3. How to relate our faith to readiness to make choice;
4. The task of the YWCA in a non-Christian environment.[53]

Hall Xuma was assigned to the first group. Members "agreed that as a Christian movement the YWCA must provide a means of understanding the Christian faith, or meeting the spiritual, as well as the physical and mental needs of the individuals, of helping them grow into fullness of life, and must try to meet the many deep and pressing needs of the present day, even if there is at the time no visible response" and looked at several important problems that the YWCA faced in its mission to provide Christian education. One of them spoke to some of the difficulties that Hall Xuma and the South African Council YWCA encountered, particularly in rural areas: "The difficulty of having a Christian impact on modern man in a secular culture and one which may sometimes be greatly influenced by traditional cultural patterns, e.g. tribal authority." While the group did not have time to discuss these issues, members listed the weighty questions of "How can we help individuals who are not now church members into church membership?" as well as "Can one be a Christian without being a member of a church?" and "Can one expect leaders who are not [C]hristians to give responsible leadership in the YWCA?" among other important issues that needed to be addressed. Hall Xuma, seemingly operating as the secretary, saw great value in the meeting and the deliberation exercises. She meticulously crafted summaries of each group's discussion and conclusions. She also handwrote comments of her own on her documents, noting, "Some of the illustrations of the work of the various national associations were very helpful to the group. It was seen that anything and method or program can be used as a starting point if the reasons or motivations are clear if they are well used and if the ultimate goals are understood. The openness of young people to go deeper, not to be satisfied with the superficial level of life is an asset on which the YWCA can build in its work."[54]

When the Executive Committee convened a contingent of World YWCA Council members from Sweden, Italy, Denmark, and Great Britain, consultants from the World Council of Churches and visitors from Mexico, Belgium, the United States, Great Britain, Greece, the World Alliance of the YMCA, and others joined them.[55] One of the most noteworthy items on the agenda provided an update about an ambitious training program that made it possible for four young women from Argentina, Canada, Jamaica, and New Zealand to spend a year working at the World YWCA headquarters. The goals were twofold. The young women were to gain intimate knowledge about the inner workings of the World YWCA and the international organizations connected to the YWCA's mission such as the United Nations and the high commissioner for refugees. In turn, the young women offered the World YWCA staff the opportunity to learn firsthand about their home communities and countries. Moreover, the committee urged national YWCAs to sponsor training opportunities, both in the home country and abroad, and provide scholarships.[56]

The committee also focused attention on "Ecumenical Questions" that had led to the creation of the consultation committee in 1955. Charged with examining "'the understanding of a commitment to Christian unity in the YWCA as an ecumenical lay movement,' and the questions raised in regard to the working of the Preamble of the World YWCA Constitution," the consultation committee understood the magnitude of their role in the reforms that were taking place among Christian organizations like the YWCA. Members ultimately recommended that changes to the wording of the preamble needed further review and circulated among all of the national organizations before being presented at the 1963 quadrangle meeting.[57]

The Mutual Service and Extension Subcommittee that met three days prior to the Executive Committee meeting on November 7–9 had been busy. Members deliberated over how to assist associations in places like in Africa, India, Indonesia, Iraq, Israel, Korea, Lebanon, and the Philippines and extension programs in the South Pacific Islands, Aruba, Cuba, Paraguay, Tangier, and Tanganyika. Subcommittee members often fought their way through very difficult determinations about ways in which member associations received resources. On the one hand, the committee made a recommendation to request that the American YWCA contribute $6,000 toward the completion of the building for a training-camp project in Egypt and, on the other hand, tabled a request for funds for a building project in Johannesburg, South Africa. The committee also recommended seeking aid from American, Canadian, and other YWCAs to provide the branch in Brazil with $1,500 to build a training-camp unit while also supporting the Alliance des Equipes Unionistes of France intention to dispatch a liaison to Africa to create stronger links among women and girls with the World YWCA. Hall Xuma must have chafed at the recommendation to table the Johannesburg project because she was one of the key architects of the proposal, yet she had come to understand and embrace the idea that the whole organization's interest outweighed the interest of one branch or individual. So she moved that both the recommendations for cobbling together a coalition of multiple branches from Australia to Thailand to assist the Middle Eastern YWCAs in Iraq, Israel, Jordan, Egypt, and Lebanon with cash and staff and that the French project in Africa be accepted.[58]

The four years that she served on the Executive Committee had been quite fulfilling, so she agreed to a second four-year term in the summer of 1959, even as South Africa became a far more dangerous place. The arrests and subsequent Treason Trials of more than 150 individuals that included ANC member Nelson Mandela began in 1956 and lasted until 1961. And her neighborhood disintegrated as more families were removed and homes vacated. In 1959 she was finally forced to move out of the Toby Street home that she had shared with Xuma for nearly twenty years. Her new ten-room house, situated on a large nice lot in Dube on Mtipa Street, was such a showplace that YWCA friend Rosalie Oakes told her that she was "anxious to see it again!" The Italian contractor who built the house ensured that it had all of the modern amenities. "It looked," Steven Gish, notes, "as if it belonged in an upper-middle class white suburb rather than on the dusty street of Soweto."[59] But the apartheid policy that had forced her out of Sophiatown reminded her of the precarious life she lived.

Another reminder remained tied to her travel for the World YWCA. When she applied to travel to Geneva in 1958, Jacqueline van Stoetwegen, the associate general secretary of the World YWCA, stood in for Elizabeth Palmer and verified her travel plans for the Department of the Interior.[60] For the "Application for Passport Facilities" in Cuernavaca, Mexico, meeting in 1959, Elizabeth Palmer wrote to the Department of the Interior on her behalf. "Once again," Palmer began, "I am writing to ask your assistance in arranging passport facilities for Mrs. A. B. Xuma (Madie Hall Xuma), to travel as a member of the World YWCA Executive Committee." "The Council meeting of the World YWCA is being held in September of this year in Mexico. We have asked Mrs. Xuma to visit Associations both before and immediately following this meeting, in the Caribbean Area," and, she continued, "It is also possible that Mrs. Xuma will be needed in Geneva for Committee meetings in the middle of 1960, and we would hope that she could make some visits to National Association in connection with that trip. We would be very grateful if passport facilities could be arranged for Mrs. Xuma so that she can undertake these responsibilities on behalf of the World YWCA."[61]

FIGURE 8.6. An outside view of Madie and Alfred Xuma's Home in Sophiatown in the late 1950s. Courtesy of Historical Papers Research Archive, University of the Witwatersrand, South Africa.

She arrived at the October 1959 World Council in Cuernavaca, Mexico, as one of the most experienced and knowledgeable Executive Committee members. She continued to serve on the Mutual Service Subcommittee and supported the continuation of consultative groups that examined ecumenical questions and further development of others issues such as the establishment of YWCA Hostels and YMCA/YWCA Relations. She engaged in a host of discussions about the organization taking part in various seminars, conferences, and meetings that seemed strategically designed to maximize the World YWCA's ability to engage with other organizations, spread its own message, and provide multilayered learning environments for young female members. There was the planned World YWCA seminar in Argentina in March or April that would coincide with the United Nations Status of Women meeting in 1960 and the World Student Christian Federation, a global ecumenical movement of students first organized in Sweden in 1895, and a teaching conference in Strasburg, France, in July where the committee wanted the fifteen delegates to be "younger leaders—under 30—capable of absorbing, contributing to and profiting from this kind of teaching conference, as well as understanding how the experience could be used in their

FIGURE 8.7. Madie and Alfred Xuma, seated on far right in their home in Sophiatown. Courtesy of Historical Papers Research Archive, University of the Witwatersrand, South Africa.

own Association afterwards." Moreover, Hall Xuma was so excited about the exchange and leadership programs among young women that she moved to accept the proposal to relaunch the Leadership Training Institute that would provide "a training and refresher course for YWCA leaders of a duration of up to six weeks."[62]

There was a particular attentiveness by the committee to the growth of the YWCA movement in geographical areas dominated by women of color. The location of the council meeting, of course, certainly highlighted the interest, but so did the proposal for a conference in Africa sometime in 1960 or 1961 that Marly V. de Barros of Brazil argued would be of "great value." While the committee deferred the final decision about the specifics of such a conference to the next meeting, it was clear that the African continent remained fertile ground for the YWCA movement. South America and the Caribbean did as well. The Executive Committee focused on the development of an exchange program in South America and discussed holding a meeting in the Caribbean in 1962. Financial constraints posed a problem, but the committee determined that "if plans could be made far enough ahead, it might be possible to obtain grants from a variety of sources." To begin that process, when the conference ended Hall Xuma flew to Miami and then visited Puerto Rico and Jamaica.[63]

The Mexico Council meeting also transitioned the World YWCA from an apolitical institution to a politicized humanitarian force. The delegates who converged on Hotel Mandel spent long busy days in group discussions on social and international issues such as how the YWCA could operate successfully in non-Christian nations, the promotion of leadership skills, the development of communities, and the problems facing refugees, and they, more significantly, engaged in conversations about the World YWCA adopted policy statement concerning world peace in September 1955. Elizabeth Palmer had helped propel the policy's importance when she told the New York YWCA in March 1956, "Membership in the world-wide women's movement today is of greater importance than ever because of the need for people to learn to live peacefully together."[64] In the years since, the continued turmoil in the Middle East and Europe, the displacement of people that had led to a refugee crisis, and the successful launch of Sputnik in 1957 by the Soviet Union that stoked fears of nuclear annihilation added to the World YWCA's weariness about the fate of some of its members. It was no coincidence then that the organization publicly pursued the goals "to promote world peace and mutual understanding between peoples" and to encourage "National Associations to bring to bear whatever pressures they can on their governments in the direction of concluding enforceable permanent agreements on the suspension of nuclear testing by any nation anywhere in the world."[65] The new course broadened the scope of the organization's mission and situated it in the center of the growing power and potency of women's politicized voices around the world.

Invigorated by the conference's message and declarations, Hall Xuma joined the more than 135 delegates who attended the three-day national conference in Port Elizabeth on December 17–19, 1959. She gave the keynote address that encapsulated the conference theme titled "The Christian Purpose of the YWCA." She also began on a quest to fulfill a "dream and passion" to build a YWCA community center in Dube. The problem was Rosalie Oakes did not believe that a center should be built and was perturbed by Hall Xuma's insistence. "If I were to give you my personal and professional assessment of the need and ability of the South African YWCA to handle building plans, etc., at this time," Oakes wrote to Janet Thomson in August 1959, "I would say we have no business at all thinking of building anything." Moreover, she asked for help in trying to get Hall Xuma "to tone down" her "idea of a suitable building for Johannesburg." But Hall Xuma was far more determined and persuasive, and the fund-raising campaign was launched by the Johannesburg Branch of the Zenzele YWCA of the Transvaal and the advisory committee in 1960.[66]

Hall Xuma was committed to the completion of that project, but at the age of sixty-six she found the challenges of the health issues that plagued both her and her husband and fears about the deteriorating political situation so difficult that she began cutting back on her work in the World YWCA. In the early months of 1960, she notified the Executive Committee that she declined to serve on the Mutual Service Subcommittee. She, however, still remained engaged with the YWCA by continuing to locate donors for fund-raising endeavors that benefited the World YWCA and the South African YWCA.[67]

That effort, however, was severely hampered by the Sharpeville massacre on March 21, 1960. Four months before the deadly assault, the ANC passed resolutions against the pass laws, and the Pan-African Congress did the same. There were demonstrations by both groups as well as others, but it was the PAC's March 18, 1960, declaration of a nonviolent campaign to abolish pass laws that set in motion what became the brutal attack on Black citizens. Members of the organization were told to resist nonviolently by refusing to carry their passes and by turning themselves over to the police at the nearest station. Thousands of women and men participated in demonstrations in many major areas. Nearly seven thousand marched in Sharpeville. The police responded by throwing tear-gas bombs and charging at demonstrators, killing almost seventy unarmed pass-law demonstrators and wounding nearly two hundred.[68] The events were so horrific that when World YWCA emissary Rosalie Oakes sent a letter to Elizabeth Palmer and Fay Allan, of the Foreign Division of the YWCA in America, ten days later, she expressed both despair and hope. "I know this should have been written a few days ago but I kept hoping things would improve in the political situation in South Africa! But it seems this Government is determined to incite the African leaders to further violence! Things are quieter on the surface today, but the atmosphere is tense." She described a nation at war. What occurred in Sharpeville impacted nearly every area, institution, and organization in the country. "I am especially frustrated tonight—no urban papers and no radio available," she lamented.[69]

Continuing YWCA work proved to be nearly impossible. "I'm en route from Bloemfontein to Port Elizabeth after about five weeks in the Free State trying to lay the groundwork for the fund raising for the YWCA centre!" that, Oakes pointed out, "seems slightly ironical now, after so many churches have been burned in Worcester, one of the Johannesburg locations—£40,000 damage was done there on Monday night, according to today's papers." She was "sure the State of Emergency will prevent my going into any location in any urban areas for as long as any trouble lasts. The Executive Committee meets April 9 and will no doubt discuss what the emergency means for our work. We had a Transvaal workshop scheduled in Sharpeville location the weekend following the first demonstrations—March 26–27 and it was postponed, of course."[70]

The effect on YWCA personnel like Hall Xuma and Phyllis Mzaidume, the general secretary of the Zenzele YWCA of the Transvaal, particularly concerned her. "I have not heard from Phyllis Mzaidume nor from Madie this week—so trust no news is good news," she lamented. But she was still "hoping Phyllis did not go to work on Monday! I tried to get a call through to her and to Madie, but the Orlando telephone service is impossible at best and the delay was hours into the night—so I have written to them."[71] Ultimately, Hall Xuma and Mzaidume were fine, but the work of the YWCA in South Africa proved to be far more difficult.

YWCA women, however, refused to bow completely to apartheid. Hall Xuma, for example, attended the World YWCA Executive Committee in Switzerland in 1960 and joined the World YWCA coalition of president Isabel G. Catto, vice president Irene E. B. Ighodaro, Phoebe Shukri, and others for the first World YWCA All Africa Conference in Salisbury, Southern Rhodesia, from December 29, 1960 to January 12, 1961. Moreover, nearly six hundred South African Council members attended a workshop in 1962, and a leadership-training workshop was held in Roodeport in 1963.[72]

As apartheid tightened its grip, condemnations and sanctions from leaders around the world followed. Even the embattled secretary-general of the United Nations, Dag Hammarskjold, visited the country, met with government administrators, and consulted with three prominent Black South African men. One of them was Alfred Xuma. Moreover, leaders on the African continent played an instrumental role in the April 1961 UN General Assembly's 95–1 vote that adopted a resolution condemning apartheid and calling it "reprehensible and repugnant to human dignity."[73] In June Pulitzer Prize–winning former chief of the South African Bureau of the Associated Press Lynn Heinzerling observed, "Today South Africa is on its own. Dr. Hendrik Verwoerd, the granite-line prime minister, heads a republic that has cut all its historic ties to Britain. But much of the world condemns this government's treatment of 13 million non-whites, distrusts its economic stability and has misgivings about its future." Still, the reporter argued that although there were "frayed nerves and uncertainty" among many white South Africans about "the threat of a full-scale strike and possibly of another Sharpeville," much of the country resembled the cities and towns in America's Midwest. "There is a good road system, and excellent internal airline and adequate railroad service. There are excellent game reserves, parks, theaters, supermarkets and department stores," he wrote. Ultimately, however, he surmised that his was "a white man's view of the country. For the black man it is a different proposition. He lives in segregated locations, in a shack on a white man's farm or in the mud hut of his ancestors in a reserve."[74]

Hall Xuma and her husband were deeply disturbed by the steadily deteriorating race relations and world isolation, but their energies were focused on fighting the pancreatic cancer that had plagued Xuma since May 1961. Hall Xuma grappled with her husband's illness and at the same time still carried on her World YWCA duties. She attended the World YWCA Executive Committee meeting in Geneva that year. But the surgery that her husband underwent proved ineffective in curtailing the progress of the disease, so the couple began the process of getting their personal affairs in order. In December they jointly signed real-estate documents agreeing to the sale of property that had been part of Edna's estate. The Redevelopment Commission of Winston-Salem purchased the lot on the corner of 7½ and Hickory Streets for $3,500.[75] Afterward, Xuma's health deteriorated rapidly, and he died on Saturday, January 27, 1962. His wife was devastated by the loss, Ellen Kuzwayo, longtime YWCA member and antiapartheid activist, noted in an interview. He had been "a very worthy husband," Kuzwayo insisted, and "he meant everything in her life."[76]

For the husband who had admired his wife and had praised her for being "a devoted mother to our two children, an indispensable companion and devoted wife," Hall Xuma held a private ceremony at the home they had shared in Dube on February 1, 1962. And she must have helped orchestrate the public tribute to him that Steven Gish argues "resembled that of a head of state." "Xuma's body was taken by procession to the Donaldson Community Centre in Orlando. Schools in Orlando East and West were closed for the afternoon so African Children could form a silent guard of honor along the procession round. Several thousand people—both Black and white—crowded in the community center to pay their last respects." Francis Herman Gow, an AME Church bishop, led the congregation of mourners and the prominent cast of dignitaries who spoke at the service for a man that the *Times* of London called "one of the architects of the African National Congress." It was the end of an era in South Africa and for Hall Xuma.[77]

Conclusion

Several months after her husband died, Hall Xuma's name was listed among those in the Shaw University class of 1912 honored with the Golden Anniversary Award presented at the 1962 commencement.[1] The recognition served as a reminder of the way in which the university had shaped her life. Perhaps it also provided some solace from the pain she felt over the loss of her beloved "Dr." who had insisted that she return to North Carolina after his death. "You leave as quickly as you can," she recalled him telling her. Others also told her "to get out." She heeded their advice. By the fall of 1962, several media outlets reported that she was indeed leaving South Africa.[2]

In the months that followed, she ensured that the legacies of both her and her husband endured. She donated their papers to the South African Institute of Race Relations (now housed at the University of Witwatersrand). The vast majority of the voluminous collection detailed her husband's life and work in South Africa. Included are her own correspondence, date books, passport, and evidence of her activism.[3] She also gave a number of interviews. One of them was with the *Rand Daily Mail* that published the article "'Momma' Xuma Is Going Back Home" on February 14, 1963. In it she articulated her motivation for leaving the country where she had resided for twenty-three years. She was deeply distressed by the fact that "race relations are far worse now than when I arrived" and asserted that what she was most looking forward to in Winston-Salem was "how wonderful it will be to meet friends on a basis of equality."[4]

Her decision saddened YWCA women because "the friendships that she had in the Y.W.C.A.," Ellen Kuzwayo argued, were not strong enough for her to say "I will not go back home, because his people were my people," but they were grateful for the time to say good-bye.[5] They joined Hall Xuma in

FIGURE 9.1. This picture was taken at the official ceremony celebrating the opening of the Dube Building YWCA on February 16, 1963. Maud Piliso, a founding member of the Johannesburg branch, is the first person (*from left to right*) and Madie Hall Xuma is the third person. Other participants included white/European Johannesburg city officials. Courtesy of World Young Women's Christian Association Archives, Geneva, Switzerland.

reveling in the fact that programs thrived in YWCAs across South Africa and that the number of programs and activities offered to both youth and adults in Dube continued to expand. They showed their affection for her at one of the last and most memorable public appearances at the dedication of the opening of the Dube YWCA foyer. Joined by her friend and YWCA associate Maud Piliso, she sat on the stage with a group of prominent white dignitaries who faced an audience of her YWCA members. They had all gathered to commemorate Hall Xuma's activism, to memorialize her and witness her laying the plaque that read "Zenzele Y.W.C.A., This Stone Was Laid By Madie Hall Xuma On 16th February 1963." By May she was back in the United States.[6]

FIGURE 9.2. This is a photograph of a group of women standing beside the plaque in the Dube building that reads "Zenzele Y. W. C. A. This Stone Was Laid By Madie Hall Xuma On 16th February 1963." Courtesy of World Young Women's Christian Association Archives, Geneva, Switzerland.

* * *

Willie had warned her sister as early as 1959 that she "won't hardly know much of Winston when you come."[7] And four years later, the city was indeed a far different place than the one that Hall Xuma left in 1940 or had even seen on her visits in the decade after the war. In the city described as "the best of the old and the best of the new blend to make a progressive city still marked by a deep religious atmosphere, a love for music and arts, and a zeal for broad educational development," the population stood at 111,000 residents. It was the largest manufacturer of hosiery and knit underwear in the world and was still the leader in the production of tobacco products. The R. J. Reynolds Tobacco Company building loomed large in the downtown district. Guided tours beckoned visitors to view the production of cigarettes such as Camel, Salem, and Winston and Prince Albert smoking tobacco. Tobacco warehouses near Oak and Patterson Streets wreaked of "the pungent smell of ripe tobacco" as the daily business of auctioning marketed the city's most profitable products. There was an airport, nearly eighty-eight thousand registered motor vehicles on the roads, and buses and trains that serviced citizens of the city. The educational system, supported by four colleges—Salem College, Bowman Gray School of Medicine of Wake Forest, Winston-Salem State College, and Wake Forest College that moved there in 1956—thrived. Three hospitals and several other medical facilities supported the community's medical needs. Recreational and cultural opportunities abounded. There were parks, recreational programs, golf courses, and a coliseum with a seating capacity of eight thousand as well as concerts and lectures provided by a bevy of organizations and institutions.[8]

Like the country, Hall Xuma's hometown was also in a civil rights transition. Following similar demonstrations in Birmingham, Alabama, and nearby cities of Greensboro, Fayetteville, and Raleigh, antisegregation protests erupted in Winston-Salem in the spring of 1963. As the "racial crisis" to dismantle Jim Crow spread to other southern cities, mayors created committees of Black and white citizens to discuss racial issues. The Winston-Salem committee, appointed on May 20, consisted of nine Blacks and nine whites. They determined that "the committee accepts as its outgoing objective the achievement in Winston-Salem of access to all public facilities for all citizens, regardless of race, color or creed. We propose to advance toward this purpose through approach, discussion and negotiation." By June 6, 1963, a large number of restaurants, hotels, and motels had ended their segregation policy.[9]

The contrast between Winston-Salem and South Africa could not have been more profound, and Hall Xuma seized the moment to highlight the differences. For example, she joined the former president of Denison University in a seminar on Africa led by American Friends Service Committee at the Woman's College of the University of North Carolina (now the University of North Carolina at Greensboro). She spoke "on the struggles for independence now in progress in Southern Africa."[10]

As she continued to resettle into life as an American citizen, members of the YWCA on Patterson Avenue properly greeted her with a "Welcome Home Tea." They entertained her with the music and singing she had always enjoyed. And her longtime friend Creola Foote helped to serve the tea. She happily participated in the honor by showing slides and regaling her audience with a discussion on her international YWCA work. She did the same at the Mary McLeod Bethune YWCA in High Point the following year.[11]

In 1966 she went on one last adventure. The trip around the world took her back to South Africa. When she arrived in Johannesburg, the newspaper welcomed "Mommy's return." She visited with friends, family, and YWCA members but understood that this was probably the last time that she would see all of them.[12]

When Hall Xuma returned to the United States, she resumed her busy life speaking and participating in various organizations such as the Parent Teacher Associations, the Winston-Salem Chapter of the National Association of University Women, and the AKA. At the "Afro Fashionetta" festival sponsored by the Phi Omega chapter of the AKA in November 1968, she took great pleasure in explaining how girls in Africa lived and displayed pieces in her arts-and-craft collection. More significantly, her commitment to promoting the kind of work she and her husband had done in South Africa continued to drive her activism. In 1968 she was one of seventy-four program participants at the North Carolina Public Health Association annual meeting in Charlotte. More than a thousand attended the three-day event that highlighted several key health concerns such as nursing, mental health, nutrition, dental health, and public health management. Hall Xuma's talk was called "Social and Medical Experiences in South Africa."[13]

She also returned to the gardening that had made her so happy and attended the Along the Garden Path Flower Garden Club (earlier referred to as the Garden Path Flower Club) meetings. She even hosted the club at a restaurant for a flower show in May 1976. Moreover, she declared in a speech to the Alta Vistas Garden Club in April 1980 that flowers were an important part of gift giving.[14] A regular at Federation of Garden Clubs annual conventions, she attended the three-day convention in Asheville in August 1980 as well as one in Winston-Salem in 1981 where she earned distinction and praise from members of the sixty-three clubs who attended the event. Photographed while "tablehopping" at a garden club anniversary in June 1982, she delighted in conversing with members.[15]

By then, memories of her life in South Africa were all she had of the country. Her daughter, Elizabeth, who had married and moved to Swaziland, had died from sickle-cell anemia in 1972. Moreover, her son, Alfred Jr., who earned his medical degree, moved to the United States and opened a medical practice.[16]

And Willie had died in December 1974 at the age of seventy-six. The loss of her last sister served as a bittersweet reminder that only she and Leroy remained of the family that Humphrey and Jennie Hall had made. Determined to keep both the Hall and the Xuma legacies alive, she sat down for a series of interviews in 1979 that would become part of the book collection *Hope and Dignity: Older Black Women of the South* and the Southern Oral History Program Interview Database housed at the University of North Carolina at Chapel Hill. In them she talked about her family, recounted her life in South

Africa, and highlighted her service, activism, and sense of adventure. She still worried about race relations and the fact that even toward the end of the twentieth century, Blacks and whites did not "live together in harmony and peace." But she was clear that after having lived under Jim Crow and apartheid, the United States had "made more progress than South Africa."[17]

In 1980 she and her brother along with their nephew Harold and his wife, Annie, divested themselves of one of the last of her parents' property investments. The lot located at the intersection of Patterson Avenue and Seventh Street epitomized a legacy of wealth born during the era of Jim Crow. Equity in the property purchased in 1906 had allowed Hall Xuma, her siblings, and Alfred B. Xuma to leverage it in a deed of trust in 1959. For twenty more years, equity continued to build until she and her family decided to sell the property to R. J. Reynolds Tobacco Company in what seemed to have been a previously negotiated transfer of assets. The property sold for the minuscule amount of only "Ten Dollars and Other Valuable Considerations." It is unclear what the "other valuable considerations" included but strongly suggests that something more profitable than monetary gain was at play between the family and the company.[18]

On the morning of Friday, September 10, 1982, Hall Xuma died at 7:15 a.m. of sepsis in Forsyth Memorial Hospital at the age of eighty-eight. The memorial service to honor her life was held at Goler Metropolitan AME Zion Church, and the following Monday her remains were buried in Evergreen Cemetery.[19] She left behind an unparalleled local, state, and global legacy. When the garden club met in October, there was "a moment of meditation" to honor her memory. Her influence on the development of garden clubs had been so profound that six years after her death, the president of the Flower Niche Garden Club made a point of reminding members that Hall Xuma had spearheaded the creation of the statewide federation.[20]

The impact on South Africa and the World YWCA was far greater. The Zenzele YWCA remained such an integral part of the World YWCA, one of the largest female organizations in the world with affiliates located in more than one hundred countries in Africa, Asia, the Caribbean, Europe, Latin America, the Middle East, North America, and the Pacific, that the "Zenzele Marketplace" was a central feature at the Twenty-Ninth World YWCA Council Meeting held in Johannesburg, South Africa, on November 17–22, 2019, nearly eighty years after Madie Beatrice Hall Xuma established the first Zenzele Club.

Notes

Preface

1. In the *Twelfth Census of the United States: 1900*, schedule 1, "Population, Cleveland County, North Carolina," 6. Lavinia is listed as Leaine and Lavinia Hendrake rather than Hendricks. In "The Beginning and History of Peter Forney and Hendricks Families" that I obtained from Alma Hendricks Cardwell, her first name is spelled "Lavinia," while city directories have her first name listed in multiple ways—Lavenia, Lauvinia. *The Winston-Salem, N.C., City Directory, 1915*, 521; *Slater Industrial and State Normal School Course Catalog 1914–1915*, 20, WSSUAr-RG 10–14-WSSU, Digital Collection, Winston-Salem State C. G. O'Kelly University Archives.

2. "The Beginning and History of Peter Forney and Hendricks Families," obtained from Alma Hendricks Cardwell; *Winston-Salem, N.C., City Directory, 1915*, 521; *Winston-Salem, N.C., City Directory, 1916*, 391; *Winston-Salem, N.C., City Directory, 1918*, 435, 377, 547; *Winston-Salem, N.C., City Directory, 1920*, 511; *Winston-Salem, N.C., City Directory, 1921*, 567; *Winston-Salem, N.C., City Directory, 1922*, 586; *Winston-Salem, N.C., City Directory, 1923*, 601.

3. *General Index to Real Estate Conveyances—Forsyth County, NC, to December 31st, 1927—Grantee*, deed, bk. 169, p. 177, bk. 278, p. 159, Forsyth County Register of Deeds. See also *General Index to Real Estate Conveyances—Forsyth County, NC, to December 31st, 1927—Grantor*, deed of trusts, bk. 123, p. 137, bk. 131, p. 274, bk. 132, p. 105, bk. 133, p. 39, bk. 144, p. 2, bk. 219, p. 172, bk. 196, p. 250.

4. "The Beginning and History of Peter Forney and Hendricks Families," personally obtained from Alma Hendricks Cardwell; *Winston-Salem, N.C., City Directory, 1922*, 586; "State's Teacher Shortage," *Winston-Salem Journal*, March 14, 1920; "Teacher Shortage Is More Acute This Year," *Winston-Salem Journal*, July 24, 1920; *The Winston-Salem Teachers College (Formerly the Slater State Normal School) Annual Catalogue 1927–1928*, 59, WSSUAr-RG 10–14-WSSU, Catalog Collection—1927–28; *The Winston-Salem Teachers College (Formerly the Slater State Normal School) Annual*

Catalogue 1928–1929, 69, WSSUAr-RG 10–14-WSSU, Catalog Collection—1928–29, both Winston-Salem State C. G. O'Kelly University Archives (digital); "Personals," *Winston-Salem Journal*, December 25, 1923; *Winston-Salem, N.C., City Directory, 1923*, 601; *Miller's Winston-Salem City Directory, 1929*, 419.

5. "Miss Sawyer Entertained," *Winston-Salem Journal*, July 1, 1931; "Clyde Hendricks, Jr., Honored," *Winston-Salem Journal*, August 27, 1931; "Leaves for New York," *Winston-Salem Journal*, August 27, 1931; "Funeral of Mrs. Forney," *Winston-Salem Journal*, July 8, 1932.

Introduction

1. "Afro-American History Society to Meet," *Winston-Salem Chronicle*, June 16, 1994.

2. "When You've Got a Question . . . Start with Your Librarian," *Wilson Daily Times*, November 15, 2002.

3. D. P. Marolen to Dr. A. B. Xuma, August 9, 1954, A. B. Xuma Papers, 1917–60, Correspondence, AD843-M6, ABX 540809, Historical Papers Research Archive.

4. "The Rise of Female Candidates Ready to Lead Our Great Country," *Weekend Argus*, July 30, 2017. A different version of the article also appeared as "SA Now Better Prepared for a Woman Leader than Before," *Sunday Tribune*, July 30, 2017.

5. There are some exceptions, of course. See, for example, Pamela E. Brooks's intriguing study *Boycotts, Buses, and Passes: Black Women's Resistance in the U.S. South and South Africa*.

6. The list of African scholars who have discussed Hall Xuma is much too long to list here, but see, for example, Iris Berger, "An African American 'Mother of the Nation': Madie Hall Xuma in South Africa, 1940–1963"; Steven D. Gish, who writes extensively about her in his biography of her husband in *Alfred B. Xuma: African, American, South African*; and Alan Grego Cobley, *The Rules of the Game: Struggles in Black Recreation and Social Welfare Policy in South Africa*, 78–80.

7. Robert Trent Vinson, *The Americans Are Coming! Dreams of African American Liberation in Segregationist South Africa*, 138.

8. "Mrs. Xuma on Way Here," *New York Times*, August 22, 1947; "It Happened in Our World: African Emissaries, Following the Pattern of Globe-Trotting Americans, Come Here to See Our Democracy at Work."

9. "'Momma' Xuma Is Going Back Home," *Rand Daily Mail*, February 14, 1963.

10. Robert Rodgers Korstad, *Civil Rights Unionism: Tobacco Workers and the Struggle for Democracy in the Mid-Twentieth-Century South*, 138.

11. Jane Olcott, *The Work of Colored Women*, 48–49, 58–59, 127–28.

12. "Women of City Organize," *Winston-Salem Journal*, May 3, 1926; "State Colored Federation of Woman's Clubs Gather," *Winston-Salem Journal*, April 24, 1927; Mrs. Charlotte Hawkins Brown to Speak," *Winston-Salem Journal*, April 24, 1927; "Mass Meeting at Goler," *Winston-Salem Journal*, April 24, 1927; "Visitors Welcome at the P.W.A.," *Winston-Salem Journal*, April 24, 1927; "Mrs. Brown Speaks," *Winston-Salem Journal*, April 25, 1927.

13. Madie Hall Xuma, interview by Emily Herring Wilson, May 28, 1980, interview G-0280, audio file 2.

14. Emily Herring Wilson and Susan Mullally, *Hope and Dignity: Older Black Women of the South*, 148.

15. Gish, *Alfred B. Xuma*, 137; Wilson and Mullally, *Hope and Dignity*, 148.

16. Nat Nakasa, "'Mummy' Goes Home—but Her Job's Done," 39; Muriel Horrell, comp., *A Survey of Race Relations in South Africa, 1955–1956*, 221.

17. Nakasa, "'Mummy' Goes Home," 40.

18. Carole Seymour-Jones, *Journey of Faith: The History of the World YWCA, 1945–1994*, 173, 500–501; "Ellen Kuzwayo, Anti-Apartheid Crusader, Dies at 91," *New York Times*, April 22, 2006; Berger, "African American 'Mother of the Nation,'" 563.

Chapter 1. The Making of Madie Beatrice Hall

1. Hall Xuma, interview by Wilson, audio file 1. Humphrey Haynes Hall often signed official documents as H. H. Hall and is listed in most city directories as H. H. Hall or Humphrey H. Hall. See, for example, *Turner's Fifth Annual Winston and Salem City Directory for the Years 1891 and 1892*, 154, 190; and *Walsh's Winston-Salem, North Carolina, City Directory for 1904–5*, 381. On occasion, however, some documents referred to him as H. Humphrey Hall. In the absence of a birth certificate or a death certificate in the Forsyth County records, his newspaper obituary, "Dr. H. H. Hall Passes," *Winston-Salem Journal*, November 10, 1935, makes clear that his name was Humphrey Haynes Hall.

2. *Chas. Emerson & Co.'s Winston, Salem & Greensboro, North Carolina, Directory, 1879–'80*, xvii–xxii; Manly Wade Wellman and Larry Edward Tise, *Industry and Commerce, 1766–1896*, 16–22, 27–29; *Ninth Census of the United States: 1870*, vol. 1, *The Statistics of the Population of the United States*, table 3, "State of North Carolina," 222; *Eleventh Census of the United States: 1890*, pt. 1, *Statistics of Population*, table 23, "Native and Foreign Born and White and Colored Population, Classified by Sex, of Places Having 2,500 Inhabitants or More," 546; *Eleventh Census of the United States: 1890*, pt. 1, *Statistics of Population*, table 5, "Population of States and Territories by Minor Civil Divisions," 256.

3. Wellman and Tise, *Industry and Commerce*, 17–22, 27–29; "A Preacher to Be Tried," *Charlotte Observer*, May 2, 1895; *Turner's Winston and Salem City Directory for the Years 1894–95*, 199–200; *Tenth Census of the United States: 1880, Population of Civil Divisions Less than Counties*, table 3, "North Carolina," 280; *Twelfth Census of the United States: 1900, Minor Civil Divisions*, table 5, "Population of States and Territories by Minor Civil Divisions, North Carolina," 289; *Twelfth Census of the United States: 1900, Sex, General Nativity, and Color*, table 24, "Native and Foreign Born and White and Colored Population, Classified by Sex, for Places Having 2,500 Inhabitants or More," 671.

4. *Turner's Fifth Annual Winston and Salem City Directory for the Years 1891 and 1892*, 193. There were also a number of tobacco-leaf dealers and tobacco warehouses. James Howell Smith, *Industry and Commerce, 1896–1975*, 9; John W. Wertheimer, *Law*

and *Society in the South: A History of North Carolina Court Cases*, 45–46; Michele Gillespie, *Katharine and R. J. Reynolds: Partners of Fortune in the Making of the New South*, 180–81; Bertha Hampton Miller, "Blacks in Winston-Salem, North Carolina, 1895–1920: Community Development in an Era of Benevolent Paternalism," 10.

5. Humphrey Hall's exact year of birth is difficult to determine. In the 1870 Census, his age is listed as twelve, which means that he was born in 1858. In the 1880 Census, his age is listed as twenty, indicating that he was born in 1860. In the 1900 Census, his age is listed as thirty-five, suggesting that he was born in 1865. I have decided to use the 1870 Census age. See *Ninth Census of the United States: 1870*, schedule 1, "Inhabitants in Salisbury Township in the County of Rowan," 51; *Tenth Census of the United States: 1880*, schedule 1, "Inhabitants in Salisbury in the County of Rowan, State of N.C.," 27; and *Twelfth Census of the United States: 1900*, schedule 1, "Population, Winston Township, North Carolina, Forsyth County," all available at Ancestry.com.

6. *Tenth Census of the United States: 1880*, schedule 1, "Inhabitants in Salisbury in the County of Rowan, State of N.C.," 27; *Twelfth Census of the United States: 1900*, schedule 1, "Population, Winston Township, North Carolina, Forsyth County"; "Dr. H. H. Hall Passes," *Winston-Salem Journal*, November 10, 1935; *Biennial Report of the Superintendent of Public Instruction of North Carolina for the Scholastic Years 1885 and 1886*, 86–91.

7. See "A Medical Department Established," in *Catalogue of the Officers and Students of Shaw University, 1880–1881*, 18, Shaw University Archive; Todd Savitt, "Training the 'Consecrated, Skillful, Christian Physician': Documents Illustrating Student Life at Leonard Medical School, 1882–1918," 251–54. See also Darlene Clark Hine, "The Anatomy of Failure: Medical Education Reform and the Leonard Medical School of Shaw University, 1882–1920," 513–16; and Frenise A. Logan, *The Negro in North Carolina, 1876–1894*, 107–8.

8. *Catalogue of the Officers and Students of Shaw University, 1885–1886*, 17; *Catalogue of the Officers and Students of Shaw University, 1886–1887*, 11–12; *Catalogue of the Officers and Students of Shaw University, 1887–1888*, 11; *Fifth Annual Announcement of the Leonard Medical School (Medical Department of Shaw University), Raleigh, NC, for the Session of 1885–'85[6?]*, 8; *Seventh Annual Announcement of the Leonard Medical School (Medical Department of Shaw University), Raleigh, NC, for the Session of 1887–'88*, 7–8, 14; *Eighth Annual Announcement of the Leonard Medical School (Medical Department of Shaw University), Raleigh, NC, for the Session of 1888–'89*, 8, 14; *Ninth Annual Announcement of the Leonard Medical School (Medical Department of Shaw University), Raleigh, NC, for the Session of 1889–'90*, 8, 16; *Tenth Annual Announcement of the Leonard Medical School (Medical Department of Shaw University), Raleigh, NC, for the Session of 1890–'91*, 19, all in Shaw University Archive (all of the annual announcements are from DigitalNC); W. N. Hartshorn, ed., *An Era of Progress and Promise, 1863–1910: The Religious, Moral, and Educational Development of the American Negro since His Emancipation*, 87–92, 509; Savitt, "Training the 'Consecrated, Skillful, Christian Physician'," 251–54, 263–65.

9. *Catalogue of the Officers and Students of Shaw University, 1888–1889*, 11; *Tenth Annual Announcement of the Leonard Medical School*, 19, both Shaw University Ar-

chive; Kelly Miller, "The Historic Background of the Negro Physician," 106, 108; Todd L. Savitt, "The Journal of the National Medical Association 100 Years Ago: A New Voice of and for African American Physicians," 735. See also Thomas J. Ward Jr., *Black Physicians in the Jim Crow South*.

10. *Turner's Fifth Annual Winston and Salem City Directory*, 55, 154, 188, 190, 193; Robert W. Prichard, "Winston-Salem's Black Hospitals prior to 1830," 246.

11. There are discrepancies in Jennie Hall's place of birth and her age. See *Ninth Census of the United States: 1870*, schedule 1, "Inhabitants in Salisbury Township in the County of Rowan," 9, State of North Carolina, that shows her born in 1867; *Tenth Census of the United States: 1880*, schedule 1, "Inhabitants in Salisbury in the County of Rowan, State of N.C.," 3, that shows her born "Abt 1866"; Wilson and Mullally, *Hope and Dignity*, 144–45; Lyda Moore Merrick and Madie Hall Xuma, interview by Emily Herring Wilson, September 11, 1979, interview G-0270, audio file 3; and "The Funeral of Mrs. Hall," *Winston-Salem Journal*, August 30, 1930.

12. Wilson and Mullally, *Hope and Dignity*, 144–45; Merrick and Hall Xuma, interview by Wilson, audio file 3; "The Funeral of Mrs. Hall," *Winston-Salem Journal*, August 30, 1930.

13. Mark Wineka, *Salisbury Post*, December 2, 2009, https://www/salisburypost.com /author/staff.report/; Merrick and Hall Xuma, interview by Wilson, audio file 3; Wilson and Mullally, *Hope and Dignity*, 144–45. Jennie was referred to as Jane in the 1870 Census.

14. *Catalogue of the Officers and Students of Shaw University, 1887–1888*, 13, 18–19, Shaw University Archive; Merrick and Hall Xuma, interview by Wilson, audio file 3.

15. There are discrepancies about Cleo's birth year. Madie noted that he was born in 1892, but he is listed in the 1900 Census as Harvey, born in July 1891. See *Twelfth Census of the United States: 1900*, schedule 1, "Population, Winston Township, North Carolina, Forsyth County"; and *General Index to Real Estate Conveyances—Forsyth County, NC, to December 31st, 1927—Grantee*, deed, bk. 46, p. 119, Forsyth County Register of Deeds.

16. *General Index to Real Estate Conveyances—Forsyth County, NC, to December 31st, 1927—Grantor*, deed of trust, bk. 19, p. 572; Langdon Edmunds Oppermann, "Historic and Architectural Resources of African-American Neighborhoods in Northeastern Winston-Salem, ca. 1900–1947, National Register of Historic Places Multiple Property Documentation Form," 11–12, 24; *Turner's Winston and Salem City Directory for the Years 1894–95*, 118. I have chosen to use the birth date recorded on the unofficial death certificate for Madie Hall Xuma obtained from the Forsyth County Register of Deeds.

17. See Oppermann, "Historic and Architectural Resources," 17–18, 22. Goler was at one time listed as the "Negro Methodist Church" on the southwest corner of Depot Street that later became Patterson Avenue and Seventh Street. *Turner's Fifth Annual Winston and Salem City Directory*, 28; "Goler Memorial Church," *Winston-Salem Journal*, July 23, 1926; "Twelve Tribes Entertainment," *Winston-Salem Journal*, September 17, 1926; "Tonight at Goler," *Winston-Salem Journal*, October 4, 1926; "Goler Opens Basement," *Winston-Salem Journal*, February 8, 1927.

18. Wilson and Mullally, *Hope and Dignity*, 145.

19. Wilson and Mullally, *Hope and Dignity*, 144. See, for example, "The Colored Y.M.C.A.," *Winston-Salem Journal*, October 1, 1898; and "Trustees Endorse Rev. Jackson," *Winston-Salem Journal*, May 4, 1924.

20. Merrick and Hall Xuma, interview by Wilson, audio file 1; Wilson and Mullally, *Hope and Dignity*, 143–44. Humphrey seems to have moved the practice out of the home within a year after Madie was born. See *Turner's Winston and Salem City Directory for the Years 1894–95*, 118, 196–97. Of course, he may have continued to see patients at both locations as Madie grew up.

21. *The Thirty-Sixth Annual Session of the North Carolina Medical, Pharmaceutical and Dental Ass'n, the Oldest Negro Medical Society in the World, June 19–21, 1923, Winston-Salem North Carolina Programme*; "The Doctors with Us," *Wilmington Messenger*, May 17, 1892; "N.C. Med-Dental, Pharmaceutical Asso. Adjourns," *Charlotte News*, June 26, 1907.

22. See "Prominent Colored Man to Speak Here Next Sunday," *Winston-Salem Journal*, May 23, 1918; "Colored Medical Society," *Winston-Salem Journal*, March 15, 1923.

23. Savitt, "Journal of the National Medical Association 100 Years Ago," 734–35; "N.M.A. Communications."

24. I have chosen to use the birth dates recorded on the unofficial death certificates obtained from the Forsyth County Register of Deeds for all of the other children as well. Edna was born January 22, 1897. Willie was born November 12, 1898, and Leroy was born October 24, 1899. *General Index to Real Estate Conveyances—Forsyth County, NC, to December 31st, 1927—Grantor*, deed of trust, bk. 30, p. 372.

25. Wilson and Mullally, *Hope and Dignity*, 144; "Mrs. Hall Dead," *Winston-Salem Journal*, August 29, 1930.

26. See, for example, *General Index to Real Estate Conveyances—Forsyth County, NC, to December 31st, 1927—Grantee*, deed, bk. 66, p. 243, bk. 72, p. 32, bk. 72, p. 56, bk. 72, p. 71, bk. 117, p. 116, bk. 261, p. 271, bk. 284, p. 112. See also *General Index to Real Estate Conveyances—Forsyth County, NC, to December 31st, 1927—Grantor*, deed of trust, bk. 41, p. 438, bk. 44, p. 577, bk. 44, p. 585, bk. 74, p. 554; bk. 78, p. 17, bk. 78, p. 47, bk. 134, p. 181, bk. 199, p. 103, bk. 204, p. 258, bk. 222, p. 77, bk. 198, p. 267, bk. 223, p. 159, bk. 223, p. 227, bk. 230, p. 2; "Item from Winston Salem," *Raleigh Gazette*, May 15, 1897; Oppermann, "Historic and Architectural Resources," 11–12. The couple also took in borders at their home. See, for example, "Rev. Henry Durham," *Winston-Salem Journal*, November 22, 1900; "Local News Items," *Winston-Salem Journal*, January 12, 1902; and *Twelfth Census of the United States: 1900*, schedule 1, "Population, Winston Township, North Carolina, Forsyth County."

27. Merrick and Hall Xuma, interview by Wilson, audio file 2; Wilson and Mullally, *Hope and Dignity*, 144–45. See Buncombe County Register of Deeds, May 7, 1914, bk. 191, p. 263; and *General Index to Real Estate Conveyances—Forsyth County, NC—Grantor to December 31st, 1927*, 216, 217; *General Index to Real Estate Conveyances—Forsyth County, NC—Grantor from January 1st, 1928*, 54; "Twenty Realty

Sales Saturday," *Winston-Salem Journal*, May 9, 1926, where J. B. Dyer sold a lot on Cameron Avenue to Jennie E. Hall.

28. "Theatre for Colored Race," *Winston-Salem Journal*, October 25, 1911; "Music Festival to Depict, in Part, Negroes' Progress," *Winston-Salem Journal*, May 24, 1923; *General Index to Real Estate Conveyances—Forsyth County, NC, to December 31st, 1927—Grantee*, deed, bk. 95, p. 572; Elizabeth Herbin-Triant, "Race and Class Friction in North Carolina Neighborhoods: How Campaigns for Residential Segregation Law Divided Middling and Elite Whites in Winston-Salem and North Carolina's Countryside, 1912–1925," 560; "The Rex Theatre Looks a Success," *Winston-Salem Journal*, January 10, 1912.

29. "C. B. Cash," *Winston-Salem Journal*, January 11, 1930. See also *Turner & Co.'s Winston and Salem City Directory, for the Years 1889 and 1890*, 10, 93, 181, 186; *Turner's Fifth Annual Winston and Salem City Directory*; *Turner's Winston and Salem City Directory for the Years 1894–95*, 30, 104, 113, 123, 125, 130, 145, 183, 188–89; Logan, *Negro in North Carolina*, 98–100, 142–53; Fambrough L. Brownlee, *Winston-Salem: A Pictorial History*, 49; *Thirty-Seventh Annual Catalogue of the Officers and Students, Shaw University, Raleigh, N.C., for the Academic Year Ending May Thirty-First, Nineteen Hundred and Eleven*, 73, Shaw University Archive; "John S. Fitts, Leader in Race Harmony," *Winston-Salem Journal*, October 7, 1923; *Nineteenth Annual Catalog of the Officers and Students of Leonard Medical School, Shaw University, Academic Year Ending March 18, 1899*, 25; *Twelfth Annual Announcement of the Leonard Medical School, Medical Department, Shaw University, Raleigh, N.C., Session of 1892–1893*, 18, both Shaw University Archive; and Oppermann, "Historic and Architectural Resources," 13. See also Leslie Brown, *Upbuilding Black Durham: Gender, Class, and Black Community Development in the Jim Crow South*, chap. 4, for a discussion of the rise of a similar Black elite in a southern city near Winston.

30. *Turner's Winston and Salem City Directory for the Years 1894–95*, 104; Manly Wade Wellman and Larry Edward Tise, *Education*, 33–37.

31. "Described by Educators as One of Strongest Colored Institutions in the South," *Winston-Salem Journal*, December 19, 1926; N. C. Newbold, *Five North Carolina Negro Educators*, 4–7; Hartshorn, *Era of Progress and Promise*, 253, 292–93, 508; I. Garland Penn, *The Afro-American Press and Its Editors*, 124; "A New Race Magazine," *Cleveland Gazette*, March 15, 1890.

32. "The City School Teachers," *Weekly Sentinel*, June 4, 1892; "Winston-Salem Teachers College Enjoys Remarkable Growth," *Winston-Salem Journal*, December 19, 1926; Newbold, *Five North Carolina Negro Educators*, 5–6, 8–10; *Walsh's Directory of the Cities of Winston and Salem, N.C., for 1902–1903*, 28; E. Louise Murphy, *The History of Winston-Salem State University, 1892–1995*, 33–43.

33. "A Call for a Meeting of the Colored Educators of North Carolina on November 11th, 1886," folder 19, American Citizenship, J. C. Price Papers, Andrew Carnegie Library Archives; "The Education of Colored Youth," *New York Tribune*, March 27, 1890; "Colored Educators' Convention," *Washington Evening Star*, January 1, 1891; "Winston-Salem Teachers College Enjoys Remarkable Growth," *Winston-Salem*

Journal, December 19, 1926; "A.M.E. Zion Delegates Present," *Pittsburgh Dispatch*, May 16, 1892; "The Conference Nearing the End," *Pittsburgh Dispatch*, May 17, 1892; *Philadelphia Inquirer*, May 17, 1892; "The City School Teachers," *Western Sentinel*, June 2, 1892; "Prof. Atkins Work," *Western Sentinel*, June 2, 1892.

34. "Items of Interest," *Winston-Salem Journal*, September 22, 1898; Hall Xuma, interview by Wilson, audio file 1.

35. "New Course Added," *Winston-Salem Journal*, May 28, 1903; "Complete List of the Teachers," *Winston-Salem Journal*, July 19, 1908; *Walsh's Directory of the Cities of Winston and Salem, N.C., for 1902–1903*, 203, 246; "Mrs. Annie L. Carson Dies; Funeral Thursday," *Baltimore Afro-American*, January 17, 1956.

36. See, for example, how prominent African Americans described the school in "Mass-Meeting of Colored People Held Last Night," *Winston-Salem Journal*, November 11, 1913.

37. Merrick and Hall Xuma, interview by Wilson, audio file 1; *Slater State Colored Normal School (Winston-Salem) 1906–'07*, 42, WSSUAr-RG 10–14-WSSU, Digital Collection, Winston-Salem State C. G. O'Kelly University Archives; "Commencement of the Colored Graded Schools," *Winston-Salem Journal*, April 24, 1908. Her classmates, some of whom would remain lifelong friends, included Zula E. Patterson, Ozanize Hairston, Creola Carter, Nannie E. Whelton, and L. Maude Belcher.

38. "A Call for a Meeting of the Colored Educators of North Carolina on November 11th, 1886," folder 19, American Citizenship, Price Papers, Andrew Carnegie Library Archives.

39. "Winston-Salem Teachers College Enjoys Remarkable Growth," *Winston-Salem Journal*, December 19, 1926; "The City School Teachers," *Weekly Sentinel*, June 4, 1892; "The Slater Industrial Academy and State Normal School" (advertisement), *Winston-Salem Journal*, September 1, 1898; Newbold, *Five North Carolina Negro Educators*, 5–6, 8–10; *Walsh's Directory of the Cities of Winston and Salem, N.C., for 1902–1903*, 28; Murphy, *History of Winston-Salem State University*, 33–43.

40. "Winston-Salem Teachers College Enjoys Remarkable Growth," *Winston-Salem Journal*, December 19, 1926; *Walsh's Directory of the Cities of Winston and Salem, N.C., for 1902–1903*, 28; Murphy, *History of Winston-Salem State University*, 33–45, 93, 97, 99, 149; "Death Takes Mrs. Oleona P. Atkins," *T.C. Informer* 1, no. 1 (1936): 4; "T. C. Makes Great Progress during Ten," *T.C. Alumni Bulletin* 5, no. 3 (1944): 6, both Winston-Salem State C. G. O'Kelly University Archives.

41. *The Slater Industrial And State Normal School Winston-Salem, N. C. Annual Catalogue 1910–1911*, 6–7, 11–15, 19–20, 26, 31–34, 41–42, Winston-Salem State C. G. O'Kelly University Archives; "Music School of Kittrell Institute" (advertisement), *Raleigh Gazette*, December 4, 1897; *The Slater Industrial and State Normal School Winston-Salem, N. C. Annual Catalogue 1912–1913*, 28; *The Slater Industrial & State Normal School Winston-Salem, N. C. Annual Catalogue 1913–1914*, 20, both Digital Collection, WSSUAr-RG 10–14-WSSU catalog, Winston-Salem State C. G. O'Kelly University Archives; "Commencement Slater School," *Winston-Salem Journal*, May 6, 1909. Note that there is no actual class of 1909 students listed in *The Slater Industrial and State Normal School Annual Catalogue, Winston-Salem, 1910–1911*.

42. "Slater School Commencement," *Winston-Salem Journal*, May 12, 1910, 6. The classmates included Richard E. Reynolds, Zula E. Patterson, Ozanize Hairston, and John P. Diggs.

43. See, for example, "State Doctors Elect Officers," *Winston-Salem Journal*, June 24, 1910; and John A. Kenney, "The Negro Doctor and Organized Medicine," 252.

44. Merrick and Hall Xuma, interview by Wilson, audio file 3; Wilson and Mullally, *Hope and Dignity*, 143; Todd L. Savitt, "Entering a White Profession: Black Physicians in the New South, 1880–1920," 518; K. Miller, "Historic Background of the Negro Physician," 107.

45. "Walter Tuttle Arrested," *Western Sentinel*, December 15, 1892; "Superior Court," *Western Sentinel*, March 9, 1893; "Shot by a Policeman," *Western Sentinel*, July 26, 1894; "Walter Tuttle Dead," *Western Sentinel*, August 2, 1894; "Tuttle Dies," *Union Republican*, August 2, 1894; *Turner & Co.'s Winston and Salem City Directory, for the Years 1889 and 1890*, 113; "Indicted for Murder," *Western Sentinel*, March 7, 1895; "Hasten Murder Trial," *Western Sentinel*, May 15, 1895; "Verdict of Not Guilty," *Western Sentinel*, May 23, 1895; "Horrible Affair!" *Western Sentinel*, May 23, 1895.

46. "Horrible Affair!"; "Riflemen in Readiness," *Washington Times*, May 19, 1895; "Race Riots at Winston," *Washington Post*, August 13, 1895; "Sunday Night's Riot," *Western Sentinel*, August 15, 1895; "Murder Second Degree," *Western Sentinel*, August 15, 1895; *Charlotte Democrat*, August 16, 1895; "North Carolina News," *Charlotte Democrat*, August 23, 1895; B. Miller, "Blacks in Winston-Salem," 41; Gillespie, *Katharine and R. J. Reynolds*, 93–96, 181–86; Brownlee, *Winston-Salem*, 93.

47. "Race Riots at Winston," *Washington Post*, August 13, 1895, 1; B. Miller, "Blacks in Winston-Salem," 34, 42–44; Gillespie, *Katharine and R. J. Reynolds*, 92.

48. "A Black Fool," *Winston-Salem Journal*, October 7, 1898, 1.

49. "To the Colored People," *Winston-Salem Journal*, November 1, 1898; "Winston-Salem White Man's Club," *Winston-Salem Journal*, November 1, 1898; "The White Man's Club," *Winston-Salem Journal*, November 12, 1989. See also "City Local News," *Winston-Salem Journal*, July 2, 1900; *Winston-Salem Journal*, November 7, 1898; "Twin City Happening," *Winston-Salem Journal*, July 6, 1900; and "Indignation Meeting," *Winston-Salem Journal*, July 7, 1900. See Neil R. McMillen, *Dark Journey: Black Mississippians in the Age of Jim Crow*, 35–71.

50. Quoted in Newbold, *Five North Carolina Negro Educators*, 31–32.

51. Newbold, *Five North Carolina Negro Educators*, 8. The Black men who were actively engaged in building the Black community with assistance from white oligarchs certainly counter Glenda Elizabeth Gilmore's argument in *Gender and Jim Crow: Women and the Politics of White Supremacy in North Carolina, 1896–1920*, xxi, and make it difficult, if not impossible, to generalize about gender and race relations in North Carolina. "Colored Citizens," *Western Sentinel*, November 17, 1892; *The Slater Industrial And State Normal School Winston-Salem Annual Catalogue 1910–1911*, 34–35.

52. Prichard, "Winston-Salem's Black Hospitals," 246; Williams T. Grimes, "The History of Kate Bitting Reynolds Memorial Hospital," 376; *Turner's Winston and Salem City Directory for the Years 1894–95*, 123, 197. Jones's practice is listed as being

located on both Main and on Liberty Streets. See Iris Carlton-LaNey, "Women and Interracial Cooperation in Establishing the Good Samaritan Hospital," 65–73; W. Montague Cobb, "Saint Agnes Hospital, Raleigh, North Carolina, 1896–1961"; and Darlene Clark Hine, *Black Women in White: Racial Conflict and Cooperation in the Nursing Profession, 1890–1950*, for a discussion and analysis of the development of Black hospitals and nurse training schools.

53. "Board of Managers Minute Book, 1899–1911, 1919–1921," 1–5, Slater Hospital Records, RG 10, folder 1/6, Winston-Salem State C. G. O'Kelly University Archives; Prichard, "Winston-Salem's Black Hospitals," 246.

54. Murphy, *History of Winston-Salem State University*, 55; "Hospital and Training School," *Virginian-Pilot*, November 17, 1899; "Workers in the Educational Field," *Colored American*, February 17, 1900; "The Stage," *Colored American*, February 24, 1900; Newbold, *Five North Carolina Negro Educators*, 11.

55. "Board of Managers Minute Book, 1899–1911, 1919–1921," 9–17, Slater Hospital Records, RG 10, folder 1/6, Winston-Salem State C. G. O'Kelly University Archives; Prichard, "Winston-Salem's Black Hospitals," 246; Newbold, *Five North Carolina Negro Educators*, 11; *Walsh's Directory of the Cities of Winston and Salem, N.C., for 1902–1903*, 28.

56. "Board of Managers Minute Book, 1899–1911, 1919–1921," 14, Slater Hospital Records, RG 10, folder 1/6, Winston-Salem State C. G. O'Kelly University Archives; "Slater Normal School," *Winston-Salem Journal*, May 15, 1903; *Twenty-Eighth Annual Catalog of the Officers and Students of the Leonard Medical School, the Medical Department of Shaw University, Raleigh, North Carolina, for the Academic Year Ending May Thirty-First, Nineteen Hundred and Eight*, 31, 34, Shaw University Archive; "In Memoriam"; Prichard, "Winston-Salem's Black Hospitals," 246; Newbold, *Five North Carolina Negro Educators*, 11; *Walsh's Directory of the Cities of Winston and Salem, N.C., for 1902–1903*, 28, 161, 192, 280, 356.

57. "Board of Managers Minute Book, 1899–1911, 1919–1921," 14, Slater Hospital Records, RG 10, folder 1/6, Winston-Salem State C. G. O'Kelly University Archives; Murphy, *History of Winston-Salem State University*, 56–57; Robert W. Prichard, *Medicine*, 24–25; "New Course Added," *Winston-Salem Journal*, May 28, 1903; *Walsh's Directory of the Cities of Winston and Salem, N.C., for 1902–1903*, 27, 28, 181, 194, 205, 224, 240, 246, 269, 339. The auxiliary also included Bettie Cash, Miss L. R. Martin, Isabella Wright, Ella Foster, and teachers from the Colored Graded School Carrie Lanier, Lena B. Neal, Lillie Debnam, and Lillian Hayes.

58. Hine, *Black Women in White*, 21; "Board of Managers Minute Book, 1899–1911, 1919–1921," 23, Slater Hospital Records, RG 10, folder 1/6, Winston-Salem State C. G. O'Kelly University Archives.

59. "Board of Managers Minute Book, 1899–1911, 1919–1921," 23, 25, Slater Hospital Records, RG 10, folder 1/6, Winston-Salem State C. G. O'Kelly University Archives.

60. "Goler Memorial Church," *Winston-Salem Journal*, July 23, 1926; "Twelve Tribes Entertainment," *Winston-Salem Journal*, September 17, 1926; "Mrs. Hall Dead," *Winston-Salem Journal*, August 29, 1930; "The Funeral of Mrs. Hall," *Winston-Salem Journal*, August 30, 1930.

61. "Board of Managers Minute Book, 1899–1911, 1919–1921," 26, Slater Hospital Records, RG 10, folder 1/6, Winston-Salem State C. G. O'Kelly University Archives; Prichard, "Winston-Salem's Black Hospitals," 246; Newbold, *Five North Carolina Negro Educators*, 12–13.

62. "Board of Managers Minute Book, 1899–1911, 1919–1921," 21–22, Slater Hospital Records, RG 10, folder 1/6, Winston-Salem State C. G. O'Kelly University Archives; Murphy, *History of Winston-Salem State University*, 57; *Walsh's Winston-Salem, North Carolina, City Directory for 1906*, 56; *Walsh's Winston-Salem, North Carolina, City Directory for 1908*, 92.

63. Mark Wineka, *Salisbury Post*, December 2, 2009; "Items from Winston Salem," *Raleigh Gazette*, May 15, 1897. William A. Jones was the only Black druggist listed among the six druggists in Winston and Salem in 1903. See *Walsh's Directory of the Cities of Winston and Salem, N.C., for 1902–1903*, 241, 345; *Walsh's Winston-Salem, North Carolina, City Directory for 1906*, 374; *Walsh's Winston-Salem, North Carolina, City Directory for 1908*, 416; and Ward, *Black Physicians in the Jim Crow South*, 111.

64. *Walsh's Winston-Salem, North Carolina, City Directory for 1908*, 416, 420; *Winston-Salem, N.C., City and Suburban City Directory, 1910*, 16: 188, 189, 202; *The Winston-Salem, N.C., City Directory, 1911*, 331.

65. "New B. And L. Association," *Winston-Salem Journal*, September 16, 1903; "Annual Statement," *Winston-Salem Journal*, September 18, 1906; *Walsh's Winston-Salem, North Carolina, City Directory for 1904–5*, 357, 421; Hartshorn, *Era of Progress and Promise*, 290–91.

66. Murphy, *History of Winston-Salem State University*, 68–78, 417; Prichard, "Winston-Salem's Black Hospitals," 246; *Walsh's Winston-Salem, North Carolina, City Directory for 1906*, 55, 396; "Board of Managers Minute Book, 1899–1911, 1919–1921," 35, Slater Hospital Records, RG 10, folder 1/6, Winston-Salem State C. G. O'Kelly University Archives.

67. "Prof Washington Will Speak in This City Easter Monday," *Winston-Salem Journal*, March 12, 1905; "Booker T. Washington," *Winston-Salem Journal*, April 11, 1905; "Booker T. Washington," *Winston-Salem Journal*, April 21, 1905; "Dr. Washington at Winston," *Charlotte Observer*, April 25, 1905; "Negro Educator's Speech," *Charlotte Observer*, April 26, 1905; *Progressive Farmer and the Cotton Plant*, March 28, 1905; *Walsh's Winston-Salem, North Carolina, City Directory for 1904–5*, 185.

68. "Board of Managers Minute Book, 1899–1911, 1919–1921," 42–47, Slater Hospital Records, RG 10, folder 1/6, Winston-Salem State C. G. O'Kelly University Archives; Prichard, "Winston-Salem's Black Hospitals," 247–48; *Walsh's Winston-Salem, North Carolina, City Directory for 1908*, 391, 397, 416, 427; *Winston-Salem, N.C., City and Suburban City Directory, 1910*, 234; *The Winston-Salem, N.C., City Directory, 1912*, 353, 382.

69. "Slater Hospital under New Management," *Winston-Salem Journal*, June 1, 1909.

70. "Tag Day Set Aside for Slater Hospital," *Western Sentinel*, August 24, 1909.

71. "Board of Managers Minute Book, 1899–1911, 1919–1921," 46–50, Slater Hospital Records, RG 10, folder 1/6, Winston-Salem State C. G. O'Kelly University Ar-

chives; Prichard, "Winston-Salem's Black Hospitals," 247–48; "Aldermen Will Give Money," *Winston-Salem Journal*, November 5, 1910; "Money Desired by Committee Is Provided," *Western Sentinel*, November 8, 1910; "Slater Hospital Re-opened," *Union Republican*, March 9, 1911; "City Hospital Is to Be Erected and Equipped," *Winston-Salem Journal*, June 11, 1913. Prominent Black men, however, did not give up. Two Black physicians, John C. Williamson and Alexander Hamilton Ray, succeeded in opening small facilities, but they didn't last long term. The Williamson Sanitorium, located in Columbian Heights, for example, had begun operating by 1915 but was no longer listed in the directory by 1918. Fire destroyed the small Alexander Hamilton Ray Hospital. A new hospital was built in the wake of its demise but had limited success. See *The Winston-Salem, N.C., City Directory, 1912*, 480; *The Winston-Salem, N.C., City Directory, 1915*, 591, 622; *Winston-Salem, N.C., City Directory, 1918*, 479, 512; "Dr. A. H. Ray Hospital," *Winston-Salem Journal*, March 15, 1923; "Music Festival, to Depict, in Part, Negroes' Progress," *Winston-Salem Journal*, May 24, 1923.

72. Korstad, *Civil Rights Unionism*, 84; "City Hospital Is to Be Erected and Equipped," *Winston-Salem Journal*, June 11, 1913.

Chapter 2. "I Wanted to Be a Doctor": Coming of Age

1. *Thirty-Seventh Annual Catalogue of the Officers and Students*, 48–50, 76–77, Shaw University Archive; "For $20,000 Building," *Raleigh News and Observer*, July 27, 1910; "Building Permits for Capital City Houses," *Greensboro Daily News*, July 28, 1910; "Raleigh's Growth," *Raleigh Evening Times*, August 11, 1910; "Steady, True, and Sure Grows the Capital City, *Raleigh News and Observer*, September 14, 1910.

2. *Thirty-Seventh Annual Catalogue of the Officers and Students*, 48–50, 76–77, Shaw University Archive; "Dr. Meserve in Boston," *Raleigh News and Observer*, November 22, 1910.

3. *Thirty-Seven Annual Catalogue of the Officers and Students*, 12, Shaw University Archive; Stephanie J. Shaw, *What a Woman Ought to Be and to Do: Black Professional Women Workers during the Jim Crow Era*, 69. See also Cynthia Neverdon-Morton, *Afro-American Women of the South and the Advancement of the Race, 1895–1925*, for a discussion of Black colleges and the training of Black women.

4. *Thirty-Seventh Annual Catalogue of the Officers and Students*, 12, 24–25, Shaw University Archive; Brownlee, *Winston-Salem*, 139.

5. *Thirty-Seventh Annual Catalogue of the Officers and Students*, 49; *Thirty-Eighth Annual Catalogue of the Officers and Students, Shaw University, Raleigh, NC*, 47; *Thirty-Ninth Annual Catalogue of the Officers and Students, Shaw University, Raleigh, NC*, 63, all Shaw University Archive (all three of these are from Digital NC and from *Shaw University Bulletin* [1911–13] online). The YWCA is not listed in the catalog of the university as one of the groups on campus, but Madie notes in her oral interview and in Wilson and Mullally in *Hope and Dignity*, 143, that she first encountered the group at Shaw. Nancy Marie Robertson, *Christian Sisterhood, Race Relations, and the YWCA, 1906–1946*, 24.

6. *Thirty-Seventh Annual Catalogue of the Officers and Students*, 13–15, 12–15, 48–50, Shaw University Archive.

7. *Thirty-Seventh Annual Catalogue of the Officers and Students*, 13, 24–25, 48–49, Shaw University Archive.

8. Hall Xuma, interview by Wilson, audio file 1; Merrick and Hall Xuma, interview by Wilson, audio file 1.

9. Hall Xuma, interview by Wilson, audio file 1; Merrick and Hall Xuma, interview by Wilson, audio file 1.

10. An eighth school for white children was under construction in 1913 but had not opened. See "Winston-Salem Schools among Best in State," *Winston-Salem Journal*, June 1, 1913; "Four Thousand in City Schools," *Winton-Salem Journal*, October 28, 1913; "Teachers for City Schools Are Announced," *Winston-Salem Journal*, July 24, 1914; "Teachers for City Schools," *Winston-Salem Journal*, July 4, 1912; Brownlee, *Winston-Salem*, 140–41; *The Slater Industrial And State Normal School Winston-Salem Annual Catalogue 1910–1911*, 42; *The Winston-Salem, N.C., City Directory, 1913*, 433, 463; Hall Xuma, interview by Wilson, audio file 1. The directory for 1914 is not available, so Madie first appears as a teacher in the 1915 directory. *The Winston-Salem, N.C., City Directory, 1915*, 516, 556. See also "Faculties for City Schools Named by the School Commissioners," *Winston-Salem Journal*, June 9, 1915; and "The Faculties," *Twin-City Daily Sentinel*, June 9, 1915.

11. The Black community was committed to maintaining residential schools in their neighborhoods but pushed forcefully for modernizing them. So when the mayor announced that the Depot Street School would be torn down and students sent to Woodland School, several prominent Black men hired an attorney to fight the decision and held mass meetings of African Americans in the community. They were even supported by whites in East Winston who had advocated for a residential segregation policy to end the "invasion" of Blacks moving into their neighborhoods and objected to the Woodland School location. In the end, the Black community won the battle because the Depot Street School survived for several more years. See, for example, "Four Thousand in City Schools," *Winton-Salem Journal*, October 28, 1913; "Aldermen Will Meet Friday," *Winston-Salem Journal*, November 2, 1913; "Colored School Hearing Will Be Held on Tuesday," *Winston-Salem Journal*, November 8, 1913; "Mass-Meeting of Colored People Held Last Night," *Winston-Salem Journal*, November 11, 1913; and "Colored School Not Be Moved," *Winston-Salem Journal*, November 16, 1913. See also Herbin-Triant, "Race and Class Friction in North Carolina Neighborhoods," 538–61.

12. L. A. Williams and J. H. Johnston, *A Study of the Winston-Salem Schools*, 1–3, 10–11, 17–18, 24, 40, 49–50, 59–66, 79, 83–86; Wellman and Tise, *Education*, 40.

13. Williams and Johnston, *Study of the Winston-Salem Schools*, 4–8, 9–11, 12–15, 20; Wellman and Tise, *Education*, 41.

14. Williams and Johnston, *Study of the Winston-Salem Schools*, 4–8, 9–11, 12–15, 20, 48; Wellman and Tise, *Education*, 41.

15. Williams and Johnston, *Study of the Winston-Salem Schools*, 14, 52–56; "Faculties of the City Schools for the Next Session," *Winston-Salem Journal*, July 3, 1918.

16. Williams and Johnston, *Study of the Winston-Salem Schools*, 60–61.

17. Williams and Johnston, *Study of the Winston-Salem Schools*, 52–56, 59; "Faculties of the City Schools for the Next Session," *Winston-Salem Journal*, July 3, 1918.

18. Wellman and Tise, *Education*, 41–42.

19. "Emancipation Day Celebration in Twin-City," *Twin-City Daily Sentinel*, January 1, 1916.

20. "Great Musical Event by the Colored People Here," *Winston-Salem Journal*, December 16, 1913.

21. "Recital to Be Given at Prof. Hawkin's Studio," *Winston-Salem Journal*, February 28, 1915; "Musical Recital Will Be Given on Monday," *Winston-Salem Journal*, March 7, 1915.

22. "The Festival," *Memphis Daily Appeal*, May 14, 1883; "To Sing for Mrs. Taft," *Washington Post*, May 12, 1911.

23. "Twin City Mozart Society to Give Recital Monday," *Winston-Salem Journal*, October 1, 1910; "Classical Recital," *Winston-Salem Journal*, October 16, 1910.

24. "Classical Concert," *Winston-Salem Journal*, July 16, 1911; "A Classical Soprano Contest," *Winston-Salem Journal*, August 6, 1911; "Grand Concert at St. Paul Monday," *Winston-Salem Journal*, September 24, 1911; "Grand Jubilee Concert by Colored People Mon. Night," *Winston-Salem Journal*, April 27, 1912; "'Aunt Bell' Grogan to Star in Great Jubilee Concert" (advertisement), *Winston-Salem Journal*, April 27, 1912.

25. "A Feast of Music" (advertisement), *Winston-Salem Journal*, April 9, 1912; "Grand Jubilee Concert by Colored People Mon. Night," *Winston-Salem Journal*, April 27, 1912; "Big Concert by Mozart Society at Slater Soon," *Winston-Salem Journal*, December 7, 1913; "Big Musical Event for Colored People Monday," *Winston-Salem Journal*, February 4, 1915; "Rest Room for Colored People," *Winston-Salem Journal*, April 4, 1915.

26. "Local Colored Talent Will Give Cantata in Greensboro," *Winston-Salem Journal*, September 23, 1917; "Winston-Salem Singers Give Fine Cantata in Greensboro," *Winston-Salem Journal*, September 25, 1917; "Jepatha-Daughter Must Die" (advertisement), *Winston-Salem Journal*, October 7, 1917; "'Jepatha and His Daughter' Attracts a Large Audience," *Winston-Salem Journal*, October 9, 1917.

27. *The Slater Industrial And State Normal School Winston-Salem Annual Catalogue 1910–1911*, 31.

28. "A Feast of Music," *Winston-Salem Journal*, April 9, 1912; "Jubilee Singers Will Be Feature," *Winston-Salem Journal*, April 9, 1912.

29. Hall Xuma, interview by Wilson, audio file 1.

30. Robertson, *Christian Sisterhood, Race Relations, and the YWCA*, 74–75; "Application for Membership in the Young Women's Christian Association of the United States of America," March 18, 1908, microfilm, reel 200, microdex 2, YWCA of the U.S.A. Records, Sophia Smith Collections; "Formal Opening of New Y.W.C.A. Will Be in April," *Winston-Salem Journal*, March 23, 1917; "History of Work Is Remarkable in Its Achievement," *Winston-Salem Journal*, April 8, 1917; "List of Officers and Committees," *Winston-Salem Journal*, April 8, 1917; Smith, *Industry and Commerce*,

14–15; Gillespie, *Katharine and R. J. Reynolds*, 221–22, 263–64; "Building Is the Spanish Mission Type and Design," *Winston-Salem Journal*, April 8, 1917.

31. "History of Work Is Remarkable in Its Achievement," *Winston-Salem Journal*, April 8, 1917; "Building Is the Spanish Mission Type and Design," *Winston-Salem Journal*, April 8, 1917.

32. "Colored Y.W.C.A. Is Organized in the City," *Winston-Salem Journal*, August 9, 1917; "Building Permits," *Winston-Salem Journal*, April 27, 1917; "Corner Stone of Reynolds Temple to Be Laid Sunday," *Winston-Salem Journal*, June 13, 1917; "Laying of the Cornerstone of Reynolds Temple, Colored," *Winston-Salem Journal*, June 26, 1917.

33. "Colored Y.W.C.A. Is Organized in the City," *Winston-Salem Journal*, August 9, 1917; "Colored Y.W.C.A. Is Now Organized in Winston-Salem," *Winston-Salem Journal*, August 22, 1917. Emma A. Barnett, the general secretary of the Institutional Department and a nurse at the Colored Day nursery, played a critical role in the development. See *Winston-Salem, N.C., City Directory, 1918*, 385. Bettie Cash, the wife of C. B. Cash, headed the board of trustees, while real-estate developer Charles Jones and attorney James Lanier were among the five Black men and two white men, a judge and alderman, who served on the board of directors. Hall was not a member of Reynolds Temple and her name does not appear in the documents, so it is unclear how engaged she was in this part of the development.

34. "Colored Women to Meet This Afternoon," *Winston-Salem Journal*, September 16, 1917; "Colored Y.W.C.A. Mass Meeting Sunday at 4:30," *Winston-Salem Journal*, November 25, 1917.

35. Olcott, *Work of Colored Women*, 48–49, 58–59, 127–28; Robertson, *Christian Sisterhood, Race Relations, and the YWCA*, 202–3n97; "Annual Meeting of Y.W.C.A.," *Winston-Salem Journal*, February 2, 1928; Monroe N. Work, ed., *Negro Year Book: An Annual Encyclopedia of the Negro, 1916–1917*, 230.

36. "Grip Now Epidemic throughout Country," *New York Times*, October 16, 1918; Nancy K. Bristow, *American Pandemic: The Lost Worlds of the 1918 Influenza Epidemic*.

37. Joanne Glenn, "The Winston-Salem Riot of 1918," 8; Bristow, *American Pandemic*, 69–74; B. Miller, "Blacks in Winston-Salem," 181.

38. "Dr. A. H. Ray Hospital," *Winston-Salem Journal*, March 15, 1923; "R. J. Reynolds' Career Is Ended," *Charlotte Observer*, July 30, 1918; "Mr. Richard Joshua Reynolds," *Winston-Salem Journal*, July 30, 1918; "Colored People Express Their Gratitude for New Hospital," *Winston-Salem Journal*, August 17, 1918; Monroe N. Work, ed., *Negro Year Book: An Annual Encyclopedia of the Negro, 1918–1919*, 34.

39. "Hospital for Colored People Is Opened in Depot Street School," *Winston-Salem Journal*, October 22, 1918; *Winston-Salem, N.C., City Directory, 1918*, 246, 435, 479, 512.

40. "Total Number of Deaths during the Epidemic of Influenza Given as 159," *Winston-Salem Journal*, November 9, 1918.

41. "Columbia, S.C.," *New York Age*, September 6, 1917; "Colored Minister Claimed by Death," *Columbia Record*, October 21, 1918; Hall Xuma, interview by Wilson, audio file 1; Merrick and Hall Xuma, interview by Wilson, audio file 4; Wilson and Mullally, *Hope and Dignity*, 145–46.

42. Hall Xuma, interview by Wilson, audio file 1.

43. Charles Harris Wesley, *The History of the National Association of Colored Women's Clubs: A Legacy of Service*, 246.

44. Hall Xuma, interview by Wilson, audio file 1; Wilson and Mullally, *Hope and Dignity*, 146.

45. Hall Xuma, interview by Wilson, audio file 1; Merrick and Hall Xuma, interview by Wilson, audio file 4; Wilson and Mullally, *Hope and Dignity*, 146. The amount of money Rockefeller donated, according to Hall, was in the neighborhood of $50,000 to $100,000.

46. Hall Xuma, interview by Wilson, audio file 1; Merrick and Hall Xuma, interview by Wilson, audio file 4. Hall does note that she and Bethune had a troubled friendship because of a disagreement over a student.

47. See, for example, "Five Killed in Riot; U.S. Troops and Home Guards Ordered Out," *Tampa Tribune*, November 18, 1918; "Order Finally Restored in Winston-Salem after 4 Killed," *Lakeland Evening Telegram*, November 18, 1918; "Mob Storms Jail in North Carolina City," *Pensacola Journal*, November 18, 1918; "Mob of Lynchers Spreads Terror at Winston-Salem," *Atlanta Constitution*, November 18, 1918; "5 Dead, 20 Hurt in N.C. Race Riot," *Washington Times*, November 18, 1918; "Southern Race Riot Costs Five Lives," *New York Times*, November 18, 1918; and "Five Are Killed and 25 Were Injured Here Last Night in Tragedy Following Attempt to Lynch Negro at City Jail," *Winston-Salem Journal*, November 18, 1918.

48. "Five Are Killed and 25 Were Injured Here Last Night"; Glenn, "Winston-Salem Riot of 1918," 9–11.

49. "Five Are Killed and 25 Were Injured Here Last Night"; Glenn, "Winston-Salem Riot of 1918," 14–15, 17.

50. "Five Are Killed and 25 Were Injured Here Last Night"; "Mob of Lynchers Spreads Terror at Winston-Salem"; "5 Dead, 20 Hurt in N.C. Race Riot"; "Southern Race Riot Costs Five Lives"; Glenn, "Winston-Salem Riot of 1918," 17–19, 31. Russell High was removed from the jail and taken to Raleigh for his own safety.

51. "Five Are Killed and 25 Were Injured Here Last Night"; "Mob of Lynchers Spreads Terror at Winston-Salem"; "5 Dead, 20 Hurt in N.C. Race Riot"; "Southern Race Riot Costs Five Lives"; quote in Glenn, "Winston-Salem Riot of 1918," 17–19. See also Brownlee, *Winston-Salem*, 149, who suggests that the death toll was probably much higher because the mob also marched into the Black neighborhood.

52. "Five Are Killed and 25 Were Injured Here Last Night"; "Other Alleged Rioters Placed under Arrest," *Winston-Salem Journal*, November 19, 1918; Glenn, "Winston-Salem Riot of 1918," 19–21, 25–29, 34–36; Brownlee, *Winston-Salem*, 149.

53. See, for example, Elliott Rudwick, *Race Riot at East St. Louis*; William M. Tuttle Jr., *Race Riot: Chicago in the Red Summer of 1919*; Robert Whitaker, *On the Laps of Gods: The Red Summer of 1919 and the Struggle for Justice That Remade a Nation*; Cameron McWhirter, *Red Summer: The Summer of 1919 and the Awakening of Black America*.

54. "Sentiment of Colored People in Recent Riot," *Winston-Salem Journal*, November 28, 1918; "Guns and Ammunition Taken by Members of Crowd from Streets,"

Winston-Salem Journal, November 18, 1918; Glenn, "Winston-Salem Riot of 1918," 29, 57–58.

55. "Many Changes among the Negroes in Line of Steady Progress," *Winston-Salem Journal*, December 28, 1919.

56. [Pneu]monia Cases [illegible] an Increase [illegible] Winston-Salem," *Winston Salem Journal*, February 12, 1920; "Course of Flu [illegible] yet Unchanged," *Winston-Salem Journal*, February 14, 1920; "Aldermen Grant Permit to Change Street Car Line," *Winston-Salem Journal*, March 13, 1920; *Winston-Salem, N.C., City Directory, 1918*, 445.

57. See, for example, "Reynolda School Remains Closed," *Winston-Salem Journal*, March 1, 1920; "Board of Trade Discusses Many Vital Matters," *Winston-Salem Journal*, March 12, 1920; "Colored Hiking Clubs Go on Several Hikes," *Winston-Salem Journal*, December 1, 1920; "Meeting Tonight of East Winston Voters," *Winston-Salem Journal*, April 28, 1921; and "Faculties for City's Schools Named by Board," *Winston-Salem Journal*, July 11, 1921. Hall, who was actually in Lynchburg, Virginia, in 1920, was still listed in the *Winston-Salem, N.C., City Directory, 1920*, 505, but has no occupation.

58. Hall claimed that she "didn't know any women's doctors," but she did develop a friendship with Ruth B. Caroll. Merrick and Hall Xuma, interview by Wilson, audio file 1; Wilson and Mullally, *Hope and Dignity*, 143–44.

59. Note that Hall states that her desire to go to medical school occurred while she was at Shaw or shortly after, but the time line of the discussion with her father is questionable. Her reference to Leroy's application to Howard strongly indicates that the discussion with her father occurred after World War I when Leroy graduated from Livingstone College in 1922. If she had applied during her time at Shaw, Leroy would have been only about twelve or thirteen years old. This strongly suggests that Hall could not have applied to Howard until she was nearly twenty-seven or twenty-eight years old, long after she earned the normal-school certificate from Shaw. See Wilson and Mullally, *Hope and Dignity*, 144; Hall Xuma, interview by Wilson, audio file 1; and Hine, "Anatomy of Failure," 521–25.

60. Darlene Clark Hine, "Co-laborers in the Work of the Lord: Nineteenth-Century Black Women Physicians," 150–51, 154–55; Darlene Clark Hine, "The Corporal and Ocular Veil: Dr. Matilda A. Evans (1872–1935) and the Complexity of Southern History," 3–18; *Anderson Intelligencer*, December 15, 1897; "In Counties Adjoining," *Yorkville Enquirer*, May 25, 1898; "The Negro Physicians," *Columbia State*, May 6, 1906; "N.M.A. Communications."

61. Hine, "Corporal and Ocular Veil," 18–19; "The Negro Physicians," *Columbia State*, May 6, 1906; "N.M.A. Communications."

62. I am assuming that the Ruth B. Carroll listed in *Walsh's Columbia, South Carolina, City Directory for 1905*, 415, as a nurse at Taylor Lane Hospital is the same person. "Columbia, S.C.," *New York Age*, September 6, 1917; "Paragraphic News," *Washington Bee*, July 24, 1909; Geraldine Rhodes Beckford, comp., *Biographical Dictionary of American Physicians of African Ancestry, 1800–1920*, 60; *Walsh's Columbia, South Carolina, City Directory for 1910*, 362; *Walsh's Columbia, South Carolina, City Directory for 1911*, 369; *Walsh's Columbia, South Carolina, City Directory for 1914*,

404; "Women Physicians Graduated from Meharry Medical College," 154; *Southern Indicator*, February 15, 1913.

63. *The Slater Industrial and State Normal School Winston-Salem, N. C. Annual Catalogue 1912–1913*, 21, Digital Collection, WSSUAr-RG 10–14-WSSU catalog, Winston-Salem State C. G. O'Kelly University Archives; Brownlee, *Winston-Salem*, 139; "Personal," *Winston-Salem Journal*, September 29, 1923; "Ninety-Three Candidates Are Given License to Practice Medicine in N.C.," *Winston-Salem Journal*, July 19, 1927; *Miller's Winston-Salem, N.C., City Directory, 1930*, 384–85; Hall Xuma, interview by Wilson, audio file 1.

64. Manly Wade Wellman, *Transportation and Communication*, 29–32; "Twenty Years Advancement of Colored People in City," *Winston-Salem Journal*, October 7, 1923.

65. "New Theatre Opens Tomorrow," *Winston-Salem Journal*, April 20, 1924; "At the Lincoln Theatre" (advertisement), *Winston-Salem Journal*, September 7, 1924. The Rex, Dunbar, and Lafayette Theatres had preceded the Lincoln Theatre.

66. Mary G. Rolinson, *Grassroots Garveyism: The Universal Negro Improvement Association in the Rural South, 1920–1927*, 60–62, 69–70, 197, 199. See also "The U.N.I.A.," *Winston-Salem Journal*, August 3, 1924; "St. Johns Baptist Church," *Winston-Salem Journal*, October 13, 1923; "U.N.I.A. Woman's Department," *Winston-Salem Journal*, March 23, 1928, "Spencer Memorial Church Program," *Winston-Salem Journal*, August 1, 1924, and "Independent Order of Tents," *Winston-Salem Journal*, September 5, 1924, on how integrated the UNIA was in the Black community.

67. "Alderman Name City Officials," *Winston-Salem Journal*, September 6, 1924; "The U.N.I. Association," *Winston-Salem Journal*, September 17, 1924; "Marcus Garvey, Negro Leader, Urges Black to Africa Movement for Race," *Winston-Salem Journal*, September 22, 1924. Garvey's followers remained committed to him even after he was sent to the Atlanta Penitentiary in February 1925. See "Big Mass Meeting," *Winston-Salem Journal*, March 1, 1925.

68. "A Study," microfilm, reel 200, microdex 2, YWCA of the U.S.A. Records, Sophia Smith Collections.

69. Smith, *Industry and Commerce*, 18–20; "A Study," microfilm, reel 200, microdex 2, YWCA of the U.S.A. Records, Sophia Smith Collections; "Mr. Richard Joshua Reynolds, *Winston-Salem Journal*, July 30, 1918.

70. *Winston-Salem, N.C., City Directory, 1920*, 505; *Winston-Salem, N.C., City Directory, 1921*, 560; *Winston-Salem, N.C., City Directory, 1923*, 593.

71. "Fifth Avenue Fashion Shop," *Winston-Salem Journal*, March 21, 1924; Wendy Gamber, *The Female Economy: The Millinery and Dressmaking Trades, 1860–1930*, 220.

72. Gamber, *Female Economy*, 193.

73. "Close Their Institute with a Splendid Program," *Winston-Salem Journal*, September 6, 1902; "Mr. and Mrs. C. H. Jones Entertains," *Winston-Salem Journal*, August 2, 1908; *The Slater Industrial And State Normal School Winston-Salem Annual Catalogue 1910–1911*, 41; "Exercises of Negro School," *Winston-Salem Journal*, April 30, 1910; "Personals," *Winston-Salem Journal*, September 11, 1924; "Alumni and

Anniversary," *Winston-Salem Journal*, June 4, 1926; "Deeds," *Winston-Salem Journal*, August 23, 1913 (I am assuming that this is the same Roberta Carr). See "Mrs. Annie L. Carson Dies; Funeral Thursday," *Baltimore Afro-American*, January 17, 1956.

74. See *Winston-Salem, N.C., City Directory, 1921*, 516, where she is first listed as the cashier; *General Index to Real Estate Conveyances—Forsyth County, NC, to December 31st, 1927—Grantor*, deed, bk. 127, p. 236; "Deeds," *Winston-Salem Journal*, August 23, 1913; *General Index to Real Estate Conveyances—Forsyth County, NC, to December 31st, 1927—Grantor*, deed, bk. 262, p. 59; "Conference," *Winston-Salem Journal*, July 25, 1923; "Business League Committees," *Winston-Salem Journal*, April 1, 1926; "Captains of League to Meet," *Winston-Salem Journal*, April 23, 1926; "Negro League Business Week," *Winston-Salem Journal*, April 25, 1926.

75. *Thirteenth Census of the United States: 1910, Population, Virginia, Campbell County, Lynchburg, Ward of City 3*; "Bishop Kyles Weds Virginia Girl," *Winston-Salem Journal*, June 18, 1926; "Bishop to Reside Here," *Winston-Salem Journal*, February 14, 1923; "Hold Funeral Service in N.C. for Bishop L. W. Kyles, Senior Bishop, A.M.E. Zion Connection," *Kansas City Plaindealer*, July 25, 1941; "D.C. Church Council to Honor Mrs. Kyles," *Washington Evening Star*, June 6, 1964.

76. "Spring Announcement" (advertisement), *Winston-Salem Journal*, March 21, 1924; *Winston-Salem, N. Carolina, City Directory, 1926*, 357, 358, 865–66; *Miller's Winston-Salem, N. Carolina, City Directory, 1928*, 403, 992.

77. "Fifth Avenue Fashion Shop," *Winston-Salem Journal*, March 21, 1924; *Winston-Salem Journal*, March 22, 1925; The *Winston-Salem Journal* continued to refer to the business as "the local millinery shop," suggesting that the dressmaking side of the shop had either ended or shifted to hats. See "Leaves for Miami and Cuba," *Winston-Salem Journal*, January 13, 1926; See also Gamber, *Female Economy*, 190–228.

78. "Personals," *Winston-Salem Journal*, September 11, 1924; "Mrs. Xuma Visiting from South Africa," *Baltimore Afro-American*, March 27, 1948; "Mrs. Annie L. Carson Dies; Funeral Thursday," *Baltimore Afro-American*, January 17, 1956. Some of the relatives included Annie Carson and her daughters Ann Payne, Emma Henson, Loretta Bell, and Christine Anderson. "Real Estate Office," *Winston-Salem Journal*, June 6, 1923; "Announcement," *Winston-Salem Journal*, November 11, 1924; "Big Wedding Tonight," *Winston-Salem Journal*, November 25, 1924; "Kennedy-Hall Marriage," *Winston-Salem Journal*, November 26, 1924; Murphy, *History of Winston-Salem State University*, 59, 78–85, 417.

79. "News of Colored People in the City and County," *Winston-Salem Journal*, January 13, 1926.

80. Frank Andre Guridy, *Forging Diaspora: Afro-Cubans and African Americans in a World of Empire and Jim Crow*, 124. See also Mark S. Foster, "In the Face of 'Jim Crow': Prosperous Blacks and Vacations, Travel and Outdoor Leisure, 1890–1945," 130–34; Hiliary Mac Austin, "The Defender Brings You the World: The Grand European Tour of Patrick B. Prescott Jr.," 57–58; Roi Ottley, *The Lonely Warrior: The Life and Times of Robert S. Abbott*, 228–40; and Ethan Michaeli, *The Defender: How The Legendary Black Newspaper Changed America from the Age of the Pullman Porters to the Age of Obama*, 150–51.

81. Guridy, *Forging Diaspora*, 155, 158–59.

82. "Leave for Hot Springs," *Winston-Salem Journal*, April 5, 1928; "Halls Returns to City," *Winston-Salem Journal*, April 30, 1928; Hall Xuma, interview by Wilson. Hall and Hall no longer appears in the city directory in 1928. See *Miller's Winston-Salem, N. Carolina, City Directory, 1928*, 403, 992.

83. *Miller's Winston-Salem, N.C., City Directory, 1929*, 389, 959; *Miller's Winston-Salem, N.C., City Directory, 1930*, 384–85, 962. Note that the address for Madie Hall's business was listed as 315 East Seventh in 1928 but as 305 in subsequent directories.

84. "Easter Cantata at Goler Memorial," *Winston-Salem Journal*, April 12 1925. Note that Goler by then was one of the most prominent and engaged Black churches in the city. Much of that was due to the very active congregants, numbering 545 by 1933, and the ministers who guided them after World War I. They included Henry H. Jackson, Stephen G. Spottswood, Earnest O. Cowan, and Dorsey G. Garland. See "Figures Given," *Winston-Salem Journal*, December 9, 1931; "Ministerial Resolution," *Winston-Salem Journal*, January 10, 1924; "Rev. Jackson Honored," *Winston-Salem Journal*, May 4, 1924; "Personal Glimpses"; "Rev. Cowan Goes Higher," *Winston-Salem Journal*, July 17, 1932; "Dr. D. G. Garland Attends," *Winston-Salem Journal*, December 4, 1932; and "Dr. H. H. Hall Passes," *Winston-Salem Journal*, November 10, 1935. See also Larry Edward Tise, *The Churches*, 34–37, for a discussion of the development and growth of the extraordinary number of Black churches in the city; and Mary L. Mason, "The World of Women," who wrote a 1930 column for the *Star of Zion* where she argued that dramas and pageants were "legitimate children of the Church" and "contribute to the highest powers of appreciation and enjoyment."

85. "Rehearsal for Pageant," *Winston-Salem Journal*, March 15, 1930; "Musical Organization," *Winston-Salem Journal*, February 19, 1928; "Grand Musical," *Winston-Salem Journal*, November 18, 1924; "Million Dollar Wedding," *Winston-Salem Journal*, April 3, 1927; "White House Mock Wedding," *Winston-Salem Journal*, March 25, 1928; "White House Mock Wedding," *Winston-Salem Journal*, April 5, 1928.

86. "Queens Wedding," *Winston-Salem Journal*, February 18, 1930; "Queens Wedding," *Winston-Salem Journal*, February 25, 1930; "Queens Wedding," *Winston-Salem Journal*, February 27, 1930.

87. "Ruth Ellis to Appear," *Winston-Salem Journal*, April 20, 1933; "Ruth Ellis Concert," *Winston-Salem Journal*, May 10, 1933; "Ruth Ellis to Appear," *Winston-Salem Journal*, May 16, 1933; "Ruth Ellis to Appear," *Winston-Salem Journal*, May 19, 1933; "'Hagar' Presented Last Night," *Winston-Salem Journal*, May 25, 1933. Hall also teamed up with members of Winston-Salem Teachers College (formerly Slater) as she starred in the biblical play *Half of My Goods* at Goler. See "Dr. D. G. Garland to Speak," *Winston-Salem Journal*, April 8, 1933; "The *Half of My Goods*," *Winston-Salem Journal and Sentinel*, April 9, 1933; "*Half of My Goods*," *Winston-Salem Journal*, April 11, 1933.

Chapter 3. "Women Are Awakening":
Shaping the Parameters of Black and White Alliances

1. Olcott, *Work of Colored Women*, 5–6.

2. Thirteenth Census of the United States: 1910, vol. 3, *Population—North Carolina*, table 1, "Population of Minor Civil Divisions: 1910, 1900, and 1890," and table 3, "Composition and Characteristics of the Population for Cities of 10,000 to 25,000," 275, 313; *Fourteenth Census of the United States: 1920*, vol. 3, *Composition and Characteristics of the Population by States*, table 8, "Age, for Cities of 10,000 or More," table 10, "Composition and Characteristics of the Population, for Cities of 10,000 or More," 734, 745; *Fifteenth Census of the United States: 1930*, vol. 3, pt. 2, *Population—North Carolina*, table 12, "Population by Age, Color, Nativity, and Sex, for Cities and Towns of 10,000 or More," 352.

3. "Preliminary Figures Put Charlotte in the Lead," *Winston-Salem Journal and Sentinel*, June 1, 1930; *Fourteenth Census of the United States: 1920*, vol. 3, *Composition and Characteristics of the Population by States*, table 8, "Age, for Cities of 10,000 or More," table 10, "Composition and Characteristics of the Population, for Cities of 10,000 or More," 734; *Fifteenth Census of the United States: 1930*, vol. 3, pt. 2, *Population—North Carolina*, table 12, "Population by Age, Color, Nativity, and Sex, for Cities and Towns of 10,000 or More," 352.

4. These figures appear in the detailed "Winston-Salem, N.C., Study, 1921," 4–5, microfilm, reel 200, microdex 2, YWCA of the U.S.A. Records, Sophia Smith Collections; "Safe Homes Needed for Working Girls," *Winston-Salem Journal*, November 13, 1917.

5. "Annual Meeting of Y.W.C.A. Held Last Night in Association Building," *Winston-Salem Journal*, January 11, 1919; "Colored Work"; Olcott, *Work of Colored Women*, 58.

6. Work, *Negro Year Book, 1918–1919*, 256; "Juanita Saddler of Y.W.C.A. Dies," *New York Times*, January 13, 1970; Robertson, *Christian Sisterhood, Race Relations, and the YWCA*, 202–32n108.

7. Catherine S. Vance, *The Girl Reserve Movement of the Young Women's Christian Association: An Analysis of the Educational Principles and Procedures Used throughout Its History*, 34–37.

8. Olcott, *Work of Colored Women*, 58; "Colored Branch of the Y.W.C.A. Is Organized," *Winston-Salem Journal*, January 14, 1919.

9. "Colored Branch of the Y.W.C.A. Is Organized," *Winston-Salem Journal*, January 14, 1919. Other scholars argue that the idea for the Black YWCA evolved out of an earlier meeting between Black women and white YWCA members about "implementing a weekly study session for young black women on Bible, health and hygiene." The success of the session encouraged white members to develop a Black branch. See, for example, Gillespie, *Katharine and R. J. Reynolds*, 264; and B. Miller, "Blacks in Winston-Salem," 181.

10. See Robertson, *Christian Sisterhood, Race Relations, and the YWCA*, 31–33, 62–65; and Marion W. Roydhouse, "Bridging Chasms: Community and the Southern

YWCA," for a broader discussion of the relationship between Black and white YWCA women.

11. "Ladies Here Form a Civic Improvement League," *Winston-Salem Journal*, May 14, 1908; "Aldermen to Co-operate," *Winston-Salem Journal*, February 20, 1913.

12. "Colored Women's Civic Improvement League Organized Here," *Twin-City Daily Sentinel*, March 8, 1913; "Mass-Meeting Colored Wom'n," *Winston-Salem Journal*, March 6, 1913. See also Gilmore, *Gender and Jim Crow*, 165–69, for a discussion of the creation of a similar organization in Salisbury by the summer of 1913.

13. "Teachers in Civic Work," *Winston-Salem Journal*, March 13, 1913.

14. "Sanitary Force Breaks Records in the Twin-City," *Winston-Salem Journal*, May 14, 1913; "Revolutionize Colored Homes," *Winston-Salem Journal*, May 11, 1913.

15. "Sanitary Force Breaks Records in the Twin-City," *Winston-Salem Journal*, May 14, 1913.

16. "Will Hold Meeting for Colored Women," *Winston-Salem Journal*, May 29, 1913; "Mass-Meeting of Colored People," *Winston-Salem Journal*, August 22, 1913.

17. "One Hundred Thousand Dollars to be Raised for Institutions Here," *Winston-Salem Journal*, February 5, 1919; "Movement Was Launched Tuesday Night to Raise $2,500 to Carry on Work of the Organization in City," *Winston-Salem Journal*, April 29, 1920 [note this article lists the address as 717 Depot [S]treet, a year before the 1921 directory]. The address is listed as 717 [North] Depot in *Winston-Salem, N.C., City Directory, 1921*, 560, 676, then as 717 Patterson [Avenue] in *Winston-Salem, N.C., City Directory, 1922*, 903. The address is listed as 621 [North] Chestnut Av[enue] in *Winston-Salem, N.C., City Directory, 1923*, 934, then as 619 Chestnut in *Winston-Salem, N. Carolina, City Directory, 1926*, 59.

18. "Report of the Industrial Secretary, Winston-Salem, North Carolina," October 27–30, 1925, Winston-Salem, NC, Visitation Reports, microfilm, reel 200, microdex 2, YWCA of the U.S.A. Records, Sophia Smith Collections.

19. "Colored Organizations Co-operate Splendidly," *Winston-Salem Journal*, August 1, 1920.

20. "Colored Mass Meeting Sunday," *Winston-Salem Journal*, July 27, 1918; "One Hundred Thousand Dollars to be Raised for Institutions Here," *Winston-Salem Journal*, February 5, 1919; "Colored Organizations Co-operate Splendidly," *Winston-Salem Journal*, August 1, 1920; "Phyllis Wheatley Home," *Winston-Salem Journal*, May 5, 1923; "Founders Day Program," *Winston-Salem Journal*, March 10, 1930; Hall Xuma, interview by Wilson, audio file 1.

21. According to a tribute in the newspaper, Eugenia Conner, who died in 1921, was the "founder of the Phyllis Wheatley Home." See "Tribute to Founder Phyllis Wheatley Home," *Winston-Salem Journal*, May 17, 1921; and *Winston-Salem, N.C., City Directory, 1918*, 402, but Lena B. Neal remained the most prominent member pushing for the home's development. Biographical information on Lena Neal has been difficult to obtain, but a number of public documents provide a means of piecing together her life when she arrived in Winston-Salem. See, for example, *Thirteenth Census of the United States: 1910, Population, North Carolina, Forsyth County, Winston Township* and *Fourteenth Census of the United States: 1920—Population, North Carolina, Forsyth*

County, Winston Salem, both available at Ancestry.com; *Walsh's Directory of the Cities of Winston and Salem, N.C., for 1902–1903*, 269. See also *Walsh's Winston-Salem, North Carolina, City Directory for 1906*, 395; *Walsh's Winston-Salem, North Carolina, City Directory for 1908*, 438; and *The Winston-Salem, N.C., City Directory, 1911*, 387, 429. Note that in this latter directory, Neal is listed as Selina B. Neal, boarding 539 Depot, home 608 Vine, not Lena Neal.

22. Note that "Phyllis" is spelled in numerous different ways, including "Phillis" and "Philis." See Alexandria Russell, "Sites Seen and Unseen: Mapping African American Women's Public Memorialization," chap. 1, for the most recent and detailed analysis of the spread of Phyllis Wheatley brand of institutions and the social welfare practices developed among Black women.

23. Booker T. Washington and Fannie Barrier Williams, *A New Negro for a New Century*, 393, 406–14; Neverdon-Morton, *Afro-American Women of the South*, 169–71; Wesley, *History of the National Association of Colored Women's Clubs*, 51–53; Elizabeth Lindsey Davis, *The Story of the Illinois Federation of Colored Women's Clubs, 1900–1922*, 16–17; Anne Meis Knupfer, *Toward a Tenderer Humanity and a Nobler Womanhood: African American Women's Clubs in Turn-of-the-Century Chicago*, 81–84; Deborah Gray White, *Too Heavy a Load: Black Women in Defense of Themselves, 1894–1994*, 29–31; Wanda A. Hendricks, *Fannie Barrier Williams: Crossing the Borders of Region and Race*, 129–30; Wanda A. Hendricks, *Gender, Race, and Politics in the Midwest: Black Club Women in Illinois*, 54.

24. "Colored Mass Meeting Sunday," *Winston-Salem Journal*, July 27, 1918.

25. "Sum Raised for Erection of Home for Colored Girls," *Winston-Salem Journal*, July 31, 1918; "A Phyllis Wheatley Appeal to Our White Friends," *Winston-Salem Journal*, August 10, 1921; "Home for Colored Girls," *Winston-Salem Journal*, September 22, 1921; *Winston-Salem, N.C., City Directory, 1921*, 616, 666.

26. See Adrienne Lash Jones, *Jane Edna Hunter: A Case Study of Black Leadership, 1910–1950*, chaps. 3–4; "One Hundred Thousand Dollars to Be Raised for Institutions Here," *Winston-Salem Journal*, February 5, 1919; "Program Rendered for Phylis [*sic*] Wheatly [*sic*] Home," *Winston-Salem Journal*, June 10, 1919; "Campaign Begins for Colored Girls Home," *Winston-Salem Journal*, December 14, 1919.

27. "Phyllis Wheatley Home Secures Homes for Girls," *Winston-Salem Journal*, May 30, 1920; "A Phyllis Wheatley Appeal to Our White Friends," *Winston-Salem Journal*, August 10, 1921; "Home for Colored Girls," *Winston-Salem Journal*, September 22, 1921; *Winston-Salem, N.C., City Directory, 1921*, 616, 666.

28. In August 1921, for example, a series of appeals specifically to whites appeared in "A Phyllis Wheatley Appeal to Our White Friends," *Winston-Salem Journal*, August 10, 18, 23, and 28, 1921. See also the long-term struggle in "Founders Day Program," *Winston-Salem Journal*, March 10, 1930; "Phyllis Wheatley Makes Appeal," *Winston-Salem Journal and Sentinel*, December 21, 1930; and Olcott, *Work of Colored Women*, 58.

29. "Colored Organizations Co-operate Splendidly," *Winston-Salem Journal*, August 1, 1920.

30. "Colored Women Hold Monthly Joint Session," *Winston-Salem Journal*, Au-

gust 26, 1920; "Musical Recital," *Winston-Salem Journal*, May 6, 1930; "Founders Day Program," *Winston-Salem Journal*, March 10, 1930. By October 1927, the Black branch is referred to as the Phyllis Wheatley Branch. See "Report of Miss Louise Leonard, the Industrial Supervisor," Winston Salem, NC, Visitation Reports, microfilm, reel 200, microdex 2, YWCA of the U.S.A. Records, Sophia Smith Collections.

31. "Winston-Salem, January 1913–1927," microfilm, reel 200, microdex 2, YWCA of the U.S.A. Records, Sophia Smith Collections.

32. "Musical Recital," *Winston-Salem Journal*, May 6, 1930; "Founders Day Program," *Winston-Salem Journal*, March 10, 1930.

33. Merrick and Hall Xuma, interview by Wilson, audio file 4; Hall Xuma, interview by Wilson, audio file 1.

34. Hayes Allen and others also joined Anne Spencer in developing the Black YWCA in Lynchburg. Merrick and Hall Xuma, interview by Wilson, audio file 4; Hall Xuma, interview by Wilson, audio file 1; "History of the Girl Reserve, Lynchburg, VA, Phyllis Wheatley Branch" and "Lynchburg, VA, Affiliation, History and Constitution, Application for Membership in the Young Women's Christian Association," microfilm, reel 218, microdex 2, YWCA of the U.S.A. Records, Sophia Smith Collections.

35. "History of the Girl Reserve, Lynchburg, VA, Phyllis Wheatley Branch" and "Chairmen of the Phyllis Wheatley Branch Y.W.C.A. Committees of Management from 1918 to Present, Lynchburg, VA, Phyllis Wheatley Branch," microfilm, reel 218, microdex 2, YWCA of the U.S.A. Records, Sophia Smith Collections; Merrick and Hall Xuma, interview by Wilson, audio file 4; Hall Xuma, interview by Wilson, audio file 1; Vance, *Girl Reserve Movement*, 43–58, 89; "Lynchburg, VA," *New York Age*, August 19, 1922; Wilson and Mullally, *Hope and Dignity*, 143; C. H. Tobias, "The Work of the Young Men's and Young Women's Christian Associations with Negro Youth," 285–86.

36. "Campaign for Colored YWCA," *Winston-Salem Journal*, June 16, 1922.

37. "Colored Fair Wins Success," *Winston-Salem Journal*, October 11, 1922; "Girls Work Dept. of the Y.W.C.A.," *Winston-Salem Journal*, May 5, 1922; "Chestnut Street Branch Y.W.C.A.," *Winston-Salem Journal*, February 25, 1925.

38. "Y.W.C.A.," *Winston-Salem Journal*, November 12, 1926; "Y.W.C.A. Notes," *Winston-Salem Journal*, March 21, 1930; "Camp Betty Hanes," *Winston-Salem Journal*, July 17, 1927; "Camp Betty Hanes," *Winston-Salem Journal*, June 18, 1930.

39. "Brisk Activities Now at Colored Y.W.C.A. This City," *Winston-Salem Journal*, October 28, 1920; "Class for Women at the Colored Y.W.C.A.," *Winston-Salem Journal*, October 7, 1921; "Work at the Colored Woman's Branch Y.W.C.A.," *Twin-City Daily Sentinel*, February 15, 1921; "Health Work in Colored YWCA," *Twin City-Daily Sentinel*, November 6, 1922; "Y.W.C.A. Notes," *Winston-Salem Journal*, March 20, 1930; "Demonstration at 'Y,'" *Winston-Salem Journal*, June 22, 1927.

40. "Colored Y.W.C.A. Asks Books and Magazines," *Twin-City Daily Sentinel*, December 10, 1920; "Negro Library to Be Opened in City," *Winston-Salem Journal*, August 19, 1926; "To Buy Books for Negroes," *Winston-Salem Journal*, January 15, 1927.

41. "Library Opening Today," *Winston-Salem Journal*, February 15, 1927; "Negro Library Opens in City," *Winston-Salem Journal*, February 16, 1927.

42. "Attend the 'Y,'" *Winston-Salem Journal*, May 16, 1930; "Business League Committees," *Winston-Salem Journal*, April 1, 1926; "Negro Business League Reception," *Winston-Salem Journal*, November 7, 1926; "Y.W.C.A.," *Winston-Salem Journal*, November 12, 1926; "Banquet Held at 'Y,'" *Winston-Salem Journal*, February 19, 1928; "Diggs Musical Recital," *Winston-Salem Journal*, April 30, 1928; "Reopening of Goler," *Winston-Salem Journal and Sentinel*, January 26, 1930, 9. *Note*: The *Journal* and *Sentinel* merged in 1927. The Monday through Friday daily paper is the *Journal*, but the weekend edition is the *Journal and Sentinel*.

43. Hall Xuma, interview by Wilson, audio file 1; "National Secretary Heard by Y.W.C.A. Directors," *Winston-Salem Journal*, April 13, 1927; "Woman's Community Service League," *Winston-Salem Journal*, May 3, 1926.

44. "White and Colored Women Co-operate."

45. "Girl Reserve Conference," *Winston-Salem Journal*, June 29, 1927; "Summer Camp," *Winston-Salem Journal*, June 29, 1927; "Camp Betty Hanes," *Winston-Salem Journal*, July 17, 1927; "Second Camp of Summer," *Winston-Salem Journal*, July 27, 1927.

46. "Y.W.C.A. News," *Winston-Salem Journal*, January 22, 1928; "Secretary Speaks," *Winston-Salem Journal*, January 23, 1928; "Mrs. Kyles Speaks, *Winston-Salem Journal*, January 23, 1928.

47. "Y.W.C.A. Makes Progress," *Winston-Salem Journal*, February 3, 1928.

48. "Industrial Work"; Roydhouse, "Bridging Chasms," 272–86; Robertson, *Christian Sisterhood, Race Relations, and the YWCA*, 124–25.

49. "Report of Miss Louise Leonard, Industrial Secretary on Winston-Salem, North Carolina," October 1927, Winston Salem, NC, Visitation Reports, microfilm, reel 200, microdex 2, YWCA of the U.S.A. Records, Sophia Smith Collections; "Union Representatives Have Conference with Officials of Company," *Winston-Salem Journal*, July 12, 1919; "To the Colored Public" (advertisement), *Winston-Salem Journal*, December 14, 1919; "Tobacco Workers on a Contract for Year," *Winston-Salem Journal*, March 31, 1920; "Form Auxiliary to Labor Union," *Winston-Salem Journal*, March 7, 1924; "Several Hundred Delegates Here Tomorrow for Meet," *Winston-Salem Journal*, August 9, 1925; "Several Unions in This City," *Winston-Salem Journal*, August 9, 1925.

50. "City Briefs," *Winston-Salem Journal*, January 26, 1928; "Report of Eleanor Copenhaver on Visit to Winston-Salem, North Carolina," February 10, 1928, Winston Salem, N.C., Visitation Reports, microfilm, reel 200, microdex 2, YWCA of the U.S.A. Records, Sophia Smith Collections; "Labor Leaders Have Returned," *Winston-Salem Journal*, April 16, 1928; "RJR Company Shows Record Earnings, 1929," *Winston-Salem Journal*, January 14, 1930. See also Korstad, *Civil Rights Unionism*, 120–25.

51. Prominent Black businessmen like J. S. Hill, however, had publicly expressed their distaste for the union and discouraged African Americans from joining. See "Colored Business Man Urges Colored People to Let Union Alone," *Winston-Salem Journal*, March 21, 1919; "Report of Eleanor Copenhaver on Visit to Winston-Salem,

North Carolina," March 5[?], 1929, Winston Salem, N.C., Visitation Reports, micro-film, reel 200, microdex 2, YWCA of the U.S.A. Records, Sophia Smith Collections.

52. "Report of Eleanor Copenhaver on Visit to Winston-Salem, North Caro-lina," January 1930, Winston Salem, N.C., Visitation Reports, Microfilmed Records, Winston-Salem, NC, reel 200, microdex 2, YWCA of the U.S.A. Records, Sophia Smith Collections.

53. Korstad, *Civil Rights Unionism*, 132; "L. E. Austin Heard," *Winston-Salem Jour-nal*, May 23, 1932. Note that the Community Chest was the forerunner to the United Way.

54. Interview with Miss Jane Skinner, General Secretary of Winston-Salem, N.C., May 11, 1935, Reported by Annie Kate Gilbert ("Community File" is handwritten in the corner), Winston Salem, N.C., Visitation Reports, Microfilmed Records, Win-ston-Salem, NC, reel 200, microdex 2, YWCA of the U.S.A. Records, Sophia Smith Collections; Korstad, *Civil Rights Unionism*, 120–41.

55. "Mass Meeting Tuesday Night," *Winston-Salem Journal*, May 5, 1928.

56. "Y.W.C.A. Meeting," *Winston-Salem Journal*, January 25, 1929; "Y.W.C.A. Notes," *Winston-Salem Journal*, February 22, 1929.

57. "Y.W.C.A. Notes," *Winston-Salem Journal*, February 22, 1929.

58. "Fashion Show Revue," *Winston-Salem Journal*, April 10, 1930; "A Correction," *Winston-Salem Journal*, April 11, 1930.

59. Robertson, *Christian Sisterhood, Race Relations, and the YWCA*, 11–20, 93–94; "Southern Women and Inter-racial Crux," *Winston-Salem Journal*, March 18, 1923.

60. Report of Miss Louise Leonard, Industrial Secretary on Winston-Salem, North Carolina, October 1927; "Convention Appointments," May 18, 1934, Winston Salem, N.C., Visitation Reports, Microfilmed Records, Winston-Salem, NC, reel 200, mi-crodex 2, both YWCA of the U.S.A. Records, Sophia Smith Collections; "Y.M.C.A. [should be "Y.W.C.A."] Conference," *Winston-Salem Journal*, January 28, 1930. Note that Jane Maxwell is also referred to as Jannie, Janie, and Jenny.

61. Report of Eleanor Copenhaver on Visit to Winston-Salem, North Carolina, April 9 to 11, 1931, Winston Salem, N.C., Visitation Reports, Microfilmed Records, reel 200, microdex 2, YWCA of the U.S.A. Records, Sophia Smith Collections. Bahnson did query "them about our advocating trade unionism" as well because, Copenhaver wrote, Mrs. Bahnson's family are connected with the largest knitting mills." Her hus-band, Fred F. Bahnson, and the family had expanded their capitalist thrust across state lines, purchasing a cotton mill in Fries, Virginia. It made for a very tense situation, Copenhaver noted, particularly because "the Winston-Salem women have insisted in all these meetings that the conditions were splendid in Winston-Salem and that there was no need for legislation. [But] On the night of the committee meeting about half of the girls were absent because they had had to work thirteen hours that day." See also *Miller's Winston-Salem, N.C., City Directory, 1931*, 126.

62. "April 9, 1932, Miss Skinner Wrote," Colored Branch, Winston Salem, N.C., Visitation Reports (has Colored Branch—General secretary: Mrs. Jenny Maxwell and Girl Reserve Miss Olivia Hampton on it), Microfilmed Records, reel 200, microdex 2, YWCA of the U.S.A. Records, Sophia Smith Collections.

63. Convention Appointments, Annie Kate Gilbert, Secretary National Services Division, May 18, 1934, Winston Salem, N.C., Visitation Reports, Microfilmed Records, reel 200, microdex 2, YWCA of the U.S.A. Records, Sophia Smith Collections. Gilbert suggests that the objection to Houston wasn't simply about regional distinctions. Race played the most prominent role. She retorted in her report, "Perhaps if Dr. Houston had been a white man the comments would have been that the approach and speech as that of a lawyer." Moreover, she also noted, even "a native of Minnesota resented the speech as much as the southern women."

64. "Reynolds Co. Shows Record Earnings, 1930," *Winston Salem Journal*, January 14, 1931; "Unemployed to Register," *Winston-Salem Journal*, November 4, 1930; "Appeal Is Made by Mayor Coan," *Winston-Salem Journal*, November 15, 1930, 1; "Jobless to Register In Schools of City Today," *Winston-Salem Journal*, November 15, 1930; "2,811 Jobless Register Here," *Winston-Salem Journal and Sentinel*, November 16, 1930. The 2,811 number was the first real record of unemployed in the city, but it was disputed because some of the data collected from those who registered revealed that some had part-time work, while others were new migrants who had lived in the city for only a short time. Regardless of the dispute over the number of unemployed, it was clear that many people were suffering.

65. "3,200 Jobless Register Here," *Winston-Salem Journal*, November 22, 1930; "Mrs. Maxwell Says," *Winston-Salem Journal*, November 27, 1930.

66. "Hund[reds] Made Glad," *Winston-Salem Journal*, November 25, 1932.

67. "Community Chest Drive," *Winston-Salem Journal*, February 20, 1931; "Community Chest Drive," *Winston-Salem Journal*, February 24, 1931.

68. "Questionnaire for Community Chest and Non Community Chest Cities," November [date unreadable?], 1935, Winston-Salem Finance; Winston Salem, N.C., Visitation Reports, President: Mrs. Robert A Moore (new), dated 3/11/33, p. 1; Jane A. Skinner, "Confidential Report," April 21, 1932, Winston Salem, N.C., Visitation Reports, all Microfilmed Records, reel 200, microdex 2, YWCA of the U.S.A. Records, Sophia Smith Collections.

69. "Report of Miss Louise Leonard, Industrial Secretary on Winston-Salem, North Carolina, October 1927; Annie Kate Gilbert, Community Files, Report of Winston-Salem, North Carolina, March 16, 1934, both Microfilmed Records, reel 200, microdex 2, YWCA of the U.S.A. Records, Sophia Smith Collections; "'Y' to Observe Health Week," *Winston-Salem Journal*, March 26, 1931; "Schedule for Negro Health Week," *Winston-Salem Journal*, April 4, 1932; "Kiddies Concert," *Winston-Salem Journal*, March 21, 1927.

70. "Women of City Organize," *Winston-Salem Journal*, May 3, 1926.

71. "*Go Slow Mary* Makes Big Hit," *Winston-Salem Journal*, November 12, 1926.

72. "*Go Slow Mary* Makes Big Hit," *Winston-Salem Journal*, November 12, 1926; "*Go Slow Mary*," *Winston-Salem Journal*, May 25, 1927.

73. "State Colored Federation of Woman's Clubs Gather," *Winston-Salem Journal*, April 24, 1927; "Mrs. Charlotte Hawkins Brown to Speak," *Winston-Salem Journal*, April 24, 1927; "Mrs. Mary McCloud [sic] Bethune to Be in City," *Winston-Salem Journal*, April 24, 1927 (note that Bethune does not appear to have come); "Mass

Meeting at Goler," *Winston-Salem Journal*, April 24, 1927; "Visitors Welcome at the P.W.A.," *Winston-Salem Journal*, April 24, 1927; "Mrs. Brown Speaks," *Winston-Salem Journal*, April 25, 1927.

74. "Federation to Meet," *Winston-Salem Journal*, April 15, 1927; "N.C. Federation Women's Clubs," *Winston-Salem Journal*, April 23, 1927; "Reception at the Y.W.C.A.," *Winston-Salem Journal*, April 25, 1927.

75. Madie B. Hall to Mrs. M. M. Bethune, November [date unclear?], 1927, in *Records of the National Association of Colored Women's Clubs, 1895–1992*, edited by Lillian Serece Williams, microfilm reel 6, frame 0600.

76. "Local Citizens Interested at Shaw," *Winston-Salem Journal*, August 14, 1931.

77. "Flower and Vegetable Gardens," *Winston-Salem Journal*, May 19, 1932; *Hill's Winston-Salem (North Carolina) City Directory, 1932*, 260; "Path Flower Club," *Winston-Salem Journal*, May 18, 1933; "Along the Garden Path," *Winston-Salem Journal*, June 7, 1933.

78. "Flower Gardens Too," *Winston-Salem Journal and Sentinel*, May 15, 1932; "Shady Rest Gardens," *Winston-Salem Journal*, August 5 1932.

79. "Shady Rest Gardens," *Winston-Salem Journal*, August 5 1932.

80. "Path Flower Club," *Winston-Salem Journal*, May 18, 1933; "Along the Garden Path," *Winston-Salem Journal*, June 7, 1933; "Garden Club Members Take Home Honors from Statewide Convention," *Henderson Daily Dispatch*, September 6, 2012; "Daisy Garden Club Members Take Home Honors from Statewide Meeting," *Henderson Daily Dispatch*, September 9, 2010.

81. "Music Festival Set for Armory," *Charlotte Observer*, February 27, 1933; "Community Festival Provokes Applause," *Charlotte Observer*, February 28, 1933; "To Repeat Festival," *Charlotte Observer*, March 1, 1933; "Crowd Hears Negro Singers in Concert," *Charlotte Observer*, March 6, 1933; "Music Festival Set for Tonight," *Charlotte News*, February 27, 1933; "Negro Concert to Be Repeated," *Charlotte News*, February 28, 1933; "Expect Crowd at Concert Sunday," *Charlotte News*, March 1, 1933; "Mrs. Bright Back to Charlotte," *Winston-Salem Journal*, March 2, 1933, 9; "Four Thousand Attend," *Winston-Salem Journal*, March 7, 1933.

Chapter 4. The Bridge between Jim Crow and Apartheid

1. "Mrs. Hall Dead," *Winston-Salem Journal*, August 29, 1930; "The Funeral of Mrs. Hall," *Winston-Salem Journal*, August 30, 1930.

2. Hall Xuma, interview by Wilson, audio file 1; *Slater State Colored Normal School (Winston-Salem) 1906–'07*, WSSUAr-RG 10–14-WSSU, Digital Collection, Winston-Salem State C. G. O'Kelly University Archives; *Winston-Salem, N.C., City and Suburban City Directory, 1910*, 188–89; *The Winston-Salem, N.C., City Directory, 1913*, 463.

3. Hall Xuma, interview by Wilson, audio file 1; "Dr. H. H. Hall Ill," *Winston-Salem Journal*, June 11, 1931; "Dr. Hall's New Location," *Winston-Salem Journal and Sentinel*, September 25, 1932; "Negro Social Service Council," *Winston-Salem Journal*, February 11, 1932; "Pageant Sunday Afternoon," *Winston-Salem Journal*, February 26, 1932; "Pageant Sunday," *Winston-Salem Journal*, February 29, 1932; "Old North State Meet-

ing," *Winston-Salem Journal*, June 9, 1932; "Dr. Atkins Improving," *Winston-Salem Journal*, August 12, 1932; "Atkins Out at Winston-Salem Son Succeeds," *Baltimore Afro American*, June 9, 1934; Murphy, *History of Winston-Salem State University*, 148. Simon Atkins's wife, Oleona, died in 1936. See "Death Takes Mrs. Oleona P. Atkins," *T.C. Informer* 1, no. 1 (1936): 4, Winston-Salem State C. G. O'Kelly University Archives; and Murphy, *History of Winston-Salem State University*, 149.

4. "A.M.E. Zion Conference Closed," *Winston-Salem Journal*, November 22, 1926; "Miss Hall to Conference," *Winston-Salem Journal*, November 12, 1931.

5. Bettye Collier-Thomas, *Jesus, Jobs, and Justice: African American Women and Religion*, 179–87. See also Bishop L. W. Kyles, ed., *The Doctrines and Discipline of the African Methodist Episcopal Zion Church*, 251–68, Andrew Carnegie Library Archives.

6. "Church Women in Interracial Cooperation"; Collier-Thomas, *Jesus, Jobs, and Justice*, 336–39.

7. "Two Bishops at Goler Memorial Church," *Winston-Salem Journal*, January 7, 1928; "Bishop W. W. Mathews," *Winston-Salem Journal*, April 6, 1931.

8. Hall Xuma, interview by Wilson audio file 2. Hall was an avid bridge player and was elected president of the bridge club in 1933. "Thursday Bridge Club," *Winston-Salem Journal*, May 28, 1933; "Bridge Entertainment," *Winston-Salem Journal*, January 2, 1933.

9. Murphy, *History of Winston-Salem State University*, 115–16, 148–49, 181–82, 417; Hall Xuma, interview by Wilson. See *Hill's Winston-Salem (Forsyth County, N.C.) City Directory, 1935*, 191, where her occupation is listed as student and also see *1935 Yearbook, T.C. Pedagogue*, 35, 44, Winston-Salem State C. G. O'Kelly University Archives, where she is listed in the junior class.

10. Newbold, *Five North Carolina Educators*, 12–15; Murphy, *History of Winston-Salem State University*, 101–28; B. Miller, "Blacks in Winston-Salem," 165–72. The college also became a way to "solve the race relations in Dixie" as reported in "Winston-Salem Teachers' College Example of the Evolution of Negro Education in South," *Pittsburgh Courier*, November 16, 1929.

11. Newbold, *Five North Carolina Negro Educators*, 15–16, 29; Murphy, *History of Winston-Salem State University*, 184–89.

12. *1935 Yearbook, T.C. Pedagogue*, 35, 44; "Honor Roll, Spring Quarter, 1935–1936," *T.C. Informer* 1 no. 2 (1936): 3, both Winston-Salem State C. G. O'Kelly University Archives.

13. "Dr. Hall Here 42 Years," *Winston-Salem Journal and Sentinel*, July 17, 1932; "Dr. Hall Laid to Rest," *Winston-Salem Journal*, November 13, 1935.

14. Hall Xuma, interview by Wilson, audio file 2.

15. Madie Hall, "Assignment Slip—Works Progress," "Notice of Change in Work Status," and "Works Progress Administration—Individual Earnings Record," Works Progress Administration, National Archives and Records Administration; "Forty Per Cent of WPA Workers in State Women," *Greensboro Record*, August 13, 1936; "Many Teachers Find Work through WPA," *Greensboro Daily News*, May 13, 1936. See also *Report on Present Conditions and Trends in Adult Education for Negroes: The Works Progress Administration and State Department of Public Instruction of North Carolina*

(1938), 1–2, 5, about the continuation of an educational program that encouraged the development of conference sites for teachers. One of the sites was Winston-Salem Teachers College.

16. Commencement programs, May 25, 1937, WSSUAr-RG 10-4-Commencement Programs-1937 May_page_3, Digital Collection, Winston-Salem State C. G. O'Kelly University Archives; *Columbia University One Hundred and Eighty-Fourth Annual Commencement, June 1, 1938*, 36, Columbia University Rare Book and Manuscript Library.

17. Cally L. Waite and Margaret Smith Crocco, "Fighting Injustice through Education," 573–74, 578–81. Also note that North Carolina was one of several southern states that encouraged the migration, offering financial assistance for tuition, housing, and even travel to some of those seeking better educational opportunity. It is unclear whether Hall applied for or received that kind of assistance.

18. "Supplement to Directory of Students," in *Columbia University in the City of New York Catalogue Number for the Sessions of 1936–1937*, 257, Columbia University Rare Book and Manuscript Library; "To Africa for Her Nuptials," *New York Amsterdam News*, May 4, 1940; "Society," *New York Amsterdam News*, January 22, 1938; *T.C. Alumni Bulletin* (May 1960): 8; *Slater Industrial and State Normal School Course Catalog, 1914–1915*, 26; *The Slater State Normal School Winston-Salem, N. C. Annual Catalogue 1921–1922*, 58; *The Slater Industrial And State Normal School Winston-Salem Annual Catalogue 1910–1911*, 27, 42; *The Winston-Salem Teachers College Annual Catalogue 1930–1931*, 11, all WSSUAr-RG 10-14-WSSU, Winston-Salem State C. G. O'Kelly University Archives; "C. B. Cash Passes," *Winston-Salem Journal*, January 11, 1930; "N. B. Kimbrough Home," *Winston-Salem Journal*, January 30, 1931.

19. "To Africa for Her Nuptials," *New York Amsterdam News*, May 4, 1940; "Society," *New York Amsterdam News*, January 22, 1938; *T.C. Alumni Bulletin* (May 1960): 8, Winston-Salem State C. G. O'Kelly University Archives; "Many Out to Opening of New Fine Arts Club," *New York Amsterdam News*, March 5, 1930; "Society," *New York Amsterdam News*, December 6, 1933; "Kimbrough in Form Wins Mimms Cup," *New York Amsterdam News*, December 8, 1934; "Holds Annual Dinner," *New York Amsterdam News*, December 28, 1935.

20. *Thirty-Seventh Annual Catalogue*, 47, 49, 51, Shaw University Archive; David Henry Anthony III, *Max Yergan: Race Man, Internationalist, Cold Warrior*, 5–77, 154–62; "Max Yergan at College," *Winston-Salem Journal*, April 9, 1927; "Max Yeargan Sails for Afri-Work," *Dallas Express*, November 26, 1921 (note that the paper spelled his name with an *a*, as in "Yeargan," rather than "Yergan"); "First Y.M.C.A. Secretary to Africa Off for Duty," *Washington Evening Star*, December 10, 1921; Berger, "African American 'Mother of the Nation,'" 548, 550; "Given International Tea," *New York Amsterdam News*, April 14, 1934.

21. Anthony, *Max Yergan*, 58–59, 73–74, 146–50, 172; Gish, *Alfred B. Xuma*, 86; Barbara Ransby, *Eslanda: The Large and Unconventional Life of Mrs. Paul Robeson*, 111.

22. Anthony, *Max Yergan*, 154–62.

23. *Columbia University in the City of New York Catalogue Number for the Sessions of 1937–1938*, 260, Columbia University Rare Book and Manuscript Library.

24. Richard Glotzer, "A Long Shadow: Frederick P. Keppel, the Carnegie Corporation and the Dominions and Colonies Fund Area Experts, 1923–1943," 630.

25. Glotzer, "Long Shadow," 630, 632–35, 638, 639.

26. Glotzer, "Long Shadow," 633–34. See also James Silbey to Dr. Thomas Jesse Jones, chairman, January 21, 1929, MG 162, box 23 (127), folder 23/1, Phelps-Stokes Collection, Schomburg Center for Research in Black Culture.

27. Walter G. Daniel, "Current Trends and Events of National Importance in Negro Education: Section A, Negro Welfare and Mabel Carney at Teachers College, Columbia University," 560–61; Glotzer, "Long Shadow," 633–34; Richard Glotzer, "The Career of Mabel Carney: The Study of Race and Rural Development in the United States and South Africa," 316–17.

28. "Columbia Starts Course on Negro," *New York Amsterdam News*, February 26, 1930.

29. "Give Course on Northern Negro," *New York Amsterdam News*, March 21, 1936.

30. Daniel, "Current Trends and Events," 561–62.

31. Hall Xuma, interview by Wilson, audio file 2; "Rockfeller [*sic*] Bids World Have Faith," *New York Times*, November 20, 1937. Other International Houses that would open before 1937 were in Chicago, Paris, and Berkeley, California. See, for example, "Manual of International House 1933–1934," 3, 4, 5, 11, International House-Member Manuals & ID Cards 1920–1980s, box 392, folder 7, series XIX, Columbia University Rare Book and Manuscript Library.

32. See, for example, "Manual of International House 1933–1934," 7, 12, 13, 15–16, Columbia University Rare Book and Manuscript Library.

33. "Manual of International House 1933–1934," 13–14, Columbia University Rare Book and Manuscript Library.

34. "Harmon Foundation Art Exhibit Ready," *New York Amsterdam News*, January 1, 1930.

35. William D. Carter to Xuma, July 14, 1937, Xuma Papers, Correspondence, AD843.B4, ABX 370714; K. P. Damlamian to Xuma, July 29, 1937, Xuma Papers, Correspondence, AD843.B4, ABX 370729, both Historical Papers Research Archive.

36. See, for example, A. B. Xuma to My dear Professor Carney [Mabel Carney], March 24, 1937, Xuma Papers, Correspondence, AD843.B4, ABX 370324c; and Mabel Carney to Dr. Xuma [A. B. Xuma], June 27, 1937, ABX 370324c, Xuma Papers, Correspondence, AD843.B4, ABX 370324c, both Historical Papers Research Archive; A. B. Xuma, M.D., "Bridging the Gap between White and Black in South Africa, 27th June to 3rd July, 1930," 3, 19, MG 162, box 23 (127), folder 23/16, Phelps-Stokes Collection, Schomburg Center for Research in Black Culture.

37. Anthony, *Max Yergan*, 170, 196–97; Gish, *Alfred B. Xuma*, 92; "'Colour Bar' Voted Down in South African Mines.'"

38. A. E. Swanson to C. W. Patterson, January 8, 1934, and Registrar [C. W. Patterson] to E. R. Moore Company, January 11, 1934, Xuma File, folder 1, Northwestern University Archives; Passport and Certificate of Mrs. Xuma, Xuma Papers, file Q31.1, Historical Papers Research Archive.

39. Madie B. Hall to Alfred B. Xuma, August 2, 1937, Xuma Papers, Correspondence, AD843.B4, ABX 370802, Historical Papers Research Archive.

40. Gish, *Alfred B. Xuma*, 91–92.

41. Anthony, *Max Yergan*, 170, 196–97; Gish, *Alfred B. Xuma*, 92; Max Yergan to Xuma, September 3, 1937, Xuma Papers, Correspondence, AD843.B4, ABX 370903, Historical Papers Research Archive.

42. Roy Wilkins to Dr. A. B. Xuma, March 13, 1937, Xuma Papers, Correspondence, AD843-B4, ABX 370313b, Historical Papers Research Archive; "Watchtower," *New York Amsterdam News*, September 18, 1937. Xuma wrote a rebuttal to some of the reporting on the event in "Takes Exception," *New York Amsterdam News*, September 18, 1937.

43. "Watchtower," *New York Amsterdam News*, September 18, 1937.

44. "Watchtower," *New York Amsterdam News*, September 18, 1937.

45. "Watchtower," *New York Amsterdam News*, September 18, 1937.

46. "Watchtower," *New York Amsterdam News*, September 18, 1937.

47. "Dr. Xuma Autobiography" [1954], 2–3, Xuma Papers, AD843-P24.1, Historical Papers Research Archive.

48. "Dr. Xuma Autobiography" [1954], 4–16, Xuma Papers, AD843-P24.1, Historical Papers Research Archive; Gish, *Alfred B. Xuma*, 15–25; "Maj. Moton Is Installed," *Washington Bee*, June 3, 1916. See also "Former Local Student Attends Mayo Clinic, July 23–Aug. 7," *Saint Paul Echo*, July 31, 1926, which states that Xuma arrived in the United States in 1914.

49. *Fourteenth Census of the United States: 1920*, vol. 3, *Composition and Characteristics of the Population by States*, table 13, "Composition and Characteristics of the Population for Wards of Cities of 50,000 or More," 524; Evelyn Riley Nicholson to Charles W. Patterson, April 7, 1923, Xuma File, folder 1, Northwestern University Archives; "Dr. Xuma Autobiography" [1954], 16–17, Xuma Papers, AD843-P24.1, Historical Papers Research Archive; Gish, *Alfred B. Xuma*, 33–36.

50. Gish, *Alfred B. Xuma*, 34–36. He also held Alpha Phi Alpha membership at Marquette University, Milwaukee, Wisconsin, in Alpha Phi Alpha's *Sphinx Magazine* (October 1923): 3–4. Xuma would also assist with establishing the Beta Psi Chapter at Oxford University in London in August 1938; "'Webster' Name of New AG. Club," *Minnesota Daily*, January 12, 1917; "Webster Discuss Rural Schools," *Minnesota Daily*, March 15, 1918; *The Gopher Yearbook*, vol. 32 (1919), 340, all University of Minnesota Libraries.

51. Gish, *Alfred B. Xuma*, 36. See also, for example, James T. Campbell, *Songs of Zion: The African Methodist Episcopal Church in the United States and South Africa*; and Vinson, *Americans Are Coming!*, for links between Black South Africans, the African Methodist Church, and African Americans.

52. *The Gopher Yearbook*, vol. 33 (1920), 164, University of Minnesota Libraries; "Official Statement of College Credits, Lewis Institute, Chicago, Ill."; J. B. Modesitt to Charles W. Patterson, April 5, 1923; Evelyn Riley Nicholson to Charles W. Patterson, April 7, 1923; and M. L. Melzer, Registrar, Office of the Registrar Marquette

University to Whom It May Concern, September 23, 1923, all in Xuma File, folder 1, Northwestern University Archives; "Dr. Xuma Autobiography" [1954], 17–20, Xuma Papers, AD843-P24.1, Historical Papers Research Archive; Gish, *Alfred B. Xuma*, 36–40.

53. Evelyn Riley Nicholson to Charles W. Patterson, April 7, 1923; J. B. Modesitt to Charles W. Patterson, April 5, 1923; Theodore R. Van Dellen to Olin E. Oeschger, August 6, 1956; A. Bitini Xuma to Charles W. Patterson, April 3, 1923; Charles A. Chandler to the Registrar of the Medical School Northwestern University, July 12, 1924; Registrar Northwestern University to A. W. McLellan, July 18, 1924; "College Goal Of Ex-Savage Near Failure," July 13, 1924, clipping; E. B. Hodge to Office of the Dean, August 20, 1924; Registrar to Alfred Xuma, August 26, 1924, all in Xuma File, folder 1, Northwestern University Archives.

54. Theodore R. Van Dellen to Olin E. Oeschger, August 6, 1956; Xuma to Charles W. Patterson, April 3, 1923; Charles A. Chandler to the Registrar of the Medical School Northwestern University, July 12, 1924; Registrar Northwestern University to A. W. McLellan, July 18, 1924; "Northwestern University Weekly Calendar," *Daily Northwestern*, November 7, 1924, all in Xuma File, folder 1, Northwestern University Archives; "Dr. Xuma Autobiography" [1954], 19–20; Xuma Papers, AD843-P24.1, Historical Papers Research Archive.

55. Alfred B. Xuma to I. Cutter, October 31, 1927, Xuma File, folder 1, Northwestern University Archives; Gish, *Alfred B. Xuma*, 42–43.

56. Gish, *Alfred B. Xuma*, 53–59.

57. "Young African Physician Marries," *Pittsburgh Courier*, January 9, 1932; "Wed in Africa," *Chicago Defender*, January 9, 1932.

58. "Dr. Xuma Autobiography" [1954], 34, Xuma Papers, AD843-P24.1, Historical Papers Research Archive; Gish, *Alfred B. Xuma*, 68, 78–79; *The Forcean, 1921*, 42, 123–24, Wilberforce University Rembert E. Stokes Library Archives; "Wilberforce," *Xenia Evening Gazette*, December 3, 1919; "City Godspeed to Students. Hosts Recall War Days," *Bystander*, January 9, 1920; "St. Paul Notes," *Bystander*, January 9, 1920; "Liberia," *Kansas City Sun*, February 21, 1920; "'Aim High' Urges Speaker Sunday at Wilberforce," *Xenia Evening Gazette*, June 13, 1921. See also "East End News," *Xenia Evening Gazette*, September 25, 1919; "African Girl Will Speak Here Aug. 3," *Kalamazoo Gazette*, August 2, 1921; and "Bethel A.M.E. Church, Thirtieth and Dearborn Streets, Rev. S. L. Birt, Pastor," *Chicago Whip*, August 27, 1921.

59. "Dr. Xuma Autobiography" [1954], 34, Xuma Papers, AD843-P24.1, Historical Papers Research Archive; Gish, *Alfred B. Xuma*, 68, 78–79.

60. Max Yergan to Xuma, November 27, 1936, Xuma Papers, Correspondence, AD843.B3, ABX 361127c, Historical Papers Research Archive; Gish, *Alfred B. Xuma*, 89, 235n35; Anthony, *Max Yergan*, 146.

61. "Dr. Xuma Autobiography" [1954], 36–37, Xuma Papers, AD843-P24.1; Max Yergan to Xuma, June 18, 1935, Xuma Papers, Correspondence, AD843.B2, ABX 350618; [Mayne?] Sims to Alfred B. Xuma, June 24, 1936, Xuma Papers, Correspondence, AD843.B3, ABX 360624a; Eva B. M. Morake to Xuma, June 25, 1936, Xuma

Papers, Correspondence, AD843.B3, ABX 360625; Max Yergan to Xuma, February 4, 1937, Xuma Papers, Correspondence, AD843.B4, ABX 370204, all in Historical Papers Research Archive.

62. *Woods v. Hall*, 214 N.C. 16, 197 S.E. 557 (1938).

63. "Supplement to Directory of Students," in *Columbia University in the City of New York Catalogue Number for the Sessions of 1936–1937*, 257; "Supplement to Directory of Students" (Morningside Heights, NY), in *Columbia University in the City of New York Catalogue Number for the Sessions of 1937–1938*, 20; "Directory of Students," in *Columbia University in the City of New York Catalogue Number for the Sessions of 1937–1938*, 143; "Degrees Conferred" (Morningside Heights, NY), in *Columbia University in the City of New York Catalogue Number for the Sessions of 1938–1939*, 235; *Columbia University One Hundred and Eighty-Fourth Annual Commencement, June 1, 1938*, 36, all in Columbia University Rare Book and Manuscript Library; Hall Xuma, interview by Wilson, audio file 2.

64. Madie B. Hall to Xuma, June 10, 1938, Xuma Papers, 1917–60, Correspondence, AD843-C1, ABX 380610, Historical Papers Research Archive.

65. Madie B. Hall to Xuma, June 10, 1938, Xuma Papers, 1917–60, Correspondence, AD843-C1, ABX 380610, Historical Papers Research Archive.

66. Gish, *Alfred B. Xuma*, 96; Madie B. Hall to Xuma, June 10, 1938, Xuma Papers, 1917–60, Correspondence, AD843-C1, ABX 380610, Historical Papers Research Archive.

67. Susie W. Yergan to Dr. Xuma [Alfred B. Xuma], June 20, 1938, Xuma Papers, 1917–60, Correspondence, AD843-C1, ABX 380620a, Historical Papers Research Archive.

68. Madie B. Hall to Xuma, August 8, 1938, Xuma Papers, 1917–60, Correspondence, AD843-C2, ABX 380808, Historical Papers Research Archive.

69. Madie B. Hall to Xuma, August 26, 1938, Xuma Papers, 1917–60, Correspondence, AD843-C2, ABX 380826, Historical Papers Research Archive; *Hill's Winston-Salem (Forsyth County, N. C.) City Directory, 1939*, 189, 206.

70. Hall to Xuma, August 26, 1938, Xuma Papers, 1917–60, Correspondence, AD843-C2, ABX 380826, Historical Papers Research Archive.

71. Hall to Xuma, August 26, 1938, Xuma Papers, 1917–60, Correspondence, AD843-C2, ABX 380826, Historical Papers Research Archive.

Chapter 5. "If I Had Wings I Would Truly Fly Over": The Courtship

1. Hall to Xuma, November 4, 1938, Xuma Papers, 1917–60, Correspondence, AD843-C1, ABX 381104c, Historical Papers Research Archive.

2. Hall to Xuma (Dear Alfred), January 1, 1939, Xuma Papers, 1917–60, Correspondence, AD843-C2, ABX 390101a, Historical Papers Research Archive. The address of her new home is 1016 Cameron Avenue.

3. Hall to Xuma (Dear Alfred), January 1, 1939, Xuma Papers, 1917–60, Correspon-

dence, AD843-C2, ABX 390101a, Historical Papers Research Archive; Gish, *Alfred B. Xuma*, 94–95.

4. Hall to Xuma (Dear Alfred), January 1, 1939, Xuma Papers, 1917–60, Correspondence, AD843-C2, ABX 390101a, Historical Papers Research Archive.

5. Hall to Xuma (Dear Alfred), January 25, 1939, Xuma Papers, 1917–60, Correspondence, AD843-C2, ABX 390125a, Historical Papers Research Archive.

6. Hall to Xuma (Dear Alfred), January 25, 1939, Xuma Papers, 1917–60, Correspondence, AD843-C2, ABX 390125a, Historical Papers Research Archive.

7. Martin G. Haynes to Xuma (Dr. Alfred B. Xuma), February 17, 1939, Xuma Papers, 1917–60, Correspondence, AD843-C2, ABX 390217[?], Historical Papers Research Archive.

8. Hall to Xuma, March 2, 1939, Xuma Papers, 1917–60, Correspondence, AD843-C2, ABX 390302, Historical Papers Research Archive.

9. Hall to Xuma, March 2, 1939, Xuma Papers, 1917–60, Correspondence, AD843-C2, ABX 390302, Historical Papers Research Archive.

10. Hall to Xuma, March 2, 1939, Xuma Papers, 1917–60, Correspondence, AD843-C2, ABX 390302 (emphasis in the original), Historical Papers Research Archive.

11. Hall to Xuma, March 12, 1939, Xuma Papers, 1917–60, Correspondence, AD843-C2, ABX 390312, Historical Papers Research Archive.

12. Quoted in Vinson, *Americans Are Coming!*, 32.

13. Hall to Xuma, April 21, 1939, Xuma Papers, 1917–60, Correspondence, AD843-C2, ABX 390421, Historical Papers Research Archive; Wilson and Mullally, *Hope and Dignity*, 146; Hall Xuma, interview by Wilson, audio file 2.

14. Wilson and Mullally, *Hope and Dignity*, 146–47; Hall Xuma, interview by Wilson, audio file 2.

15. Hall to Xuma, August 13, 1939, Xuma Papers, 1917–60, Correspondence, AD843-C2, ABX 390813, Historical Papers Research Archive.

16. Hall to Xuma, April 21, 1939, Xuma Papers, 1917–60, Correspondence, AD843-C2, ABX 390421, Historical Papers Research Archive.

17. Hall to Xuma, April 21, 1939, Xuma Papers, 1917–60, Correspondence, AD843-C2, ABX 390421, Historical Papers Research Archive.

18. Hall to Xuma, April 21, 1939, Xuma Papers, 1917–60, Correspondence, AD843-C2, ABX 39042, Historical Papers Research Archive 1.

19. Hall to Xuma, May 5, 1939, Xuma Papers, 1917–60, Correspondence, AD843-C2, ABX 390505a, Historical Papers Research Archive.

20. Hall to Xuma, May 5, 1939, Xuma Papers, 1917–60, Correspondence, AD843-C2, ABX 390505a, Historical Papers Research Archive.

21. Hall to Xuma, May 5, 1939, Xuma Papers, 1917–60, Correspondence, AD843-C2, ABX 390505a, Historical Papers Research Archive.

22. Hall to Xuma, June 11, 1939, Xuma Papers, 1917–60, Correspondence, AD843-C2, ABX 390611, Historical Papers Research Archive.

23. Hall to Xuma, June 19, 1939, Xuma Papers, 1917–60, Correspondence, AD843-C2, ABX 390619c, Historical Papers Research Archive.

24. Hall to Xuma, July 15, 1939, Xuma Papers, 1917–60, Correspondence, AD843-C2, ABX 390715, Historical Papers Research Archive.

25. Hall to Xuma, June 25, 1939, Xuma Papers, 1917–60, Correspondence, AD843-C2, ABX 390625, Historical Papers Research Archive.

26. Hall to Xuma, June 28, 1939, Xuma Papers, 1917–60, Correspondence, AD843-C2, ABX 390628, Historical Papers Research Archive.

27. Hall to Xuma, June 28, 1939, Xuma Papers, 1917–60, Correspondence, AD843-C2, ABX 39062, Historical Papers Research Archive 8.

28. Hall to Xuma, July 4, 1939, Xuma Papers, 1917–60, Correspondence, AD843-C2, ABX 390704, Historical Papers Research Archive.

29. Hall to Xuma, July 15, 1939, Xuma Papers, 1917–60, Correspondence, AD843-C2, ABX 390715, Historical Papers Research Archive.

30. Anthony, *Max Yergan*, 78–166, 167–215, quote on 132–33, Historical Papers Research Archive.

31. Susie W. Yergan to Xuma, June 20, 1938, Xuma Papers, 1917–60, Correspondence, AD843-C1, ABX 380620a; Hall to Xuma, August 26, 1938, Xuma Papers, 1917–60, Correspondence, AD843-C2, ABX 380826; Hall to Xuma, January 25, 1939, Xuma Papers, 1917–60, Correspondence, AD843-C2, ABX 390125a; Hall to Xuma, March 12, 1939, Xuma Papers, 1917–60, Correspondence, AD843-C2, ABX 390312; Hall to Xuma, June 11, 1939, Xuma Papers, 1917–60, Correspondence, AD843-C2, ABX 390611; Hall to Xuma, June 28, 1939, Xuma Papers, 1917–60, Correspondence, AD843-C2, ABX 390628; Hall to Xuma, July 27, 1939, Xuma Papers, 1917–60, Correspondence, ABX 390727[?], AD843-C2, all in Historical Papers Research Archive; Anthony, *Max Yergan*, 215.

32. Xuma to D. L. Smit, July 5, 1939, Xuma Papers, 1917–60, Correspondence, AD843-C2, ABX 390705, Historical Papers Research Archive.

33. Smit to Xuma, July 8, 1939, Xuma Papers, 1917–60, Correspondence, AD843-C2, ABX 390708; Xuma to Smit, July 11, 1939, Xuma Papers, 1917–60, Correspondence, AD843-C2, ABX 390711, both in Historical Papers Research Archive.

34. Hall to Xuma, July 18, 1939 (Post Office Telegraphs), Xuma Papers, 1917–60, Correspondence, AD843-C2, ABX 390718; Hall to Xuma, July 31, 1939, Xuma Papers, 1917–60, Correspondence, AD843-C2, ABX 390731, both in Historical Papers Research Archive.

35. Hall to Xuma, July 27, 1939, Xuma Papers, 1917–60, Correspondence, AD843-C2, ABX 390727[?], Historical Papers Research Archive.

36. Hall to Xuma, July 27, 1939, Xuma Papers, 1917–60, Correspondence, AD843-C2, ABX 390727[?]; Hall to Xuma, July 31, 1939, Xuma Papers, 1917–60, Correspondence, AD843-C2, ABX 390731; Hall to Xuma, September 22, 1939, Xuma Papers, 1917–60, Correspondence, AD843-C2, ABX 390922, all in Historical Papers Research Archive.

37. *Fifteenth Census of the United States: 1930, Population Schedule, Winston Salem, North Carolina*. Note that Willie is listed in the Census as Willie H. Kennedy, male, head of household, and twenty-five years old.

38. Hall to Xuma, July 31, 1939, Xuma Papers, 1917–60, Correspondence, AD843-C2, ABX 390731, Historical Papers Research Archive.

39. Smit to Xuma, July 20, 1939, Department of Native Affairs, Pretoria, Xuma Papers, 1917–60, Correspondence, AD843-C2, ABX 390720; Smit to Xuma, September 6, 1939, Department of Native Affairs, Pretoria, Xuma Papers, 1917–60, Correspondence, AD843-C2, ABX 390906; Hall to Xuma, August 13, 1939, Xuma Papers, 1917–60, Correspondence, AD843-C2, ABX 390813, all in Historical Papers Research Archive.

40. Hall to Xuma, August 13, 1939, Xuma Papers, 1917–60, Correspondence, AD843-C2, ABX 390813; Hall to Xuma, August 24, 1939, Xuma Papers, 1917–60, Correspondence, AD843-C2, ABX 390824a, both in Historical Papers Research Archive.

41. Hall to Xuma, August 24, 1939, Xuma Papers, 1917–60, Correspondence, AD843-C2, ABX 390824a (emphasis in the original), Historical Papers Research Archive.

42. Hall to Xuma, August 24, 1939, Xuma Papers, 1917–60, Correspondence, AD843-C2, ABX 390824a, Historical Papers Research Archive.

43. Hall to Xuma, September 22, 1939, Xuma Papers, 1917–60, Correspondence, AD843-C2, ABX 390922, Historical Papers Research Archive.

44. Hall to Xuma, September 22, 1939, Xuma Papers, 1917–60, Correspondence, AD843-C2, ABX 390922, Historical Papers Research Archive.

45. Hall to Xuma, September 22, 1939, Xuma Papers, 1917–60, Correspondence, AD843-C2, ABX 390922, Historical Papers Research Archive.

46. Xuma to Hall, September 29, 1939, Xuma Papers, 1917–60, Correspondence, AD843-C2, [no ABX or number], Historical Papers Research Archive.

47. Hall to Xuma, October 9, 1939, Cable, Xuma Papers, 1917–60, Correspondence, AD843-C2, ABX 391009; Hall to Xuma, November 2, 1939, Xuma Papers, 1917–60, Correspondence, AD843-C2, ABX 391102b, both in Historical Papers Research Archive.

48. Neverdon-Morton, *Afro-American Women of the South*, 54; Robenia Baker Gary and Lawrence E. Gary, "The History of Social Work Education for Black People, 1900–1930," 71–75.

49. Neverdon-Morton, *Afro-American Women of the South*, 53–54; Gary and Gary, "History of Social Work Education," 74–75.

50. City of Johannesburg, Continuation Committee on Bantu Juvenile Delinquency, July 24 and 25, 1939, Xuma Papers, 1917–60, Correspondence, AD843-C2, ABX 390724b; G. Ballenden to Xuma, August 9, 1939, Xuma Papers, 1917–60, Correspondence, AD843-C2, ABX 390809; G. Ballenden to Xuma, September 23, 1939, Xuma Papers, 1917–60, Correspondence, AD843-C2, ABX 390923; Ray E. Phillips to Xuma, October 21, 1939, Xuma Papers, 1917–60, Correspondence, AD843-C2, ABX 391021; Phillips to Xuma, November 2, 1939, Xuma Papers, 1917–60, Correspondence, AD843-C2, ABX 391102a, all in Historical Papers Research Archive.

51. Hall to Xuma, November 2, 1939, Xuma Papers, 1917–60, Correspondence, AD843-C2, ABX 391102b (emphasis in the original), Historical Papers Research Archive.

52. Hall to Xuma, October 11, 1939, Xuma Papers, 1917–60, Correspondence, AD843-C2, ABX 391011; Hall to Xuma, October 15, 1939 (cable), Xuma Papers, 1917–60, Correspondence, AD843-C2, ABX 391015, both in Historical Papers Research Archive.

53. Hall to Xuma, November 2, 1939, Xuma Papers, 1917–60, Correspondence, AD843-C2, ABX 391102b, Historical Papers Research Archive.

54. Hall to Xuma, November 17, 1939, Xuma Papers, 1917–60, Correspondence, AD843-C2, ABX 391117a, Historical Papers Research Archive.

55. Hall to Xuma, November 8, 1939, Xuma Papers, 1917–60, Correspondence, AD843-C2, ABX 391108, Historical Papers Research Archive.

56. Hall to Xuma, November 8, 1939, Xuma Papers, 1917–60, Correspondence, AD843-C2, ABX 391108, Historical Papers Research Archive.

57. Hall to Xuma, November 17, 1939, Xuma Papers, 1917–60, Correspondence, AD843-C2, ABX 391117a, Historical Papers Research Archive.

58. Phillips to Xuma, March 21, 1940, Xuma Papers, 1917–60, Correspondence, AD843-C3, ABX 400321; Xuma to Phillips, March 23, 1940, Xuma Papers, 1917–60, Correspondence, AD843-C3, ABX 400323, both in Historical Papers Research Archive.

59. Xuma to L. Brink, March 28, 1940, Xuma Papers, 1917–60, Correspondence, AD843-C3, ABX 400328; [unreadable signature but secretary for the interior to] Xuma, May 20, 1940, Xuma Papers, 1917–60, Correspondence, AD843-C3, ABX 400520a, both in Historical Papers Research Archive.

60. Hall Xuma, interview by Wilson, audio file 2; *Sixteenth Census of the United States: 1940, Population Schedule, Winston-Salem, North Carolina.* Note the continued discrepancy in age for Hall; she is listed as forty-three. *Grantor General Index to Real Estate Conveyances—Forsyth County, N.C.—Grantors*, deed of trust, bk. 396, p. 319; deed, bk. 465, p. 225. The address of Leroy Hall's new home is 1009 Cameron Avenue.

61. Louise Ballou Gow to Hall, March 26, 1940, Xuma Papers, 1917–60, Correspondence, AD843-C3, ABX 400326, Historical Papers Research Archive; Dennis C. Dickerson, *The African Methodist Episcopal Church: A History*, 433.

62. Gow to Hall, March 26, 1940, Xuma Papers, 1917–60, Correspondence, AD843-C3, ABX 400326, Historical Papers Research Archive. It is unclear when Hall actually received the letter or offered a response, but its significance encouraged her to hold on to it for more than two decades and to include it in her husband's archival collection more than twenty years later.

63. Hall Xuma, interview by Wilson, audio file 2. The name of the nurse is not revealed by Xuma or Hall, but see Ruth C. Cowles to Xuma, February 17, 1939, Xuma Papers, 1917–60, Correspondence, AD843-C2, ABX 390217c; Cowles to Xuma, February 20, 1939, Xuma Papers, 1917–60, Correspondence, AD843-C2, ABX 390220a, both in Historical Papers Research Archive. Also, of the passengers listed on the ship, thirty-seven-year-old Ruth C. Cowles of Los Angeles, a white female, seems to have

been Hall's companion. Her occupation is listed in the *Fifteenth Census of the United States: 1930, Population Schedule, Winston Salem, North Carolina*, as a missionary.

64. "To Africa for Her Nuptials," *New York Amsterdam News*, May 4, 1940. See "In Celebration," *New York Amsterdam News*, October 12, 1940, for reference to the club in Harlem. "Memorials to TC-ites and Relatives of TC-ites," *T.C. Alumni Bulletin* 21, no. 3 (1960): 8, Winston-Salem State C. G. O'Kelly University Archives; "Makes Change," *New York Amsterdam News*, October 24, 1936.

65. List of Passengers, N.A.S.M. Holland-America Line, April 27, 1940, Xuma Papers, 1917–60, Correspondence, AD843-C3, ABX 400427, Historical Papers Research Archive; "To Africa for Her Nuptials," *New York Amsterdam News*, May 4, 1940.

Chapter 6. "I Had to Do Something for Women Here"

1. List of Passengers, N.A.S.M. Holland-America Line, April 27, 1940, Xuma Papers, 1917–60, Correspondence, AD843-C3, ABX 400427, Historical Papers Research Archive.

2. Hall Xuma, interview by Wilson, audio file 2.

3. Hall Xuma, interview by Wilson, audio file 2.

4. Hall Xuma, interview by Wilson, audio file 2.

5. Hall Xuma, interview by Wilson, 1980, audio file 2; "Welcome Supper," May 20, 1940, Xuma Papers, 1917–60, Correspondence, AD843-C3, ABX 400520b, Historical Papers Research Archive; "Dr Xuma Married," *Bantu World*, May 25, 1940, 13; Peter Limb, ed., *A. B. Xuma: Autobiography and Selected Works*, 35.

6. "Amalgamation of Woman's Organisations," *Bantu World*, January 6, 1940; "10,000 Miles on Y.M.[W.]C.A. Affairs," *Bantu World*, October 1, 1955; Ray E. Phillips to Xuma, July 11, 1940, Xuma Papers, 1917–60, Correspondence, AD843-C3, ABX 400711, Historical Papers Research Archive; Patricia G. Clark, "A Gendered View of the History of Professionalization in South Africa," 83; Gish, *Alfred B. Xuma*, 76.

7. "Mrs. A. B. Xuma Guest at Reception"; Nonceba Lubanga, "Nursing in South Africa: Black Women Workers Organize," 54–55; Gish, *Alfred B. Xuma*, 100.

8. Karlton C. Johnson to Mrs. A. B. Xuma, November 4, 1940, Xuma Papers, 1917–60, Correspondence, AD843-C3, ABX 401104, Historical Papers Research Archive; "Daughters of Africa." See also Dawne Y. Curry, "'What Is It That We Call the Nation': Celilia Lillian Tshabalala's Definition, Diagnosis, and Prognosis of the Nation in a Segregated South Africa," 56.

9. Zubeida Jaffer, *Beauty of the Heart: The Life and Times of Charlotte Mannye Maxeke*; Frene Ginwala, "Women and the African National Congress, 1912–1943," 89–90; Brooks, *Boycotts, Buses, and Passes*, 170–72; "Progress of Negro Americans"; Gish, *Alfred B. Xuma*, 69–70, 100.

10. "'Momma' Xuma Is Going Back Home," *Rand Daily Mail*, February 14, 1963.

11. A. De V. Herholdt to Mrs. M. B. H. Xuma, September 6, 1940, Xuma Papers, 1917–60, Correspondence, AD843-C3, ABX 400906, Historical Papers Research Archive.

12. Hall Xuma to Spencer, August 1, 1943, MSS 14204, box 6, Anne Spencer Papers,

Albert and Shirley Small Special Collections Library. Anne Spencer was a Black activist and librarian in Lynchburg and earned fame for her poetry published during the Harlem Renaissance.

13. Call Meeting of the Board of Managers Crogman Community Clinic, August 8, 1940, Xuma Papers, 1917–60, Correspondence, AD843-C3, ABX 400830b; Crogman Community Clinic Wilberforce Institute Evaton First Annual Report from September 1939 to August 1940, Xuma Papers, 1917–60, Correspondence, AD843-C3, ABX 400830b, both Historical Papers Research Archive; Gish, *Alfred B. Xuma*, 97; Merrick and Hall Xuma, interview by Wilson, audio file 2.

14. Gish, *Alfred B. Xuma*, 105.

15. Stephen Oliphant to Xuma, May 14, 1940, Xuma Papers, 1917–60, Correspondence, AD843-C3, ABX 400514a; Stephen Oliphant to Xuma, May 30, 1940, Xuma Papers, 1917–60, Correspondence, AD843-C3, ABX 400530b; A. B. Xuma to Stephen Oliphant, June 15, 1940, Xuma Papers, 1917–60, Correspondence, AD843-C3, ABX 400615; A. B. Xuma to Stephen Oliphant, November 20, 1940, Xuma Papers, 1917–60, Correspondence, AD843-C3, ABX 401120; African National Congress, December 17, 1940, Xuma Papers, 1917–60, Correspondence, AD843-C3, ABX 401217a, all Historical Papers Research Archive; Thomas Karis, *Hope and Challenge, 1935–1952*, 158–59; Gish, *Alfred B. Xuma*, 106, 117.

16. Gish, *Alfred B. Xuma*, 107–15.

17. African National Congress, June 21, 1943, Xuma Papers, 1917–60, Correspondence, AD843-G5, ABX 430621b, Historical Papers Research Archive.

18. "American Negro Revue," June 10 and 11, 1943, Xuma Papers, 1917–60, Correspondence, AD843-G5, ABX 430610b, Historical Papers Research Archive; J. W. Gibson and W. H. Crogman, *Progress of a Race; or, The Remarkable Advancement of the Colored American, from the Bondage of Slavery, Ignorance and Poverty to the Freedom of Citizenship, Intelligence, Affluence, Honor and Trust.* These kinds of celebrations and performances of freedom and emancipation were quite popular in African American communities throughout the country. See, for example, "After Thirty Years of Freedom," *Chicago Daily Tribune*, May 4, 1896; and "To Sing in Jubilee," *Daily Inter Ocean* (Chicago), May 10, 1896.

19. "American Negro Revue," June 10 and 11, 1943, Xuma Papers, 1917–60, Correspondence, AD843-G5, ABX 430610b, Historical Papers Research Archive; Gibson and Crogman, *Progress of a Race*.

20. Maurice Cohen, "With Fences around Them," undated, but probably in 1943 when the production takes place, Xuma Papers, 1917–60, AD843, N10.8; A Second Release of the American Negro Revue, Xuma Papers, 1917–60, Correspondence, AD843-P25.1; Ray E. Phillips to Hall Xuma, June 21, 1943, Xuma Papers, 1917–60, Correspondence, AD843-G5, ABX 43061e, all Historical Papers Research Archive; Hall Xuma to Spencer, August 1, 1943, MSS 14204, box 6, Spencer Papers, Albert and Shirley Small Special Collections Library.

21. A. B. P. Malunga of Gere-Brown Training School, Barkly Road, Kimberley, to Xuma, November 12, 1943, Xuma Papers, 1917–60, Correspondence, AD843-H4, ABX 431112b; A. B. Xuma to A. B. P. Malunga. November 13, 1943, Xuma Papers, 1917–60,

Correspondence, AD843-H4, ABX 431113a; A. B. Xuma to A. B. P. Malunga, December 7, 1943, Xuma Papers, 1917–60, Correspondence, AD843-H5, ABX 431207b; A. B. Xuma to A. B. P. Malunga, December 24, 1943, Xuma Papers, 1917–60, Correspondence, AD843-H5, ABX 431224b; Receiver of Revenue to Xuma, December 29, 1943, Xuma Papers, 1917–60, Correspondence, AD843-H5, ABX 431229b; A. B. Xuma to the Receiver of Revenue, January 26, 1944, Xuma Papers, 1917–60, Correspondence, AD843-I1, ABX 440126c, all Historical Papers Research Archive.

22. "Hollywood Turned Heaven Loose for This Picture," *Raleigh News and Observer*, July 12, 1936; "Film Version of Famous Stage Hit Coming," *Franklin Times*, July 31, 1936; "Theatres," *Raleigh News and Observer*, July 12, 1936; "'The Green Pastures' Will Be Presented at Carolina," *Durham Morning Herald*, August 16, 1936; "'De Lawd' Speaks at Guilford Today," *Greensboro Record*, April 7, 1936; "Starts Tomorrow!—Marc Connelly's 'The Green Pastures'" (advertisement), *Greensboro Record*, April 11, 1936.

23. "News of the Screen," *New York Times*, July 16, 1936; "'Green Pastures' at B'klyn Paramount," *New York Amsterdam News*, August 1, 1936; "'Green Pastures' Scene," *New York Amsterdam News*, August 8, 1936; "Along Radio Lane," *New York Amsterdam News*, December 26, 1936; "Bars 'Green Pastures,'" *New York Times*, June 23, 1936; "'Green Pastures' Freed," *New York Times*, September 13, 1936; "Censorship Is Lifted on 'Green Pastures,'" *New York Times*, November 4, 1936.

24. "Secretary for the Interior [name illegible] to Hall Xuma, November 5, 1943, Xuma Papers, 1917–60, Correspondence, AD843-H4, ABX 431105, Historical Papers Research Archive.

25. Secretary for the Interior [name illegible] to Hall Xuma, December 21, 1943, Xuma Papers, 1917–60, Correspondence, AD843-H5, ABX 431221b, Historical Papers Research Archive.

26. Berger, "African American 'Mother of the Nation,'" 556–57.

27. Brooks, *Boycotts, Buses, and Passes*, 134–36; Gish, *Alfred B. Xuma*, 170–71.

28. "Amalgamation of Woman's Organisations," *Bantu World*, January 6, 1940; National Council of African Women Coming of Age Conference, 1937–1958, Ernest Cole, Photographic Collection and Papers, Historical Papers Research Archive; Cherryl Walker, *Women and Resistance in South Africa*, 36–40.

29. "Amalgamation of Woman's Organisations," *Bantu World*, January 6, 1940; National Council of African Women Coming of Age Conference, 1937–1958, Ernest Cole, Photographic Collection and Papers, Historical Papers Research Archive; Walker, *Women and Resistance in South Africa*, 36–40; Jaffer, *Beauty of the Heart*; Ginwala, "Women and the African National Congress," 89–90; Brooks, *Boycotts, Buses, and Passes*, 170–72; Karis, *Hope and Challenge*, 157; Cobley, *Rules of the Game*, 76–78. See also Meghan Healy-Clancy, "Women and the Problem of Family in Early African Nationalist History and Historiography," for a discussion of the debate about Black women and engagement in politics.

30. Quoted in Nicholas Grant, "The National Council of Negro Women and South Africa: Black Internationalism, Motherhood, and the Cold War," 67; Grace V. Leslie, "'United, We Build a Free World': The Internationalism of Mary McLeod Bethune and the National Council of Negro Women," 194.

31. National Council of African Women, August, 8, 1941, Xuma Papers, 1917–60, Correspondence, AD843-D2, ABX 410829b, Historical Papers Research Archive.

32. Mina Soga to Xuma, November 18, 1942, Xuma Papers, 1917–60, Correspondence, AD843-F2, ABX 421118c, Historical Papers Research Archive.

33. Report of the Queentown's National Council of African Women, February 12, 1943, Xuma Papers, 1917–60, Correspondence, AD843-G1, ABX 430212; Ray E. Phillip to Xuma, July 11, 1940, Xuma Papers, 1917–60, Correspondence, AD843-C3, ABX 400711; South African National Council of Young Men's Christian Association, Jan H. Hofmeyr School of Social Work, South African Institute of Race Relations (SAIRR) Papers, 1892–1974, AD1715, 14.20.1; Courses of Study and Time Tables, Jan H. Hofmeyr School of Social Work, South African Institute of Race Relations (SAIRR) Papers, 1892–1974, AD1715, 14.20.4, all Historical Papers Research Archive; "Jan H. Hofmeyr School of Social Work," *Bantu World*, July 13, 1940, 4. See also Clark, "Gendered View," 82–84, for a discussion of how segregationist policies even before apartheid meant that Blacks could not attend most of the white colleges and universities. Technically, however, Black students had access to social work education at the open universities of the University of South Africa and the University of Witwatersrand. Few Black students actually attended the schools. Those like Charlotte Maxeke and Violet Sibusisiwe would leave South Africa and earn their degrees in the United States.

34. South African National Council of Young Men's Christian Association, Jan H. Hofmeyr School of Social Work, South African Institute of Race Relations (SAIRR) Papers, 1892–1974, AD1715, 14.20.1; Courses of Study and Time Tables, Jan H. Hofmeyr School of Social Work, South African Institute of Race Relations (SAIRR) Papers, 1892–1974, AD1715, 14.20.4, both Historical Papers Research Archive.

35. Walker, *Women and Resistance in South Africa*, 35–36.

36. Wilson and Mullally, *Hope and Dignity*, 148; Hall Xuma, interview by Wilson, audio file 2. See also Vinson, *Americans Are Coming!*, for an analysis of the complex history of African Americans with South Africa.

37. Catherine Higgs, "Zenzele: African Women's Self-Help Organizations in South Africa, 1927–1998," 123–25, 131–32.

38. Quotes from Berger, "African American 'Mother of the Nation,'" 562; and Seymour-Jones, *Journey of Faith*, 160–61.

39. Wilson and Mullally, *Hope and Dignity*, 147; Nat Nakasa, "'Mummy' Goes Home," 39; Ellen Kuzwayo, interviewed by Steven Gish, March 27, 1991, in Soweto; *The Tenth Anniversary Number Johannesburg Zenzele Club Year Book, 1951*, Conference Program, South African Institute of Race Relations (SAIRR) Papers, 1892–1974, AD1715–14–18–2, Historical Papers Research Archive; Seymour-Jones, *Journey of Faith*, 158.

40. Nakasa, "'Mummy' Goes Home," 39; Seymour-Jones, *Journey of Faith*, 158.

41. Higgs, "Zenzele," 121–25, 131–32; Walker, *Women and Resistance in South Africa*, 38–39; Berger, "African American 'Mother of the Nation,'" 550; Cobley, *Rules of the Game*, 78–80.

42. Hall Xuma to Spencer, August 1, 1943, MSS 14204, box 6, Spencer Papers,

Albert and Shirley Small Special Collections Library; Dorothy Maud to Hall Xuma, February 10, 1943, Xuma Papers, 1917–60, Correspondence, AD843-G1, ABX 430210a, Historical Papers Research Archive.

43. Africa House Filled to Capacity in First Public Meeting, October 20, 1947, Xuma Papers, 1917–60, Correspondence, AD843-L1, ABX 471020; *The Tenth Anniversary Number Johannesburg Zenzele Club Year Book, 1951*, Conference Program, South African Institute of Race Relations (SAIRR) Papers, 1892–1974, AD1715–14–18–2; F. J. Ndimande (Mrs.) to Mrs. Xuma, June 15, 1948, Xuma Papers, 1917–60, Correspondence, AD843-L2.1; Witbank Zenzele Club, undated, Xuma Papers, 1917–60, Correspondence, AD843-O23.4, all Historical Papers Research Archive. See also Hall Xuma Diary, 1947, Xuma Papers, 1917–60, Correspondence, AD843-Q30.3; Annual Report of the Johannesburg Zenzele Club, undated, Xuma Papers, 1917–60, Correspondence, AD843-O23.4, both Historical Papers Research Archive; World YWCA Project in South Africa, July 1956, Foreign Country—Africa—South Africa—M. Hathaway—1953–1957, microfilm, reel 230, microdex 1—M-8, YWCA of the U.S.A. Records, Sophia Smith Collections; Berger, "An African American 'Mother of the Nation': Madie Hall Xuma in South Africa, 1940–1963," 562.

44. Grant, "National Council of Negro Women and South Africa," 67; Nicholas Grant, *Winning over Freedom Together: African Americans and Apartheid, 1945–1960*, 191–93.

45. N. Msweli [spelling unclear in original] to Madie Xuma, August 21, 1947, Xuma Papers, 1917–60, Correspondence, AD843-L1.2, ABX 470821a, Historical Papers Research Archive.

46. Betty Motsepe to Madie Xuma, August 21, 1947, Xuma Papers, 1917–60, Correspondence, AD843-L1.2, ABX 470821b, Historical Papers Research Archive.

47. Witbank Zenzele Club, undated, Xuma Papers, 1917–60, Correspondence, AD843-O23.4; Annual Report of the Johannesburg Zenzele Club, undated, Xuma Papers, 1917–60, Correspondence, AD843-O23.4, both Historical Papers Research Archive.

48. Cauny Matsie [spelling unclear in original] to Hall Xuma, August 31, 1947, Xuma Papers, 1917–60, Correspondence, AD843-L1.2, ABX 470831b; Samuel J. Sibeka to Hall Xuma, September 3, 1947, Xuma Papers, 1917–60, Correspondence, AD843-L1.2, ABX 470903a; M. J. Pitoyi [spelling unclear in original] to Hall Xuma, September 8, 1947, Xuma Papers, 1917–60, Correspondence, AD843-L1.2, ABX 470908, all Historical Papers Research Archive.

49. Minutes of 4th October 1948 [Homemakers Club], Xuma Papers, 1917–60, Correspondence, AD843-L2.2, ABX 481004; Homemaker's Club Annual Report, the Year Ending December 1948, Xuma Papers, 1917–60, Correspondence, AD843-L2.2, ABX 481231; Diaries, 1948, Xuma Papers, 1917–60, Correspondence, AD843-Q30.3, all Historical Papers Research Archive. Note that it is unclear whether or not the Homemakers Club is a name for a Zenzele Club or a completely different club.

50. Karis, *Hope and Challenge*, 172. See also Ginwala, "Women and the African National Congress," 81–82, 84–91; Judy Kimble and Elaine Unterhalter, "'We Opened the Road for You. You Must Go Forward': ANC Women's Struggles, 1912–1982," 18–20;

Natasha Erlank, "Gender and Masculinity in South African Nationalist Discourse, 1912–1950."

51. Karis, *Hope and Challenge*, 186.

52. Ginwala, "Women and the African National Congress," 90–91; Karis, *Hope and Challenge*, 319–20; Kimble and Unterhalter, "'We Opened the Road for You,'" 18–21; Erlank, "Gender and Masculinity in South African Nationalist Discourse."

53. Gish, *Alfred B. Xuma*, 117; Nakasa, "'Mummy' Goes Home," 40; Hall Xuma, Diary, 1947, Xuma Papers, 1917–60, Correspondence, AD843-Q30.3; African National Congress, Bloemfontein Rally: Guest of Honour: Mrs. A. B. Xuma Programme, Xuma Papers, 1917–60, Correspondence, AD843-N2.57, both Historical Papers Research Archive; Erlank, "Gender and Masculinity in South African Nationalist Discourse," 660; Walker, *Women and Resistance in South Africa*, 88–89, 91; Brooks, *Boycotts, Buses, and Passes*, 172–73; Ginwala, "Women and the African National Congress," 90–91. See also see Healy-Clancy, "Women and the Problem of Family."

54. Draft of Hall Xuma Speech, May 3, 1944, Xuma Papers, 1917–60, Correspondence, AD843-I2, ABX 440503a, Historical Papers Research Archive.

55. Draft of Hall Xuma Speech, May 3, 1944, Xuma Papers, 1917–60, Correspondence, AD843-I2, ABX 440503a, Historical Papers Research Archive. See also A'Lelia Bundles, *On Her Own Ground: The Life and Times of Madam C. J. Walker*; and Tiffany M. Gill, *Beauty Shop Politics: African American Women's Activism in the Beauty Industry*.

56. Draft of Hall Xuma Speech, May 3, 1944, Xuma Papers, 1917–60, Correspondence, AD843-I2, ABX 440503a, Historical Papers Research Archive.

57. See, for example, A. B. Xuma to Alfred Kule, March 8, 1944, Xuma Papers, 1917–60, Correspondence, AD843-I1, ABX 440308a, Historical Papers Research Archive.

58. See, for example, A. B. Xuma to Mrs. Kry, March 8, 1944, Xuma Papers, 1917–60, Correspondence, AD843-I1, ABX 440308b, Historical Papers Research Archive.

59. Jellicoe Ntshona to Xuma, March 13, 1944, Xuma Papers, 1917–60, Correspondence, AD843-I1, ABX 440313b; A. B. Xuma to Jellicoe Ntshona, March 23, 1944, Xuma Papers, 1917–60, Correspondence, AD843-I1, ABX 440323, both Historical Papers Research Archive.

60. Gish, *Alfred B. Xuma*, 137.

61. S. D. Morokotso to Dr. A. B. Xuma, May 6, 1947, Xuma Papers, 1917–60, Correspondence, AD843-L1.1, ABX 470506b; Alfred B. Xuma to Miss S. D. Morokotso, May 30, 1947, Xuma Papers, 1917–60, Correspondence, AD843-L1.1, ABX 470530a, both Historical Papers Research Archive.

62. Ray E. Phillips to Hall Xuma, August 5, 1944, Xuma Papers, 1917–60, Correspondence, AD843-I3, ABX 440805, Historical Papers Research Archive.

63. The Xumas, for example, had a subscription to *Crisis* but because of the war had not received their copies. See A. B. Xuma to Roy Wilkins, January 6, 1943, Xuma

Papers, 1917–60, Correspondence, AD843-G1, ABX 430106a, Historical Papers Research Archive; and "South Africa Yields a Bit as Natives Riot," *Negro Star*, January 22, 1943.

64. Editorials, *Crisis* 50, no. 11 (1942): 343; L. D. Reddick, "South Africa: A Case for the United Nations" (emphasis in the original).

65. See, for example, Alphaeus Hunton to Xuma, October 4, 1946, Xuma Papers, 1917–60, Correspondence, AD843-K6, ABX 461004, Historical Papers Research Archive; Karis, *Hope and Challenge*, 209–23.

66. SAC, New York, Director, FBI, Alfred B. Xuma Registration Act, November 15, 1948, U.S. Department of Justice, Federal Bureau of Investigation Washington, DC; John Edgar Hoover to Dear Sir, December 19, 1946 [Re: Alfred B. Xuma Registration Act], U.S. Department of Justice, Federal Bureau of Investigation Washington, DC. (both obtained through the Freedom of Information Act [FOIA] dated December 31, 2019); Gish, *Alfred B. Xuma*, 146. Note that the author also submitted a FOIA to the CIA on Alfred Xuma. The CIA "determined that in accordance with Section 3.6(a) of Executive Order 13526, the CIA can neither confirm nor deny the existence or nonexistence of records responsive to your request" and denied the request in a letter dated October 23, 2020.

67. Gish, *Alfred B. Xuma*, 147; "African Plan Assailed," *New York Times*, November 18, 1946.

68. K. Ozuomba Mbadiwe to Xuma, November 12, 1946, Xuma Papers, 1917–60, Correspondence, AD843-K6, ABX 461112; W. E. B. DuBois and L. D. Reddick to Xuma, November 21, 1946, Xuma Papers, 1917–60, Correspondence, AD843-K6, ABX 461121d; African Academy of Arts and Research, Race Relations 30/11/1946, Xuma Papers, 1917–60, Correspondence, AD843-K6, all Historical Papers Research Archive; Gish, *Alfred B. Xuma*, 147; "New York This Week," *Indianapolis Recorder*, December 14, 1946; Hine, *Black Women in White*, 118–19.

69. "Seek UN Aid to Block Land Grab in Africa," *Indianapolis Recorder*, November 30, 1946; "Welcome Address to Dr. A. B. Xuma by the Residents of the Western Areas of Johannesburg at the Western Native Township on the 16th March, 1947," Xuma Papers, 1917–60, Correspondence, AD843-L1.1, ABX 470316, Historical Papers Research Archive; Gish, *Alfred B. Xuma*, 148–49.

70. T. R. Ponsford to Xuma, January 23, 1947, Xuma Papers, 1917–60, Correspondence, AD843-L1.1, ABX 470123, Historical Papers Research Archive.

71. W. Avery Jones to Hall Xuma, April 28, 1945, Xuma Papers, 1917–60, Correspondence, AD843-J1, ABX 450428, Historical Papers Research Archive.

72. Hall Xuma to W. Avery Jones, June 18, 1945, Xuma Papers, 1917–60, Correspondence, AD843-J2, ABX 450618a, Historical Papers Research Archive.

73. CooCoo [Elizabeth Nozipho Xuma] to "My dear Mummy [Hall Xuma], August 16, 1947, Xuma Papers, 1917–60, Correspondence, AD843-L1.2, ABX 470816, Historical Papers Research Archive.

74. Hall Xuma to Alice Dalgliesh, July 11, 1945, Xuma Papers, 1917–60, Correspondence, AD843-J3, ABX 450711, Historical Papers Research Archive.

75. Alice Dalgliesh to Mrs. A. B. Xuma, September 12, 1945, Xuma Papers, 1917–60, Correspondence, AD843-J5, ABX 480912, Historical Papers Research Archive.

76. Esther [Mohlabi] to My dearest Mummie [Hall Xuma], August 18, 1947, Xuma Papers, 1917–60, Correspondence, AD843-L1.2, ABX 470818a; *The Tenth Anniversary Number Johannesburg Zenzele Club Year Book, 1951,* Conference Program, South African Institute of Race Relations (SAIRR) Papers, 1892–1974, AD1715–14–18–2, both Historical Papers Research Archive, list an Esther Mohlabi from Attridgeville, and I am assuming that they are the same person.

77. Betty Motsepe to Hall Xuma, August 21, 1947, Xuma Papers, 1917–60, Correspondence, AD843-L1.2, ABX 470821b, Historical Papers Research Archive.

Chapter 7. "Prominent South African Woman Arrives in New York"

1. Pan Am had just begun flight service between New York and Johannesburg in 1947. See G. H. Pirie, "Aviation, Apartheid and Sanctions: Air Transport to and from South Africa, 1945–1989," 232; and "Mrs. Xuma on Way Here: Will Attend Women's Conference in New York," *New York Times,* August 22, 1947. See also Leila J. Rupp, *Worlds of Women: The Making of an International Women's Movement,* 15–21, for a discussion of the establishment of the ICW in 1888 that originated out of the National Woman Suffrage Association meeting in Washington. See also "New U.N. Agenda Items," *New York Times,* September 7, 1947; and Saul Dubow, "The United Nations and the Rhetoric of Race and Rights," 63–65.

2. Photo stand-alone 5, *Chicago Defender,* September 6, 1947; "Reports S. Africa Growing Worse for All Non-Whites," *Chicago Defender,* September 27, 1947.

3. "Prominent South African Woman Arrives in New York," *People's Voice,* September 6, 1947. See also James H. Meriwether, *Proudly We Can Be Africans: Black Americans and Africa, 1935–1961,* 59–73. Plagued by his communist ties Max Yergan was in serious trouble with the U.S. government. He would eventually renounce communism and help facilitate the firing of several of the leftist newspaper staff. By April 1948, the paper ceased publication. See Anthony, *Max Yergan,* 214–15, 226–31; and Farah Jasmine Griffin, *Harlem Nocturne: Women Artists & Progressive Politics during World War II,* 90–94.

4. "Prominent South African Woman Arrives in New York."

5. "Prominent South African Woman Arrives in New York."

6. Xuma Diary, 1947, Xuma Papers, 1917–60, AD843-Q30.3, Historical Papers Research Archive; Rupp, *Worlds of Women,* 74; "Report of the 18th Biennial Period National Council of Women of South Africa, July 1948," 21, South African Institute of Race Relations (SAIRR) Papers, 1892–1974, AD1715–18–6.1, Historical Papers Research Archive; "Women's Prisons, Health Discussed: Three Arrive from Argentina, South Africa and Sweden for Council Session," *New York Times,* August 26, 1947; "National Council of Negro Woman [*sic*]," *Omaha Guide,* September 6, 1947; "Eunice H. Carter among Delegates to Paris Talks," *Chicago Defender,* September 13, 1947;

"International Council in Session; Mrs. Bethune 1 of 11 Delegates," *Richmond Afro-American*, September 13, 1947.

7. Rupp, *Worlds of Women*, 45; "Truman Message to Open Women's Council Meeting," *Washington Evening Star*, August 25, 1947; "Women Will Back Individual Rights: Netherlands Delegation Plans to Propose Amendment to International Council," *New York Times*, September 5, 1947; "Aid to Greece Urgent and Vital, World Council of Women Is Told," *New York Times*, September 9, 1947; "Lack of U.N. Posts to Women Scored," *New York Times*, September 11, 1947.

8. United Nations Twenty-Ninth Plenary Meeting, February 12, 1946, 64, Declaration on the Participation of Women in the Work of the United Nations: Report of the General Committee, Document A/46, United Nations Archives and Records Management.

9. See *Second Women's International Congress*, 20–51; "AFL Requests Equal Status," *Reno Evening Gazette*, January 23, 1946; Rupp, *Worlds of Women*, 47.

10. "Mrs. Bethune Gets Report on Women's International Meet," *Indianapolis Recorder*, February 9, 1946; "Women's Council Hears Report on International Federation," *Baltimore Afro-American*, February 16, 1946.

11. *Second Women's International Congress*, 45; Leslie, "'United, We Build a Free World,'" 206–7. See also "NCNW Protests Atomic Bomb Production," *Indianapolis Recorder*, November 30, 1946.

12. Anna V. Rice, *A History of the World's Young Women's Christian Association*, 4–56, 258, 262–67; "YW in Nation-wide Observance of 50th Anniversary Sunday," *Blizzard*, November 17, 1944; Seymour-Jones, *Journey of Faith*, 1–21.

13. "Y.W.C.A. Aide to Go to Germany," *New York Times*, January 24, 1946; "Y.W.C.A. Votes Aid for Needy Nations," *New York Times*, March 8, 1946; "Adds to World Aid Fund," *New York Times*, March 6, 1947; "Y.W.C.A. Nearing Goal," *New York Times*, April 3, 1947; "To Study Y.W.C.A. Work in War-Ravaged Europe," *New York Times*, July 31, 1947; "Miss Height to Work in Y Drive," *Richmond Afro-American*, February 8, 1947. See also "Langston Hughes Speaks for Drive," *Richmond Afro-American*, February 22, 1947.

14. Seymour-Jones, *Journey of Faith*, 72–73; *World YWCA Statements of Policy Adopted at Legislative Meetings, 1894–2015*, 16–17.

15. Seymour-Jones, *Journey of Faith*, 329–30, 508.

16. Mummy [Madie] to dear Daddy [Xuma], September 17, 1955, Xuma Papers, 1917–60, Correspondence, AD843-M7, ABX 550917, Historical Papers Research Archive; World Young Women's Christian Association Minutes of the Meeting of the Executive Committee 17th–19th September, 1955, p. 1, Appendix I, II, III, (Box) World YWCA Executive Committee Minutes, 1945–49, 1950–59, World Young Women's Christian Association Archives; Seymour-Jones, *Journey of Faith*, 74.

17. Robertson, *Christian Sisterhood, Race Relations, and the YWCA*, 162–74; "Racial Equality in Y.W.C.A. Urged," *New York Times*, March 6, 1946; "YWCA Votes to Drop Color Lines," *New York Amsterdam News*, March 9, 1946; "Protestants, YWCA Drop Race Segregation Policy," *Chicago Defender*, March 16, 1946.

18. Xuma Diary, 1947, Xuma Papers, 1917–60, AD843-Q30.3, Historical Papers Research Archive. Hall Xuma's visit home was also important because she made a request from the minister at Goler to move her membership to the AME Church in Johannesburg. See Rev. W. F. Witherspoon, April 29, 1948, Xuma Papers, 1917–60, Correspondence, AD843-L2, ABX 480429, Historical Papers Research Archive; as well as Campbell, *Songs of Zion*, who provides a comprehensive discussion of the AME in South Africa. Also note that a fire destroyed Goler Memorial in 1941. The congregation held services at the Black YWCA on Chestnut Street and began a campaign to raise money to rebuild. Part of the congregation that included Leroy Hall decided to purchase a white Baptist church for sale on East Fourth Street in an East Winston-Salem community that was steadily transitioning from white to Black. The church was later named Goler Metropolitan AME Zion, while the original congregation rebuilt its own church and became known as Old Goler or Goler Memorial. See Langdon Edmunds Oppermann, "Goler Metropolitan A.M.E. Zion Church, Forsyth County, NC, National Register of Historic Places Registration Form," sec. 8, pp. 5–9; "Mt. Pleasant Methodist Church Presents Mrs. Madie Hall Xuma Johannesburg, S. Africa," September 21, 1947, Xuma Papers, 1917–60, Correspondence, AD843-L1.2, ABX 470921, Historical Papers Research Archive. See also *Hill's Winston-Salem (Forsyth County, N.C.) City Directory, 1947–48*, 1058, 1059.

19. Hall Xuma to Josephus Coan [she refers to him as Dr. Coan], November 15, 1947, box 1, folder 9, Josephus Roosevelt Coan Papers, Stuart A. Rose Manuscript, Archives, and Rare Book Library; K. Ozuomba Mbadiwe to Xuma, September 13, 1947, Xuma Papers, 1917–60, Correspondence, AD843-L1.2, ABX 470913; K. Ozuomba Mbadiwe to Xuma, October 14, 1947, Xuma Papers, 1917–60, Correspondence, AD843-L1.2, ABX 471014a; Xuma Diary, 1947, Xuma Papers, 1917–60, AD843-Q30.3, all Historical Papers Research Archive.

20. "Africa House Here to Serve Students," *New York Times*, October 13, 1947; "Tobias Urges Support of Africa House," *Atlanta Daily World*, October 18, 1947.

21. Africa House Filled to Capacity in First Public Meeting, October 20, 1947, Xuma Papers, 1917–60, Correspondence, AD843-L1.2, ABX 471020, Historical Papers Research Archive.

22. Africa House Filled to Capacity in First Public Meeting, October 20, 1947, Xuma Papers, 1917–60, Correspondence, AD843-L1.2, ABX 471020, Historical Papers Research Archive.

23. Xuma Diary, 1947, Xuma Papers, 1917–60, AD843-Q30.3, Historical Papers Research Archive; Dubow, "United Nations and the Rhetoric of Race and Rights," 45–46, 67–68; "India Rips South Africa," *Chicago Defender*, September 13, 1947, 13.

24. "South Africa Defies UN Assembly on Jim Crow Issue," *Chicago Defender*, October 4, 1947; Gish, *Alfred B. Xuma*, 143–50; Dubow, "United Nations and the Rhetoric of Race and Rights," 45–46, 67–71; Vinson, *Americans Are Coming!*, 141–43.

25. Xuma Diary, 1947, Xuma Papers, 1917–60, AD843-Q30.3, Historical Papers Research Archive; "Dr. Alma Haskina [*sic*] Fetes Visitors from South Africa and Bermuda," *New York Amsterdam News*, October 25, 1947.

26. Xuma Diary, 1947, Xuma Papers, 1917–60, AD843-Q30.3, Historical Papers Research Archive; "Business and Professional Women's Clubs In Convention Here Oct. 24–26th," *New York Amsterdam News*, October 11, 1947; "Two Special Awards to Be Given by National Women's Clubs," *New York Amsterdam News*, October 25, 1947.

27. Mary McLeod Bethune to Mrs. Xuma [Hall Xuma], October 31, 1947, Xuma Papers, 1917–60, Correspondence, AD843-L1.2, ABX 471031a, Historical Papers Research Archive; "Women Mass for All-Out Attack on Race Problems," *Chicago Defender*, November 22, 1947; "Minorities' Chances for Jobs Improving, Schwellenback Says," *Washington Evening Star*, November 10, 1947; "Negro Women to Visit White House Today," *Washington Evening Star*, November 13, 1947; "Negro Women to End Council Session Today," *Washington Evening Star*, November 14, 1947.

28. Xuma Diary, 1947, Xuma Papers, 1917–60, AD843-Q30.3, Historical Papers Research Archive. Note pages missing from the diary/datebook from Wednesday, November 12 to Wednesday, November 26.

29. Hall to Xuma, March 12, 1939, ABX 390312, Xuma Papers, 1917–60, Correspondence, AD843-C2, Historical Papers Research Archive; Marjorie H. Parker, *Past Is Prologue: The History of Alpha Kappa Alpha, 1908–1999*, 338.

30. Bernice K. Howard, a graduate of Atkins High School, received the scholarship in 1943–44 (while a student at Atkins High School) and in the subsequent years of 1944–45, 1945–46, and 1946–47. See *Winston-Salem Teachers College Commencement Day Program, May 25, 1944*, 4; *Winston-Salem Teachers College Commencement Day Program, May 25, 1945*, 4; *Winston-Salem Teachers College Commencement Day Program, May 28, 1946*, 4, WSSUAr-RG10-4—Commencement Programs, 4, all Winston-Salem State C. G. O'Kelly University Archives; "Winston-Salem, N.C."; Grimes, "History of Kate Bitting Reynolds Memorial Hospital," 377.

31. Hall Xuma had alluded to being "inducted" into the Phi Omega chapter of the AKA in a letter to Xuma in 1939, but it was not until 1948 that she was officially inducted. See Hall to Xuma, March 12, 1939, ABX 390312, Xuma Papers, 1917–60, Correspondence, AD843-C2; 1948, Xuma Papers, 1917–60, Correspondence, AD843-Q30.3; Passport and Certificate of Mrs. Xuma, Xuma Papers, 1917–60, AD843-Q31.1; "Winston-Salem, N.C."; Alpha Kappa Alpha Messages, Xuma Papers, 1917–60, AD843-Q30.1, all Historical Papers Research Archive.

32. Xuma Diary, 1948, Xuma Papers, 1917–60, AD843-Q30, Historical Papers Research Archive. The radio station began in 1947 and was the third radio station in Winston-Salem. "Describes Life in South Africa," *Wilson Daily Times*, February 28, 1948, 9; Brown, *Upbuilding Black Durham*, 35, 100, 162; Wilson and Mullally, *Hope and Dignity*, 69–73; "Daughters of Dorcas Club of Durham."

33. Xuma Diary, 1948, Xuma Papers, 1917–60, AD843-Q30.3, Historical Papers Research Archive; "Our Negro Community," *Annapolis Evening Capital*, March 16, 1948; advertisement, *Baltimore Afro-American*, March 13, 1948; "Our Negro Community," *Annapolis Evening Capital*, March 23, 1948. Hall Xuma also stayed with relatives in Baltimore. See "Gadabouting in Baltimore," *Baltimore Afro-American*, March 27, 1948.

34. 1948, Xuma Papers, 1917–60, Correspondence, AD843-Q30.3, Historical Papers Research Archive.

35. Hall Xuma to Josephus Coan [she refers to him as Dr. Coan], April 29, 1948, Coan Papers, Stuart A. Rose Manuscript, Archives, and Rare Book Library.

36. Xuma Diary, 1948, Xuma Papers, 1917–60, AD843-Q30.3, Historical Papers Research Archive; *T.C. Alumni Bulletin* 9, no. 4 (1948): 2, Winston-Salem State University Archives C. G. O'Kelly Library.

37. "Apartheid"; 1948, Xuma Papers, 1917–60, Correspondence, AD843-Q30.3, Historical Papers Research Archive [note that Hall Xuma refers to her in her date book as Ethel Brown Ballentine]; "News of Interest to Colored People," *High Point Enterprise*, May 28, 1948.

38. Xuma Diary, 1948, Xuma Papers, 1917–60, AD843-Q30.3, Historical Papers Research Archive; "Bon Voyage Breakfast," *Philadelphia Tribune*, May 29, 1948, 7; "Pennsylvania," *Chicago Defender*, June 12, 1948, 20.

39. Xuma Diary, 1948, Xuma Papers, 1917–60, AD843-Q30.3, Historical Papers Research Archive.

40. Xuma Diary, 1948, Xuma Papers, 1917–60, AD843-Q30.3, Historical Papers Research Archive; "Pitter Patter," *Baltimore Afro-American*, June 5, 1948, 11; "Daughters of Dorcas Club of Durham."

41. Xuma Diary, 1948, Xuma Papers, 1917–60, AD843-Q30.3, Historical Papers Research Archive; "Bon Voyage Breakfast," *Philadelphia Tribune*, May 29, 1948, 7; "Pennsylvania," *Chicago Defender*, June 12, 1948.

42. Annual Report of the Johannesburg Zenzele Club, undated, Xuma Papers, 1917–60, AD843-O23.4; Homemaker's Club Annual Report, the Year Ending December 1948, Xuma Papers, 1917–60, AD843-L2.2, ABX 481231; The Roodepoort Zenzele Club Annual Report, 1948, Xuma Papers, 1917–60, AD843-L2.2; Brief Annual Report of the Johannesburg Zenzele Club—1948, Xuma Papers, 1917–60, AD843-L2.2, all Historical Papers Research Archive.

43. "South Africa's Color Fight Is Battle for Survival," *Sun* (Sydney), July 21, 1947; "By a South African Journalist Who Has Covered Parliament for Many Years," *Sun* (Sydney), July 21, 1947.

44. Karis, *Hope and Challenge*, 368–69, 288–300, 321–23, 323–31, 337–39, 362–68, 370–88; Gish, *Alfred B. Xuma*, 158–64.

45. Edmund Mlotywa to Dr. and Mrs. Xuma, March 28, 1951, Xuma Papers, 1917–60, AD843-M3, ABX 510328, Historical Papers Research Archive; Gish, *Alfred B. Xuma*, 165–67.

46. Seymour-Jones, *Journey of Faith*, 158.

47. *The Y.W.C.A. Today and Yesterday: A Handbook of National Associations, 1855–1955*, 139–42; Seymour-Jones, *Journey of Faith*, 159–60, 510.

48. Elizabeth Lester to Helen Roberts, June 12, 1950, binder 2 on South Africa, Durban, Port Elizabeth, 1947–, World Young Women's Christian Association Archives.

49. *Y.W.C.A. Today and Yesterday*, 140–41; "World's YWCA Project for South Africa," November 11, 1954, Foreign Country—Africa—South Africa—miscellaneous,

reel 230, microdex M-8, YWCA of the U.S.A. Records, Sophia Smith Collections; "Gets South African Job as Y.W.C.A. Secretary," *New York Times*, September 9, 1950; *The Tenth Anniversary Number Johannesburg Zenzele Club Year Book, 1951*, Conference Program, South African Institute of Race Relations (SAIRR) Papers, 1892–1974, AD1715–14–18–2, Historical Papers Research Archive; Seymour-Jones, *Journey of Faith*, 159–65; Minutes of the Coordinating Committee Of YWCAs of South Africa Affiliated With the World's YWCA, March 6, 1954, microfilm reel 230, microdex M-8, file separator, YWCA of the U.S.A. Records, Sophia Smith Collections.

50. Helen Roberts to A. M. Neilson, July 19, 1951, and Carrie Meares to Dear Geneva [World's Y.W.C.A.], June 29, 1951, binder 2 on South Africa, Durban, Port Elizabeth, 1947–, World Young Women's Christian Association Archives.

51. Uncertified copy of certificate of death of Edna Florence Hall, Forsyth County Register of Deeds; Xuma Diary, 1948, Xuma Papers, 1917–60, Correspondence, AD843-Q30.3; Mummy to My dear Daddy [Hall to Xuma], June 24, 1951, Xuma Papers, 1917–60, Correspondence, AD843-C2, ABX 510624, both Historical Papers Research Archive.

52. [Post Office Telegraphs], May 19, 1951, Xuma Papers, 1917–60, Correspondence, AD843-M3, ABX 510519; Mummy to My dear Daddy [Hall to Xuma], June 24, 1951, Xuma Papers, 1917–60, Correspondence, AD843-C2, ABX 510624, both Historical Papers Research Archive; "43 Die as Airliner, Navy Plane Crash in Air at Key West," *New York Times*, April 26, 1951.

53. Mummy to My dear Daddy [Hall to Xuma], June 24, 1951, Xuma Papers, 1917–60, Correspondence, AD843-C2, ABX 510624, Historical Papers Research Archive.

54. "The World's Most Prejudiced Nation," 96.

55. "Mrs. Madie Hall Xuma Will Address Session," *Durham Morning Herald*, April 23, 1951; "Missionary to Speak," *Statesville Daily Record*, May 9, 1951, 8; "Apartheid." See also "Evidence Given before the Commission Enquiring Johannesburg 1/3/50 into the Riots on Newlands, Krugersdorp and Randfontein by Dr. Xuma," Xuma Papers, 1917–60, Correspondence, AD843-M2, ABX 500301, Historical Papers Research Archive.

56. *Chicago Defender*, August 18, 1951.

57. "AMEZ Women Elect Mrs. Rosa Weller at Winston-Salem," *Pittsburgh Courier*, August 18, 1951; "World's Woes Laid to Weak Moral Values," *Durham Morning Herald*, August 30, 1951.

58. Gill, *Beauty Shop Politics*, 82–92, 95–96; Xuma Diary, 1948, Xuma Papers, 1917–60, AD843-Q30.3, Historical Papers Research Archive.

59. "Woman Who Made S. Africa Hair Conscious Returns," *Atlanta Daily World*, July 3, 1951.

60. Gill, *Beauty Shop Politics*, 105–6.

61. "Women's World," *Bantu World*, December 8, 1951; Helen Roberts to Whom It May Concern, August 27, 1951, and Carrie Meares to Dear Geneva Friends [World's YWCA], June 29, 1951, binder 2 on South Africa, Durban, Port Elizabeth, 1947–; (Box) World YWCA Council Minutes/Reports till 1934: World's Committee Biennial

Meetings 1920–71, (folder) Minutes of World's Council Meeting of the Young Women's Christian Association Held at Beirut, Lebanon October 14–24, 1951, 3–4, all World Young Women's Christian Association Archives; Gish, *Alfred B. Xuma*, 168–69. See also *We Meet in Lebanon: The Story of the World's YWCA Council Meeting, 1951*; and Seymour-Jones, *Journey of Faith*, 506.

62. "It Happened in Our World: African Emissaries, Following the Pattern of Globe-Trotting Americans, Come Here to See Our Democracy at Work," 10–11; Miriam Penn to Xuma, December 11, 1951, Xuma Papers, 1917–60, Correspondence, AD843-M3, ABX 511211, Historical Papers Research Archive.

63. Seymour-Jones, *Journey of Faith*, 165; "Death Calls Clubwoman," *Portland Oregonian*, October 17, 1946; "Chefoo Troubles Scrutinized Here," *Portland Oregonian*, October 6, 1937; "YWCA Officials Visit USO Here," *Columbia Record*, August 2, 1951; "YWCA Workshop Leader Is World Staff Member," *Corpus Christi Caller-Times*, September 9, 1956; "YW Foreign Staff Member to Visit LR," *Arkansas Democrat*, November 13, 1960; "YW's Role in Africa Will Be Told Here," *New Orleans Times-Picayune*, October 6, 1968.

64. "From Letters and Reports from the World's YWCA Secretary in South Africa received between April 1 and August 1, 1953," Foreign Country—Africa—South Africa—Miscellaneous, reel 230, microdex M-8, YWCA of the U.S.A. Records, Sophia Smith Collections; Elizabeth Lester to Miss [Jacqueline van] Stoetwegen, January 16, 1952 [should be 1953—stamped date of receipt is 21 Jan 1953], and Jacqueline van Stoetwegen to Elizabeth Lester, January 5, 1953, binder 2 on South Africa, Durban, Port Elizabeth, 1947–, World Young Women's Christian Association Archives; *Y.W.C.A. Today and Yesterday*, 140–41; "World's YWCA Project for South Africa," November 11, 1954, Foreign Country—Africa—South Africa—Miscellaneous; Minutes of the Coordinating Committee of YWCAs of South Africa Affiliated with the World's YWCA, March 6, 1954, both reel 230, microdex M-8 file separator, both YWCA of the U.S.A. Records, Sophia Smith Collections.

65. "Women's World," *Bantu World*, May 17, 1952; Silver Tea, Tickets—Zenzele Y.W.C.A. of Johannesburg, April 5, 1952, Xuma Papers, 1917–60, Correspondence, AD843-M4, ABX 520405; Xuma to Dr. C. W. DeKiewiet, July 22, 1952, Xuma Papers, 1917–60, Correspondence, AD843-M4, ABX 520722, both Historical Papers Research Archive; "World's YWCA Project for South Africa," Foreign Country—Africa—South Africa—Miscellaneous, reel 230, microdex M-8, YWCA of the U.S.A. Records, Sophia Smith Collections; "Program Exchange Sheet," YWCA, November 12, 1953, binder 2 on South Africa, Durban, Port Elizabeth, 1947–, World Young Women's Christian Association Archives.

66. "From Letters and Reports from the World's YWCA Secretary in South Africa received between April 1 and August 1, 1953," Foreign Country—Africa—South Africa—Miscellaneous; "World's YWCA Project for South Africa," Foreign Country—Africa—South Africa—Miscellaneous, reel 230, microdex M-8, both YWCA of the U.S.A. Records, Sophia Smith Collections.

67. See Xuma to Dr. C. W. DeKiewiet, July 22, 1952, Xuma Papers, 1917–60, Correspondence, AD843-M4, ABX 520722, Historical Papers Research Archive.

68. Seymour-Jones, *Journey of Faith*, 165.

69. Seymour-Jones, *Journey of Faith*, 168–69.

70. Conference to Promote Women's Rights. To be held on Saturday 17th April 54, April 17, 1954, Federation of South African Women 1954–1963 Papers, AD1137, Ac1, Historical Papers Research Archive; Horrell, *Survey of Race Relations in South Africa, 1955–1956*, 85–87; Julia C. Wells, "Why Women Rebel: A Comparative Study of South African Women's Resistance in Bloemfontein (1913) and Johannesburg (1958)"; Brooks, *Boycotts, Buses, and Passes*, 202–38; Muriel Horrell, comp., *A Survey of Race Relations in South Africa, 1962*, 109–10. See also Jacqueline Castledine, "'In a Solid Bond of Unity': Anticolonial Feminism in the Cold War Era."

71. Quoted in Seymour-Jones, *Journey of Faith*, 166.

72. "African Women Are Awakening," *Bantu World*, February 7, 1953.

73. "African Women Are Awakening," *Bantu World*, February 7, 1953.

74. "African Women Are Awakening," *Bantu World*, February 7, 1953.

Chapter 8. A Transnational Nexus: The World YWCA

1. Minutes of the Coordinating Committee of YWCAs of South Africa Affiliated with the World's YWCA, March 6, 1954, reel 230, microdex M-8 file separator, YWCA of the U.S.A. Records, Sophia Smith Collections; Xuma Diary, 1954, Xuma Papers, 1917–60, AD843-Q30.3, Historical Papers Research Archive. The other members of the committee included Agnes Neilson, Coral A. Haley, Miss Lester of Durban, Cora Phillips, Mrs. Pule, Mrs. Mbomba and Phyllis Mzaidume from Johannesburg, Mrs. Kennelly, Mrs. Binning, Mrs. Barrowman, Mrs. Kama, Mrs. Peterson and Mrs. Grylls from Port Elizabeth, and Margaret Hathaway.

2. See, for example, Muriel Horrell, comp., *A Survey of Race Relations in South Africa, 1951–1952*, 48–49; Horrell, *Survey of Race Relations in South Africa, 1955–1956*, 85–87, 194; Muriel Horrell, comp., *A Survey of Race Relations in South Africa, 1959–1960*, 213, 227.

3. Horrell, *Survey of Race Relations in South Africa, 1951–1952*, 7–8, 25, 27; "South Africa Denies Student Passport," *New York Times*, July 22, 1955; "South Africa Backs Negro Passport Ban," *New York Times*, July 23, 1955.

4. Secretary for the Interior [illegible name] to A. B. Xuma, August 27, 1953, Xuma Papers, 1917–60, Correspondence, AD843-M5, ABX 530827, Historical Papers Research Archive; Gish, *Alfred B. Xuma*, 190–97. See also Xuma to Dr. C. W. DeKiewiet, July 22, 1952, Xuma Papers, 1917–60, Correspondence, AD843-M4, ABX 520722, Historical Papers Research Archive.

5. Minutes of the Coordinating Committee of YWCAs of South Africa Affiliated with the World's YWCA, March 6, 1954, reel 230, microdex M-8 file separator, YWCA of the U.S.A. Records, Sophia Smith Collections.

6. Coral A. Haley to Miss Thompson [*sic*], April 9, 1955, binder 2 on South Africa, Durban, Port Elizabeth, 1947–, World Young Women's Christian Association Archives; Minutes of the Coordinating Committee of YWCAs of South Africa Affili-

ated with the World's YWCA, March 6, 1954, reel 230, microdex M-8 file separator, YWCA of the U.S.A. Records, Sophia Smith Collections.

7. Coral A. Haley to Miss Thompson [Janet Thomson—note the misspelling of Thomson by Haley], April 9, 1955, binder 2 on South Africa, Durban, Port Elizabeth, 1947–, World Young Women's Christian Association Archives; Xuma Diary, 1954, Xuma Papers, 1917–60, AD843-Q30.3; South African Police, Witwatersrand Divisional Naturalization Staff to Hall Xuma, December 2, 1954, Xuma Papers, 1917–60, Correspondence, AD843-M6, ABX 541202b; Dr. A. B. Xuma to Mr. Honck [Secretary of the Interior], April 12, 1955, Xuma Papers, 1917–60, Correspondence, AD843-M7, ABX 550412a; Madie Beatrice Hall Xuma Passport, Xuma Papers, 1917–60, Correspondence, AD843-Q31.1, all Historical Papers Research Archive.

8. Memorandum to the Ad Hoc Committee on the Removal of Non Europeans from the Western Areas Presented by the African Anti-Expropriation Ratepayers Association and Proper Housing Movement, October 8, 1952, Xuma Papers, 1917–60, Correspondence, AD843-M4, ABX 521008 Historical Papers Research Archive; Limb, *A. B. Xuma*, 364–67. See also draft of a letter by Alfred Xuma dated March 21, 1954, Xuma Papers, 1917–60, Correspondence, AD843, ABX 54031, Veronica Keating to Dr. A. B. Xuma, January 3, 1955, Xuma Papers, 1917–60, Correspondence, AD843, ABX 550103, both Historical Papers Research Archive; "The Grim Drama at Johannesburg," *New York Times*, February 27, 1955.

9. "South African Govt. Starts Early to Move Out Natives," *Atlanta Daily World*, February 15, 1955; "Despondent Africans Discuss Intolerance," *Greensboro Daily News*, March 10, 1955; "Johannesburg Shift Catches N.C. Woman," *Asheville Citizen-Times*, March 10, 1955; "Negro Couple of Johannesburg Facing Ruin in Race Struggle," *Burlington Free Press*, March 10, 1955; "South Africa Negro Couple Defies Mass Removal Order," *Cumberland News*, March 10, 1955; "African Unity Champion Sees Life Work Shattered," *Winnipeg Free Press* (Canada), March 11, 1955; "They'll Come and Take Us Then Destroy This Home as Others," *Medicine Hat News*, March 16, 1955. See also "South Africa Segregates Negroes; Doctors, Others Will Lose Homes," *Democrat and Chronicle*, March 10, 1955; "How Africa's Segregation Policy Affects Doctor and Wife," *Des Moines Register*, March 11, 1955; "Despondent Africans Discuss Intolerance," *Greensboro Daily News*, March 10, 1955; Tom Lodge, "The Destruction of Sophiatown"; Willie H. Kennedy to Dear Dr. [Xuma], March 15, 1955, Xuma Papers, 1917–60, Correspondence, AD843-M7, ABX 550315, Historical Papers Research Archive.

10. "South Africa Segregates Negroes; Doctors, Others Will Lose Homes," *Democrat and Chronicle*, March 10, 1955; "Negro Couple of Johannesburg Facing Ruin in Race Struggle," *Burlington Free Press*, March 10, 1955; "South Africa Negro Couple Defies Mass Removal Order," *Cumberland News*, March 10, 1955; "Johannesburg Shift Catches N. C. Woman," *Asheville Citizen-Times*, March 10, 1955; "Despondent Africans Discuss Intolerance," *Greensboro Daily News*, March 10, 1955; "How Africa's Segregation Policy Affects Doctor and Wife," *Des Moines Register*, March 11, 1955; "African Unity Champion Sees Life Work Shattered," *Winnipeg Free Press*, March 11, 1955; "They'll Come And Take Us Then Destroy This Home As Others," *Medicine Hat News*, March 16, 1955.

11. "By Way of Report," *New York Times*, August 13, 1950; "What Price Race," *Chicago Defender*, September 16, 1950; "Canada Lee, Sidney Poitier Find South Africa Is Tough," *Chicago Defender*, October 28, 1950; "Only Negro Servants Allowed in S. Africa," *New York Amsterdam News*, October 28, 1950; "Canada Lee to S. Africa," *Indianapolis Recorder*, August 26, 1950.

12. "Apartheid."

13. "Y.W.C.A. Observes 100th Birthday," *New York Times*, April 21, 1955; "Colored Women Take Top Roles at N.Y. YWCA Meet," *Atlanta Daily World*, May 5, 1955; "Top Roles Won by Noted YWCA Women throughout Nation at New York Meet," *Pittsburgh Courier*, May 7, 1955.

14. Mummy [Madie] to Dear Daddy [Xuma], April 13, 1955, Xuma Papers, 1917–60, Correspondence, AD843-M7, ABX 550413; Mummy [Madie] to Dear Daddy [Xuma], April 26, 1955, Xuma Papers, 1917–60, Correspondence, AD843-M7, ABX 550426, both Historical Papers Research Archive.

15. Madie to My dearest Margaret [Hathaway], May 25, 1955, Xuma Papers, 1917–60, Correspondence, AD843-M7, ABX 550525, Historical Papers Research Archive.

16. Mummy [Madie] to Dear Daddy [Xuma], May 8, 1955, Xuma Papers, 1917–60, Correspondence, AD843-M7, ABX 550508, Historical Papers Research Archive.

17. Madie to My dearest Margaret [Hathaway], May 25, 1955, Xuma Papers, 1917–60, Correspondence, AD843-M7, ABX 550525, Historical Papers Research Archive.

18. Mummy [Madie] to Dearest Daddy [Xuma], May 28, 1955, Xuma Papers, 1917–60, Correspondence, AD843-M7, ABX 550528, Historical Papers Research Archive.

19. Mummy [Madie] to Dear Daddy [Xuma], June 25, 1955, Xuma Papers, 1917–60, Correspondence, AD843-M7, ABX 550625, Historical Papers Research Archive.

20. Unofficial Death Certificate of Death for Edna Florence Hall, Forsyth County Register of Deeds; In Memoriam Miss Edna Florence Hall, September 18, 1953, Goler Metropolitan A. M. E. Zion Church, Xuma Papers, 1917–60, Correspondence, AD843-M5, ABX 530918, Historical Papers Research Archive.

21. Mummy [Madie] to Dear Daddy [Xuma], May 5, 1955, Xuma Papers, 1917–60, Correspondence, AD843-M7, ABX 550505, Historical Papers Research Archive; Howard University, *The Bison: 1951*, Howard University Yearbooks, 120, https://dh.howard.edu/bison_yearbooks/120 (a picture of Harold appears on 140 and his name on 152); Mummy [Madie] to My dearest Daddy [Xuma], May 23, 1955, Xuma Papers, 1917–60, Correspondence, AD843-M7, ABX 550523, Historical Papers Research Archive.

22. See, for example, "Mary Bethune, 79, Educator, Is Dead," *New York Times*, May 19, 1955; "Mrs. Mary Bethune Dies," *Pittsburgh Courier*, May 21, 1955; and Mummy [Madie] to My dearest Daddy [Xuma], May 23, 1955, Xuma Papers, 1917–60, Correspondence, AD843-M7, ABX 550523, Historical Papers Research Archive.

23. Mummy [Madie] to Dear Daddy [Xuma], May 8, 1955, Xuma Papers, 1917–60, Correspondence, AD843-M7, ABX 550508; Mummy [Madie] to Dear Daddy [Xuma], May 15, 1955, Xuma Papers, 1917–60, Correspondence, AD843-M7, ABX 550515; Mummy [Madie] to My dearest Daddy [Xuma], May 23, 1955, Xuma Papers,

1917–60, Correspondence, AD843-M7, ABX 550523; Madie to My dearest Margaret [Hathaway], May 25, 1955 (emphasis in the original), Xuma Papers, 1917–60, Correspondence, AD843-M7, ABX 550525, all Historical Papers Research Archive.

24. Mummy [Madie] to Dear Daddy [Xuma], May 23, 1955, Xuma Papers, 1917–60, Correspondence, AD843-M7, ABX 550523, Historical Papers Research Archive.

25. Mummy [Madie] to Dear Daddy [Xuma], June 25, 1955, Xuma Papers, 1917–60, Correspondence, AD843-M7, ABX 550625, Historical Papers Research Archive. The travel plans changed, so see Mummy [Madie] to Dear Daddy [Xuma], June 10, 1955, Xuma Papers, 1917–60, Correspondence, AD843-M7, ABX 550610, Historical Papers Research Archive, for early itinerary. Mummy [Madie] to Dear Daddy [Xuma], June 18, 1955, Xuma Papers, 1917–60, Correspondence, AD843-M7, ABX 550618; Mummy [Madie] to Dear Daddy [Xuma], July 8, 1955, Xuma Papers, 1917–60, Correspondence, AD843-M7, ABX 550708; Madie to My dearest Margaret [Hathaway] May 25, 1955, Xuma Papers, 1917–60, Correspondence, AD843-M7, ABX 550525; Mummy [Madie] to dear Daddy [Xuma], July 21, 1955, Xuma Papers, 1917–60, Correspondence, AD843-M7, ABX 550721, all Historical Papers Research Archive. Madie seems to have been registered as an Alien of South Africa, hence the Aliens Registration Book, and may not have been a dual citizen.

26. "South African Racism," *New York Times*, June 25, 1955.

27. Mummy [Madie] to my dear Daddy [Xuma], July 25, 1955, Xuma Papers, 1917–60, Correspondence, AD843-M7, ABX 550725, Historical Papers Research Archive.

28. Mummy [Madie] to my dear Daddy [Xuma], July 25, 1955, Xuma Papers, 1917–60, Correspondence, AD843-M7, ABX 550725; Mummy [Madie] to My dear Daddy [Xuma], August 11, 1955, Xuma Papers, 1917–60, Correspondence, AD843-M7, ABX 550811; Mummy [Madie] to Dear Daddy [Xuma], August 16, 1955, Xuma Papers, 1917–60, Correspondence, AD843-M7, ABX 550816; Mummy [Madie] to My dear Daddy [Xuma], August 23, 1955, Xuma Papers, 1917–60, Correspondence, AD843-M7, ABX 550823a; Mummy [Madie] to My dear Daddy [Xuma], July 16, 1955, Xuma Papers, 1917–60, Correspondence, AD843-M7, ABX 550716; Mummy [Madie] to Dear Daddy [Xuma], August 26, 1955, Xuma Papers, 1917–60, Correspondence, AD843-M7, ABX 550826a, all Historical Papers Research Archive; 1955 Annual Report of the South African Council of World Affiliated Y.W.C.A., box 323, folder 8, YWCA of the U.S.A. Records, Sophia Smith Collections; "Dorothy Height Named to New Position as Associate Director—National YWCA," *New York Amsterdam News*, December 3, 1955, 11.

29. Mrs. Madie-Hall Xuma, "World Y.W.C.A. Council Meets in London," *Bantu World*, October 1, 1955, 9–10 [note that her first and family middle name is hyphenated in the newspaper]; "Constitution of Y.W.C.A.," *Times* (London), August 26, 1955, 8; "Points from Letters," *Times* (London), September 5, 1955, 14. See also Dorothy Height, *Open Wide the Freedom Gates: A Memoir*, 224.

30. Mummy [Madie] to My dear Daddy [Xuma], August 8, 1955 [incorrect month—should be September 8, 1955 as noted in archival number], Xuma Papers,

1917–60, Correspondence, AD843-M7, ABX 550908, Historical Papers Research Archive.

31. 1955 Annual Report of the South African Council of World Affiliated Y.W.C.A., box 323, folder 8, YWCA of the U.S.A. Records, Sophia Smith Collections; *A Meeting of the World YWCA Council: Royal Holloway College Surrey England, September 1955*, 3, 17; Mummy [Madie] to Dear Daddy [Xuma], September 13, 1955, Xuma Papers, 1917–60, Correspondence, AD843-M7, ABX 550913a, Historical Papers Research Archive.

32. Mummy [Madie] to Dear Daddy [Xuma], September 13, 1955, Xuma Papers, 1917–60, Correspondence, AD843-M7, ABX 550913a; Mummy [Madie] to dear Daddy [Xuma], September 17, 1955, Xuma Papers, 1917–60, Correspondence, AD843-M7, ABX 550917, both Historical Papers Research Archive. Note that the president of the World YWCA made number 20 as ex-officio member.

33. Marly V. de Barros from Brazil, R. Nita Barrow from Barbados, Annie Baeta Jiagge from Ghana, and Virginia Sanchez from the Philippines were also among those elected to the Executive Committee. See Seymour-Jones, *Journey of Faith*, 323, 499; and "Wrong to Jeer at Victorians," *Times* (London), September 17, 1955.

34. Mummy [Madie] to dear Daddy [Xuma], September 17, 1955, Xuma Papers, 1917–60, Correspondence, AD843-M7, ABX 550917, Historical Papers Research Archive; World Young Women's Christian Association Minutes of the Meeting of the Executive Committee, 17th–19th September, 1955, p. 1, Appendix I, II, III, box World YWCA Executive Committee Minutes, 1945–49, 1950–59, World Young Women's Christian Association Archives; Seymour-Jones, *Journey of Faith*, 74.

35. World Young Women's Christian Association Minutes of the Meeting of the Executive Committee, 17th–19th September, 1955, p. 1, Appendix I, II, III, box World YWCA Executive Committee Minutes, 1945–49, 1950–59, World Young Women's Christian Association Archives.

36. "World Leader of YWCA Stresses Universal Welfare," *Los Angeles Times*, September 25, 1957; World Young Women's Christian Association Minutes of the Meeting of the Executive Committee 17th–19th September, 1955, p. 1, Appendix I, II, III, box World YWCA Executive Committee Minutes, 1945–49, 1950–59, World Young Women's Christian Association Archives.

37. "Constitution of Y.W.C.A.," *Times* (London), August 26, 1955; "Wrong to Jeer at Victorians," *Times* (London), September 17, 1955; Mrs. Madie-Hall Xuma, "World Y.W.C.A. Council Meets in London," *Bantu World*, October 1, 1955; "10,000 Miles on YWCA Affairs," *Bantu World*, October 1, 1955, 9. See also "New Y.W.C.A. Clubs Springing Up All over the Country," *Bantu World*, July 30, 1955; 1955 Annual Report of the South African Council of World Affiliated Y.W.C.A., box 323, folder 8, YWCA of the U.S.A. Records, Sophia Smith Collections.

38. Horrell, *Survey of Race Relations in South Africa, 1955–1956*, 221; "New Y.W.C.A. Clubs Springing Up All over the Country," *Bantu World*, July 30, 1955; Janet Thomson to Gwen Grindler, November 14, 1955, binder 2 on South Africa, Durban, Port Elizabeth, 1947–, World Young Women's Christian Association Archives.

39. "South Africa—Planning Ahead."

40. Zenzele Young Women's Christian Association of the Transvaal, June 4, 1957, Xuma Papers, 1917–60, Correspondence, AD843-M9, ABX 570604, Historical Papers Research Archive; Newsletter from South African Council of World Affiliated YWCA, January 1957, reel 230, microdex M-8 file separator, YWCA of the U.S.A. Records, Sophia Smith Collections.

41. "People in the News."

42. Elizabeth Palmer to Mrs. Madie Hall Xuma and Mrs. Ray Phillips, October 22, 1956, reel 230, microdex M-8 file separator; Madie Hall Xuma and Cora A. Phillips to Mrs. [Elizabeth] Palmer, April 9, 1957, reel 230, microdex M-8 file separator; Mrs. A. B. Xuma and Mrs. Margaret Hathaway to Dear Friends of Riverside Church, January 27, 1957, reel 230, microdex M-8 file separator; Janet Thomson to Madames M. H. Xuma and Dora [Cora] Phillips, July 1, 1957, reel 230, microdex M-8 file separator, all YWCA of the U.S.A. Records, Sophia Smith Collections; Elizabeth Palmer to Miss Gwen Grindler, November 2, 1956, binder 2 on South Africa, Durban, Port Elizabeth, 1947–, World Young Women's Christian Association Archives.

43. Elizabeth Palmer to Mrs. Madie Hall Xuma and Mrs. Ray Phillips, October 22, 1956, reel 230, microdex M-8 file separator; Madie Hall Xuma and Cora A. Phillips to Mrs. [Elizabeth] Palmer, April 9, 1957, reel 230, microdex M-8 file separator; Mrs. A. B. Xuma and Mrs. Margaret Hathaway to Dear Friends of Riverside Church, January 27, 1957, reel 230, microdex M-8 file separator, all YWCA of the U.S.A. Records, Sophia Smith Collections.

44. Xuma to Claudia Haines Marsh, December 2, 1954, Xuma Papers, 1917–60, Correspondence, AD843-M6, ABX 541202c, Historical Papers Research Archive.

45. Madie Hall Xuma and Cora A. Phillips to Mrs. [Elizabeth] Palmer, April 9, 1957, reel 230, microdex M-8 file separator; Mrs. A. B. Xuma and Mrs. Margaret Hathaway to Dear Friends of Riverside Church, January 27, 1957, reel 230, microdex M-8 file separator, both YWCA of the U.S.A. Records, Sophia Smith Collections.

46. National Council of African Women Coming of Age Conference 1937–1958, Ernest Cole, Photographic Collection and Papers, Historical Papers Research Archive.

47. Passport and Certificate of Mrs. Xuma, Xuma Papers, AD843-Q31.1; Clary Elfving to Mrs. A. B. Xuma [Madie], August 25, 1958, Xuma Papers, 1917–60, Correspondence, AD843-M9, ABX 580825, both Historical Papers Research Archive. The young woman's name was Edith Hlstshayo—see Clary Elfving to Mrs. A. B. Xuma, June 8, 1959, Xuma Papers, 1917–60, Correspondence, AD843-M10, ABX 590608, Historical Papers Research Archive.

48. "Great Union Ambassador Flies to Europe," *World*, June 30, 1956, 6 (formerly the *Bantu World*).

49. World Young Women's Christian Association Minutes of the Meeting of the Executive Committee 1st–13 July 1956, pp. 11–12, box World YWCA Executive Committee Minutes, 1945–49, 1950–59, World Young Women's Christian Association Archives.

50. "Great Union Ambassador Flies to Europe."

51. World Young Women's Christian Association Minutes of the Meeting of the

Executive Committee 12th–24th May 1957, pp. 3, 5–7, box World YWCA Executive Committee Minutes, 1945–49, 1950–59, World Young Women's Christian Association Archives; "World Leader of YWCA Stresses Universal Welfare," *Los Angeles Times*, September 25, 1957.

52. Jacqueline van Stoetwegen to Mrs. M. H. Xuma, September 15, 1958, Xuma Papers, 1917–60, Correspondence, AD843-M9, ABX 580915a; Jacqueline van Stoetwegen to Whom It May Concern, September 15, 1958, Xuma Papers, 1917–60, Correspondence, AD843-M9, ABX 580915b; Consultation of the Christian Task of The YWCA, October 30th–November 6th, 1956, Xuma Papers, 1917–60, Correspondence, AD843-M9, ABX 581106, all Historical Papers Research Archive.

53. Consultation of the Christian Task of the YWCA, October 30th–November 6th, 1958, Xuma Papers, 1917–60, Correspondence, AD843-M9, ABX 5801106, Historical Papers Research Archive.

54. Consultation of the Christian Task of the YWCA, October 30th–November 6th, 1958, Xuma Papers, 1917–60, Correspondence, AD843-M9, ABX 5801106, Historical Papers Research Archive.

55. See, for example, Report of the Sub-Committee for Mutual Service and Extension, November 7–9, 1958, Xuma Papers, 1917–60, Correspondence, AD843-M9, ABX 5801109, Historical Papers Research Archive.

56. World Young Women's Christian Association Minutes of the Meeting of the Executive Committee, November 9–22, 1958, pp. 1–3, 21–22, box World YWCA Executive Committee Minutes, 1945–49, 1950–59, World Young Women's Christian Association Archives.

57. World Young Women's Christian Association Minutes of The Meeting of The Executive Committee November 9–22, 1958, pp. 25–26, box World YWCA Executive Committee Minutes, 1945–49, 1950–59, World Young Women's Christian Association Archives.

58. World Young Women's Christian Association Minutes of the Meeting of the Executive Committee November 9–22, 1958, pp. 19–20, box World YWCA Executive Committee Minutes, 1945–49, 1950–59, World Young Women's Christian Association Archives; Report of the Sub-Committee for Mutual Service and Extension, November 7–9, 1958, Xuma Papers, 1917–60, Correspondence, AD843-M9, ABX 581109 Historical Papers Research Archive. See, for example, excerpts from July 8, 1958 letter from Rosalie Oakes to Fay Allen, Rosalie Oakes to Madie [Xuma], July 2, 1959, and Rosalie [Oakes] to Janet Thomson, August 3, 1959, all binder 2 on South Africa, Durban, Port Elizabeth, 1947–, World Young Women's Christian Association Archives.

59. Rosalie Oakes to Madie [Xuma], July 2, 1959, binder 2 on South Africa, Durban, Port Elizabeth, 1947–, World Young Women's Christian Association Archives; Gish, *Alfred B. Xuma*, 197–198; Wilson and Mullally, *Hope and Dignity*, 148; Elizabeth Palmer to Mrs. Madie Hall Xuma, May 4, 1959, Xuma Papers, 1917–60, Correspondence, AD843-M10, ABX 590504a, Historical Papers Research Archive.

60. Jacqueline van Stoetwegen to Mrs. M. H. Xuma, September 15, 1958, Xuma Papers, 1917–60, Correspondence, AD843-M9, ABX 580915a; Jacqueline van Stoetwe-

gen to Whom It May Concern, September 15, 1958, Xuma Papers, 1917–60, Correspondence, AD843-M9, ABX 580915b; Passport and Certificate of Mrs. Xuma, Xuma Papers, AD843-Q31.1, both Historical Papers Research Archive.

61. Elizabeth Palmer to Mrs. Madie Hall Xuma, May 4 1959, Xuma Papers, 1917–60, Correspondence, AD843-M10, ABX 590504a; Elizabeth Palmer to the Secretary, the Department of the Interior, May 4 1959, Xuma Papers, 1917–60, Correspondence, AD843-M10, ABX 590504b; South African Police, Witwatersrand Divisional Naturalization Staff to Madie Hall Xuma, May 22, 1959, Xuma Papers, 1917–60, Correspondence, AD843-M10, ABX 590522, all Historical Papers Research Archive.

62. Minutes of the Meeting of the Executive Committee, October 9–10, 1959, Hotel Mandel, Cuernavaca, Mexico, p. 3, box World YWCA Executive Committee Minutes, 1945–49, 1950–59, World Young Women's Christian Association Archives.

63. Minutes of the Meeting of the Executive Committee, October 9 and 10, 1959, Hotel Mandel, Cuernavaca, Mexico, p. 3, box World YWCA Executive Committee Minutes, 1945–49, 1950–59, World Young Women's Christian Association Archives. See also "Y.W.C.A. Exchange Set: Latin American Program Is Aimed at Understanding," *New York Times*, October 16, 1960.

64. "World Role Hailed by Y.W.C.A. Leader," *New York Times*, March 8, 1956.

65. From the Statement of World YWCA Policy in Regard to World Peace Adopted by the World YWCA Council, September 1955; Minutes of the Meeting of the Executive Committee, October 9 and 10, 1959, Hotel Mandel, Cuernavaca, Mexico, pp. 1, 2, 3, box World YWCA Executive Committee Minutes, 1945–49, 1950–59, World Young Women's Christian Association Archives; Carmen Lusan, "The West Indies at the World Council of the Y.W.C.A.," *Daily Gleaner*, October 21, 1959, 8.

66. "South Africa—National Conference"; Rosalie V. Oakes, "Epistle from South Africa," *YWCA Magazine*, February 1963, YWCA Records, box 323, folder 8.; Rosalie [Oakes] to Janet Thomson, August 3, 1959, binder 2 on South Africa, Durban, Port Elizabeth, 1947–, both World Young Women's Christian Association Archives.

67. Janet Thomson to Rosalie Oakes, March 11, 1960, reel 230, microdex M-8 file separator, YWCA of the U.S.A. Records, Sophia Smith Collections; Rosalie Oakes to Janet Thomson, March 5, 1960, binder 2 on South Africa, Durban, Port Elizabeth, 1947–, World Young Women's Christian Association Archives. Steven Gish notes that Alfred Xuma "received medical treatment from Dr. Charles W. Mayo, head of the world-famous Mayo Clinic" while traveling in the United States in 1960. See Gish, *Alfred B. Xuma*, 196.

68. Sharpeville did not occur in a vacuum. Black people had been mounting campaigns against oppression for some time in both rural and urban areas. In Bizana between February and May 1960, for example, two white constables sent to investigate Africans using land designated by the government for other purposes were attacked. Opposition to the polices that deprived native Africans/Bantus of land prompted some members of the community to retaliate against those charged with enforcing government policies by assaulting them and even burning down their huts. As the protests escalated, many whites feared for their safety and fled the area.

In response, law enforcement sent in heavily armed police where there were often deadly clashes with the community. Reports of similar incidents with authorities for those angry about the Bantu policy system appeared in Tembuland, Gcalekaland, and the Northern Transvaal. See Horrell, *Survey of Race Relations in South Africa, 1959–1960*, 39–48, 52–58.

69. Rosalie Oakes to Miss Elizabeth Palmer and Miss Fay Allan, March 31, 1960, box 323, folder 8, YWCA of the U.S.A. Records, Sophia Smith Collections.

70. Rosalie Oakes to Miss Elizabeth Palmer and Miss Fay Allan, March 31, 1960, box 323, folder 8, YWCA of the U.S.A. Records, Sophia Smith Collections.

71. Rosalie Oakes to Miss Elizabeth Palmer and Miss Fay Allan, March 31, 1960, box 323, folder 8, YWCA of the U.S.A. Records, Sophia Smith Collections.

72. World YWCA Executive Committee, Bossey, Switzerland, 1960, Photographs World YWCA Executive Committee, World YWCA Council Meetings, 1922–1966, World Young Women's Christian Association Archives; "World YWCA Mutual Service Programme: Lists of Projects." Seymour-Jones, *Journey of Faith*, notes incorrect date on page 145. The YWCA was fortunate because other groups like the Federation of South African Women that had been established in 1954 did not fare as well. See Walker, *Women and Resistance in South Africa*, 165–66, 228, 272–74; 1959 Banning of M. Goldberg, March 20, 1959, Federation of South African Women Papers, 1954–63, AD1137, Ad1.5, Historical Papers Research Archive; and Horrell, *Survey of Race Relations in South Africa, 1962*, 24, 240.

73. "U.N. Chief Offers to Quit If the Assembly Requests," *New York Times*, April 6, 1961; "Bantus Show Dislike for Hammarskjold," *Pittsburgh Courier*, April 15, 1961. W. M Nkomo and K. T. Masemola also attended the meeting with Xuma. See Gish, *Alfred B. Xuma*, 199; and "U.N. Vote Scores South Africa, 95–1," *New York Times*, April 14, 1961.

74. See reprint in, for example, "South Africa on Its Own, but Bubble Is Vulnerable," *High Point Enterprise*, June 9, 1961; "Afrikaner Dream Is a Nightmare," *Robesonian*, June 13, 1961; "Fear Dominant Feeling in New Republic of S. Africa," *Fergus Falls Daily Journal*, June 14, 1961; and "Afrikaners Dream into a Nightmare," *Denton Record-Chronicle*, June 16, 1961.

75. Gish, *Alfred B. Xuma*, 201–2; Photographs, World YWCA Executive Committee, Bossey, Switzerland, 1960, World YWCA Council Meetings, 1922–66, World Young Women's Christian Association Archives; *Grantor General Index to Real Estate Conveyances—Forsyth County, NC*, deed, bk. 834, p. 346; *General Index to Real Estate Conveyances—Forsyth County, NC, to December 31st, 1927—Grantee*, deed, bk. 284, p. 112.

76. Gish, *Alfred B. Xuma*, 201–3; Kuzwayo, interview by Gish; Limb, *A. B. Xuma*, 35.

77. Limb, *A. B. Xuma*, 35; Gish, *Alfred B. Xuma*, 201–3; "Dr. A. B. Xuma," *Times* (London), January 30, 1962, 15. See also Nat Nakasa, "Who Was Dr. Xuma? An Intimate Profile," 37, 39; and "African Leader Xuma Is Dead," *Washington Post*, February 8, 1962.

Conclusion

1. "Shaw Finals Speaker Sees Advancement for Negroes," *Carolinian*, June 2, 1962.

2. Wilson and Mullally, *Hope and Dignity*, 148; Gish, *Alfred B. Xuma*, 204. See, for example, "She's Leaving Africa after 20 Years' Work," *Durham Morning Herald*, October 28, 1962; "Negro Woman Returning to N.C. after South African Service," *Danville Register*, October 28, 1962; and "African Leader to Return to N.C.," *Carolina Times*, November 10, 1962.

3. Gish, *Alfred B. Xuma*, 204.

4. "'Momma' Xuma Is Going Back Home," *Rand Daily Mail*, February 14, 1963.

5. Kuzwayo, interview by Gish.

6. Seymour-Jones, *Journey of Faith*, 173, 177; Photographs, World YWCA, Box—Africa—Sierra Leone, South Africa, Uganda, Tanzania, Zaire, Zambia, Zimbabwe, World Young Women's Christian Association Archives. See, for example, "Africa Seminar Slated for WUNC," *Carolina Times*, May 4, 1963.

7. Willie [H. Kennedy] to Madie Hall Xuma, May 12, 1959, A. B. Xuma Papers, 1917–1960, Correspondence, AD843-M10, ABX 590512, Historical Papers Research Archive. See also *Hill's Winston-Salem (Forsyth County, N.C.) City Directory, 1963*, 433, 888.

8. See the description of the city in "Winston-Salem City of Culture, History and Industry," in *Hill's Winston-Salem (Forsyth County, N.C.) City Directory, 1963*, ix–xix.

9. "Over 250 Nabbed in Birmingham," *Burlington Daily Times-News*, May 4, 1963; "Chief Judge Reverses District Judge's Ruling in Alabama Integration Controversy," *Raleigh Register*, May 23, 1963; "Expelled Negro Students Flock Back to School," *Galesburg Register-Mail*, May 23, 1963; "4,000 Stage Protest for 12th Night," *Galesburg Register-Mail*, May 23, 1963; "Greensboro Awaits Racial Report," *Burlington Daily Times-News*, May 23, 1963; "Raleigh, W-S Announce New Integration," *Gastonia Gazette*, June 6, 1963.

10. "Africa Seminar Slated for WUNC," *Carolina Times*, May 4, 1963.

11. "Mrs. Xuma Feted at Tea," *Baltimore Afro-America*, October 29, 1963, 9; "Mary Bethune YWCA Holds Annual Meet," *High Point Enterprise*, January 26, 1964, 36.

12. Wilson and Mullally, *Hope and Dignity*, 149.

13. "PTA News," *Burlington Daily Times-News*, March 9, 1966; "University Women Host Program," *Winston-Salem Chronicle*, March 5, 1977; "Afro-Fashionetta," *Carolina Times*, November 16, 1968; "North Carolina Public Health Association Fifty-Seventh Annual Meeting, October 9–11, White House Inn, Charlotte, NC," 11, 26; "Meeting Opens," *Greensboro Record*, October 9, 1968.

14. "Garden Club Holds Flower Show," *Winston-Salem Chronicle*, May 15, 1976; "Garden Path Holds Meeting," *Winston-Salem Chronicle*, November 19, 1977; "Alta Vistas Plan Flower Show," *Winston-Salem Chronicle*, April 26, 1980; "Along Garden Path Holds Dinner," *Winston-Salem Chronicle*, March 11, 1982.

15. "45th Annual Convention," *Asheville Citizen-Times*, August 5, 1980; "Garden Council Praised for Best Confab," *Winston-Salem Chronicle*, August 15, 1981; "Flower

Niche Garden Club Has 7th Anniversary," *Winston-Salem Chronicle*, June 17, 1982; "Along the Garden Path," *Winston-Salem Chronicle*, July 1, 1982.

16. Gish, *Alfred B. Xuma*, 204; "Deaths and Funerals," *Winston-Salem Journal*, September 11, 1982.

17. Unofficial certificate of death for Willie Corine Kennedy, Forsyth County Register of Deeds; Wilson and Mullally, *Hope and Dignity*, 149; Merrick and Hall Xuma, interview by Wilson, G-0270 and G-0280.

18. *Forsyth County Register of Deeds Grantor—Grantee Index*, Code-Book-Page RE-1321-1183; *Grantor General Index to Real Estate Conveyances—Forsyth County, NC*, deed of trust, bk. 788, p. 180; *General Index to Real Estate Conveyances—Forsyth County, NC, to December 31st, 1927—Grantee*, deed, bk. 81, p. 123, all Forsyth County Register of Deeds.

19. Unofficial certificate of death for Madie Hall Xuma, Forsyth County Register of Deeds; "Deaths and Funerals," *Winston-Salem Journal*, September 12, 1982. Note that Leroy died in 1984 at the age of eighty-four. See unofficial copy of certificate of death, Forsyth County Register of Deeds.

20. "Along the Garden Path Club Meets," *Winston-Salem Chronicle*, October 14, 1982; "Guests Present Variety of Discussion Topics at Flower Niche Meeting," *Winston-Salem Chronicle*, March 3, 1988.

Bibliography

Archival Collections

Albert and Shirley Small Special Collections Library, University of Virginia, Charlottesville

    Anne Spencer Papers

Andrew Carnegie Library Archives, Livingstone College, Salisbury, NC

    J. C. Price Papers

    Kyles, Bishop L. W., ed. *The Doctrines and Discipline of the African Methodist Episcopal Zion Church*. Charlotte: A.M.E. Zion Publication House, 1925.

Buncombe County Register of Deeds, Asheville, NC

    Jennie E. Hall

Central Intelligence Agency

    Alfred Bitini Xuma

Columbia University Rare Book and Manuscript Library, New York

    Columbia University in the City of New York Catalogue Number for the Sessions of 1936–1937. Morningside Heights, NY.

    Columbia University in the City of New York Catalogue Number for the Sessions of 1937–1938. Morningside Heights, NY.

    Columbia University in the City of New York Catalogue Number for the Sessions of 1938–1939. Morningside Heights, NY.

    Columbia University One Hundred and Eighty-Fourth Annual Commencement, June 1, 1938

    International House-Member Manuals and ID Cards, 1920–1980s, box 392, folder 7, series XIX

Forsyth County Register of Deeds, Forsyth County Government Center, Winston-Salem, NC

    General Index to Real Estate Conveyances

    Unofficial certificates of death: Edna Florence Hall, Leroy Langston Hall, Madie Hall Xuma, and Willie Corine Kennedy

Historical Papers Research Archive, William Cullen Library, University of the Wit-
    watersrand, Johannesburg, South Africa (digital)
    A. B. Xuma Papers
    Ernest Cole Photographic Collection and Papers
    Federation of South African Women Papers
    South African Institute of Race Relations (SAIRR) Papers
National Archives and Records Administration, National Personnel Records, St.
    Louis, MO
    Madie Hall, Works Progress Administration
North Carolina Supreme Court
    Woods et al v. Hall et al., 214 N.C. 16 197 S.E. 557, No. 755 Supreme Court of
        North Carolina
Northwestern University Archives, Evanston, IL
    Alfred Bitini Xuma File
Schomburg Center for Research in Black Culture, New York Public Library
    Phelps-Stokes Collection
Shaw University Archive, Raleigh, NC
    Catalogue of the Officers and Students of Shaw University, 1880–1881. Raleigh, NC:
        Edwards, Broughton, 1881.
    Catalogue of the Officers and Students of Shaw University, 1885–1886. Raleigh, NC:
        Edwards, Broughton, 1886.
    Catalogue of the Officers and Students of Shaw University, 1886–1887. Raleigh, NC:
        Edwards, Broughton, 1887.
    Catalogue of the Officers and Students of Shaw University, 1887–1888. Raleigh, NC:
        Edwards & Broughton, 1888.
    Catalogue of the Officers and Students of Shaw University, 1888–1889. Raleigh, NC:
        Edward & Broughton, 1889.
    *Eighth Annual Announcement of the Leonard Medical School (Medical Depart-
        ment of Shaw University), Raleigh, NC, for the Session of 1888–'89.* Raleigh,
        NC: Edward, Broughton, 1888.
    *Fifth Annual Announcement of the Leonard Medical School (Medical Department
        of Shaw University), Raleigh, NC, for the Session of 1885–'85[6?].* Raleigh, NC:
        Edward, Broughton, 1885[6?].
    *Nineteenth Annual Catalog of the Officers and Students of Leonard Medical School,
        Shaw University, Academic Year Ending March 18, 1899.* Raleigh, NC: Brough-
        ton.
    *Ninth Annual Announcement of the Leonard Medical School (Medical Department
        of Shaw University), Raleigh, NC, for the Session of 1889–'90.* Raleigh, NC:
        Edward, Broughton, 1889.
    *Seventh Annual Announcement of the Leonard Medical School (Medical Depart-
        ment of Shaw University), Raleigh, NC, for the Session of 1887–'88.* Raleigh, NC:
        Edward, Broughton, 1887.
    *Tenth Annual Announcement of the Leonard Medical School (Medical Department
        of Shaw University), Raleigh, NC, for the Session of 1890–'91.* Raleigh, NC: Shaw
        University Printing Department, 1890.

Thirty-Eighth Annual Catalogue of the Officers and Students, Shaw University, Raleigh, NC. Raleigh, NC: Edward & Broughton, 1912.

Thirty-Ninth Annual Catalogue of the Officers and Students, Shaw University, Raleigh, NC. Raleigh, NC: Edward & Broughton, 1913.

Thirty-Seventh Annual Catalogue of the Officers and Students, Shaw University, Raleigh, N.C., for the Academic Year Ending May Thirty-First, Nineteen Hundred and Eleven. Raleigh, NC: Edward & Broughton, 1911.

Twelfth Annual Announcement of the Leonard Medical School, Medical Department, Shaw University, Raleigh, N.C., Session of 1892–1893. Raleigh, NC: Shaw University Printing Department, 1892.

Twenty-Eighth Annual Catalog of the Officers and Students of the Leonard Medical School, the Medical Department of Shaw University, Raleigh, North Carolina, for the Academic Year Ending May Thirty-First, Nineteen Hundred and Eight. Raleigh, NC: Edwards & Broughton, 1908.

Sophia Smith Collections, Smith College, Northampton, MA

1955 Annual Report of the South African Council of World Affiliated Y.W.C.A., YWCA of the U.S.A. Records

YWCA of the U.S.A. Records. Microfilm.

Stuart A. Rose Manuscript, Archives, and Rare Book Library, Emory University, Atlanta

Josephus Roosevelt Coan Papers

United Nations Archives and Records Management, New York

United Nations Twenty-Ninth Plenary Meeting, Tuesday, 12 February 1946, 64. Declaration on the Participation of Women in the Work of the United Nations: Report of the General Committee, Document A/46 (online digital).

University of Minnesota Libraries, University Archives, Minneapolis

The Gopher Yearbook, vol. 32, 1919

The Gopher Yearbook, vol. 33, 1920

Minnesota Daily (student newspaper)

U.S. Department of Justice, Federal Bureau of Investigation, Washington, DC: Alfred Bitini Xuma

Wilberforce University Rembert E. Stokes Library Archives, Wilberforce, OH

The Forcean Yearbook, 1921

Winston-Salem State University Archives, C. G. O'Kelly Library, Winston-Salem State University, Winston-Salem, NC

1935 Yearbook, T.C. Pedagogue

"Board of Managers Minute Book, 1899–1911, 1919–1921," Slater Hospital Records

Commencement Day Program Winston-Salem Teachers College Tuesday, May 25, 1937

The Slater Industrial And State Normal School Winston-Salem. Annual Catalogue 1910–1911

The Slater Industrial and State Normal School Winston-Salem, N. C. Annual Catalogue 1912–1913

The Slater Industrial & State Normal School Winston-Salem, N. C. Annual Catalogue 1913–1914

Slater Industrial and State Normal School Course Catalog, 1914–1915

Slater State Colored Normal School (Winston-Salem) 1906–'07

The Slater State Normal School Winston-Salem, N. C. Annual Catalogue 1921–1922

The T.C. Alumni Bulletin 5, no. 3 (1944): 6.

The T.C. Alumni Bulletin, 9, no. 4 (1948): 2.

The T.C. Alumni Bulletin 21, no. 3 (1960): 8.

The T.C. Informer 1, no. 1 (1936): 4.

The T.C. Informer 1, no. 2 (1936): 3.

The Winston-Salem Teachers College (Formerly the Slater State Normal School) Annual Catalogue 1927–1928

The Winston-Salem Teachers College (Formerly the Slater State Normal School) Annual Catalogue 1928–1929

The Winston-Salem Teachers College Annual Catalogue 1930–1931

Winston-Salem Teachers College Commencement Day Program Thursday, May 25, 1944

Winston-Salem Teachers College Commencement Day Program Friday, May 25, 1945

Winston-Salem Teachers College Commencement Day Program Tuesday, May 28, 1946

World Young Women's Christian Association Archives, Geneva

Photographs, World YWCA Executive Committee, Bossey, Switzerland, 1960, World YWCA Council Meetings, 1922–66

Photographs, World YWCA, Box—Africa—Sierra Leone, South Africa, Uganda, Tanzania, Zaire, Zambia, Zimbabwe

South Africa, Durban, Port Elizabeth, 1947–, binder 2

World YWCA Council Minutes/Reports till 1934: World's Committee Biennial Meetings, 1920–71

World YWCA Executive Committee Minutes, 1945–49, 1950–59

Interviews

Hall Xuma, Madie. Interview by Emily Herring Wilson, May 28, 1980. G-0280, audio files 1–2. Southern Oral History Program Interview Database, University of North Carolina at Chapel Hill.

Kuzwayo, Ellen. Interviewed by Steven Gish, March 27, 1991, in Soweto.

Merrick, Lyda Moore, and Madie Hall Xuma. Interview by Emily Herring Wilson, September 11, 1979. G-0270, audio files 1–4. Southern Oral History Program Interview Database, University of North Carolina at Chapel Hill.

City Directories

COLUMBIA, SC

Walsh's Columbia, S.C., Directory, 1916. Charleston, SC: Walsh Directory, n.d.

Walsh's Columbia, South Carolina, City Directory for 1905. Charleston, SC: Walsh Directory, 1905.

Walsh's Columbia, South Carolina, City Directory for 1910. Charleston, SC: Walsh Directory, 1909.

Walsh's Columbia, South Carolina, City Directory for 1911. Charleston, SC: Walsh Directory, 1911.

Walsh's Columbia, South Carolina, City Directory for 1914. Charleston, SC: Walsh Directory, 1913.

Walsh's Columbia, South Carolina, City Directory for 1915. Charleston, SC: Walsh Directory, 1913.

Walsh's Columbia, South Carolina, City Directory for 1917. Charleston, SC: Walker, Evans & Cosewell, 1917.

WINSTON-SALEM, NC

Chas. Emerson & Co.'s Winston, Salem & Greensboro, North Carolina, Directory, 1879–'80. Raleigh, NC: Edwards, Broughton, 1879.

Hill's Winston-Salem (Forsyth County, N.C.) City Directory, 1935. Richmond, VA: Hill Directory, 1934.

Hill's Winston-Salem (Forsyth County, N.C.) City Directory, 1939. Richmond, VA: Hill Directory, 1939.

Hill's Winston-Salem (Forsyth County, N.C.) City Directory, 1947–48. Richmond, VA: Hill Directory, 1948.

Hill's Winston-Salem (Forsyth County, N.C.) City Directory, 1963. Richmond, VA: Hill Directory, 1963.

Hill's Winston-Salem (North Carolina) City Directory, 1932. Richmond, VA: Hill Directory, 1932.

Hill's Winston-Salem (North Carolina) City Directory, 1933. Richmond, VA: Hill Directory, 1932.

Miller's Winston-Salem, N.C., City Directory, 1929. Asheville, NC: Commercial Service, 1928.

Miller's Winston-Salem, N.C., City Directory, 1930. Asheville, NC: Commercial Service, 1929.

Miller's Winston-Salem, N.C., City Directory, 1931. Asheville, N. C.: Commercial Service, 1931.

Miller's Winston-Salem, N. Carolina, City Directory, 1928. Asheville, NC: Commercial Service, 1927.

Turner & Co.'s Winston and Salem City Directory, for the Years 1889 and 1890. Yonkers, NY: E. F. Turner, 1889.

Turner's Fifth Annual Winston and Salem City Directory for the Years 1891 and 1892. Yonkers, NY: E. F. Turner, 1891.

Turner's Winston and Salem City Directory for the Years 1894–95. Yonkers, NY: Turner & Co., 1894.

Walsh's Directory of the Cities of Winston and Salem, N.C., for 1902–1903. Charleston, SC: W. H. Walsh Directory, 1902.

Walsh's Winston-Salem, North Carolina, City Directory for 1904–5. Charleston, SC: W. H. Walsh Directory, 1904.

Walsh's Winston-Salem, North Carolina, City Directory for 1906. Charleston, SC: Walsh Directory, 1906.

Walsh's Winston-Salem, North Carolina, City Directory for 1908. Charleston, SC: Walsh Directory, 1907.

Winston-Salem, N.C., City and Suburban City Directory, 1910. Asheville, NC: Piedmont Directory, n.d.

The Winston-Salem, N.C., City Directory, 1911. Asheville, NC: Piedmont Directory, 1911.

The Winston-Salem, N.C., City Directory, 1912. Asheville, NC: Piedmont Directory, 1912.

The Winston-Salem, N.C., City Directory, 1913. Asheville, NC: Piedmont Directory.

The Winston-Salem, N.C., City Directory, 1915. Asheville, NC: Piedmont Directory, 1915.

Winston-Salem, N.C., City Directory, 1916. Asheville, NC: Commercial Service, 1916.

Winston-Salem, N.C., City Directory, 1918. Asheville, NC: Commercial Service, n.d.

Winston-Salem, N.C., City Directory, 1920. Asheville, NC: Commercial Service, n.d.

Winston-Salem, N.C., City Directory, 1921. Asheville, NC: Commercial Service, n.d.

Winston-Salem, N.C., City Directory, 1922. Asheville, NC: Commercial Service, 1922.

Winston-Salem, N.C., City Directory, 1923. Asheville, NC: Commercial Service, 1923.

Winston-Salem, N. Carolina, City Directory, 1926. Asheville, NC: Commercial Service, 1926.

Government Documents

Eleventh Census of the United States: 1890. Pt. 1, Statistics of Population. Table 5, "Population of States and Territories by Minor Civil Divisions." Washington, DC: Government Printing Office.

———. Eleventh Census of the United States: 1890. Pt. 1, Statistics of Population. Table 23, "Native and Foreign Born and White and Colored Population, Classified by Sex, of Places Having 2,500 Inhabitants or More." Washington, DC: Government Printing Office.

———. Fifteenth Census of the United States: 1930. Vol. 3, pt. 2, Population—North Carolina. Table 12, "Population by Age, Color, Nativity, and Sex, for Cities and Towns of 10,000 or More." Washington, DC: Government Printing Service.

———. Fifteenth Census of the United States: 1930, Population Schedule, Winston Salem, North Carolina. Washington, DC: Government Printing Office.

———. Fourteenth Census of the United States: 1920. Vol. 3, Composition and Characteristics of the Population by States. Table 8, "Age, for Cities of 10,000 or More." Washington, DC: Government Printing Office.

———. Fourteenth Census of the United States: 1920. Vol. 3, Composition and Characteristics of the Population by States. Table 10, "Composition and Characteristics of the Population, for Cities of 10,000 or More." Washington, DC: Government Printing Office.

———. Fourteenth Census of the United States: 1920. Vol. 3, Composition and Characteristics of the Population by States. Table 13, "Composition and Characteristics of the Population for Wards of Cities of 50,000 or More." Washington, DC: Government Printing Office.

———. *Fourteenth Census of the United States: 1920—Population, North Carolina, Forsyth County, Winston Salem*. Washington, DC: Government Printing Office.

———. *Ninth Census of the United States: 1870*. Schedule 1, "Inhabitants in Salisbury Township in the County of Rowan," 9, 51. Washington, DC: Government Printing Office.

———. *Ninth Census of the United States: 1870*. Vol. 1, *The Statistics of the Population of the United States*. Table 3, "State of North Carolina." Washington, DC: Government Printing Office.

———. *Sixteenth Census of the United States: 1940, Population Schedule, Winston-Salem, North Carolina*. Washington, DC: Government Printing Office.

———. *Tenth Census of the United States: 1880, Population of Civil Divisions Less than Counties*. Table 3, "North Carolina." Washington, DC: Government Printing Office.

———. *Tenth Census of the United States: 1880*. Schedule 1, "Inhabitants in Salisbury in the County of Rowan, State of N.C.," 3, 27. Washington, DC: Government Printing Office.

———. *Thirteenth Census of the United States: 1910*. Vol. 3, *Population—North Carolina*. Table 1, "Population of Minor Civil Divisions: 1910, 1900, and 1890." Washington, DC: Government Printing Office.

———. *Thirteenth Census of the United States: 1910*. Vol. 3, *Population—North Carolina*. Table 3, "Composition and Characteristics of the Population for Cities of 10,000 to 25,000." Washington, DC: Government Printing Office.

———. *Thirteenth Census of the United States: 1910, Population, North Carolina, Forsyth County, Winston Township*. Washington, DC: Government Printing Office.

———. *Thirteenth Census of the United States: 1910, Population, Virginia, Campbell County, Lynchburg, Ward of City 3*. Washington, DC: Government Printing Office.

———. *Twelfth Census of the United States: 1900*. Schedule 1, "Population, Cleveland County, North Carolina." Washington, DC: National Archives and Records Administration.

———. *Twelfth Census of the United States: 1900*. Schedule 1, "Population, Winston Township, North Carolina, Forsyth County." Washington, DC: Government Printing Office.

———. *Twelfth Census of the United States: 1900, Minor Civil Divisions*. Table 5, "Population of States and Territories by Minor Civil Divisions, North Carolina." Washington, DC: U.S. Census Office.

———. *Twelfth Census of the United States: 1900, Sex, General Nativity, and Color*. Table 24, "Native and Foreign Born and White and Colored Population, Classified by Sex, for Places Having 2,500 Inhabitants or More." Washington, DC: U.S. Census Office.

Newspapers

Amarillo Sunday News and Globe
Anderson (SC) Intelligencer
Annapolis (MD) Evening Capital

Arkansas Democrat (Little Rock)
Asheville Citizen-Times
Atlanta Constitution
Atlanta Daily World
Baltimore Afro-American
Bantu World
Blizzard (Oil City, PA)
Burlington (NC) Daily Times-News
Burlington (VT) Free Press
Bystander (Des Moines)
Carolina Times
Carolinian (Raleigh)
Charlotte Democrat
Charlotte News
Charlotte Observer
Chicago Daily Tribune
Chicago Defender
Chicago Whip
Colored American
Columbia (SC) Record
Columbia (SC) State
Corpus Christi Caller-Times
Cumberland (MD) News
Daily Gleaner (Kingston, Jamaica)
Daily Inter Ocean (Chicago)
Dallas Express
Danville (VA) Register
Denton (TX) Record-Chronicle
Des Moines (IA) Register
Durham (NC) Morning Herald
Fergus Falls (MN) Daily Journal
Franklin Times (Louisburg, NC)
Galesburg (IL) Register-Mail
Gastonia (NC) Gazette
Greensboro (NC) Daily News
Greensboro (NC) News & Record
Greensboro (NC) Record
Henderson (NC) Daily Dispatch
High Point (NC) Enterprise
Indianapolis Recorder
Kalamazoo (MI) Gazette
Kansas City (KS) Plaindealer
Kansas City (MO) Sun
Lakeland (FL) Evening Telegram

Los Angeles Times
Medicine Hat (Alberta) News
Memphis Daily Appeal
Negro Star (Wichita)
New Orleans Times-Picayune
New York Age
New York Amsterdam News
New York Times
New York Tribune
Omaha (NE) Guide
Palmetto Leader (Columbia, SC)
Pensacola Journal
People's Voice (New York)
Philadelphia Inquirer
Philadelphia Tribune
Pittsburgh Courier
Pittsburgh Dispatch
Portland Oregonian
Progressive Farmer and the Cotton Plant (Raleigh)
Raleigh Evening Times
Raleigh Gazette
Raleigh News and Observer
Raleigh Register (Beckley, WV)
Raleigh Times
Rand Daily Mail (South Africa)
Reno Evening Gazette
Richmond (VA) Afro American
Robesonian (Lumberton, NC)
Rochester (NY) Democrat and Chronicle
Salisbury (NC) Post
Southern Indicator (Columbia, SC)
Sphinx Magazine (Alpha Phi Alpha fraternity)
St. Paul (MN) Echo
Statesville (NC) Daily Record
Sun (Sydney, Australia)
Sunday Tribune (South Africa)
Times (London)
Twin-City (NC) Daily Sentinel
Union Republican (Winston-Salem, NC)
Virginian-Pilot (Norfolk)
Washington Bee
Washington Evening Star
Washington Post
Washington Times

Weekend Argus (South Africa)
Western Sentinel (NC)
Wilmington (NC) Messenger
Wilson (NC) Daily Times
Winnipeg Free Press
Winston-Salem (NC) Chronicle
Winston-Salem (NC) Journal
Winston-Salem (NC) Journal and Sentinel
Winston-Salem (NC) Weekly Sentinel
World (South Africa)
Xenia (OH) Evening Gazette
Yorkville (SC) Enquirer

Microfilm

Williams, Lillian Serece, ed. *Records of the National Association of Colored Women's Clubs, 1895–1992*. Pt. 1, *Minutes of National Conventions, Publications, and President's Office Correspondence*. Bethesda, MD: University Publications of America, 1993.

Other Sources

Anthony, David Henry, III. *Max Yergan: Race Man, Internationalist, Cold Warrior*. New York: New York University Press, 2006.

"Apartheid." *Federation Journal* 12 (April 1955): 2.

Austin, Hiliary Mac. "The Defender Brings You the World: The Grand European Tour of Patrick B. Prescott Jr." In *The Black Chicago Renaissance*, edited by Darlene Clark Hine and John McCluskey Jr., 57–75. Urbana: University of Illinois Press, 2012.

Beckford, Geraldine Rhodes, comp. *Biographical Dictionary of American Physicians of African Ancestry, 1800–1920*. Cherry Hill, NJ: Africana Homestead Legacy, 2011.

Berger, Iris. "An African American 'Mother of the Nation': Madie Hall Xuma in South Africa, 1940–1963." *Journal of Southern African Studies* 27, no. 3 (2001): 547–66.

———. *Threads of Solidarity: Women in South African Industry, 1900–1980*. Bloomington: Indiana University Press, 1992.

Biennial Report of the Superintendent of Public Instruction of North Carolina for the Scholastic Years 1885 and 1886. Raleigh: P. M. Hale, State Printer and Binder, 1887.

Bristow, Nancy K. *American Pandemic: The Lost Worlds of the 1918 Influenza Epidemic*. New York: Oxford University Press, 2012.

Brooks, Pam. "'But Once They Are Organized, You Can Never Stop Them': 1950s Black Women in Montgomery and Johannesburg Defy Men and the State." *Agenda*, no. 58 (2003): 84–97.

Brooks, Pamela E. *Boycotts, Buses, and Passes: Black Women's Resistance in the U.S. South and South Africa*. Amherst: University of Massachusetts Press, 2008.

Brown, Leslie. *Upbuilding Black Durham: Gender, Class, and Black Community De-*

velopment in the Jim Crow South. Chapel Hill: University of North Carolina Press, 2008.

Brownlee, Fambrough L. *Winston-Salem: A Pictorial History.* Norfolk, VA: Donning, 1977.

Bundles, A'Lelia. *On Her Own Ground: The Life and Times of Madam C. J. Walker.* New York: Washington Square Press, 2001.

Campbell, James T. *Songs of Zion: The African Methodist Episcopal Church in the United States and South Africa.* New York: Oxford University Press, 1995.

Carlton, David L. "The Revolution from Above: The National Market and the Beginning of Industrialization in North Carolina." *Journal of American History* (September 1990): 464–67.

Carlton-LaNey, Iris. "Women and Interracial Cooperation in Establishing the Good Samaritan Hospital." *Affilia* 15, no. 1 (2000): 65–81.

Castledine, Jacqueline. "'In a Solid Bond of Unity': Anticolonial Feminism in the Cold War Era." *Journal of Women's History* 20, no. 4 (2008): 57–81.

"Church Women in Interracial Cooperation." *Federal Council Bulletin: A Journal of Religious Cooperation and Interchurch Activities* 11, no. 8 (1928): 13–14.

Clark, Patricia G. "A Gendered View of the History of Professionalization in South Africa." *Africa Development* 23, nos. 3–4 (1998): 77–93.

Cobb, W. Montague. "Saint Agnes Hospital, Raleigh, North Carolina, 1896–1961." *Journal of the National Medical Association* 53, no. 5 (1961): 439–46.

Cobley, Alan Gregory. *The Rules of the Game: Struggles in Black Recreation and Social Welfare Policy in South Africa.* Westport, CT: Greenwood Press, 1997.

Collier-Thomas, Bettye. *Jesus, Jobs, and Justice: African American Women and Religion.* New York: Alfred A. Knopf, 2011.

"Colored Work." *Blue Triangle News,* no. 85 (January 16, 1920).

"'Colour Bar' Voted Down in South African Mines." *Star of Zion* 50, no. 1 (1926): 5.

Cook, Dawn. "Aprons and Tobacco Leaves: The Agency of Black Women in Winston-Salem and the North Carolina Piedmont, 1855–1920." Master's thesis, California State University, Fullerton, 2014.

Curry, Dawne Y. "'What Is It That We Call the Nation': Celilia Lillian Tshabalala's Definition, Diagnosis, and Prognosis of the Nation in a Segregated South Africa." *Safundi: The Journal of South African and American Studies* 19, no. 1 (2018): 55–76.

Daniel, Walter G. "Current Trends and Events of National Importance in Negro Education: Section A, Negro Welfare and Mabel Carney at Teachers College, Columbia University." *Journal of Negro Education* 11, no. 4 (1942): 560–62.

"Daughters of Africa." *Umteteli* 21, no. 1 (1940): 4.

"Daughters of Dorcas Club of Durham." *Federation Journal* 5 (April 1, 1949): 4.

Davis, Elizabeth Lindsay. *The Story of the Illinois Federation of Colored Women's Clubs, 1900–1922.* Chicago: n.p., 1922.

Dickerson, Dennis C. *The African Methodist Episcopal Church: A History.* Cambridge: Cambridge University Press, 2020.

Dubow, Saul. "The United Nations and the Rhetoric of Race and Rights." *Journal of Contemporary History* 43, no. 1 (2008): 45–74.

Erlank, Natasha. "Gender and Masculinity in South African Nationalist Discourse, 1912–1950." *Feminist Studies* 29, no. 3 (2003): 653–71.

Foster, Mark S. "In the Face of 'Jim Crow': Prosperous Blacks and Vacations, Travel and Outdoor Leisure, 1890–1945." *Journal of Negro History* 84, no. 2 (1999): 130–49.

"From the Statement of World YWCA Policy in Regard to World Peace Adopted by the World YWCA Council, September 1955." *World Y.W.C.A. Monthly* 34, no. 11 (1956): 275–77.

Gamber, Wendy. *The Female Economy: The Millinery and Dressmaking Trades, 1860–1930*. Urbana: University of Illinois Press, 1997.

Gary, Robenia Baker, and Lawrence E. Gary. "The History of Social Work Education for Black People, 1900–1930." *Journal of Sociology & Social Welfare* 21, no. 1 (2015): 67–81.

Gatewood, Willard B. *Aristocrats of Color: The Black Elite, 1880–1920*. 1990. Reprint, Fayetteville: University of Arkansas Press, 2000.

Gibson, J. W., and W. H. Crogman. *Progress of a Race; or, The Remarkable Advancement of the Colored American, from the Bondage of Slavery, Ignorance and Poverty to the Freedom of Citizenship, Intelligence, Affluence, Honor and Trust*. Rev. ed. Naperville, IL: J. L. Nichols, 1912.

Gill, Tiffany M. *Beauty Shop Politics: African American Women's Activism in the Beauty Industry*. Urbana: University of Illinois Press, 2010.

Gillespie, Michele. *Katharine and R. J. Reynolds: Partners of Fortune in the Making of the New South*. Athens: University of Georgia Press, 2012.

Gilmore, Glenda Elizabeth. *Gender and Jim Crow: Women and the Politics of White Supremacy in North Carolina, 1896–1920*. Chapel Hill: University of North Carolina Press, 1996.

Ginwala, Frene. "Women and the African National Congress, 1912–1943." *Agenda: Empowering Women for Gender Equity* 8 (1990): 77–93.

Gish, Steven D. *Alfred B. Xuma: African, American, South African*. New York: New York University Press, 2000.

Glenn, Joanne. "The Winston-Salem Riot of 1918." Master's thesis, University of North Carolina, 1979.

Glotzer, Richard. "The Career of Mabel Carney: The Study of Race and Rural Development in the United States and South Africa." *International Journal of African Historical Studies* 29, no. 2 (1996): 309–36.

——. "A Long Shadow: Frederick P. Keppel, the Carnegie Corporation and the Dominions and Colonies Fund Area Experts, 1923–1943." *History of Education* 38, no. 5 (2009): 621–48.

Grant, Nicholas. "The National Council of Negro Women and South Africa: Black Internationalism, Motherhood, and the Cold War." *Palimpsest: A Journal on Women, Gender, and the Black International* 5, no. 1 (2016): 59–87.

——. *Winning over Freedom Together: African Americans and Apartheid, 1945–1960*. Chapel Hill: University of North Carolina Press, 2017.

Griffin, Farah Jasmine. *Harlem Nocturne: Women Artists & Progressive Politics during World War II*. New York: Basic Civitas, 2013.

Grimes, William T. "The History of Kate Bitting Reynolds Memorial Hospital." *Journal of the National Medical Association* 64, no. 4 (1972): 376–81.

Guridy, Frank Andre. *Forging Diaspora: Afro-Cubans and African Americans in a World of Empire and Jim Crow*. Chapel Hill: University of North Carolina Press, 2010.

Hartshorn, W. N., ed. *An Era of Progress and Promise, 1863–1910: The Religious, Moral, and Educational Development of the American Negro since His Emancipation*. Boston: Priscilla, 1910.

Healy-Clancy, Meghan. "Women and the Problem of Family in Early African Nationalist History and Historiography." *South African Historical Journal* 64, no. 3 (2012): 450–71.

Height, Dorothy. *Open Wide the Freedom Gates: A Memoir*. New York: Public Affairs, 2003.

Hendricks, Wanda A. *Fannie Barrier Williams: Crossing the Borders of Region and Race*. Urbana: University of Illinois Press, 2014.

———. *Gender, Race, and Politics in the Midwest: Black Club Women in Illinois*. Bloomington: Indiana University Press, 1998.

Herbin-Triant, Elizabeth A. "Race and Class Friction in North Carolina Neighborhoods: How Campaigns for Residential Segregation Law Divided Middling and Elite Whites in Winston-Salem and North Carolina's Countryside, 1912–1925." *Journal of Southern History* 83, no. 3 (2017): 531–72.

Higgs, Catherine. "Zenzele: African Women's Self-Help Organizations in South Africa, 1927–1998." *African Studies Review* 47, no. 3 (2004): 119–41.

Hine, Darlene Clark. "The Anatomy of Failure: Medical Education Reform and the Leonard Medical School of Shaw University, 1882–1920." *Journal of Negro Education* 54, no. 4 (1985): 512–25.

———. *Black Women in White: Racial Conflict and Cooperation in the Nursing Profession, 1890–1950*. Bloomington: Indiana University Press, 1989.

———. "Co-laborers in the Work of the Lord: Nineteenth-Century Black Women Physicians." In *HineSight: Black Women and the Re-construction of American History*, edited by Darlene Clark Hine, 147–61. Brooklyn: Carlson, 1994.

———. "The Corporeal and Ocular Veil: Dr. Matilda A. Evans (1872–1935) and the Complexity of Southern History." *Journal of Southern History* 70, no. 1 (2004): 3–34.

Horrell, Muriel, comp. *A Survey of Race Relations in South Africa, 1951–1952*. Johannesburg: South African Institute of Race Relations.

———, comp. *A Survey of Race Relations in South Africa, 1955–1956*. Johannesburg: South African Institute of Race Relations.

———, comp. *A Survey of Race Relations in South Africa, 1959–1960*. Johannesburg: South African Institute of Race Relations.

———, comp. *A Survey of Race Relations in South Africa, 1962*. Johannesburg: South African Institute of Race Relations, 1963.

"Industrial Work." *Blue Triangle News*, no. 85 (January 16, 1920).

"In Memoriam." *Journal of the National Medical Association* 34, no. 4 (1942): 174.

"It Happened in Our World: African Emissaries, Following the Pattern of Globe-

Trotting Americans, Come Here to See Our Democracy at Work." *Our World Magazine* 12, no. 6 (1951): 10–11.

J. P. R. "A Successful Negro School." *Outlook* 85, no. 9 (1907): 529.

Jaffer, Zubeida. *Beauty of the Heart: The Life and Times of Charlotte Mannye Maxeke.* Bloemfontein, South Africa: Sun Press, 2016.

Jones, Adrienne Lash. *Jane Edna Hunter: A Case Study of Black Leadership, 1910–1950.* Vol. 12 of *Black Women in United States History,* edited by Darlene Clark Hine. New York: Carlson, 1990.

Karis, Thomas. *Hope and Challenge, 1935–1952.* Vol. 2 of *From Protest to Challenge: A Documentary History of African Politics in South Africa, 1882–1964,* edited by Thomas Karis and Gwendolen M. Carter. Stanford, CA: Hoover Institution Press, 1973.

Kenney, John A. "The Negro Doctor and Organized Medicine." *Journal of the National Medical Association* 31, no. 6 (1939): 252–54.

Kimble, Judy, and Elaine Unterhalter. "'We Opened the Road for You. You Must Go Forward': ANC Women's Struggles, 1912–1982." *Feminist Review* 12 (1982): 11–35.

Knupfer, Ann Meis. *Toward a Tenderer Humanity and a Nobler Womanhood: African American Women's Clubs in Turn-of-the-Century Chicago.* New York: New York University Press, 1996.

Korstad, Robert Rodgers. *Civil Rights Unionism: Tobacco Workers and the Struggle for Democracy in the Mid-Twentieth-Century South.* Chapel Hill: University of North Carolina Press, 2003.

Leslie, Grace V. "'United, We Build a Free World': The Internationalism of Mary McLeod Bethune and the National Council of Negro Women." In *To Turn the Whole World Over: Black Women and Internationalism,* edited by Keisha N. Blain and Tiffany M. Gill, 192–218. Urbana: University of Illinois Press, 2019.

Limb, Peter, ed. *A. B. Xuma: Autobiography and Selected Works.* Cape Town, South Africa: Van Riebeeck Society, 2012.

Lodge, Tom. "The Destruction of Sophiatown." *Journal of Modern African Studies* 19, no. 1 (1981): 107–32.

Logan, Frenise Avedis. *The Negro in North Carolina, 1876–1894.* Chapel Hill: University of North Carolina Press, 1964.

Lubanga, Nonceba. "Nursing in South Africa: Black Women Workers Organize." In *Women and Health in Africa,* edited by Meredith Turshen, 51–77. Trenton, NJ: Africa World Press, 1991.

Lundeen, Elizabeth Ann. "Accommodation Strategies of African American Educational Leaders in North Carolina, 1890–1930." Master's thesis, Cambridge University, 2008.

Mason, Mary L. "The World of Women." *Star of Zion* 50, no. 4 (1926): 2.

———. "The World of Women." *Star of Zion* 54, no. 40 (1930): 2.

McMillen, Neil R. *Dark Journey: Black Mississippians in the Age of Jim Crow.* Urbana: University of Illinois Press, 1990.

McWhirter, Cameron. *Red Summer: The Summer of 1919 and the Awakening of Black America.* New York: Henry Holt, 2011.

A Meeting of the World YWCA Council: Royal Holloway College, Surrey, England, September 1955. Available from Women and Social Movements International—1840 to Present, Alexander Street Press.

Meriwether, James H. *Proudly We Can Be Africans: Black Americans and Africa, 1935–1961.* Chapel Hill: University of North Carolina Press, 2002.

Michaeli, Ethan. *The "Defender": How the Legendary Black Newspaper Changed America from the Age of the Pullman Porters to the Age of Obama.* New York: Houghton Mifflin Harcourt, 2016.

Miller, Bertha Hampton. "Blacks in Winston-Salem, North Carolina, 1895–1920: Community Development in an Era of Benevolent Paternalism." PhD diss., Duke University, 1981.

Miller, Kelly. "The Historic Background of the Negro Physician." *Journal of Negro History* 1, no. 2 (1916): 99–109.

"Mrs. A. B. Xuma Guest at Reception." *Umteteli*, 21, no. 1058 (1940): 4.

Murphy, E. Louise. *The History of Winston-Salem State University, 1892–1995.* Rev. ed. Virginia Beach: Donning, 1999.

Nakasa, Nat. "'Mummy' Goes Home—but Her Job's Done." *Drum Magazine* (March 1963): 39–41.

———. "Who Was Dr. Xuma? An Intimate Profile." *Drum*, no. 132 (March 1962): 37, 39.

Neverdon-Morton, Cynthia. *Afro-American Women of the South and the Advancement of the Race, 1895–1925.* Knoxville: University of Tennessee Press, 1989.

Newbold, N. C. "Common Schools for Negroes in the South." *Annals of the American Academy of Political and Social Science* 140 (November 1928): 209–23.

———. *Five North Carolina Negro Educators.* Chapel Hill: University of North Carolina Press, 1939.

"N.M.A. Communications." *Journal of the National Medical Association* 13, no. 1 (1921): 39–41.

"North Carolina Public Health Association Fifty-Seventh Annual Meeting, October 9–11, White House Inn, Charlotte, NC."

Olcott, Jane. *The Work of Colored Women.* New York: Colored Work Committee War Work Council National Board Young Womens [*sic*] Christian Association, n.d.

Oppermann, Langdon Edmunds. "Goler Metropolitan A.M.E. Zion Church, Forsyth County, NC, National Register of Historic Places Registration Form." U.S. Department of the Interior National Park Service, March 1998.

———. "Historic and Architectural Resources of African-American Neighborhoods in Northeastern Winston-Salem, ca. 1900–1947, National Register of Historic Places Multiple Property Documentation Form." Historic Preservation Planning, 1997. https://www.cityofws.org/DocumentCenter/View/6825/Historic-and -Architectural-Resources-of-African-American-Neighborhoods-in-Northeastern -Winston-Salem—-1900-to-1947-PDF.

Ottley, Roi. *The Lonely Warrior: The Life and Times of Robert S. Abbott.* Chicago: Henry Regnery, 1955.

Parker, Marjorie H. *Past Is Prologue: The History of Alpha Kappa Alpha, 1908–1999.* Washington, DC: Alpha Kappa Alpha Sorority, 1999.

Penn, I. Garland. *The Afro-American Press and Its Editors*. 1891. Reprint, New York: Arno Press and the New York Times, 1969.

"People in the News." *Ghana Today* 1, no. 11 (1957): 8.

"Personal Glimpses." *Star of Zion* 50, no. 1 (1926): 5.

Pirie, G. H. "Aviation, Apartheid and Sanctions: Air Transport to and from South Africa, 1945–1989." *GeoJournal* 22, no. 3 (1990): 231–40.

Prichard, Robert W. *Medicine*. Vol. 11 of *Winston-Salem in History*. Winston-Salem, NC: Historic Winston, 1976.

———. "Winston-Salem's Black Hospitals prior to 1930." *Journal of the National Medication Association* 68, no. 3 (1976): 246–49.

"Progress of Negro Americans." *Umteteli* 21, no. 1 (1940): 4.

Ralston, Richard D. "American Episodes in the Making of an African Leader: A Case Study of Alfred B. Xuma (1893–1962)." *International Journal of African Historical Studies* 6, no. 1 (1973): 72–93.

Ransby, Barbara. *Eslanda: The Large and Unconventional Life of Mrs. Paul Robeson*. New Haven, CT: Yale University Press, 2013.

Reddick, L. D. "South Africa: A Case for the United Nations." *Crisis* 50, no. 5 (1943): 137–39, 56.

Report on Present Conditions and Trends in Adult Education for Negroes: The Works Progress Administration and State Department of Public Instruction of North Carolina. Washington, DC: Library of Congress, 1938.

Rice, Anna V. *A History of the World's Young Women's Christian Association*. New York: Woman's Press, 1947.

Rich, Paul B. *State Power and Black Politics in South Africa, 1912–51*. New York: St. Martin's Press, 1996.

Rief, Michelle. "Thinking Locally, Acting Globally: The International Agenda of African American Clubwomen, 1880–1940." *Journal of African American History* 89, no. 3 (2004): 203–22.

Robertson, Nancy Marie. *Christian Sisterhood, Race Relations, and the YWCA, 1906–1946*. Urbana: University of Illinois Press, 2007.

Rolinson, Mary G. *Grassroots Garveyism: The Universal Negro Improvement Association in the Rural South, 1920–1927*. Chapel Hill: University of North Carolina Press, 2007.

Roydhouse, Marion W. "Bridging Chasms: Community and the Southern YWCA." In *Visible Women: New Essays on American Activism*, edited by Nancy A. Hewitt and Suzanne Lebsock, 270–95. Urbana: University of Illinois Press, 1993.

Rudwick, Elliott. *Race Riot at East St. Louis*. 1964. Reprint, Urbana: University of Illinois Press, 1982.

Rupp, Leila J. *Worlds of Women: The Making of an International Women's Movement*. Princeton, NJ: Princeton University Press, 1997.

Russell, Alexandria. "Sites Seen and Unseen: Mapping African American Women's Public Memorialization." PhD diss., University of South Carolina, 2018.

Savitt, Todd L. "Entering a White Profession: Black Physicians in the New South, 1880–1920." *Bulletin of the of History of Medicine* 61 (1987): 507–40.

———. "Four African-American Proprietary Medical Colleges, 1888–1923." *Journal of the History of Medicine and Allied Sciences* 55 (July 2000): 203–55.

———. "The Journal of the National Medical Association 100 Years Ago: A New Voice of and for African American Physicians." *Journal of the National Medical Association* 102, no. 8 (2010): 734–44.

———. "Training the 'Consecrated, Skillful, Christian Physician': Documents Illustrating Student Life at Leonard Medical School, 1882–1918." *North Carolina Historical Review* 75, no. 3 (1998): 250–76.

Second Women's International Congress. Paris: Women's International Democratic Federation, [1948]. Available from Women and Social Movements International—1840 to Present, Alexander Street Press.

Sehat, David. "The Civilizing Mission of Booker T. Washington." *Journal of Southern History* 73, no. 2 (2007): 322–62.

Seymour-Jones, Carole. *Journey of Faith: The History of the World YWCA, 1945–1994.* London: Allison & Busby, 1994.

Shaw, Stephanie. *What a Woman Ought to Be and to Do: Black Professional Women Workers during the Jim Crow Era.* Chicago: University of Chicago Press, 1996.

Smith, James Howell. *Industry and Commerce, 1896–1975.* Vol. 8 of *Winston-Salem in History.* Winston-Salem, NC: Historic Winston, 1977.

"South Africa—National Conference." *World Y.W.C.A. Monthly* 38, no. 5 (1960): 146–47.

"South Africa—Planning Ahead." *World Y.W.C.A. Monthly*, 34, no. 11 (1956): 293.

The Thirty-Sixth Annual Session of the North Carolina Medical, Pharmaceutical and Dental Ass'n, the Oldest Negro Medical Society in the World, June 19–21, 1923, Winston-Salem North Carolina Programme. North Carolina digital collection.

Tise, Larry Edward. *The Churches.* Vol. 10 of *Winston-Salem in History.* Winston-Salem, NC: Historic Winston, 1976.

Tobias, C. H. "The Work of the Young Men's and Young Women's Christian Associations with Negro Youth." *Annals of the American Academy of Political Science* 140 (1926): 283–86.

Tuttle, William M., Jr. *Race Riot: Chicago in the Red Summer of 1919.* New York: Atheneum, 1970.

Vance, Catherine S. *The Girl Reserve Movement of the Young Women's Christian Association: An Analysis of the Educational Principles and Procedures Used throughout Its History.* New York: Bureau of Publications, Teachers College, Columbia University, 1937.

Vinson, Robert Trent. *The Americans Are Coming! Dreams of African American Liberation in Segregationist South Africa.* Athens: Ohio University Press, 2012.

Waite, Cally L., and Margaret Smith Crocco. "Fighting Injustice through Education." *History of Education* 33, no. 5 (2004): 573–83.

Walker, Cherryl Walker. *Women and Resistance in South Africa.* London: Onyx Press, 1982.

Ward, Thomas J., Jr. *Black Physicians in the Jim Crow South.* Fayetteville: University of Arkansas Press, 2003.

Washington, Booker T., and Fannie Barrier Williams. *A New Negro for a New Century*. Chicago: American Publishing House, 1900.

Wellman, Manly Wade. *Transportation and Communication*. Vol. 4 of *Winston-Salem in History*. Winston-Salem, NC: Historic Winston, 1976.

Wellman, Manly Wade, and Larry Edward Tise. *Education*. Vol. 3 of *Winston-Salem in History*. Winston-Salem, NC: Historic Winston, 1976.

———. *Industry and Commerce, 1766–1896*. Vol. 7 of *Winston-Salem in History*. Winston-Salem, NC: Historic Winston, 1976.

Wells, Julia C. "Why Women Rebel: A Comparative Study of South African Women's Resistance in Bloemfontein (1913) and Johannesburg (1958)." *Journal of Southern African Studies* 10, no. 1 (1983): 55–70.

We Meet in Lebanon: The Story of the World's YWCA Council Meeting, 1951. Geneva: World's Young Women's Christian Association, [1951]. Available from Women and Social Movements International—1840 to Present, Alexander Street Press.

Wertheimer, John W. *Law and Society in the South: A History of North Carolina Court Cases*. Lexington: University Press of Kentucky, 2009.

Wesley, Charles Harris. *The History of the National Association of Colored Women's Clubs: A Legacy of Service*. Washington, DC: National Association of Colored Women's Clubs, 1984.

Whitaker, Robert. *On the Laps of Gods: The Red Summer of 1919 and the Struggle for Justice That Remade a Nation*. New York: Crown, 2008.

White, Deborah Gray. *Too Heavy a Load: Black Women in Defense of Themselves, 1894–1994*. New York: W. W. Norton, 1999.

"White and Colored Women Co-Operate." *Star of Zion* 50, no. 48 (1926): 7.

Williams, L. A., and J. H. Johnston. *A Study of the Winston-Salem Schools*. [Winston-Salem, NC]: High School Press, 1918.

Wilson, Emily Herring, and Susan Mullally. *Hope and Dignity: Older Black Women of the South*. Philadelphia: Temple University Press, 1983.

"Winston-Salem, N.C." *Ivy Leaf Magazine* 26, no. 3 (1948): 13.

"Women Physicians Graduated from Meharry Medical College." *Journal of the National Medical Association* 60, no. 2 (1968): 154.

Work, Monroe N., ed. *Negro Year Book: An Annual Encyclopedia of the Negro, 1916–1917*. Tuskegee, AL: Negro Year Book, 1916.

———, ed. *Negro Year Book: An Annual Encyclopedia of the Negro, 1918–1919*. Tuskegee, AL: Negro Year Book, 1919.

"The World's Most Prejudiced Nation." *Ebony Magazine*, February 1, 1951, 96–100.

"World YWCA Mutual Service Programme: Lists of Projects." *World Y.W.C.A. Monthly* 38, no. 8 (1960): 198–203.

World YWCA Statements of Policy Adopted at Legislative Meetings, 1894–2015. Geneva: World Young Women's Christian Association, [2015].

The Y.W.C.A. Today and Yesterday: A Handbook of National Associations, 1855–1955. Geneva: World's Young Women's Christian Association, [1955]. Available from Women and Social Movements International—1840 to Present, Alexander Street Press.

Index

DuBois, W. E. B., 63, 84, 140–41
Dunbar, Paul Lawrence, 27, 63

Ebony Magazine, 158
Evans, Matilda A., 46, 47

fascism, 140, 145
Federation of South African Women, 163
feminism, 2
Fitts, Amelia J., 21
Fitts, John, 21
Foote, Creola, 196
Fries, Henry, 26

Gamber, Wendy, 49
Garvey, Marcus, 47, 89
gender norms/roles, 32, 45–47, 136. *See also* African National Congress (ANC): and gender; apartheid: and gender
Gilbert, Annie Kate, 66, 67, 68
Gill, Tiffany, 159, 160
Gillespie, Michele, 14
Gilmore, Glenda, 26, 207n51
Gish, Steven, 93, 124, 185, 191
Glotzer, Richard, 83, 84
Goler Memorial AME Zion Church (Winston-Salem), 17, 51, 52, 63, 71, 77, 78, 80, 218n84, 246n18
Goler Metropolitan AME Zion Church (Winston-Salem), 148, 159, 198, 246n18
Gow, Francis Herman, 117, 191
Gow, Louise Ballou, 117, 118
Great Migration, 90
Green Pastures, The (Connelly), 128–29
Grier, Eliza A., 46
Guridy, Frank Andre, 51

Hairston, Lula C., 27
Hairston, Mary L., 70
Haley, Cora A., 167
Hall, Abraham, 14
Hall, Cleo Harvey, 17, 29, 77
Hall, Edna Florence, 19, 48, 50, 51, 103, 117, 141, 158, 170–71, 191
Hall, Eleanor, 103, 117, 150, 171
Hall, Harriet, 14
Hall, Humphrey Haynes, 13–17, 23, 49, 50, 70, 77, 80, 197, 201n1, 202n5; children, 16–17, 18, 19; community activism/support, 22, 26, 27, 62, 78; encounters with white supremacy, 23, 24; entrepreneurship, 20, 29–30; as physician, 16, 17–18,

19, 23–24, 27, 45, 204n20; property ownership, 17, 19–20
Hall, Jennie Estelle Cowan, 13, 50, 77, 203n11,13; community activism/support, 17, 18, 20–21, 22, 27–29, 58; entrepreneurship, 19–20, 49; motherhood, 17–18, 19, 197; Shaw University, 16–17, 30
Hall, Leroy Langston, 19, 45, 47, 70, 77, 101, 103, 117, 150, 171, 197, 198
Hall, Robert B., 40
Hall, Willie Corine, 19
Hall & Hall (fashion shop), 48–52
Hall Drug Company, 29
Hall Xuma, Madie Beatrice, 1, *44*, *153*, 164, *173*, *174*, *175*, *186*, *187*, *194*, 198; African National Congress Women's League, 7, 141, 143; Atlanta School of Social Work, 6, 114–15, 116–17, 131; Christianity, 2–3, 4, 5–6, 104, 108, 152, 181, 183, 184; City Federation of Colored Women (Winston-Salem), 70–71; Columbia University's Teacher College, 5, 6, 81, 83–84, 97–98; courtship of/marriage to Alfred Bitini Xuma, 6–7, 98–108, 110–18, 121–22, 124, 131, 191, 193; criticism of, 3, 66, 132, 137; early life/education, 17, 22, 23, 28–29; encounters with racism, 4, 54–55, 68–69, 123, 163, 167–70; empowerment of Black women, 130, 132, 133, 136, 145–46, 164; encounters with sexism, 45–46, 47; entrepreneurship, 48–50, 51, 116; gardening, 72, 73, 98, 134, 197, 198; influenza pandemic, 40–41, 44, 54; interracial partnerships, 3, 5, 37, 64, 67–68, 78–79, 86; Mary McLeod Bethune friendship, 41, 63–64, 72, 130, 145, 171; medical school ambitions, 45–46, 215n59; music/dramatic skills, 35–37, 41, 52–53, 71, 73, 106, 125–27; return trips to United States, 141, 143, 148–51, 158–59, 169, 171–72, 193; Shaw University, 4, 30, 31–33, 36, 79, 171, 215n59; Slater School/Winston-Salem State Teachers College, 4, 31, 33, 36, 37, 79–80, 97, 151, 152; social activism, 69–70, 72, 77–78, 114–15, 148–49, 196–98; South Africa activism, 1–2, 3, 122–23, 125–31, 138–40, 143–44, 181–82, 198; South African Council of World Affiliated YWCA, 8, 157, 162, 175, 177, *178*, 179, *179*; teaching career, 33, 81, 99, 109, 113–14; World YWCA, 4, 8, 157, 159, 160, 161, 167, 173, 175–77, 180–82, 185, 189, 191; Works Progress Adminis-

WANDA A. HENDRICKS is a distinguished professor emerita of history at the University of South Carolina. Her books include *Fannie Barrier Williams: Crossing the Borders of Region and Race* and *Gender, Race and Politics in the Midwest: Black Club Women in Illinois*.

Women, Gender, and Sexuality in American History

The University of Illinois Press
is a founding member of the
Association of University Presses.

———————————————

Composed in 10.5/13 Adobe Minion Pro
with Avenir display
by Jim Proefrock
at the University of Illinois Press
Manufactured by Versa Press, Inc.

University of Illinois Press
1325 South Oak Street
Champaign, IL 61820-6903
www.press.uillinois.edu